ETHICAL QUESTIONS IN NAME AUTHORITY CONTROL

ETHICAL QUESTIONS IN NAME AUTHORITY CONTROL

Jane Sandberg, Editor

LIBRARY JUICE PRESS
SACRAMENTO, CA

Published in 2019 by Library Juice Press

Library Juice Press
PO Box 188784
Sacramento, CA 95822

http://libraryjuicepress.com/

This book is printed on acid-free paper.

Library of Congress Cataloging-in-Publication Data

Names: Sandberg, Jane, 1989- editor.
Title: Ethical questions in name authority control / edited by Jane Sandberg.
Description: Sacramento, CA : Library Juice Press, 2019. | Includes
    bibliographical references and index.
Identifiers: LCCN 2018035657 | ISBN 9781634000543 (acid-free paper)
Subjects: LCSH: Name authority records (Information retrieval) |
    Cataloging--Moral and ethical aspects.
Classification: LCC Z693.3.A88 E86 2019 | DDC 025.3/222--dc23
LC record available at https://lccn.loc.gov/2018035657

Contents

Part III: Gender Variance and Transgender Identities

Part IV: Challenges to the Digital Scholarly Record

Part V: Emancipatory Collaborations

INTRODUCTION

Jane Sandberg

On the surface, catalogers perform name authority control by identifying several possible forms of a name, selecting one to be the authorized form, and recording other information about the name using rules and their judgment. However, if you scratch beneath the surface, you will find that this work asks catalogers to interact with rich webs of stories that surround every form of every name.

Names have a way of collecting stories. If you take a moment to sit back and think about the stories surrounding your names, you will probably think of several. Your stories might touch on values and aspirations that you or the people that named you hold. They might be tied to painful histories of colonialism, enslavement, or government naming policies. Perhaps you use different names in different contexts, or have changed your name, or represent your name in specific ways when using different languages and scripts. You could probably tell stories about how people have gotten your name wrong, or of unexpected reactions others have had to your names. If we sat down to share these stories with each other, I am sure we would have moments of identification, resonance, surprise, and learning. We could probably go on for some time!

Catalogers who do personal name authority work are often in a position to actively seek out these stories, to decide which stories to include in an authority record (with some stories represented explicitly and others only hinted at), and sometimes to tell a story of their own within an authority record. This gives catalogers a very specific type of power over the people they describe, which comes with ethical questions. What considerations should catalogers take when they encounter a story about a name that is told by somebody other than that person? Which stories should a cataloger share with other library workers and patrons? How can catalogers know that a story is not theirs to share? Are there times when we do our patrons a disservice by not sharing one of those stories?

The contributors to this volume have come together to provide analysis, tools, taxonomies, and advice for navigating ethical questions like these, filling a gap in the literature. Prior to this monograph, a handful of scholars have explored ethical dimensions of name authority control in very illuminating ways.[1] Others have brought up foundational questions of what the term "author" means in a bibliographic context,[2] and what a "real name" is in an online environment shaped by identity registrars.[3] However, this is the first time that scholars have come together to look at multiple facets of name authority control with the goal of working toward an ethical framework. Such a framework is a timely project. Linked open data projects, researcher profiles, and author name

---

1. For discussion of North American indigenous names, see Frank Exner, Little Bear, "North American Indian Personal Names in National Bibliographies," in *Radical Cataloging*, ed. K.R. Roberto (Jefferson, N.C.: McFarland, 2008), 150-164 and Hannah Buckland, "Decolonizing Catalogs in Tribal College Libraries," YouTube video, 30:00, posted by the Association for Library Collections & Technical Services (ALCTS), June 5, 2017, https://www.youtube.com/watch?v=sUmS2dmngE0. For discussion of recording gender in authority records and problematic descriptions of gender variant people, see Amber Billey, Emily Drabinski, and K. R. Roberto, "What's Gender Got to Do with It? A Critique of RDA Rule 9.7," *Cataloging & Classification Quarterly* 52, no. 4 (2014): 412-421, doi: 10.1080/01639374.2014.882465 and Kelly J. Thompson, "More Than a Name: A Content Analysis of Name Authority Records for Authors Who Self-Identify as Trans," *Library Resources & Technical Services* 60, no. 3 (2016): 140-155, doi: 10.5860/lrts.60n3.

2. Carla Mara Hilário, Daniel Martínez-Ávila, Maria Cláudia Cabrini Grácio, and Dietmar Wolfram, "Authorship in Science: A Critical Analysis from a Foucauldian Perspective," *Research Evaluation* 27, no. 2 (2017), 63-72, doi: 10.1093/reseval/rvx041.

3. Oliver L. Haimson and Anna Lauren Hoffmann, "Constructing and Enforcing 'Authentic' Identity Online: Facebook, Real Names, and Non-Normative Identities," *First Monday* 21, no. 6 (2016), http.//firstmonday.org/ojs/index.php/fm/article/view /6791/5521.

disambiguation algorithms now use name authority data and concepts in unforeseen and impactful ways; this is a particularly urgent time to make sure that our commitments to ethically describing people, corporate bodies, and families are widely understood and stated explicitly.

The first part of this volume takes up questions of privacy violations and the consent of people described in authority files to include information about themselves. Some of these issues have emerged with the new RDA fields, while others have been with name authority control throughout its history.

The second part explores two specific histories of colonialism in Colorado and Kurdistan. While colonialism—both past and current—is discussed throughout this volume, these two chapters provide particularly rich case studies of how colonial mentalities shape name authority files. Both chapters apply Duarte and Belarde Lewis' *imagining* technique to the important task of decolonizing authority files.[4]

The third part of this monograph is a response to the PCC Ad Hoc Task Group on Gender in Authority Records, which attempted to take a more humane approach to how authority files describe gender variant and transgender people. These chapters take issue with how the Task Group's recommendations center Western understandings of gender and the English language. These chapters ask critical questions about how necessary it is to record gender at all in various contexts, and encourage catalogers to think beyond the oversimplified dichotomy of hiding or outing gender variant people to envision new ways that catalogs can connect with gender variant users.

The fourth part of this monograph takes up three emerging technologies: massive indexing databases, linked data authorities, and researcher profiles. The chapters in this part explore how English dominance and cataloging practices challenge the scholarly record and the livelihoods of individual authors. They also show how solutions that should theoretically

4. Marisa Elena Duarte and Miranda Belarde-Lewis, "Imagining: Creating Space for Indigenous Ontologies," *Cataloging & Classification Quarterly* 53, no. 5-6 (2015): 687, doi: 10.1080/01639374.2015.1018396.

help problems of representation, such as linked data descriptions and researcher-maintained profiles, also have their own problems.

The fifth and final part of this monograph proposes some answers to the questions posed in this volume. From collaborating with authors to conducting racism audits, centering indigenous language, learning from community archivists, and applying protocols developed by indigenous communities, these four chapters all describe how communities can come together to do ethical name authority work.

I hope that this monograph encourages you to do some more learning and research of your own. In particular, further research is necessary when it comes to the ethical dimensions of corporate and family name authority control. Furthermore, this volume cannot claim to provide a comprehensive global perspective. While contributors discuss the description of authors in Canada, Egypt, Iran, and Israel; and of places in Australia, Canada, Kurdistan, and New Zealand; this volume is still most comprehensive when discussing the context of the United States. Research about bibliographic representation of names and naming traditions in additional cultural contexts is still needed.

Working with the contributors on this project has been a wonderful experience, and I deeply appreciate all of their efforts on these chapters. My wish is that while reading this volume, you are also able to experience some of the joy I felt while working with these thoughtful scholars. I am so glad that you are joining us in thinking about ethical approaches to name authority control.

Acknowledgements

My heartfelt appreciation goes to my colleagues Richenda Hawkins, Michaela Willi Hooper, and especially Bryan Miyagishima, and to my partner Leo. They all provided an incredible amount of support during this project.

Bibliography

Billey, Amber, Emily Drabinski and K.R. Roberto. "What's Gender Got to Do with It? A Critique of RDA 9.7." *Cataloging and Classification Quarterly* 52, no. 4 (2014): 412-421. doi: 10.1080/01639374.2014.882465.

Buckland, Hannah. "Decolonizing Catalogs in Tribal College Libraries." YouTube video, 30:00. Posted by the Association for Library Collections & Technical Services (ALCTS), June 5, 2017. https://www.youtube.com/watch?v=sUmS2dmngE0

Duarte, Marisa Elena, and Miranda Belarde-Lewis. "Imagining: Creating Spaces for Indigenous Ontologies." *Cataloging & Classification Quarterly* 53, no. 5-6 (2015): 677-702. doi: 10.1080/01639374.2015.1018396.

Frank Exner, Little Bear, "North American Indian Personal Names in National Bibliographies." In *Radical Cataloging*, edited by K.R. Roberto, 150-164. Jefferson, N.C.: McFarland, 2008.

Haimson, Oliver L., and Anna Lauren Hoffmann. "Constructing and Enforcing 'Authentic' Identity Online: Facebook, Real Names, and Non-Normative Identities." *First Monday* 21, no. 6 (2016). http://firstmonday.org/ojs/index.php/fm/article/view/6791/5521

Hilário, Carla Mara, Daniel Martínez-Ávila, Maria Cláudia Cabrini Grácio, and Dietmar Wolfram. "Authorship in Science: A Critical Analysis from a Foucauldian Perspective." *Research Evaluation* 27, no. 2 (2017): 63-72. doi: 10.1093/reseval/rvx041

Thompson, Kelly J. "More Than a Name: A Content Analysis of Name Authority Records for Authors Who Self-Identify as Trans." *Library Resources and Technical Services* 60, no. 3 (2016): 140-155. doi: 10.5860/lrts.60n3.

PART I:
SELF-DETERMINATION
AND PRIVACY

Chapter 1

"My Zine Life is my Private Life": Reframing Authority Control from Detective Work to an Ethics of Care

Violet B. Fox and Kelly Swickard

Introduction

The essence of authority control is authoritatively correlating people with the works they create—but what happens when people don't want to be paired with their work? Contemporary artists and authors who create controversial or private artwork and literature have concerns around controlling their identity which may change over time and require thoughtful policies which give them as much autonomy as possible. The authors of this chapter have experience cataloging resources that illuminate privacy challenges in name authority work: protest art, artists' books, and zines. The Maryland Institute College of Art (MICA)'s Decker Library is an example of a small art and design college library which provides many opportunities to reflect on ethical name authority issues.

Kelly Swickard is a librarian with master's degrees in library science as well as archaeology and art history. Her career began with working at the archive of a female artist, where she learned to respect even a deceased artist's wishes for privacy. Swickard now works as the Resource Description Librarian at Decker Library, where she curates the zine and artists' books collections. Violet Fox is a NACO-trained metadata librarian who has a long history in zine librarianship, particularly focusing on the intricacies of zine cataloging. She is also one of the administrators for critlib Twitter chats, a community of library workers who are dedicated to bringing social justice principles into library work.

Collection Development

Collection practices of libraries and archives change over time, as ideas for what is important to include in cultural institutions shift. At MICA, previous library administrations considered graffiti and street art to be vandalism, but cultural recognition has shifted enough that the current administration is open to viewing street art as a form of protest art. Decker Library acquisitions have followed the changes in the college's focus from fine art to design, illustration, and practical art.

Alternative press materials such as zines have slowly gained purchase in library and archival collections as a relatively inexpensive way to document contemporary culture from more diverse viewpoints than traditionally published works.[1] Decker Library began acquiring zines in 2016, with a collection policy focused on work created by students and alumni, created by and/or about people of color and/or members of the LGBTQ+ community, and zines focusing on activism.[2]

Artists' books have a longer history of being accepted within library collections, especially at institutions with strong arts programs; Decker Library's artists' books collection supports MICA's active book arts program.[3] At Decker Library, artists' books were collected as part of student courses or events in the mid- to later part of the 20th century, however it was not until the mid-2000s that the collection was fully

---

1. David Tkach and Carolyn Hank, "Before Blogs, There Were Zines: Berman, Danky, and the Political Case for Zine Collecting in North American Academic Libraries." *Serials Review* 40 (1) (2014): 12-20, doi: 10.1080/00987913.2014.891866.

2. "Decker Library Zine Collection Policy," https://docs.google.com/document/d/1_WanrCg6X69tjboeOqQ2mIARJHpeOEV06ehiO1N6H4I/edit.

3. Louise Kulp, "Artists' Books in Libraries: A Review of the Literature," *Art Documentation: Journal of the Art Libraries Society of North America* 24 (1) (2005): 5-10, doi: 10.1086/adx.24.1.27949342.

inventoried or cataloged. The artists' books collection was recently assessed and the library determined the need to actively collect works created by people of color, especially women of color.[4]

Protest artwork is a common theme in the college's nearly 200-year history, and current students' artwork content and themes increasingly demonstrate a focus on political engagement and active protest. Decker Library's current library director and staff are dedicated to collecting student artwork that addresses political and social justice issues.[5]

Metadata Differences

Zines, artists' books, and protest art differ from traditional books and media in a number of ways, including with respect to a work's intended audience. People usually create books and media with the goal of producing something that people will want to purchase; creators generally want their name visible and recognizable. This sentiment applies to artwork as well. MICA students and alumni sell their artwork (including zines, comics, and artists' books) and actively promote themselves online. In these instances, differences in the descriptive cataloging of resources such as zines, artists' books, and protest art versus traditional materials are generally manageable with not much difficulty. Potential cataloging challenges that can occur are when zines or artists' books lack traditional access points such as an easily identifiable title, as well as problems in subject description (for example, applying Library of Congress Subject Headings to countercultural material creates the potential for using terms that do not provide sufficient access, or that creators would find inappropriate). Protest art often lacks creator(s) names, for a variety of reasons including potential illegality.

For authority work, the primary difference in cataloging zines, artists' books, and protest art are the multifaceted challenges that arise when

---

4. "Collection Development Policy," Accessed June 7, 2018, https://docs.google.com/document/d/1EoOlRmCPy_cSIW82QWatOWs17p8o_dt2rbGwrBxk_NA/edit.

5. Decker Library, "Collection Development Policy."

the creator of a work does not want their legal name associated with their work.

Creators' Privacy Concerns

To fully understand the privacy concerns of creators around their artwork, we asked several zinesters and artists about their identities. We inquired about the type of artwork they created and whether they use pseudonyms. We also asked creators if their privacy was more or less important than having their work seen by the greatest number of people, as well as any concerns they might have about what people know about them.

A recent case of a MICA alumni being "outed" by the institution was one of the reasons Kelly Swickard was interested in researching this topic. "Gaia" is a MICA alumnus who has created mural and graffiti work throughout Baltimore. The college sent out an email about a charity auction and Gaia's real name was used without their permission.[6]

In discussing their concerns with us, Gaia said that they use a pseudonym primarily because:

> I have spent a majority of my life committing crimes against property. Whilst most of my illegal works followed the path of least resistance in the wake of divestment, an abandoned building is still property, and thus many of my activities have amounted to potential felonies. Also, there is of course something liberating about maintaining a pseudonym: it precludes judgement.[7]

When specifically asked about privacy issues, Gaia discussed the importance of "political alliance"; they shared that "advocating for

---

6. Laura Vozzella, "Unmasked: Gaia, Street Artist Specializing in Leatherclad Roosters," *The Baltimore Sun*, July 11, 2011, http://www.baltimoresun.com/bal-unmasked-gaia-the-street-artist-specializing-in-leatherclad-roosters-cradling-john-the-baptists-head-20110708-story.html.

7. Gaia, "Privacy Concerns," email interview by Kelly Swickard, March 15, 2018.

people on the margin is important to me, and thus secrecy is imperative in planning stages."

Another MICA alumni and self-described "zine maker/wall writer/ outsider artist" goes by the pseudonym AVOID or Adam Void. AVOID talked about having adopted their pseudonym in high school, which allows "the freedom to self-define my abilities and my voice."[8] AVOID also appreciated that using a pseudonym "allows for the audience to build the mystery for this character that I am using." AVOID went on to say "I don't see the conflict between privacy and having one's work seen, or the reason my they would be mutually exclusive. Many more (if not all of the) people are looking for my work under my pseudonym than are looking for my government name."

Many of the zinesters we talked with had written pseudonymously (or just using a first name), taking advantage of their anonymity to write about very private matters. Zinester Michelle described how important her privacy was by describing the consequences that would arise if the information in her zine were revealed:

> My main concern is that my family will somehow find out my sexual orientation, which I intend to keep private. I also worry about whether or not my critiques of my workplace will somehow end up in the hands of my boss. I also don't like many people knowing about my past drug-use, for fear of judgement, so I like to keep that information private as well.[9]

Another zinester, R. Logios, shared that her work was highly informed by her identity as a queer woman, a survivor of domestic abuse, and someone with chronic mental illnesses, writing: "I don't really have a strong drive to have my work seen by a large audience. I see zines as more about personal connection, so I really only distribute them face to face at zine fests, instead of trying to get distributed through shops,

---

8. Adam Void, "Privacy Concerns," email interview by Kelly Swickard, March 19, 2018.

9. Michelle, interview by Violet Fox, Questions about zines and privacy, March 12, 2018.

online, etc."[10] She concluded by explaining that she uses a pseudonym in large part because of concerns about safety.

Current Rules and Interpretation

Contributions to the Library of Congress's National Authority File (NAF) are governed by standards maintained by the Program for Cooperative Cataloging's (PCC) Name Authority Cooperative Program (NACO) as well as guidelines within Resource Description & Access (RDA).[11] Pseudonymous entries are allowed in the name authority record (NAR) as preferred names when creators have a "commonly known" identity.[12] The problem in current practice regarding privacy for creators lies in both RDA guidance and the mindset of catalogers.

RDA 9.2.3.4, regarding "Real Name" gives the following guidance: "If: the preferred name or names for an individual are pseudonyms, and the individual does not use his or her real name as a creator or contributor, and the individual's real name is known, then: record the individual's real name as a variant name for each pseudonym."[13] Similarly, RDA 9.2.2.8 instructs the cataloger: "If an individual uses only one pseudonym and does not use his or her real name as a creator or contributor, choose the pseudonym as a preferred name for person. Record the individual's real name as a variant name for person."[14]

In addition, the FAQ-LC/PCC practice for creating NARs for persons who use pseudonyms explicitly states in A1.1 that when a "person uses one pseudonym and never uses the real name," that the cataloger should "use the pseudonym as the 100 (Heading—personal name) and

---

10. R. Logios, interview by Violet Fox, Questions about zines and privacy, March 25, 2018.

11. "Frequently Asked Questions on Creating Personal Name Authority Records (NARs) for NACO," https://www.loc.gov/aba/pcc/naco/personnamefaq.html.

12. RDA, "section 9.2.3.4 Real Name."

13. RDA, "section 9.2.3.4 Real Name."

14. RDA, "section 9.2.2.8 Individuals with More Than One Identity."

add the un-used real name as a variant name in a 400 field (see reference) in the NAR."[15]

The RDA and LC/PCC verbiage of "real name" could be considered problematic in itself, as it apparently conflates legal name with a sense of realness or authenticity. But the main problem is the instruction in RDA and LC/PCC guidelines that if the real name is known by the cataloger, the cataloger should include that name as a variant name.

As seen in the responses from our interviewees, assigning a creator's name to works may jeopardize the creator. Many respondents stated they feel the need for privacy and separation of identities is key to their ability to continue their work. But there are no explicit instructions to NAF contributors to reflect on the needs of the subject of the authority work. As with other aspects of cataloging, the emphasis is primarily on the needs of the information seeker and little thought is given to the safety or security of the creator.

Diligence / Detective Work

Beyond the stated guidelines that instruct catalogers, a challenge lies in the mindset that catalogers bring to their work. In the case of zines, artists' books, and protest art, resources often lack stated information about creators, leaving the cataloger to either leave off information about creators, or, more likely, to turn to Internet searches to find information. In a presentation given at ALA Midwinter 2018, Mississippi State University cataloger Ilda Cardenas described preliminary results from a survey of catalogers as indicating that catalogers often use information they find on social media instead of contacting authors or publishers directly.[16] Cardenas described this relationship between cataloging and

---

15. "FAQ – LC/PCC practice for creating NARs for persons who use pseudonyms," http://www.loc.gov/catdir/cpso/pseud.pdf.

16. Ilda Cardenas, "Catalogers Cyberstalking Authors: Relationship Between Cataloging and Social Media," paper presented at ALCTS CaMMS Cataloging Norms Interest Group program at the American Library Association Midwinter meeting, Denver, CO, February 10, 2018.

social media in the title of her presentation "Catalogers Cyberstalking Authors."

There is often a great wealth of information about creators available to catalogers who are willing to spend time looking through social media accounts or long dormant websites. In the authors' experience, this can be a pleasurable part of our job duties, becoming "detectives" looking for clues about the creator. Is the Jasmine Smith who wrote the zine about gender norms the same as the Jasmine Smith who wrote their doctoral thesis on bioluminescence? There is a sense of satisfaction that comes with making definitive statements either confirming or refuting connections to creators and works.

The NACO program gives catalogers great latitude in deciding how much information should be added. The NACO FAQs for personal name authority records include questions such as "Should catalogers add references beyond those called for by the rules and the LCRIs, if those references would enable automatic conflict detection and updating of known bibliographic records, which use a variant heading for the same person?," the answer to which is that catalogers' judgement in adding headings is appropriate as long as those variant headings are consistent with cataloging policies.[17] Again, the FAQs fail to mention any consideration about the creators' needs about confidentiality or safety.

Catalogers are often loath to leave information unknown; our entire raison d'etre is to provide as much information as possible to those who are looking for resources. We delight in tracking down information. But this detective work has the potential to do harm when we are dealing with resources outside the traditional publishing of books and media. Catalogers need to understand the very real danger posed by sharing inappropriate relationship about, for example, street artists who are protesting police violence or city inaction against economic hardships, or transgender artists who do not want previous art created under a dead name connected to their current art.

---

17. PCC, "Frequently Asked Questions on creating Personal Name Authority Records (NARs) for NACO."

Technological and Administrative Solutions

There are a few administrative improvements that could be made to
the Name Authority File contribution process that would ameliorate
some of the challenges involved in respectfully addressing privacy concerns. First and foremost, the creation and maintenance of the name
authority file needs to become more transparent to the people whose
names are a part of the file. Information about the NACO program
is available at LC's website, but the site is exclusively designed to be a
resource for people contributing to NACO, not to non-NACO catalogers, non-cataloging library workers, or the public.

In order to accurately reflect people's identities, NACO contributors
should err on the side of contacting creators whenever there is a concern
about privacy issues. That task would be greatly eased if there were a
public-facing NACO website that clearly stated the goals of NACO,
and, imperatively, information about how people can contact NACO
administrators if the information on their authority record is incorrect
or contains information that the creator does not want reflected. To
empower people to understand how and why information about them
is being created and shared, and to provide access to requesting prompt
changes to that information, is the best practice that cataloging librarians
need to provide to the public to reflect our ideals. (The fact that once
information has been shared on the Internet it is in many instances
impossible to remove is an important consideration, discussed in the
next section.)

Along with the ability for people to have the ability to request changes
to their own information, the concept of data provenance should be
incorporated into the NAF's structure. A clear history of when and
how changes to authority records were made should be readily available
to NACO contributors, and ideally, the public as well. The lineage of
the information provided should be able to be ranked by the level of
confidence in the data provided. Data provided by the subject of the
authority record should be considered the most reliable data possible,
and decisions regarding conflicting information should be decided by

giving that data highest priority. For example, the legal name of one of our interviewees, Gaia, was "outed" by a publicly accessible email to MICA alumni, but Gaia's wishes should be reflected in their authority record by not recording their legal name as a variant name.

Another archival concept, the idea of information embargoes, could also be incorporated within the NAF to provide flexibility in sharing information about people. Those with authority records could request that information about them be made available at a certain point in the future. There also seems to be a need to reflect information in an authority record that is *never* available to the public. For example, Violet Fox was contacted by an author who had transitioned genders, did not want information about their dead name in an authority record, and did not want any reflection of their transgender status in an authority record. A note was added to reflect that the author requested no further information be added to the authority record, but unfortunately, there is no way to ensure that NACO contributors will understand and respect this essential request. The concept of the MARC field 667 ("Nonpublic General Note") is a nod to this idea, but the MARC format does not have a way to secure sensitive information. Future iterations of the NAF, based on linked data formats, may provide alternatives that allow for the sharing of private information between institutions. The idea of storing sensitive information in the NAF is not without potential downsides, so these ideas would need to be considered in the light of data security issues.

Introducing an Ethics of Care Framework to Authority Work

We know that technological solutions will not solve societal problems, and in essence, the challenge discussed above can only be solved by reframing the way that catalogers think about information. The real shift that needs to happen is training NAF contributors to reframe their approach to information, shifting their perspective from considering only the information seeker to considering both the information seeker as well as the subject of the information at hand. NACO contributors need to reflect on potential problems before adding any information to an authority record, or, indeed, before creating the record in the first place. Once information is shared, especially in a linked data environment, there is little hope of removing it from the Internet—it is a bell that can't be unrung.

The authors would like to introduce the concept of radical empathy to the practice of cataloging and creation of authority records, as first outlined in respect to information work by Michelle Caswell and Marika Cifor's 2016 article "From Human Rights to Feminist Ethics: Radical Empathy in Archives." The framework of an ethics of care was first introduced by Carol Gilligan, an American psychologist, in her 1982 book, *In a Different Voice: Psychological Theory and Women's Development.* Gilligan's initial ethics of care framing has been critiqued as relying on gender essentialism, but its emphasis on revealing the devaluation and exploitation of traditionally women's work, as well as fully understanding the context of justice and injustice in which we do our work, makes it an appealing ethical structure for those who are interested in highlighting and critiquing the power relations that underlie the status quo.[18]

Gilligan's ethics of care framework centers interpersonal relationships and care as the foundation of moral action.[19] As Caswell and Cifor argue that archivists have an affective responsibility to the subject of their records, we argue that those creating authority records must recognize and seriously consider their responsibility to the subjects of those records. Catalogers must resist the temptation to see the records they create as simply about information and categorization; instead, they should take the time to recognize and empathize with the persons that information is describing.

---

18. Maureen Sander-Staudt, "Care Ethics." *Internet Encyclopedia of Philosophy*, http://www.iep.utm.edu/care-eth/.

19. Michelle Caswell and Marika Cifor, "From Human Rights to Feminist Ethics: Radical Empathy in the Archives," https://escholarship.org/uc/item/0mb9568h.

By thinking of the creator as a person and not a piece of data that one is entitled to discover, catalogers can be more mindful of the privacy and safety of the people being described. Catalogers should not hesitate to contact living artists and creators to confirm how they would like to be described. Our interviewees said over and over that their names are very important to them as well as their privacy. The ALA Code of Ethics confirms our profession's commitment to respecting privacy: "We protect each library user's right to privacy and confidentiality with respect to information sought or received and resources consulted, borrowed, acquired or transmitted."[20] This principle has most frequently been interpreted as a front-of-the-house issue, meaning that circulation records should not be revealed. But there needs to be full cooperation and understanding of this cooperation throughout library and archives staff, including catalogers. Those who are creating and editing personal name authority records need to take privacy rights of our subjects seriously, in both our guidelines and our practice.

Conclusion

Because of our position as workers in technical services, usually at least somewhat removed from the public, the idea of radical empathy can seem irrelevant to our work as catalogers. Taking the time to listen to the subjects of our authority control work can help us understand the consequences of introducing inappropriate information into our systems and can give us insight into the responsibilities we have towards the people we describe. Embracing the idea of an ethics of care can help us understand our work in the context of the larger information ecosystem and in emphasizing the importance of relationship building in the work we do in libraries.

---

20. American Library Association, "Code of Ethics," http://www.ala.org/tools/ethics.

Acknowledgements

We would like to thank each of the artists and zinesters who graciously shared their thoughts with us: Michelle, Saorsa Free Press, Thomas Kula, Ed Blair, Mark Beechill, johnnie b. baker, R. Logios, Christian Valles, Gaia, and AVOID. Thanks also to Mel Leverich, Archivist & Collections Librarian at the Leather Archives & Museum, and Joshua Barton, Head of Cataloging and Metadata Services at Michigan State University Libraries.

Bibliography

American Library Association. "Code of Ethics." http://www.ala.org/ tools/ethics.

Cardenas, Ilda. "Catalogers Cyberstalking Authors: Relationship Between Cataloging and Social Media." Paper presented at ALCTS CaMMS Cataloging Norms Interest Group program at the American Library Association Midwinter meeting, Denver, CO, February 10, 2018.

Caswell, Michelle, and Marika Cifor. "From Human Rights to Feminist Ethics: Radical Empathy in the Archives." https://escholarship.org/ uc/item/0mb9568h.

Decker Library. "Collection Development Policy." https://docs.google. com/document/d/1EoOlRmCPy_cSIW82QWatOWs17p8o_ dt2rbGwrBxk_NA/edit.

———. "Decker Library Zine Collection Policy." https://docs.google.com/ document/d/1_WanrCg6X69tjboeOqQ2mIARJHpeOEV06e- hiO1N6H4I/edit.

Gaia. "Privacy Concerns." Email interview by Kelly Swickard. March 15, 2018.

Kulp, Louise. "Artists' Books in Libraries: A Review of the Literature." *Art Documentation: Journal of the Art Libraries Society of North America*, 24 (1) (2005): 5-10. doi: 10.1086/adx.24.1.27949342.

Library of Congress Policy and Standards Division. "FAQ – LC/PCC practice for creating NARs for persons who use pseudonyms." http://www.loc.gov/catdir/cpso/pseud.pdf.

Logios, R., interview by Violet Fox. Questions about zines and privacy, March 25, 2018.

Michelle, interview by Violet Fox. Questions about zines and privacy, March 12, 2018.

Program for Cooperative Cataloging. "Frequently Asked Questions on creating Personal Name Authority Records (NARs) for NACO." https://www.loc.gov/aba/pcc/naco/personnamefaq.html.

———. "NACO - Name Authority Cooperative Program." Accessed June 7, 2018. https://www.loc.gov/aba/pcc/naco/.

RDA Board. "section 9.2.2.8 "Individuals with More Than One Identity"." RDA: Resource Description and Access.

RDA Board. "section 9.2.3.4 "Real Name"." RDA: Resource Description and Access.

Sander-Staudt, Maureen. "Care Ethics." *Internet Encyclopedia of Philosophy.* . http://www.iep.utm.edu/care-eth/.

Tkach, David, and Carolyn Hank. "Before Blogs, There Were Zines: Berman, Danky, and the Political Case for Zine Collecting in North American Academic Libraries." *Serials Review* 40 (1) (2014): 12-20. doi: 10.1080/00987913.2014.891866.

Void, Adam. "Privacy Concerns." Email interview by Kelly Swickard. March 19, 2018.

Vozzella, Laura. "Unmasked: Gaia, Street Artist Specializing in Leather-clad
    Roosters." *The Baltimore Sun*, July 11, 2011. http://www.balti-
    moresun.com/bal-unmasked-gaia-the-street-artist-specializing-in-
    leatherclad-roosters-cradling-john-the-baptists-head-20110708-sto-
    ry.html.

Chapter 2

IDENTITY THEFT: HOW AUTHORITY CONTROL UNDERMINES WOMEN'S AGENCY

Michelle M. Kazmer

Introduction

At the intersection of name authority control and the undermining of women's agency, two basic conceptual approaches exist in tension. The first of these is that, entirely independent of and separate from authority control, individual people have multiple identities in real life all the time. As part of their multiple identities, individuals have *internal* identities associated with who/what they feel inside that they are (I am a mother; I am a professor; I am a left-handed person; I am a woman). People also have *external* identities that manifest to outsiders. These external identities are the identities that others see, and which can appear as names, titles, positions, roles, activities, behaviors, and so forth. People both *feel* and *present* different identities throughout their lives, and they usually also have different preferences and experiences about what identities are appropriate for what settings. For example, I am happy to be "David's Mom" at my child's school. I am happy to be "Mrs. Marty" to a hotel room service delivery person, although I do not regularly use my husband's surname in either my professional or my private life. I am unaccepting of anything other than "Dr. Kazmer" or "Professor Kazmer" in the undergraduate classroom at work, but my faculty colleagues, also at work, call me Michelle and I am pleased at that. My own idiosyncratic preferences, how I comport myself, the role I am occupying in a given space, and the roles of those around me, all determine how my identity can be named and used in a context and how acceptable that naming and use is to me. I am able to assert agency, with varying degrees of success to be sure, over how I am named.

Now to the second conceptual basis that exists in tension with this: the conceptual basis of authority control. We generally start teaching the conceptual foundations of authority control in what, I assume, are the same basic ways, in which the process goes like this: you identify all the potential "variants" of the thing you wish to name; use the standards to determine the "correct" name and its form; and link all variants to the "correct" authority form. In other words, authority control in the way we have practiced it has by definition involved the flattening and narrowing of identity, privileging some names and roles over others. Such privileging is done with what are stated as the best of intentions; as Bennett and Williams succinctly express it, "The use of widely variant forms of authors' names without reference or linkage to alternatives causes hardship for searchers."[1] We flatten, narrow, privilege, and erase, all with the goal of creating and maintaining more robust, persistent linkages among our data to lead to better retrieval.

This privileging does not occur within a static universe, either. Names of things, places, and people change over time. As a simple yet telling geographic example (intentionally chosen to allow us to focus momentarily on a non-personal context), there is a 667 (nonpublic general) note in the Library of Congress Name Authority File (LCNAF) under the heading "Slovakia" that indicates: "Name heading valid for the 1993+ sovereign nation, the 1939-1945 independent republic, and the pre-1918 entity belonging to the Austro-Hungarian Empire." In other words, names of entities in general are definitely not static and there is established authority control practice to identify timelines for name

---

1. Denise Beaubien Bennett and Priscilla Williams, "Name Authority Challenges for Indexing and Abstracting Databases," *Evidence Based Library and Information Practice* 1, no. 1 (March 15, 2006): 37–57.

changes. Using a famous and familiar example of a personal name, the "See From" (400) fields in the entry for English American actor Elizabeth Taylor show seven additional surnames associated with her husbands. Finally, staying personal but using a more scholarly example of a content creator, the authority record for LIS scholar and author Karen Markey shows a series of intentional and explicit communications from Markey to the Library of Congress requesting name changes in her NAR upon her marriage and divorce.

The contribution of this chapter to this volume's overall framework for ethical name authority control practice is to attempt to expose and explicate the tensions between (a) thorough authority control that leads to dense networks of linked data to facilitate effective retrieval and (b) threats to privacy, identity enactment, and compensation for creative work.

In this chapter, I am focusing specifically on Western, primarily Anglo-American, authority control of women's names, and predominantly white women's names; more detailed analyses of additional name authority problems for women globally (where surnaming conventions differ from what is typical in Anglo-American cultures), and the unique harm via naming that has been systemically inflicted on African-American women through the long history of enslavement and its subsequences, are best tackled when they can be foregrounded directly by scholars with appropriate expertise.[2] I also do not argue that threats to personal agency, privacy, and creative ownership as a result of name authority control *only* affect women, but rather that they *disproportionately* affect women compared with men both in numbers (more women are affected than men) and in magnitude (systemic social biases that persist in society mean that the potentially negative results will affect women to a greater degree). Gender goes well beyond men/women and again, issues of authority control and the gender spectrum are more effectively handled

---

2. John C. Inscoe, "Carolina Slave Names: An Index to Acculturation," *Journal of Southern History* 49, no. 4 (1983): 527–54, https://doi.org/10.2307/2208675; Shirley A. Hill, "Marriage among African American Women: A Gender Perspective," Journal of Comparative Family Studies 37, no. 3 (2006): 421–40.

when they can be foregrounded directly. I will often in this chapter refer to "male" and "female" identities and names as that usage is reflected in the literature to which I refer and is used by the people whose names I invoke as examples.

I assert that Anglo-American name authority control undermines the self-presentation choices of white women who engage in creative activity and whose work thus leaves them vulnerable to having authority control exerted on their names. It is impossible to state with certainty the complete set of potential harms of the long-term persistence of linked identities, especially as harm may largely be judged by the individual experience of the author in their life context, rather than by an external metric. The primary ethical concern with authority control as I have described it is the basic violation of authors' autonomy, which I think is paramount compared with any specific measurable harms. This primary concern of violation of autonomy does, however, affect women disproportionately as I noted already. I will deal in turn with three specific problems that arise from the persistence of connections among bibliographic identities that is achieved by name authority control. First: women's work in actively managing their bibliographic identities is undercut by authority control; second: name authority control has a disproportionate effect in violating the privacy of women when compared with men; and third: women's "true" identities are hidden for a variety of economic and social reasons and inscribing a persistent link between the true identity and the bibliographic identity can serve to reallocate credit for intellectual endeavor to the true creator or it can pose measurable harm to a writer's livelihood.

Women's Identity Management Is Undercut

The seed of motivation from this chapter came from my scholarly work on Agatha Christie, which involved my spending many hours doing research in her business papers archive at the University of Exeter. As one result of my time spent in that archive, I take Agatha Mallowan as my starting point in the discussion of intentional identity management.

Although it is not strictly a name authority example (and I will invoke several examples that are not "pure" authority examples throughout the chapter), it is an authorial identity violation involving the Library of Congress. Agatha Mallowan was born Agatha Mary Clarissa Miller, but her most famous authorial name is Agatha Christie. Dame Agatha was married to Archie Christie when she became famous as a detective writer, and after his infidelity and their divorce she preserved her ability to be compensated for her work by continuing to use the already-famous authorial name "Agatha Christie." Upon her second marriage, to Max Mallowan, she used the name and identity Agatha Mallowan in her personal and professional life (and as the authorial name on her auto-biography). And when she wrote semi-autobiographical non-detective novels, she used the authorial name "Mary Westmacott." Her papers make clear that her very firm intention was that the Westmacott identity stay separate from the Christie (formerly personal, now authorial) and Mallowan (personal) identities. Her dismay at the Mary Westmacott identify being connected explicitly with the Agatha Christie identity (and thus to Agatha Mallowan, her "real self") was palpable as I read her correspondence with her literary agent, as was her ire that it was apparently the US copyright office of the Library of Congress who facilitated the connection to be made public.

Copyright records have long been blamed as the tool also used to expose the "true" identity of mystery author Amanda Cross, who was the separate and intentionally secret bibliographic identity maintained by Columbia University professor Carolyn Heilbrun. Heilbrun was concerned about the effect on her academic livelihood if Cross's mystery fiction novels were publicly connected to the Heilbrun name, and intentionally maintained the Cross authorial identity as a separate one. And in both cases, now—Christie/Mallowan/Westmacott and Heilbrun/Cross—the authority records in the LCNAF maintain explicit connections among the identities. Long-term persistence of "fact" and the need for thorough retrieval has outweighed the agency and original intention of these women.

On the topic of identify management by authors, the popular press has also offered explanations. In 2013, *The Economist* published an article explaining "why some writers use pseudonyms." This article, under the gender-neutral byline "E.H.," was motivated by the release of a book written by J.K. Rowling under the pseudonym "Robert Galbraith."[3] *The Economist* largely glossed over the issue of gender in pseudonymous identity management, even as they presented examples of women using male pseudonyms and men using…male pseudonyms. But also in 2013, in describing the same Rowling/Galbraith example, J.K. Rowling offered a quite gender-inflected interview to *The Guardian* in which she described her intentional choice of "Robert Galbraith" for the explicitly male-sounding pseudonym under which to publish a detective novel.[4] In this case her identity work was compromised when a reporter asked a computer scientist to engage in computational analysis to find underlying similarities between texts written by Galbraith and Rowling.[5] Tools, whether older tools such as copyright records or new tools such as computational text analysis, have offered ways for readers and other interested people to unearth connections between "true" and authorial identities and among multiple authorial identities. It is, therefore, not so much up to the library authority control worker in creating the name authority records to reveal multiple bibliographic identities, but to locate them, document them, and keep them organized and persistent. To what extent the good achieved by doing so outweighs the intention of authors is an open question but one that needs to be continuously considered.

An idea about intentional authorial identity management that comes up repeatedly in the popular and semi-academic literature is

---

3. E. H. "Why Do Some Writers Use Pseudonyms?," *The Economist*, July 24, 2013, https://www.economist.com/blogs/economist-explains/2013/07/economist -explains-18.

4. Liz Bury, "JK Rowling Tells Story of Alter Ego Robert Galbraith," *The Guardian*, July 24, 2013, http://www.theguardian.com/books/2013/jul/24/jk-rowling -robert-galbraith-harry-potter.

5. Patrick Juola, "How a Computer Program Helped Reveal J. K. Rowling as Author of *A Cuckoo's Calling*," *Scientific American*, https://www.scientificamerican.com/article/ how-a-computer-program-helped-show-jk-rowling-write-a-cuckoos-calling/.

that publishing under a male pseudonym allows a female author to have her writing judged by readers and critics "without preconceived notions." I find it baffling that the obvious and vital tweak need to make this statement accurate--"with a different and perhaps more tacit set of preconceived notions"-- is rarely made. This argument, focused as it is on "male" and "female" identities, also obscures issues that emerge for authors who are transgender, non-binary, or otherwise do not have a male or female gender (for more explication of these issues, which include but are not limited to misgendering, outing, and deadnaming, one may refer to the works of Amber Billey, Emily Drabinski, K. R. Roberto, and Kelly Thompson, as a starting point). As late as 2013, the prevailing argument in the popular press, made in the publicity swirl around Rowling/Galbraith, was that women (Nora Roberts = J.D. Robb, Ann Rule=Andy Stack, Louisa May Alcott=A. M. Barnard) used male or non-specific names when writing suspense thrillers in particular (as distinct from the detective genre that had been in both male and female hands practically since its inception).[6] But then, fast forward four years to the summer of 2017, when *The Atlantic* and *The Guardian* both published pieces about what they refer to as a "decade-long" trend toward men using *female* pseudonyms to write suspense fiction.[7] *The Atlantic* article is buttressed by a (truly nauseous) example about Martyn Waites and his "alter-ego" Tania Carver (Waites-as-Waites is reported to have said: "Martyn books," he explains, "were more complex, more metaphorical. The kind of things I like in writing." Tania books [he said] were "simpler: mainstream commercial thrillers aimed at a female audience.").[8] Waites's internalization of gender stereotypes notwithstanding, of most interest

---

6. Bury, "JK Rowling Tells Story of Alter Ego Robert Galbraith"; E. H., "Why Do Some Writers Use Pseudonyms?"

7. Paula Cocozza, "Forget George Eliot: Now It's Male Authors Disguising Their Sex to Sell More Books," *The Guardian*, July 18, 2017, http://www.theguardian.com/books/shortcuts/2017/jul/18/riley-sager-and-other-male-authors-benefiting-from-a-gender-neutral-pen-name; Sophie Gilbert, "Why Men Pretend to Be Women to Sell Thrillers," *The Atlantic*, August 3, 2017, https://www.theatlantic.com/entertainment/archive/2017/08/men-are-pretending-to-be-women-to-write-books/535671/.

8. Gilbert, "Why Men Pretend to Be Women to Sell Thrillers."

here is that, as of May 2018 anyway, Tania Carver and Martyn Waites have separate authority records in the Library of Congress Name Authority File (LCNAF). Martyn Waites' identity is safely kept separate from the "lowbrow" Carver—which seems to contravene established rules such as RDA 9.2.2.8 which specifies that "if an individual has more than one identity, record the relationships between these separate identities." In contrast to the Waites/Carver example and in line with name authority rules, Nora Roberts and J.D. Robb have connected authority records, as do Ann Rule and Andy Stack; A. M. Barnard is a reference in Louisa May Alcott's record.

Several other issues emerged as I examined some specific examples. I work through them here as synecdochic cases. First is the case of scholar and author Ann Peterson-Kemp. Peterson-Kemp is frozen in the LCNAF as Ann Peterson Bishop although her most recently-used scholarly name is Ann Peterson-Kemp. MIT Press has, in their author list, corrected her name to Peterson-Kemp, and this name is associated with a book she co-edited called *Digital Library Use*—on which her name is listed as Ann Peterson Bishop. Without active identity management by Peterson-Kemp with respect to her NAR, her LCNAF record will likely stay frozen in time. Second is the case of scholar and author Caroline Haythornthwaite. Although the vast preponderance of use in published books (as well as articles and other documents) shows the form Caroline Haythornthwaite, her NAR encodes the authority form as Caroline A. Haythornthwaite. Haythornthwaite herself says that she quite strongly prefers not to include the middle initial; the middle initial is in the NAR because the form of name reflects that used during her master's degree." In fact, often for purposes of record-keeping or their internal name disambiguation needs, universities and colleges regularly require non-preferred forms of name to be included on theses and dissertations (my own dissertation lists me as Michelle Marie Kazmer, a form I strongly dis-prefer and which fortunately did not make it into my NAR). The mismatch for Haythornthwaite between the NAR form and the form she regularly uses in her published materials can hinder or confuse retrieval, as well as violating the integrity of her identity management. (Note: the absence in the LCNAF of a way to capture "frequent misspellings" also places it at a disadvantage when compared with a tool such as Google Scholar, flawed as it may be, because Google Scholar easily links "Caroline Haythornthwaite" with the frequent misspelling "Caroline Haythornwaite" – a misspelling that appears both in search queries and in many hundreds of published references to Haythornthwaite's work. That said, such connections also privilege the human assumptions behind the algorithm over the author's intentional identity management.)

These examples are not offered to prove that authority work only serves to hinder identity management. The record for LIS scholar Pauline Atherton Cochrane clearly connects an older form of use – Pauline Atherton – with the later form of use – Pauline Atherton Cochrane – in a way that tracks closely with Cochrane's publication trace and familiar professional use. Similarly, the NAR for LIS scholar Karen E. Fisher connects two other forms of name (Karen E. Pettigrew and Karen E. Pettigrew-Fisher) based closely on use, culminating in a form of name that reflects current usage in literary and real life.

Other examples, from index databases rather than name authority records, are worked through by Bennett and Williams, demonstrating how women's specific work in presenting their identities in publications after a name change is undercut by attempts at author name management in index databases.[9] Systems such as Google Scholar and ORCID shift the burden of identity management onto authors – the vast majority of whom are not LIS people and therefore have probably not been explicitly educated on the nuances of name authority control – who therefore need to do work that in one way they may ill understand but on the other hand they are uniquely qualified to do since they know their own identity preferences and practices best.

---

9. Bennett and Williams, "Name Authority Challenges for Indexing and Abstracting Databases."

Women's Privacy Is Disproportionately Violated

Another facet of the identity management issue is that even as women engage actively in intentional identity management, their privacy is disproportionately violated by the very authority work that closely tracks their public identities. I wish to revisit the deceptively simple example provided in the introduction, the name authority record for English American actor Elizabeth Taylor, which contains seven 400 (See From) fields that pair her given name of Elizabeth with the surnames (family names) of her husbands (like so: "Hilton, Elizabeth"; "Wilding, Elizabeth"; and so forth). I must here issue the caveat that using American actors as examples for name authority control is a fraught endeavor, as name authority work conducted on the LIS side is affected by name authority work conducted by the actors' union called the Screen Actors Guild. As actors do offer easily-recognized examples, I will proceed, but a reader should be aware that the Screen Actors Guild requires that actor members have a unique name upon their joining the union, so that substantial disambiguation is handled on the SAG end. In any event, it is "well known" in public that Elizabeth Taylor had many husbands; an ongoing part of the media coverage of her life and career was focused on her frequent marriages. That said, Elizabeth Taylor was not known to any reasonable extent as, for example, "Elizabeth Jenkins" although this is offered as another one of the See From references in her authority record.

Some of Taylor's married names carry slightly more familiarity in popular culture (e.g., Todd, Fisher, Burton), but she was not commonly known or credited as Elizabeth Todd, Elizabeth Fisher, or Elizabeth Burton. And yet – those forms of name sit in her authority record for all to see – and as public See From references, not modestly hidden nonpublic notes. What happens when we compare this situation to the authority records of some of her famous husbands? Richard Burton's and Mike Todd's authority records each contain a mention of Elizabeth Taylor in a 670 field (in which "Citations and information in this field are often not written in a form adequate for public user display") but

no direct 400 "See From" references to "Richard Taylor" or "Mike
Taylor", and indeed such invented forms of name feel absurd, although
it is purely cultural norms that make them feel so. Eddie Fisher's record
contains no reference to Elizabeth Taylor at all. In other words, white
Anglo-American naming conventions lead to asymmetries in the authority records that may seem reasonable to someone entrenched in those
conventions but really are not. [An aside: the record was last touched
after her death in 2011, but there is no reference to the name "Elizabeth
Fortensky" to account for her final husband.]

As a partial counter example, the actor Courteney Cox self-identified
and was explicitly credited in her work (for example in the television
series *Friends*) as Courteney Cox Arquette during her marriage to actor
David Arquette. Her name authority record indicates this—as well as
the current form of name, which is again Courteney Cox subsequent to
their divorce. We are back to the asymmetry in revelation of information,
however, as David Arquette's authority record makes no mention at all
of Courteney Cox. To offer two more scholarly examples—at the risk of
compounding the damage to privacy, but acknowledging that the NARs
are already public—I highlight the records of Anne Gilliland and Toni
Carbo. For Gilliland, dates in the NAR demonstrate a shift from Gilliland to Gilliland-Swetland sometime between 1987 and 1991, and back
to Gilliland at some unspecified time between 1991 and 2014. Similarly
for Carbo, the NAR offers the information that this person was Toni
Carbo Bearman (with a 400 see reference) in 1979 but at some point
dropped the Bearman to become Toni Carbo by 1997 (David Bearman
does have a record in the LCNAF, which carries no mention of Carbo).

Taking these examples as symptoms of a more pervasive problem, I
argue that name authority control has a disproportionate effect in violating the privacy of women when compared with men. Women (white
Anglo-American women) are more likely than men are to change their
names upon marriage, divorce, and repetitions thereof, and to have these
name changes tracked in painstaking detail in their authority records.
The privacy of men, without their having to make any effort to do so,
is tacitly protected through similar life changes when they do not result

in a change of the man's name. The disproportionality is not restricted to authority work done for the LCNAF; for example, it is drawn to stark attention in instructive works in indexing and abstracting such as Wellisch's, which despite an explicit attempt at feminist framing still describes the case of a married woman who changed her surname after becoming famous as a separate case from a person who "was well-known also under a previous name."[10]

Citation systems outside the authority control structure vary in their treatment of gender. Some, especially those used in the physical and social sciences, require only initials of authors, making the establishment of a bibliographic identity more challenging for the author and any indexing systems, but affording additional privacy for the perceived gender of the author. Compare this with the needed ado that has been raised about RDA 9.7 and its requirement for gender in the authority record (and note that while the "Report of the PCC Ad Hoc Task Group on Gender in Name Authority Records" was submitted in 2016, there is still not a final LC-PCC PS for 9.7.1.3, as of April 9, 2018; see also the extensive body of public scholarship on RDA and gender, especially the writings of Drabinski, Roberto, and Billey).[11] The citation system has routinely offered an opportunity for authors to transcend limitations of perceived gender, while the RDA rule as originally written does the exact opposite.

Reallocating Intellectual Credit Is Not a Universal Boon

Finally, it is important to understand that issues of identity management cross personal/professional lines, and that active and intentional identity management occurs in many ways and for many reasons – and the wishes of the person engaging in identity management are sometimes in conflict with the desire of authority control to select "the"

---

10. Hans H. Wellisch, *Indexing from A to Z* (New York: H.W. Wilson, 1991).

11. Amber Billey, Matthew Haugen, John Hostage, Nancy Sack, and Adam L. Schiff. "Report of the PCC Ad Hoc Task Group on Gender in Name Authority Records."

authority form of name, "dig" for disambiguating details, and explicitly
link ALL possible identities together persistently (note that even once
we get beyond the idea that there has to be one main authority form
and instead proceed with robustly linked forms, two of these issues
will still be in play). One reason, although not the only reason, for such
identity management on the part of content creators is to protect the
ability to claim or hide intellectual credit.

Both in cases where it was done intentionally for reasons of publication (e.g., the Brontë sisters publishing as Acton, Ellis, and Currer Bell),
and in cases where it was done through social norm (a woman, Christina
Smith, named on a title page as "Mrs. James Smith"), women's "true"
identities are hidden for a variety of economic and social reasons. In
some cases, linking the true identity to the bibliographic identity is a
way to reallocate credit for intellectual endeavor to the true creator; in
other cases, such linking can pose real harm to a writer's livelihood.

Ohmann reminds us that it was Charlotte Brontë who, after the
premature deaths of her sisters Anne and Emily, revealed that all three
sisters were women who had used the authorial pseudonyms Acton,
Currer, and Ellis Bell.[12] Ohmann points out that the names chosen
were not "avowedly masculine." Charlotte's words from the Biographical Note that was published with the second edition of Wuthering
Heights indicated that "we had a vague impression that authoresses
are liable to be looked on with prejudice"—in other words, they chose
pseudonyms that did not broadcast their identities clearly as women,
specifically to manage the critical and commercial responses to their
writing by managing their presentations of identity. We can turn back
to the case of Carolyn Heilbrun, already described above, for another
example of an author attempting to preserve their livelihood through
identity management. The Heilbrun example is different for two specific and significant reasons: she used a female pseudonym, and thus
was not attempting to present her detective fiction as being written by

---

12. Carol Ohmann, "Emily Brontë in the Hands of Male Critics," *College English* 32,
no. 8 (1971): 906–13, https://doi.org/10.2307/375629.

a male to improve its sales; rather, she was attempting to preserve her livelihood and scholarship in a male-dominated industry – Ivy League academia – by keeping the two authorial identities separate. Heilbrun is quoted by Mann thus: "There was no question in my mind then, nor is there any now, that had those responsible for my promotion to tenure in the English department of the University where I teach known of the novels, they would have counted heavily against me; I would probably have been rejected."[13]

Similarly, Mary Ann Evans published as George Eliot to attempt to provoke a fairer assessment of her work by readers and by critics all of whom were operating in a male-dominated society. Even to this day, when our society is still dominated by male communication and narrative norms, a reader may pick up a book by George Eliot and, not knowing about Mary Ann Evans, engage with the book per the original authorial intent. In other words, even a fairly commonly-known link between a male pseudonym and a female author does not necessarily indicate universal awareness on the part of readers, and such a linkage being reified in an authority record certainly does not. (If online library catalogs had been built from the start to take better advantage of our authority structures of all types, this might be a different story needing to be written.)

NARs that include honorifics such as "Mrs" have been flagged with 667s indicating that "THIS 1XX FIELD CANNOT BE USED UNDER RDA UNTIL THIS RECORD HAS BEEN REVIEWED AND/OR UPDATED," as part of an attempt to align authority practice in such a way that one result would be that women's identity would no longer be elided; that said, entries for women predominantly known by a married honorific, e.g., "Mrs. Beeton," are both kept and retrievable in that usage. The decision to universally flag possibly non-RDA NARs also means that scary-looking all-capitals "yelling" notes appear needlessly: my cousin "Mimi's" NAR (authority form of name: Kazmer, Margaret

---

13. Jessica Mann, *The Fifties Mystique* (The Cornovia Press, 2013).

M.) is also similarly flagged, although I know personally that the form of name captured in it is correct both in fact and in literary use.

Finally, we find a distinct yet important point made by Graban, whose argument leads to the conclusion that name authority also privileges contributions of women who make it onto the title page, and disprivileges the contributions of women whose names appear only in the acknowledgements or not at all.[14] Similarly, we know that citation and indexing practices disproportionately affect how intellectual credit is allocated to women;[15] what I have argued here is that authority control practices, which are intended in part to ensure that credit is allocated accurately, also work against women's agency and intentionality in their own identity management.

Conclusions

Although I made the conscious choice to organize my argument around specific examples, I hope that my intention for those examples to serve synecdochically to highlight larger issues of women's identity management and the way it can be thwarted or inappropriately highlighted by authority work was clear. I wish to return to the constraints I offered in the introduction about the content of this chapter. While I believe the effects of name authority control on women who are not white, western, cisgender, and married to men is best addressed by scholars who have the appropriate expertise, I do wish to stress that some of the issues I have raised in this chapter surely apply readily beyond the women I have identified. Societal assumptions about the

14. Tarez Samra Graban, "From Location(s) to Locatability: Mapping Feminist Recovery and Archival Activity through Metadata," *College English* 76, no. 2 (2013) 171-193.

15. Susan M. Tescione, "Research News And Comment: A Woman's Name: Implications for Publication, Citation, and Tenure," *Educational Researcher* 27, no. 8 (November 1, 1998): 38–42, https://doi.org/10.3102/0013189X027008038; Lorraine J. Pellack and Lori Osmus Kappmeyer, "The Ripple Effect of Women's Name Changes in Indexing, Citation, and Authority Control," *Journal of the American Society for Information Science and Technology* 62, no. 3 (March 1, 2011): 440–48, https://doi.org/10.1002/asi.21469.

lower intellectual quality and financial worth of materials written by authors with "female" names are pervasive. Conventions of name changing with marriage and divorce are not restricted to white women who marry men, although those conventions vary substantially with culture and geography. The fundamental issue of violating authors' autonomy by revealing, connecting, or keeping persistent connections between multiple identities and names has the potential to affect everyone.

Our desires to facilitate retrieval most effectively, to give intellectual credit appropriately, and our inclination to engage in increasingly invasive detective work to saturate the values and connections in an authority record, all generally come from an urge to serve users and maintain a rigorous and accurate cultural record. But as admirable as that may sound, it can also be a way to erase women's labor in identity management, expose or reallocate intellectual credit in unintended or harmful ways, and to ossify societal imbalances in how we deal with women's marital status.

Bibliography

Bennett, Denise Beaubien, and Priscilla Williams. "Name Authority Challenges for Indexing and Abstracting Databases." *Evidence Based Library and Information Practice* 1, no. 1 (March 15, 2006): 37–57.

Billey, Amber, Matthew Haugen, John Hostage, Nancy Sack, and Adam L. Schiff. "Report of the PCC Ad Hoc Task Group on Gender in Name Authority Records." https://www.loc.gov/aba/pcc/documents/Gender_375%20field_RecommendationReport.pdf

Bury, Liz. "JK Rowling Tells Story of Alter Ego Robert Galbraith." *The Guardian*, July 24, 2013. http://www.theguardian.com/books/2013/jul/24/jk-rowling-robert-galbraith-harry-potter.

Cocozza, Paula. "Forget George Eliot: Now It's Male Authors Disguising Their Sex to Sell More Books." *The Guardian*, July 18, 2017. http://www.theguardian.com/books/shortcuts/2017/jul/18/riley-sager-and-other-male-authors-benefiting-from-a-gender-neutral-pen-name.

E. H. "Why Do Some Writers Use Pseudonyms?" *The Economist*, July 24, 2013. https://www.economist.com/blogs/economist-explains/2013/07/economist-explains-18.

Gilbert, Sophie. "Why Men Pretend to Be Women to Sell Thrillers." *The Atlantic*, August 3, 2017. https://www.theatlantic.com/entertainment/archive/2017/08/men-are-pretending-to-be-women-to-write-books/535671/.

Graban, Tarez Samra. "From Location(s) to Locatability: Mapping Feminist Recovery and Archival Activity through Metadata." *College English* 76, no. 2 (2013): 171-193. http://www.jstor.org/stable/24238148.

Hill, Shirley A. "Marriage among African American Women: A Gender Perspective." *Journal of Comparative Family Studies* 37, no. 3, 2006: 421–40.

Inscoe, John C. 1983. "Carolina Slave Names: An Index to Acculturation." *Journal of Southern History* 49, no. 4, 1983: 527–54. https://doi.org/10.2307/2208675.

Juola, Patrick. "How a Computer Program Helped Reveal J. K. Rowling as Author of *A Cuckoo's Calling*." *Scientific American* August 20, 2013. https://www.scientificamerican.com/article/how-a-computer-program-helped-show-jk-rowling-write-a-cuckoos-calling/.

Mann, Jessica. *The Fifties Mystique*. The Cornovia Press, 2013.

Ohmann, Carol. "Emily Brontë in the Hands of Male Critics." *College English* 32, no. 8 (1971): 906–913. https://doi.org/10.2307/375629.

Pellack, Lorraine J., and Lori Osmus Kappmeyer. "The Ripple Effect of Women's Name Changes in Indexing, Citation, and Authority Control." *Journal of the American Society for Information Science and Technology* 62, no. 3 (2011): 440–48. https://doi.org/10.1002/asi.21469.

Tescione, Susan M. "Research News and Comment: A Woman's Name: Implications for Publication, Citation, and Tenure." *Educational Researcher* 27, no. 8 (1998): 38–42. https://doi.org/10.3102/0013189X027008038.

Wellisch, Hans H. *Indexing from A to Z*. New York: H.W. Wilson, 1991.

Chapter 3

When Public Identity Meets Personal Privacy: Ethical Considerations for the Use of Dates of Birth in Name Authority Records for Living Persons

Jennifer M. Martin

The roots of authority control predate the modern understanding of privacy by almost half a century,[1] and thus early authority control took no heed of privacy considerations. This foundational independence of authority control from privacy considerations has persisted through the intervening century and a quarter to the present day.[2] However, if we wish to establish ethical practices of authority control, we must examine authority control from the ground up in the light of privacy because privacy ethics are an important part of ethical practice when dealing with personal information.

This chapter tackles one long-standing aspect of authority control: the use of birth dates in personal name authority records for living persons. After explaining the boundaries of this chapter and exploring

---

1. Panizzi's "Rules for Compilation of the Catalogue" was published in 1841 and Cutter's *Rules for a Dictionary Catalog* was originally published in 1876, whereas the seminal article on privacy, Warren and Brandeis' "The Right to Privacy," was published in 1890.

2. Some of the newer changes to authority control practice (such as RDA's introduction of gender as a recorded element) have been given privacy-based scrutiny by some in the library world, but the long-standing practices seem to have been taken as a given and thus never examined.

the inherent tension between authority control and privacy, the chapter provides an overview of the current use of birth dates in personal name authority records and reflects on the privacy ethics at play. The chapter concludes with recommendations for ways we as catalogers can use birth dates in a more ethical manner.

Before proceeding, two limitations of this chapter need to be addressed. First, the boundaries of what is considered private are culturally defined.[3] As a result, the discourse around privacy ethics depends heavily on cultural privacy norms and can therefore be difficult to generalize, as each culture can and will have different boundaries for what is considered private. This chapter is written from the cultural perspective of the United States but will likely also find resonance among those in cultures with similar or stricter privacy norms.

Second, the ethics of privacy for the deceased is a complicated and contested issue.[4] Legally, the dead do not have privacy rights.[5] Most philosophical and ethical arguments for privacy require an agent who is capable of exerting active control over their personal information and capable of being harmed by a lack of such control. The dead inherently cannot exert active control, and the question of whether the dead can be harmed by a lack of privacy is a complicated philosophical question. Discussions of posthumous privacy also encounter the problem of how to handle situations where explicit directions or wishes are not known, which closely ties into the ethics of respecting the wishes of

3. Ellen Frankel Paul, Fred D. Miller, Jr., and Jeffrey Paul, eds., *The Right to Privacy* (Cambridge, England: Cambridge University Press, 2000), 9, 42, 68, 203; Scott J. Shackelford, "Fragile Merchandise: A Comparative Analysis of the Privacy Rights for Public Figures," *American Business Law Journal* 49, no. 1 (2012): 135, doi:10.1111/j.1744-1714.2011.01129.x.

4. See, for instance, Antoon De Baets, "A Historian's View on the Right to be Forgotten," *International Review of Law, Computers & Technology* 30, no. 1 (Mar, 2016): 63; Natasha Chu, "Protecting Privacy After Death," *Journal of International Human Rights* 13, no. 2 (2015); and T. M. Wilkinson, "Last Rights: The Ethics of Research on the Dead," *Journal of Applied Philosophy* 19, no. 1 (2002).

5. L. Lee Byrd, "Privacy Rights of Entertainers and Other Celebrities: A Need for Change," *University of Miami Entertainment & Sports Law Review* 5, no. 1 (April 1, 1988): 100-101, http://repository.law.miami.edu/umeslr/vol5/iss1/6; and Chu, "Protecting Privacy," 269-70.

the deceased in general. These complications would require a chapter of their own to address properly; therefore, this chapter focuses exclusively on privacy for living persons.

Privacy, at its core, is the ability or right to control what, when, how, and to whom personal information is shared.[6] This includes (at the extreme end) the ability to be anonymous, as well as the ability to be "pseudonymous," that is, the ability to have a recognizable identity which is at the same time separate from the identity of your actual self. Full control of privacy therefore allows an individual to obscure their identity as much or as little as desired. As a result, any ethic of privacy must afford the individual the power to control their own personal information and must not allow others to make decisions regarding that personal information without the individual's consent. The practice of authority control, on the other hand, involves identifying persons as fully and accurately as possible, in a way that links together all of their identities (including any pseudonymous identities). Authority control seeks to bring clarity and precision to issues of identity and is opposed to obscuration of information about persons, as obscurity can only lead to confusion over identities. As a result, privacy and authority control exist in a state of inherent tension, as authority control by nature seeks to expose that which privacy may wish to leave hidden.

Until now, authority control has dealt with this tension by operating as though privacy is not an issue—or at least by assuming that the information needs of the catalog user override almost any desire for privacy on the part of the subject of the authority record. The use of birth dates in personal name authority records is a case in point. The instructions for creating a personal name authority record states that if a birth date can be found from any (legal) source, then it should

---

6. See, for instance, Louis Hodges, "The Journalist and Privacy," *Journal of Mass Media Ethics* 9, no. 4 (1994): 198; Richard A. Glenn, *The Right to Privacy: Rights and Liberties under the Law* (Santa Barbara, CA: ABC-CLIO, 2003), 205; Raymond Wacks, *Privacy: A Very Short Introduction* (Oxford: Oxford University Press, 2010), 40-47; and Paul, Miller, and Paul, *The Right to Privacy*, 34. On the issue of whether privacy is a moral right, see Paul, Miller, and Paul, *The Right to Privacy*.

be included in the authority record.[7] Additionally, once entered into a record, birth date information is never removed, although according to an anecdotal discussion on AUTOCAT, no subject of an authority record has ever requested that their date of birth be fully removed from their authority record.[8] This default position of including birth dates no matter the source implicitly treats birth dates as public information and thus implies that any objections to their use is an unusual demand.

However, birth dates, including just birth years, are held to be private information in the United States. This cultural norm of privacy revolves around two issues. First, birth dates are considered private because they reveal age, and age is considered a private matter, particularly in most professional contexts. Reflecting this, discussions on AUTOCAT suggest that the most common reason an individual requests that their birth date be removed from their authorized heading is because the individual is uncomfortable with their age being known in a professional context.[9] Second, birth dates are considered private because they are a class of personally identifying information, which is legally and by definition personal. As awareness of the risk of identity theft has grown, the cultural norms regarding the privacy of personally identifying information, including birth dates, have tightened in response, and privacy has become inextricably tied to issues of information security. Information security recommendations advise keeping one's birth date as close to the vest as possible, only revealing it when absolutely necessary.[10] Due to these two factors, birth dates are private information.

However, birth dates being private is not in and of itself enough to establish that authority control practices need to change. The issue of

7. RDA Toolkit, 9.1.1, last modified April 11, 2017.

8. "Objection to author's birth year," emails sent to AUTOCAT email list, September 26, 2011-September 30, 2011.

9. "Objection to author's birth year," February 15, 2008-February 22, 2008 and September 26, 2011-September 30, 2011; and "Personal info in authority records," emails sent to AUTOCAT email list, August 3, 2015-August 11, 2015.

10. See, for example, Frank W. Abagnale, *Stealing Your Life: The Ultimate Identity Theft Prevention Plan* (New York: Broadway Books, 2007), 109.

privacy for subjects of personal name authority records is complicated
by the fact that those individuals are, to at least some degree, public
figures, and public figures have more limited privacy rights than private
individuals. Public figures do not give up all claim to privacy, though, so
the question becomes one of where the balance point is between what
becomes ethically available to the public and what remains purely private.
The range of privacy afforded to public figures does vary according to
the type of public figure;[11] for instance, a politician, a local hero, and a
celebrity each have different claims to privacy. I hold that all subjects
of authority records are, for the purposes of those records, one of two
types of public figure: a creator of media, or a person discussed in media.
Further, I believe that these two categories of public figure should be
afforded equal privacy. Therefore, I treat all subjects of authority records
as having equal claim to privacy.

As no literature exists specifically addressing privacy as related to
public figures in light of authority control, I approach the question by
considering the standards of journalism ethics relating to privacy. Journalism privacy ethics focus on case-by-case analyses because journalists
must consider each piece of information disclosed in each article they
write in light of privacy, and the circumstances surrounding that use
of information varies every time. In contrast, the circumstances and
information involved in the use of birth names in authority records
are essentially stable; as a result, I argue for a broad and generalized
application of these principles to authority work, although individual
catalogers could certainly perform their own analyses if desired.

In journalism, the primary question at stake is whether the informational needs of the reader outweigh the subject's desire for privacy.[12]
This is weighed on whether the information is necessary for the stated

11. See Hodges, "The Journalist and Privacy," 205-11; and Shackelford, "Fragile Merchandise," 144-51.

12. See Hodges, "The Journalist and Privacy;" and Candace Cummins Gauthier, "Privacy Invasion by the News Media: Three Ethical Models," *Journal of Mass Media Ethics*
17, no. 1 (2002).

purpose and provides information which the public needs to "live well"[13] or to make their own (ethical) decisions[14] and involves weighing the harms to the public of not releasing the information against the harm to the individual from having their privacy invaded.[15] Under this analysis, then, we must consider what the public gains from having birth dates in authority records, what the subjects of those records lose, and how the two compare.

Without birth dates, the public might lose some precision in authority control, meaning that some identities could be split across two or more unlinked records or separate identities with the same name could erroneously end up on the same record (although these scenarios are not a certainty; alternative methods for identification do exist). While such errors are clearly less than ideal, the consequences are also generally going to be minor: someone might be inconvenienced by wading through extra results or might not discover one of the books by the author they are looking up. On the whole, the impact on the public of keeping birth dates entirely private would likely be minimal, and any losses relatively small.

On the flip side, the impact on the subjects of the authority records could be greater. Some subjects of authority records could be particularly uncomfortable with having their age publicly known, in which case the presence of their date of birth in the authority record could cause them distress, if they knew about it. More significantly, having their date of birth publicly available puts the subjects of authority records at greater risk of identity theft. Some might object to this premise, claiming that having the date of birth exposed in an authority file provides little greater risk given all the other (not always legal) places such information can be found, or saying that if the date of birth is in the catalog record, it must already be public and therefore it does not matter if it is also publicly in the authority record. To the first, I would respond

---

13. Hodges, "The Journalist and Privacy," 203-5.

14. Gauthier, "Privacy Invasion," 24.

15. Ibid., 25.

that taking information security seriously has to start somewhere—if
everyone continues to be lax because everyone else is also being lax,
then we will never get anywhere and have no chance of ever stemming
identity theft. As to the second, while in some cases the birth date is
already public, in many cases the information is provided to the cataloger by the publisher.[16] Information coming from the publisher is not
generally public; instead, the publisher is specifically revealing the date
of birth to the cataloger, who then makes it public by adding it to the
authority record. This means that the birth date may not, in fact, be
publicly available prior to the creation of the authority record. Thus, the
subject risks having their birth date exposed when it may not have been
previously, which represents a real, even if small, increase in their risk
of having their identity stolen. In considering the needs of the public
against the risks to the subjects of the authority records, the small but
definitely present risks to the subject outweigh the potential small losses
to the public and, therefore, an ethical authority control practice should
treat birth dates as private information.

Given the privacy issues, it is worth considering whether birth dates
are even necessary to meet the goals of authority control. Five features
make date of birth attractive as a means of identification of persons for
authority control. First, date of birth is generally[17] factual. Second, date
of birth is often relatively easy to ascertain for living people because of
the option of contacting the individual to ask directly. Third, it is stable,
meaning that it will stay the same from when it is first entered through
the demise of the authority record. Fourth, it is unique enough to have
high discriminatory ability; that is, a date of birth alone is usually enough

16. Among a convenience sample of 101 personal name authority records (collected
while doing routine cataloging work) which contain either the full date of birth or
solely the birth year, 55% had the birth date information provided by the publisher
(63% from CIP information, 32% from direct inquiry, and 5% from the publisher's
website), 19% of birth date information came from the subject of the record themselves (42% from direct inquiry, 32% from US copyright files, and 26% published
either online or in a book), and the remaining 26% of records had copied the birth
date from some other source of information such as Wikipedia.

17. Sometimes people give out a false date of birth, and occasionally the legal date of
birth differs from the date the individual considers their actual date of birth.

to distinguish between two otherwise identical names (although it is possible for people with the same name to have the same birth date, so it is not perfect). Fifth, information about a range for date of birth can often be surmised from information in the material (for instance, a highly technical academic piece is unlikely to have been written by a 20-year-old), which means that date of birth can be of use to help distinguish names even if the precise date or year is not actually known by the user. As a result, birth dates work quite well as a means of identifying people.

Unfortunately, no other single element carries all of the advantages of birth dates, although RDA lists sixteen other elements for use in personal name authority records.[18] Many of the elements, such as place of residence or field of activity, are subject to variation over time or to repeated changes. Other elements are more likely to be shared by people with the same name and thus of little use in distinguishing among them, such as gender or language. Most of the elements cannot be surmised, which means that if a user doesn't already know the information, it will not help them distinguish between the identities in the authority records. Additionally, many of these elements have privacy concerns of their own associated with them, meaning that they face much the same ethical issues as birth dates, particularly gender, place of birth, place of residence, address, and biographical information. As a result, the use of birth dates still stands out as a uniquely powerful method of identification and differentiation, and, for that reason, I do not recommend completely dropping their use.

I do recommend placing more emphasis on using those alternate means for differentiating names, though. Under AACR2, date of birth was prescribed as the primary means of differentiating names,[19] and

---

18. See RDA, 9. The elements are fuller form of name, titles (such as of nobility), profession or occupation, unique identifiers, period of activity, variant forms of name, "other designation[s] associated with a person," gender, place of birth, associated country, place of residence, address, affiliation, language, field of activity, and biographical information.

19. Joint Steering Committee for Revision of AACR, *Anglo-American Cataloguing Rules*, Second edition, 2002 revision, 2005 update (Chicago: American Library Association, 2005), 22.17-22.20.

this mindset has persisted under RDA, even though RDA itself does
not privilege one method of name differentiation over another. Moving
towards a multifaceted habit of disambiguation would diminish the need
for birth dates, indirectly alleviating some of the problem by reducing
its spread. However, simply reducing the scope of the problem is not
enough.

To address the root of the problem, I recommend that catalogers
switch from obtaining birth date information from any place it is available to obtaining birth date information solely from the subject of
the authority record. If the birth date is not available from the subject
of the authority record, do not include it in the authority record. An
expansive meaning of "from the subject" is intended, aligning with the
recommendation of the PCC Ad Hoc Task Group on Gender in Name
Authority Records to use (only) "self-identifie[d] and explicitly disclose[d]
[…] information from readily and publicly available sources."[20] In practice, this means that in addition to birth dates determined by asking the
subject of the authority record directly, birth dates which have been
published by the subject (for instance, as happens in some genealogi-
cal books) and birth dates which the subject has voluntarily entered
into the public sphere (such as birth year in the US copyright files[21] or
information published on the individual's website) can also be used. By
restricting the source of information to the subject of the authority
record themselves, catalogers can be certain that any birth dates which
are posted in the authority files are present by consent of the subject.
Recall that privacy is the ability of a person to control where and how
their personal information is used; therefore, if the person has consented
to the information being used and shared, the use of that information
is not a violation of privacy. When the date of birth is sought, the fact

---

20. PCC Ad Hoc Task Group on Gender in Name Authority Records, *Report of
the PCC Ad Hoc Task Group on Gender in Name Authority Records*, October 4, 2016, 2,
https://www.loc.gov/aba/pcc/documents/Gender_375%20field_Recommendation-
Report.pdf.

21. Inclusion of the birth year is optional, per the instructions on the US copyright
registration forms.

that the information will be made publicly available, likely permanently,[22] must be plainly disclosed; without that information, the subject of the authority record cannot make a fully informed (and therefore fully consensual) decision about whether or not to share their birth date. If the subject of the authority record declines to provide their birth date, then other means of differentiating the record must be used, and the subject's decision regarding their date of birth should be recorded so that other catalogers do not make additional queries on the matter (to respect both the subject's decision and the other catalogers' time). By respecting the wishes of the subjects of the authority records, catalogers would both be respecting the subjects' ability to control what information about themselves is made publicly available (their privacy) and be respecting the subjects' level of risk tolerance with respect to identity theft and exposing personally identifying information. If the subject of the authority record would rather remain in a mix with other people with the same name than expose themselves to risk by revealing private information, that is their prerogative under an ethic of privacy. Following this single recommendation would go a long way towards creating a more ethical practice surrounding the use of birth dates in personal name authority records for living persons.

An important corollary to the previous recommendation is that catalogers must stop asking publishers for the birth dates of subjects of authority records. This includes no longer requesting birth information

---

22. While in most cases consent is something which can be revoked, if the date becomes part of the authorized form of the name, the current nature of authority files makes any such revocation of consent difficult to carry out in practice. It is necessary to retain past headings for continuity; otherwise, catalogs would be left with formerly authorized forms in place and have no clear indication of what the new authorized form is. In addition, the changes propagating out to everyone who has a copy of the heading in their catalog is not guaranteed. Dates of birth which reside solely in a note field are able to be removed completely, but face the same challenge regarding distribution as dates in headings.

In a linked data system, it might be easier to remove the birth date from the locally controlled authority graph (given that there is no need for continuity between authorized forms of the name), but if that information has been copied elsewhere, it may be difficult to impossible to remove it from all the places it has spread to. "Once on the web, always on the web" applies to linked data, too.

on CIP applications, which are filled out by publishers. Unless the subject of the authority record has specifically authorized the publisher to distribute their birth date, the publisher does not have the ethical right to decide whether or not to make that individual's birth date public. While this is ultimately an ethical issue on the publisher's end, it is still unethical for catalogers to take advantage of this lack of respect for privacy—catalogers can respect privacy even if the publishers do not care.

Additionally, other sources for birth dates, such as Wikipedia or biographical resources, should be used with caution, as the consent or lack thereof of the subject of the authority record is generally not clear within those sources. It is tempting to assume that since the birth date has entered other public sources, it is okay to use it, but if the birth date was posted without the subject's consent, then all uses of it constitute a violation of the subject's privacy. Someone else committing a violation of privacy does not make it ethical for catalogers to propagate that violation of privacy.

Ideally, this ethical standard would be applied retroactively by going back through the authority file and seeking permission, where not already granted, from existing subjects of authority files for the use of their birth dates. Unfortunately, completing such a project is likely not realistic, mostly because of the prohibitive time commitment involved. However, nothing but inertia ultimately prevents implementing these recommendations moving forward, and that alone would be a huge gain in the ethical treatment of birth dates in authority records.

To implement these recommendations, we must navigate a major shift in practice for many[23] and a minor change in standards for all. Currently, in the United States, directly asking the subject of an authority record for their date of birth is generally a last resort when trying to differentiate a personal name authority record;[24] catalogers would have

---

23. Some cataloging communities already routinely correspond with the subjects of authority records and thus would have a much smaller adjustment to make to align themselves with the recommended practice regarding birth dates.

24. See, for instance, Joseph C. Lin, "Undifferentiated Names: A Cataloging Rule Overlooked by Catalogers, Reference Librarians, and Library Users," *Cataloging &*

to adjust to usually[25] directing a request for a birth date to the subject of the authority record. A likely outcome of this shift would be that birth dates are more frequently only included when actually needed to break a conflict or, rarely,[26] to establish identity in cases where overlap or lack thereof is not clear. This reduction would not necessarily be contrary to RDA: although birth dates are a core element,[27] RDA instructions only require that core elements be recorded when "readily ascertainable."[28] While the precise definition of "readily ascertainable" could certainly be debated, it does not seem unreasonable to think that having to contact an author would fall outside the bounds of "readily ascertainable." Birth dates would clearly be less readily ascertainable once CIP applications no longer requested birth date information. However, the clearest way to ensure an ethical practice of authority control related to birth dates would be to rewrite RDA 9.3.2.2 (and 9.3.1.2) to specify that the only allowed sources of information are the subject of the authority record or sources in which the subject has voluntarily made their birth date public. Until such a change is made, an ethical practice of authority control will stand in conflict with the rules we are supposed to be following.

In the end, we as catalogers must face the universal question of whether we place greater value on our own and the library users' convenience or on acting ethically. If we wish to act ethically, we must acknowledge that the current use of dates of birth in name authority records violates privacy ethics by publicly exposing the personal information of the living subjects of authority records without those subjects' consent. The remedy is simple: only include birth dates in

---

Classification Quarterly 19, no. 2 (1995): 41, doi:10.1300/J104v19n02_03; and Jonathan Tuttle, "Cataloger Research for Name Authority Control," University of North Carolina at Chapel Hill, 2013.

25. If the subject of the authority record has previously chosen to make their birth date public, that source can be used instead of contacting the subject directly.

26. Often, such uncertainty would be at least as easily resolved by using one of the other personal name elements, such as field of activity, as by birth date.

27. RDA, 9.3.

28. RDA, 8.3 and 0.6.7.

authority records if the subject of the authority record has consented
to the public exposure of their birth date. This can be accomplished by
only gathering birth date information directly from the subject of the
authority record. Bringing our standards in line with this recommended
practice would allow us to begin acting ethically while using birth dates
in personal name authority records for living persons.

Bibliography

Abagnale, Frank W. *Stealing Your Life: The Ultimate Identity Theft Prevention Plan.*
New York: Broadway Books, 2007.

Byrd, L. Lee. "Privacy Rights of Entertainers and Other Celebrities: A Need
for Change." *University of Miami Entertainment & Sports Law Review*
5, no. 1 (April 1, 1988): 95-116. http://repository.law.miami.edu/
umeslr/vol5/iss1/6.

Chu, Natasha. "Protecting Privacy After Death." *Journal of International Human Rights* 13, no. 2 (2015): 255-75.

Cutter, Charles A. *Rules for a Dictionary Catalog.* Washington, D.C.: Government Printing Office, 1876.

De Baets, Antoon. "A Historian's View on the Right to be Forgotten." *International Review of Law, Computers & Technology* 30, no. 1 (Mar, 2016):
57-66.

Gauthier, Candace Cummins. "Privacy Invasion by the News Media: Three
Ethical Models." *Journal of Mass Media Ethics* 17, no. 1 (2002): 20-
34.

Glenn, Richard A. *The Right to Privacy: Rights and Liberties under the Law.* Santa
Barbara, CA: ABC-CLIO, 2003.

Hodges, Louis. "The Journalist and Privacy." *Journal of Mass Media Ethics* 9,
no. 4 (1994): 197-212.

Joint Steering Committee for Revision of AACR. *Anglo-American Cataloguing
Rules.* 2nd ed., 2002 rev., 2005 update. Chicago: American Library
Association, 2002–2005.

Lin, Joseph C. "Undifferentiated Names: A Cataloging Rule Overlooked by Catalogers, Reference Librarians, and Library Users." *Cataloging & Classification Quarterly* 19, no. 2 (1995): 23-48. doi:10.1300/ J104v19n02_03.

"Objection to author's birth year." AUTOCAT mailing list archives. February 15, 2008-February 22, 2008 and September 26, 2011–September 30, 2011.

Panizzi, A. "Rules for the Compilation of the Catalogue." In *Catalogue of Printed Books in the British Museum*, vol. 1, v–ix. London: The British Museum, 1841.

Paul, Ellen Frankel, Fred D. Miller, Jr., and Jeffrey Paul, eds. *The Right to Privacy*. Cambridge: Cambridge University Press, 2000.

PCC Ad Hoc Task Group on Gender in Name Authority Records. *Report of the PCC Ad Hoc Task Group on Gender in Name Authority Records*. October 4, 2016. https://www.loc.gov/aba/pcc/documents/Gender_375%20field_RecommendationReport.pdf.

"Personal info in authority records." AUTOCAT mailing list archives. August 3, 2015–August 11, 2015.

RDA Toolkit. Last modified April 11, 2017.

Shackelford, Scott J. "Fragile Merchandise: A Comparative Analysis of the Privacy Rights for Public Figures." *American Business Law Journal* 49, no. 1 (2012): 125-208. doi:10.1111/j.1744-1714.2011.01129.x.

Tuttle, Jonathan. "Cataloger Research for Name Authority Control." University of North Carolina at Chapel Hill, 2013. https://cdr.lib.unc.edu/record/uuid:f16614b9-2900-490f-970b-6585e7db02cf.

Wacks, Raymond. *Privacy: A Very Short Introduction*. Oxford: Oxford University Press, 2010.

Warren, Samuel, and Louis Brandeis. "The Right to Privacy." *Harvard Law Review* IV, no. 5 (December 15, 1890): 193-220.

Wilkinson, T. M. "Last Rights: The Ethics of Research on the Dead." *Journal of Applied Philosophy* 19, no. 1 (2002): 31-41.

Chapter 4

DEMOGRAPHIC CHARACTERISTICS IN PERSONAL NAME AUTHORITY RECORDS AND THE ETHICS OF A PERSON-CENTERED APPROACH TO NAME AUTHORITY CONTROL

Thomas A. Whittaker

Research indicates that libraries' approach to personal name authority control[1] is in the process of transitioning from a "name-centered" approach, whose primary purposes are disambiguation, differentiation, and collocation, to a "person-centered" approach that supports a more comprehensive description of the persons represented in name authority records (NARs).[2] *Resource Description & Access* (RDA) chapter nine, "Identifying Persons," and the subsequent changes to the MARC 21 Authority Format to accommodate the attributes defined therein substantiate this claim. These attributes range from the seemingly innocuous

---

1. For the purposes of this work, name authority control (and all variations) refers specifically to the type of authority control practiced by libraries that relies (at time of writing) on creating authority records using MARC 21 Authority Format for inclusion in the Library of Congress-Name Authority Cooperative Name Authority File.

2. Heather Lea Moulaison, "The Expansion of the Personal Name Authority Record under Resource Description and Access: Current Status and Quality Considerations," *IFLA Journal* 41, no. 1 (2015): 13-24; Heather Lea Moulaison, Felicity Dykas, and John M. Budd, "Foucault, the Author, and Intellectual Debt: Capturing the Author-Function Through Attributes, Relationships, and Events in Knowledge Organization Systems," *Knowledge Organization* 41, no. 1 (2014): 30-43; Jinfang Niu, "Evolving Landscape in Name Authority Control," *Cataloging & Classification Quarterly* 51, no. 4 (2013): 404-419; Kelly J. Thompson, "More Than a Name: A Content Analysis of Name Authority Records for Authors Who Self-Identify as Trans," *Library Resources & Technical Services* 60, no. 3 (2016): 140-55, doi: 10.5860/lrts.60n3.

"Profession or Occupation" (RDA 9.16) to the ethically fraught and contentious "Gender" (RDA 9.7).[3]

In addition to these specifically enumerated attributes, RDA has also incorporated the poorly defined concept of "Other Designation Associated with Person" (RDA 9.6). Research conducted into the use of MARC 21 Authority Format field 368, subfield c (hereafter MARC 368c) in NARs for personal names suggests that some catalogers have interpreted "Other Designation" in a manner that supports recording additional demographic characteristics of a person, including sexual orientation, ethnicity, and religion.[4] Personal information of this nature is characteristically sensitive, as historically it has been used as the basis for discrimination and in the perpetration of violence against specific groups of individuals. While consistent with a person-centered approach, the practice of including sensitive information such as this in NARs should not be engaged in without a thorough examination of the possible consequences. By focusing specifically on how sexual orientation has been recorded in NARs, we can begin to comprehend the range of ethical problems inherent to this type of person-centered approach to name authority control.

Scope and Context

Out of 6899 total usages of MARC 368c in personal name authority records in the Library of Congress/Name Authority Cooperative Name Authority File (LCNAF), there were eighty-seven individual instances in which sexual orientation information was recorded in the source data. In three of those cases, sexual orientation was included on records for fictitious characters and were excluded for the purposes of this

---

3. Amber Billey, Emily Drabinski, and K. R. Roberto, "What's Gender Got to Do with It? A Critique of RDA 9.7," *Cataloging & Classification Quarterly* 52, no. 4 (2014): 412-21, doi: 10.1080/01639374.2014.882465; Thompson, "More Than a Name."

4. Complete analysis is pending, but the dataset is available: Thomas A. Whittaker, *MARC 21 Authority 368 Subfield 'C' Data* (Bloomington, IN: IUScholarWorks, 2018) http://hdl.handle.net/2022/22031.

analysis.[5] **Table 1** shows the number of occurrences of each term and
the thesaurus from which they were taken.

Thesaurus

	LCDGT	LCSH	Total
Gay men	35	25	60
Lesbians	14	5	19
Bisexual men	0	2	2
Bisexuals	1	1	2
Gays	0	1	1
Total	50	34	84

Term

Table 1. Terms Used in 368c in Personal Name Authority Records
in LCNAF

The low number of occurrences of sexual orientation demographic
terms in NARs, even as a percentage of the total usage of MARC 368c
(1.26 percent), should not detract from their significance in a critique
of person-centered authority control. It is important to remember that
MARC 368c was only approved for use in personal name authority
records in 2012.[6] Additionally, the preferred use of *Library of Congress
Demographic Group Terms* (LCDGT) as the source for sexual orientation
demographic terms indicates that a majority of this data was recorded
in NARs post-June 2015, when the first LCDGT terms were approved.[7]

This suggests that the practice of recording sexual orientation demographic terms in NARs is trending upward. This trend is likely to be
encouraged by recommendations contained in the 2016 *Report of PCC*

5. I acknowledge that RDA's definition of "person" is inclusive of fictitious and
non-human entities.

6. "368 – Other Attributes of Person or Corporate Body," MARC 21 Format for
Authority Data, Library of Congress, last updated December 2017, http://www.loc.
gov/marc/authority/ad368.html.

7. Policy and Standards Division, Library of Congress, *Introduction to Library of
Congress Demographic Group Terms*, 2018 edition (Washington, D.C.: Policy and Stan-
dards Division, Library of Congress, 2018) https://www.loc.gov/aba/publications/
FreeLCDGT/2018%20LCDGT%20intro.pdf.

Ad Hoc Task Group on Gender in Name Authority Records. In "Appendix A," the task group presents a draft of *Descriptive Cataloging Manual Z1* for MARC 375 that includes guidance to, "use field 368 $c (Other designation) for attributes such as sexual orientation, ethnicity, religion, etc., that do not fit into any other RDA elements."[8] While not yet adopted, the possibility that the Program for Cooperative Cataloging and the Library of Congress could, at any moment, endorse the practice of recording sexual orientation and other sensitive demographic information in NARs increases the urgency with which this practice should be evaluated.

The literature critical of RDA's gender attribute and its use in NARs raises legitimate concerns regarding risks to personal privacy and safety. These concerns are equally applicable to any criticism of recording sexual orientation information in NARs. So as not to belabor that point, the analysis presented in this chapter will instead focus on the issue of recording sexual orientation in NARs with reference to two challenges that are inherent to the cataloging profession: consistency and accuracy. What results is an investigation into the feasibility of an ethically conscious approach to person-centered authority control.

The Challenge of Consistency

Consistency is a foundational principle of cataloging, and one that is of perpetual concern for catalogers. As a profession, we have created rules, interpretations of those rules, best practices, and local practices, all in an effort to tame the chaos of the bibliographic universe and to give our users as consistent an experience as possible. There is a widely expressed sentiment that if you ask five catalogers to independently catalog the same item; you will end up with five different records. The truth (and humor) in this statement comes from the fact that while members the cataloging profession are notoriously consistent about

---

8. Amber Billey, Matthew Haugen, John Hostage, Nancy Sack, and Adam L. Schiff, "Report of the PCC Ad Hoc Committee on Gender in Name Authority Records" (report, Program for Cooperative Cataloging, October 4, 2016): 5, http://www.loc. gov/aba/pcc/documents/Gender_375%20field_RecommendationReport.pdf.

some aspects of metadata creation, they are just as notoriously inconsistent about others.

Subject analysis is one facet of cataloging that is especially prone to problems of inconsistency. Inconsistent application of subject headings can lead to inaccurate assumptions about the nature of a library's collection. However, when using demographic terms in authority records to characterize people, the consequences of inconsistency can lead to far more troubling interpretations of our data.

Problematic Othering

From a sociopolitical standpoint, othering is the act by which an individual or group is labelled as being distinct from and subordinate to the dominant social category. Historically, the practice of othering has rationalized the marginalization and disenfranchisement of significant populations of peoples. Catalogers should be conscious of this effect when adopting a person-centered approach to name authority control, as inconsistent application of demographic terms in NARs can lead to othering in the authority file.

The potential for othering in the authority file is illustrated by the inconsistency with which sexual orientation demographics have been assigned. In all eighty-four instances where sexual orientation information was recorded in the MARC 368c, the person being characterized was a member of a sexual minority group. By only recording the sexual orientation of individuals who do not identify as heterosexual, we unconsciously reify and validate a worldview that normalizes hetero identities, assuming them as the default category. While it is reasonable to assume that this was not the intended result, it nevertheless represents a form of othering based upon the unconscious privilege of the majority, which is summarized by Marilyn Frye: "One of the privileges of being normal and ordinary is a certain unconsciousness. When one is that which is taken as the norm in one's social environment, one does not have to think about it ... If one is the norm, one does not have to know what

one is. If one is marginal, one does not have the privilege of not notic-
ing what one is."[9]

Problematic Spotlighting

Another undesirable effect of inconsistency is spotlighting, or gra-
tuitously directing attention to one demographic attribute, giving that
attribute disproportionate significance. Sexual orientation demographic
terms were included as the sole "Other Designation" attribute in sixty-
one of the eighty-four total instances (approximately seventy-three
percent). Keeping in mind that demographic group terms of all types
(religion, nationality, ethnicity, etc.) have been used in NARs, the inclusion of a single particular demographic group signifies that in those
sixty-one cases, sexual identity is disproportionately important to those
persons' comprehensive identities. While not discounting that there
are likely individuals who do place more importance on their sexuality
over other characteristics such as religion, nationality, or ethnicity, an
ethically conscious cataloger should have a strong aversion to making
this determination in an authority record.

Problematic Associations

The inconsistent application of demographic group terms in personal
name authority records can also lead to unintentional, but regrettable
associations. It is possible to see how assigning medical, psychological,
or disability related demographic group terms as an intended audience
characteristic in bibliographic records could be extremely helpful for
identification and selection of resources. However, to record these terms
in authority records, to identify a person on the basis of their condition
or affliction, is insensitive at best. The MARC 368c research identified
twenty-one instances where medical, psychological, or disability related

---

9. Marilyn Frye, "Lesbian Feminism and the Gay Rights Movement: Another View
of Male Supremacy, Another Separatism," in *The Politics of Reality: Essays in Feminist
Theory* (Trumansburg, N.Y.: The Crossing Press, 1983), 146-47.

terms were recorded in NARs (**Table 2)**, but those concerning HIV/
AIDS were especially problematic.

	Thesaurus		
Term	LCDGT	LCSH	Total
AIDS (Disease)--Patients	0	4	4
Blind	0	2	2
Cerebral palsied	0	2	2
Parkinson's disease patients	2	0	2
People with disabilities	1	1	2
AIDS patients	1	0	1
Alcoholics	1	0	1
Asperger's syndrome patients	1	0	1
Deafblind people	0	1	1
Diabetics	0	1	1
HIV-positive persons	1	0	1
Patients	0	1	1
Recovering alcoholics	0	1	1
Schizophrenics	0	1	1
Total	7	14	21

Table 2. Medical, Psychological, or Disability Related Terms
in LCNAF

In all six NARs where HIV/AIDS information was recorded (AIDS
(Disease)—Patients (4), AIDS patients (1), HIV-positive persons (1)),
it was found that the sexual orientation demographic group term "Gay
men" was also included. Associating HIV/AIDS only with gay men
"only serves to perpetuate harmful stereotypes about people living with
HIV and members of the LGBT community,"[10] and the homophobia
that this stereotype supports "continues to be a major barrier to ending
the global AIDS epidemic."[11] Without consistent application of demographic information in NARs, authority data is highly susceptible to
this type of interpretation that acts to further marginalize vulnerable
populations.

---

10. "Debunking Common Myths About HIV," Human Rights Campaign, last updated
February 2017, https://www.hrc.org/resources/debunking-common-myths-about-hiv.

11. "Homophobia and HIV," Avert, last updated March 16, 2018, https://www.avert.
org/professionals/hiv-social-issues/homophobia.

The Challenge of Accuracy

Accuracy is another foundational principle of cataloging, and one that is no less challenging for catalogers to achieve than consistency. In validation of this principle, it is general best practice in name authority work for catalogers to provide sufficient evidence for recording attributes of a person in a NAR. This is usually achieved by citing information from an authoritative source in a MARC 670 field. Failing to provide this justification can damage the integrity of our data, which could be viewed as unscrupulous when that data is sensitive and susceptible to misuse as is the case with sexual orientation demographics.

Problematic Credibility

In forty-three of the cases where sexual orientation was recorded, this information was justified solely based on a citation from Wikipedia. There are very practical reasons for citing Wikipedia in NARs, and, anecdotally, Wikipedia citations in NARs are becoming more prevalent in general, but the fact that it is being used as an authoritative source for sexual orientation information is concerning. If the cataloging profession as a whole decides that this information is worth including in NARs, there is a moral obligation to get it right. Depending on a site whose data is highly volatile, is prone to vandalism[12] and editing wars,[13] and whose own general disclaimer states that it, "makes no guarantee of validity"[14] is not good enough to meet this obligation. To its credit, Wikipedia has developed specific guidelines regarding the categorization of individuals by ethnicity, gender, religion and sexuality and its crowdsourcing model

12. Wikipedia, s.v. "Wikipedia:Vandalism," last edited April 27, 2018, https://en.wikipedia.org/wiki/Wikipedia:Vandalism.

13. Wikipedia, s.v. "Wikipedia:Edit Warring," last edited April 20, 2018, https://en.wikipedia.org/wiki/Wikipedia:Edit_warring.

14. Wikipedia, s.v. "Wikipedia:General Disclaimer," last edited December 17, 2015, https://en.wikipedia.org/wiki/Wikipedia:General_disclaimer.

for content generation allows for greater participation from more diverse populations than the LCNAF model.[15] However, Wikipedia's relative openness is susceptible to abuse from bad-faith actors and is cause for greater scrutiny of its content. Ultimately, getting a birth or death date wrong is one thing, the possibility of falsely outing someone based on information cited from a questionable source is another matter entirely.

Problematic Justification

Taking an ethically conscious approach to including demographic information NARs relies not only on the use of credible sources, but also on providing proper justification for the demographic terms used. An evaluation of the content of information recorded in the MARC 670 citations of those NARs containing sexual orientation terms found several instances of inadequate justification. There is no agreed upon definition of what is considered adequate justification in this context, so it is necessary to discuss specific examples.[16]

In nearly all cases where sexual orientation was included in the MARC 368c, there was at least some attempt to justify the sexual orientation term with information in a MARC 670 citation; the lone exception being the NAR for *Cooper, Dennis, 1953-* (LCCN: n 80049015). Citations in several records (e.g. LCCNs: n 80045876, no 99015852) offered no explicit reference to sexual orientation, evidently relying on terms like "partner" and "companion" to justify including the term "Gay men." Assuming a person's sexual orientation based solely on the nature of past or current relationships is reductive and irresponsible. Furthermore, this line of reasoning can result in discrediting bisexual identities or any sexual orientation identity that does not adhere to a gay-straight dichotomy.[17]

---

15. Wikipedia, s.v. "Wikipedia:Categorization/Ethnicity, gender, religion and sexuality," last edited March 18, 2018, https://en.wikipedia.org/wiki/Wikipedia:Categorization/Ethnicity,_gender,_religion_and_sexuality.

16. Name authority records are subject to change. The analysis contained here is based on how the records existed as of March 28, 2018.

17. "Erasure of Bisexuality," GLAAD, accessed June 1, 2018, https://www.glaad.org/bisexual/bierasure.

The NAR for *Allen, Paula* Gunn (LCCN: n 81139185) is an example
of problematic justification that also highlights the concern of relying
on Wikipedia for sensitive demographic information. Allen's authority
record includes the sexual orientation demographic group term "Lesbians" in a MARC 368c. This piece of information was justified by a
December 14, 2015 citation from Wikipedia that identifies Allen as a
"lesbian activist." This language is ambiguous in its own right. "Lesbian
activist" could mean an activist that is a lesbian or an activist for lesbian
causes. To complicate matters further, Allen's Wikipedia page has since
been edited and has removed "lesbian" from that particular statement.[18]
Regardless of Allen's true sexual identity,[19] making claims in NARs
based on ambiguous language from questionable sources runs the risk
of perpetuating and legitimizing falsehoods.

Addressing the Challenges

Demographic terms are becoming more common in personal name
authority records, providing additional evidence of a transition to a
person-centered approach to authority control. However, the examination of how sexual orientation has been recorded in NARs raises
legitimate concerns about the feasibility of incorporating demographic
terms in a way that is equitable and ethical. It is unreasonable to expect
that the Library of Congress or the Program for Cooperative Cataloging
would require the type of rigid uniformity that would be necessary to
prevent othering and spotlighting. It is equally unreasonable to assume
that catalogers could maintain accurate demographic information in
NARs given the fluid nature of identity.

The most salient argument for including demographic characteristics
in personal name authority records relies upon a vision of the future in
which a library's authority file can be queried (directly or indirectly) to

18. Wikipedia, s.v. "Paula Gunn Allen," last edited March 18, 2018, https://
en.wikipedia.org/wiki/Paula_Gunn_Allen.

19. Allen did identify as lesbian, see: Annette Van Dyke, "A Tribute to Paula Gunn
Allen (1939-2008)," *Studies in American Indian Literatures* Series 2, 20, no. 4 (2008): 71.

identify a set of creators sharing common attributes (e.g. find all Lesbian chemists) or to collocate resources based on creator attributes (e.g. find all resources created by Chinese Muslims). It is a compelling vision that promises new and interesting uses for authority data. However, without a guarantee of either consistency or accuracy the use of demographic characteristics in name authority records is difficult to defend.

Bibliography

Billey, Amber, Emily Drabinski, and K. R. Roberto. "What's Gender Got to Do with It? A Critique of RDA 9.7." *Cataloging & Classification Quarterly* 52, no. 4 (2014): 412-21. doi: 10.1080/01639374.2014.882465.

Billey, Amber, Matthew Haugen, John Hostage, Nancy Sack, and Adam L. Schiff. "Report of the PCC Ad Hoc Task Group on Gender in Name Authority Records." 2016. http://www.loc.gov/aba/pcc/documents/Gender_375%20field_RecommendationReport.pdf.

Drabinski, Emily. "Queering the Catalog: Queer Theory and the Politics of Correction." *Library Quarterly: Information, Community, Policy* 83, no. 2 (2013): 94-111.

Frye, Marilyn. "Lesbian Feminism and the Gay Rights Movement: Another View of Male Supremacy, Another Separatism." In *The Politics of Reality: Essays in Feminist Theory*, 128-51. Trumansburg, NY: The Crossing Press, 1983.

Library of Congress. "368 – Other Attributes of Person or Corporate Body." MARC 21 Format for Authority Data. Updated December 2017. http://www.loc.gov/marc/authority/ad368.html.

Library of Congress, Policy and Standards Division. *Introduction to Library of Congress Demographic Group Terms, 2018* edition. Washington, D.C.: Policy and Standards Division, Library of Congress, 2018. https://www.loc.gov/aba/publications/FreeLCDGT/2018%20LCDGT%20intro.pdf.

Moulaison, Heather Lea. "The Expansion of the Personal Name Authority Record under Resource Description and Access: Current Status and Quality Considerations." *IFLA Journal* 41, no. 1 (2015): 13-24.

Moulaison, Heather Lea, Felicity Dykas, and John M. Budd. "Foucault, the Author, and Intellectual Debt: Capturing the Author-Function through Attributes, Relationships, and Events in Knowledge Organization Systems." *Knowledge Organization* 41, no. 1 (2014): 30-43.

Niu, Jinfang. "Evolving Landscape in Name Authority Control." *Cataloging & Classification Quarterly* 51, no. 4 (2013): 404-19.

Thompson, Kelly J. "More Than a Name: A Content Analysis of Name Authority Records for Authors Who Self-Identify as Trans." *Library Resources & Technical Services* 60, no. 3 (2016): 140-55. doi: 10.5860/lrts.60n3.

Van Dyke, Annette. "A Tribute to Paula Gunn Allen (1939-2008)." *Studies in American Indian Literatures* Series 2, 20, no. 4 (2008): 68-75.

Whittaker, Thomas A. "MARC 21 Authority 368 Subfield 'C' Data." IU-ScholarWorks, 2018. http://hdl.handle.net/2022/22031.

PART II:

IMPACTS OF COLONIALISM

Chapter 5

THIS IS THE OPPRESSOR'S LANGUAGE YET I NEED IT TO TALK TO YOU:[1] NATIVE AMERICAN NAME AUTHORITIES AT THE UNIVERSITY OF DENVER

Erin Elzi and Katherine M Crowe

Abstract

Critiques of the cataloging and classification of materials by and about Native American peoples in United States libraries have proliferated in the academic literature in recent years, often written by non-Native librarians. Alternative classification systems, thesauri, protocols and federal law regulating practices around archival and other cultural heritage materials, exist, albeit primarily in special libraries. Libraries have rarely, however, dealt with name authorities in ways that are consistent with tribal nation-specific practices.

This chapter will propose a "middle way" that, while problematizing dominant culture's approach to creating name authorities, suggests a re-envisioning of practice within existing systems that builds on the work in Frank Exner, Little Bear's "North American Indian Personal Names in National Bibliographies."[2] This re-envisioned practice proposes that,

---

1. Adrienne Cecile Rich, *The Will to Change: Poems 1968-70* (London, 1972): 41.

2. K.R. Roberto, *Radical Cataloging: Essays at the Front* (Jefferson, N.C.: McFarland &

rather than relying on or waiting for the National Authority Cooperative (NACO) of the Program for Cooperative Cataloging (PCC) for changes or updates to existing authorities, that universities and consortia should embrace creation, application, and maintenance of local name authorities, in coordination with local and regional tribal representatives.

The authors, an archivist/curator and a cataloging and user experience librarian, both of whom identify as white, will include examples of this re-envisioned practice in the University of Denver (DU) Libraries' catalog as a proof of concept that could be implemented at like institutions. Examples focus specifically on name authorities related to tribal nations with roots in the un-ceded and ancestral territories in the state of Colorado, as well as Native American individuals with deep and sustained connections to the University. The authors also will also touch on the development process for an MOU (Memorandum of Understanding) between the University of Denver and the Cheyenne and Northern Arapaho nations, a necessary step to address the University's complex and brutal history with these nations. Examples of similar relationships and projects in the museum and archival community at other institutions will further illustrate how this mechanism might be utilized to establish other libraries' working relationships with tribal representatives in other institutions. This chapter builds on the evolving process outlined in "'If You Want the History of a White Man, You Go to a Library'"[3] where the librarians and archivists at the University of Denver—many of whom identify as white women – work to disrupt, or at least mitigate, the impact of systemic racism, specific to Native American-related collections in academic libraries and archives in Predominantly White Institutions (PWIs).

Co., 2008): 150.

3. Jennifer Bowers, Katherine Crowe, and Peggy Keeran, "'If You Want the History of a White Man, You Go to the Library': Critiquing Our Legacy, Addressing Our Library Collections Gaps," *Collection Management* 42, no. 3-4 (2017): 159.

Introduction

Theoretical Framework

The authors employ two theoretical frameworks for their work on Native American name authorities: Tribal Critical Race Theory (TribalCrit)[4] and feminist theory, specifically the feminist ethic of care.[5] These frameworks provide necessary underpinnings for our work given its focus on Native American name authorities and related ontologies, as both authors identify as white women with limited personal connections to Native communities and work at a Predominantly White Institution (PWI) with low numbers of Native American students, faculty, and staff. Though several authors in the literature review note an understandable tension between theory and practice, bell hooks' work as a feminist scholar engages with just this kind of theorizing—using lived experience and practice to inform theory and vice versa—and is ideal for the kind of work where "[a] blended method reflects the dynamic interrelationship between theory and practice we learn from our daily professional activities that in turn inform theoretical frameworks."[6] The authors interweave Tuck and Yang's reminder that "decolonization is not a metaphor"[7] throughout. We recognize that this work should, first and foremost, recognize contemporary Indigenous struggle for sovereignty. As Tuck and Yang remind us, "Solidarity is an uneasy, reserved, and

---

4. Bryan McKinley Jones Brayboy, "Toward a Tribal Critical Race Theory in Education," *The Urban Review* 37, no. 5 (2005): 425.

5. Bergis, Jules, "Confronting Our Failure of Car Around the Legacies of Marginalized People in the Archives," *Medium* (blog), November 11, 2016, https://medium.com/on-archivy/confronting-our-failure-of-care-around-the-legacies-of-marginalized-people-in-the-archives-dc4180397280.

6. Ann M. Doyle, Kimberley Lawson, and Sarah Dupont, "Indigenization of Knowledge Organization at the Xwi7xwa Library," *Journal of Library and Information Studies* 13, no. 2 (2015): 107.

7. Eve Tuck and K. Wayne Yang, "Decolonization is Not a Metaphor," *Decolonization: Indigeneity, Education & Society* 1, no. 1 (2012): 1.

unsettled matter that neither reconciles present grievances nor forecloses future conflict."[8] We are conscious of Tuck and Yang's outlined "settler moves to innocence," which attempt to "relieve the settler of feelings of guilt or responsibility without giving up land or privilege or power."[9] We will discuss how "settler moves to innocence" show up in actions taken by the University of Denver as it wrestles with its founders' brutal history with the Cheyenne and Arapaho nations, as well as within this work on Native American name authorities. We also remain conscious of Tuck and Yang's reminder that colonization is a historical process which requires material and systemic disruption. We also recognize that our project is not ambitious enough to extend into the logical end result of decolonization: the repatriation of land and restoration of full Native American sovereignty.

The foundational theoretical framework and lens for our work with Native American name authorities is TribalCrit, which extends the lens of critical race theory (CRT) to "address the specific needs of tribal people" by dealing directly with "American Indians' liminality as both legal/political and racialized beings [and] the experience of colonization."[10] Bryan Joseph McKinley Brayboy, who developed TribalCrit, describes it as a necessary evolution from CRT, which arose from the civil rights struggles of the African American community and "is [often] oriented toward an articulation of race issues along a 'black-white' binary."[11] According to Brayboy, "while [CRT has] developed to meet the specific needs of Latinos/as and Asian Americans, they largely maintain the basic premise of CRT that racism is endemic in society. In contrast, the basic tenet of TribalCrit emphasizes that colonization is endemic to society."[12] TribalCrit also maintains that "stories are not separate

---

8. Tuck and Yang, "Decolonization is not a Metaphor," 3.

9. Ibid., 10.

10. Brayboy, "Toward a Tribal Critical Race Theory," 425.

11. Ibid., 429.

12. Ibid.

from theory; they make up theory and are, therefore, real and legitimate sources of data and ways of being."[13] In addition, "theory and practice are connected in deep and explicit ways such that scholars must work towards social change."[14]

TribalCrit has some epistemic overlap with feminist theory, as both speak directly to the work of naming and ontologies, and connect the acts of storytelling, natural language, and naming to theory and practice. They also both call out dominant power structures for the devaluation of "nontraditional" ways of theorizing, as a way of reinforcing those same power structures. According to bell hooks, "the privileged act of naming often affords those in power access to modes of communication and enables them to project an interpretation, a definition, a description of their work and actions, that may not be accurate, that may obscure what is really taking place."[15] While hooks' work uses feminist theory for this critique, it can be logically extended to use of TribalCrit. Brayboy's work references a conversation with his mother to make this point:

> For some Indigenous scholars (and others), theory is not simply an abstract thought or idea that explains overarching structures of societies and communities; theories, through stories and other media, are roadmaps for our communities and reminders of our individual responsibilities to the survival of our communities...I once had an encounter with a colleague who told me that people like me "told good stories" and later added that because I told good stories, I might not ever be a "good theorist." I was struck by the seeming disconnect between community stories and personal narratives and "theory." After this encounter with my colleague, I returned home to Prospect, North Carolina, one of the communities of the Lumbee tribe of which I am an enrolled member, and told several of my relatives and elders about my colleagues' comments. My mother told me, "Baby, doesn't she know that our stories are our theories? And she thinks she's smarter than you because she can't tell stories?" My mother clearly hit on the reason why locating theory

---

13. Ibid, 430.

14. Ibid.

15. bell hooks, *Teaching to Transgress: Education as the Practice of Freedom* (New York: Routledge, 1994): 62.

as something absent from stories and practices is problematic in many Indigenous communities and in the work of anthropologists who seek to represent Indigenous communities.[16]

For hooks, Brayboy, and other scholars working within these theoretical frameworks, the processes are inherently dialogic and iterative. Our proposed "middle way" incorporates a community-based, natural language approach that allows for knowledge "outside of" libraries—especially as they are and have been constituted—to work its way into professional library practice.

Literature Review

The authors' "middle way" for addressing issues specific to Native American name authorities is informed by the above theoretical framework, as well as existing professional practice and projects with similar missions and goals. The literature has several gaps: much of the writing is on tribal nations outside of the United States, or deals with thesauri or classification schemes rather than names and name authorities – and much of the literature that does deal with name authorities in a bibliographic context is ten or more years old. We are also cognizant of the risk in compressing the specificity of different nations' histories and cultures during the development of practice-based solutions, especially because each community has different practices for naming and name representation. Per Marisa Elena Duarte and Miranda Belarde-Lewis, "embedded in the names [indigenous communities] call themselves are whole networks of semiotic interactions that are very likely often incommensurable with Anglo-American lists of terms and knowledge structures. Being aware of the context of names and the colonial practice of renaming helps us understand the frustration Indigenous peoples experience when attempting to research Indigenous histories through

---

16. Brayboy, "Toward a Tribal Critical Race Theory," 426.

Western-oriented classification and cataloging systems."[17] This caveat aside, the literature gives us some hope that there are consistent issues and solutions.

There is a small but powerful selection of writing on the treatment of indigenous nations as subject matter and classification, and some that address issues in the representation of indigenous names in library cataloging practices. With the exception of Duarte and Belarde-Lewis' "Imagining: Creating Spaces for Indigenous Ontologies," the articles in the excellent 2015 special issue of *Cataloging and Classification Quarterly* on Indigenous Knowledge Organization primarily address issues between libraries and indigenous communities in New Zealand, Australia and Canada. While the specifics regarding tribal traditions and institutional practices may be unique to each country and nation, there are some consistent issues and solutions that span across international lines, various tribal nations, and are reflective of the issues found in representing Indigenous communities of North America in US libraries that are working primarily with Library of Congress standards.

Of the existing literature, there is a poignant collection of writings that both discuss the inherent problems in creating thoughtful library spaces for indigenous peoples (in both the traditional sense of physical space, but also in the online, digital and knowledge organization spaces), and cover the ways in which institutions have sought solutions – including a cataloging and classification perspective. The establishment and practices taken by the X̱wi7x̱wa Library at the University of British Columbia is one example of a holistic approach to the organization of knowledge by, for, and about a specific indigenous community. Recognizing the interconnectedness between the work of technical services, and the work of instruction, reference and other "user-centered" services, this Library has taken an approach that acknowledges their subject matter and user-base as "deeply embedded in organizational, political,

---

17. Marisa Elena Duarte and Miranda Belarde-Lewis. "Imagining: Creating spaces for indigenous ontologies." *Cataloging & Classification Quarterly* 53, no. 5-6 (2015): 685, doi: 10.1080/01639374.2015.1018396.

and social contexts of a particular time and place, and within the global relations of those dimensions", and uses this to inform their methods and practices in all areas of the Library.[18] The Cline Library at Northern Arizona University has taken a similarly holistic approach; in addition to collection development and metadata work, which has focused on the inability of subject headings to address particular clans of tribal nations, the library's outreach and programming enables the community to get involved in creating community-sourced visibility for Native American authors, artists, and scholars via Wikipedia edit-a-thons.[19] In these ways, the library becomes permeable, with knowledge working its way both from outside and to the outside from within.

Other projects have involved extended dialogue and direct community consultation with tribal representatives during the design phase of collaborative projects, using many of the concepts outlined in TribalCrit. The National Research Centre for Truth and Reconciliation (NRCTR) in Canada was created to house, process and make available millions of records and documents collected from institutions involved in Canada's Residential Schools program (a 150-year program that sought to indoctrinate indigenous children and sever all ties to their communities and cultures). In the effort to "combat" the barriers that Indigenous users of libraries and archives face, the NRCTR adopted a set of five best practices for managing indigenous knowledge: "protect and preserve Indigenous knowledge(s) in a variety of mediums for use by current and future generations in a respectful and sensitive manner"; "provide a welcoming environment and assistance for First Nations, Métis, non-status, and Inuit people to access this knowledge"; "seek direction from communities on proper protocols regarding access and care of their culturally sensitive records"; "respect the First Nations, Métis, and Inuit cultural concept of copyright with regard to Aboriginal history or cultural

---

18. Ann M. Doyle, Kimberley Lawson, and Sarah Dupont, "Indigenization of Knowledge Organization at the Xwi7xwa Library," *Journal of Library and Information Studies* 13, no. 2 (2015): 108.

19.Naomi Bishop, Jonathan Pringle, and Carissa Tsosie. "Connecting Cline Library with tribal communities: A case study," *Collection Management* 42, no. 3-4 (2017): 246.

heritage, which is often located in but not limited to oral traditions, songs, dance, storytelling, anecdotes, place names, hereditary names, and other forms of Indigenous knowledges"; "provide opportunities and access to training and employment regarding the protection and preservation of Indigenous knowledge materials for First Nations."[20] The Truth and Reconciliation Commission has also issued several reports which provide a sense of the impact of names and their relationship to the destruction of language and culture for the students who survived Canadian residential schools. Peter Nakogee, Ministik, recounted a classroom experience where a nun asked the students to write their names: "I didn't know English, so…I wrote on my scribblers in Cree syllabics. And…I got the nun really mad that I was writing in Cree. And then I only knew my name was Ministik from the first time I heard my name, my name was Ministik. So I was whipped again because I didn't know my name was Peter Nakogee."[21] This example sheds some light on not only the brutality of the residential school system, but the challenges in providing respectful, ethical access to materials documenting the multiplicity of identities created by colonization in indigenous communities.

Camille Callison's chapter in *Indigenous Notions of Ownership and Libraries, Archives, and Museums* delves into this more directly, addressing Tuck and Yang's concerns about the material consequences of colonization, as well as the underpinnings of TribalCrit—namely, that libraries can function as another tool of colonization, which is endemic in the lives of indigenous peoples. According to Callison: "The strengths of these systematic cataloguing standards are obvious. If all libraries are the same throughout the nation, anyone familiar with the system can walk into any library in the country and use the catalogue to quickly find what they want. It makes cataloguing much simpler and faster,

---

20. Brett Lougheed, Ry Morgan, and Camille Callison, "Reconciliation Through Description: Using Metadata to Realize the Vision of the National Research Centre for Truth and Reconciliation," *Cataloging & Classification Quarterly* 53, no. 5-6 (2015): 597, 605-608.

21. Truth and Reconciliation Commission of Canada, *The Survivors Speak: Report of the Truth and Reconciliation Commission of Canada* (Ottawa: Truth and Reconciliation Commission of Canada), 2015: 48.

saving time and money. However, for Native American/Alaska Native people, there are concerns related to assimilation and colonization that must be considered. Colonization has resulted in rapid and traumatic cultural change – the loss of language, lands, governance, children, and community – leading to widespread social challenges. All cultures need to store and retrieve information. For cultures with a history of abuse by Western people, a Western-style library may function as one more emblem of assimilation. Libraries in these communities must overcome a variety of hurdles to collect material relevant to the community and to provide the best access they can to that material. Like any library, they must consider their community base and adjust library practice to meet the needs of their communities."[22]

The authors' work is also informed by Gina Schlesselman-Tarango's "The Legacy of Lady Bountiful"[23] and *White Mother to a Dark Race* by Margaret Jacobs,[24] both of which critique the influence of white supremacy through a gender-based lens—in Jacobs' case, as a way of drawing out the influence of white womanhood on the residential school movement in both the United States and Australia, and Schlesselman-Tarango's, the "civilizing" impulse of white female librarians and the related potential harm to the communities served by these librarians. As a profession which is 88% white-identified[25] and two white female authors, this historical resonance to this topic in particular shouldn't be ignored—and we are vigilant for its influence on our professional practice.

---

22. Camille Callison, Loriene Roy, and Gretchen Alice LeCheminant, *Indigenous Notions of Ownership and Libraries, Archives, and Museums* (Boston, MA: IFLA Publications, 2016), 182.

23. Gina Schlesselman-Tarango, "The Legacy of Lady Bountiful: White Women in the Library," *Library Trends* 64, no. 4 (2016): 667.

24. Margaret D. Jacobs, *White Mother to a Dark Race: Settler Colonialism, Maternalism, and the Removal of Indigenous Children in the American West and Australia, 1880-1940* (Lincoln: University of Nebraska Press, 2009), 148.

25. "American Library Association Releases New Data to Update Diversity Counts Report," *Targeted News Service*, September 15, 2012.

In a project that envisions a "middle way" of integrating both auto-
mation and community input, a 2008 study by Srinivasan, Pepe and
Rodriguez looked at "what methods can researchers, engineers, and
policymakers alike embrace in creating digital systems that categorize,
share, and transfer information meaningfully for diverse communities?"
while acknowledging that "the system's interface, ontologies, and deployment all must consider the larger social and cultural context within which
the user is embedded."[26] The researchers worked with the ontology that
resulted from Tribal Peace research initiative—a project that looked at
how information systems could help lessen the fragmentation among
nineteen Native American tribes in San Diego County. Developing an
approach labeled as "semi-automated," the project combined a fully
automated method of determining the terms of an ontology via an
aggregator, then gathering community feedback in the approval of the
terms, and in determining the relationships between them. The authors
acknowledge that creating purely "fluid" ontologies (ie., community
created and ever adaptable) is a highly successful method, but is time
consuming and only applicable on a small scale. In testing the merged
method of combining a fluid terminology with automated clustering
techniques, the authors found that a sustainable and relevant ontology
could be developed.[27]

An example of a highly localized and well documented classification structure is the Brian Deer Classification System. This scheme
was developed in the 1970s by A. Brian Deer, considered one of the
first Indigenous librarians in Canada. From the start, Deer sought to
create a system that applied only to the items in the collection of the
library at the National Indian Brotherhood in Ottawa.[28] However, several

---

26. Ramesh Srinivasan, Alberto Pepe, and Marko A. Rodriguez, "A Clustering-Based
Semi-Automated Technique to Build Cultural Ontologies," *Journal of the American Society for Information Science & Technology* 60, no. 3 (2009): 608.

27. Srinivasan, Pepe, and Rodriguez, "Clustering-Based Semi-Autonomous Technique," 608.

28. Alissa Cherry and Keshav Mukunda, "A Case Study in Indigenous Classification:
Revisiting and Reviving the Brian Deer Scheme," *Cataloging & Classification Quarterly*
53, no. 5-6 (2015): 552.

other institutions have adapted Brian Deer to meet the needs of their own collections, including the Cree Cultural Institute and the X̱wi7x̱wa Library.[29] Brian Deer and its applications in other institutions show both the impossibility for developing a one-schema-to-rule-them all approach for indigenous knowledge organization, as well as how, once there is a model based on indigenous knowledge in place, smaller institutions with fewer resources can often adapt it to meet their own needs. In this way, organizational systems that extend beyond the Euro-centric structure of Library of Congress Classification (LCC) can at the very least inspire the development of, structures that work for more than one indigenous group. It's also worth noting that while the Brian Deer Classification System may be the most well-known, it is not the only classification system that has been developed for indigenous groups as an alternative to LCC. Others include classification schemes developed by the Environmental Aboriginal Guardianship Through Law and Education, the BC Aboriginal Child Care Society Resource Centre, the Museum of Anthropology at the University of British Colombia, and the Southwest Museum's Braun Research Library (now at the Autry Center).[30] In addition to these, there are also a number of thesauri that have been constructed to make up for the downfalls of Library of Congress Subject Headings (LCSH), including Maori Subject Headings, the Aboriginal and Tores Strait Thesaurus, the National Indian Law Library Thesaurus, and the First Nations House of Learning Thesaurus.[31]

While all these institutions take a thoughtful approach to looking beyond what the Library of Congress provides for cataloging tools, these projects are a solution for only some of the problem. These

---

29. Raegan Swanson, "Adapting the Brian Deer Classification System for Aanischaaukamikw Cree Cultural Institute," *Cataloging & Classification Quarterly* 53, no. 5-6 (2015): 113.

30. Cherry, 552.

31. Sandra Littletree and Cheryl A. Metoyer, "Knowledge Organization from an Indigenous Perspective: The Mashantucket Pequot Thesaurus of American Indian Terminology Project," *Cataloging & Classification Quarterly* 53, no. 5-6 (2015): 642.

projects look at subject headings and classification, but do not specifically address issues in the representation of personal or tribal names. Based on a review of the public portals of several of the projects, many include multiple forms of names selectively. For example, the Plateau Peoples' Portal, which utilizes Mukurtu software, includes both the community name in the language of each tribal nation as well as the translated English language name, but the personal names included in the publicly accessible portions of the web portal show only the translated English language name form. There are certainly authors whose works address the specific issues regarding personal and tribal name of indigenous tribes of North America and their members. However, this area of the library literature is both smaller in size and older in publication date—in all cases, at least ten years prior to the publication of this chapter. Despite the age of these writings, the problems they discuss are still relevant—both in libraries, as well as in society and historical representation as a whole.

Frank Exner, Little Bear's chapter in *Radical Cataloging: Essays at the Front*, published in 2008, is primary among the existing literature for its salience to this project. The chapter covers a survey of his findings of a multitude of national library catalogs from ten countries, searching for 185 Native American names. The chapter also includes a thorough discussion on the various forms that Native American names can take: in different languages and cultures, in formal versus informal settings, and over the span of a lifetime. At the time of the writing, only 20% of the names found in the Library of Congress catalog included the traditional form of the author's name. While the author admitted that 185 is a fairly small sample of records to come to any conclusions, and that more research in this area should be done, the results of this study showed that of the ten countries searched, LC had one of the worst ratios of names found to names found with the traditional name. Furthermore, even when the traditional or mixed form name is included in an LC authority record, the strict formatting demanded by LC sometimes warps it into something other than what the author would be known by.[32] It is worth nothing that even the citation format for this publication does not do mixed name form justice (Frank Exner, Little Bear). The author's own name is often mangled in citations for the chapter; in doing this research, we found multiple citations that identify this author as two different people (Frank Exner & Little Bear),[33] or instances where, despite the correct name form listed on the article, the metadata provided by a vendor rearranged the name as incorrect inverted order rather than in direct order, to read "Exner, Little Bear, Frank."[34]

A Way Forward/Proposed Solutions

Institutional Context

The University of Denver's relationship to the Cheyenne and Arapaho nations remains fraught, violent, and continues to evolve. The University has issued several reports since 2013 related to its founders' role in the Sand Creek Massacre. The first, issued by the John Evans Study Committee in 2014, concluded that Evans, the University's primary founder and second Territorial Governor at the time of the Massacre, was culpable.[35] The University's Task Force on Native American Inclusivity issued a report in 2016,[36] calling for the inclusion of Native American history

---

32. Frank Exner, Little Bear, "North American Indian Personal Names in National Bibliographies," in *Radical Cataloging*, ed. K.R. Roberto (Jefferson, NC: McFarland, 2008), 153-157.

33. Frank Exner and Little Bear, "North American Indians: Personal Names with Semantic Meaning," *Names* 55, no. .1 (2007): 3.

34. Frank Little Bear Exner, "Indexing Integrated Manual Sets at Northern Telecom," *Bulletin of the American Society for Information Science and Technology* 23, no. 4 (1997): 20.

35. University of Denver John Evan Study Committee, *Report of the John Evans Study Committee of the University of Denver* (Denver, CO: University of Denver, 2014), 12.

36. University of Denver Task Force on Native American Inclusivity, *Strategic Recommendations of the Task Force on Native American Inclusivity for the Sustainable Development of a Native American Community Presence at the University of Denver* (Denver, CO: University of Denver, 2016), 7.

and culture into the University curriculum, as well as a Memorandum of Understanding (MOU) between the University and the Cheyenne and Arapaho nations.

The reports have produced several tangible outcomes; first, in 2016, the University hired a Director of Native American Community Relations and Programs.[37] Second, on April 2, 2018, the University held a ceremony to add the flags from Northern Cheyenne, Northern Arapaho and Southern Cheyenne and Arapaho Nations to the display in the DU student center, next to the University of Denver flag, the flag of the United States, and the state flag of Colorado. Per a press release from the University's marketing department: "According to treaties between representatives of these Nations and the United States Government, Cheyenne and Arapaho people retain legal claims to their original lands. The University of Denver acknowledges such claims. In order to signify this recognition, while also honoring the sovereign political status of the Northern Cheyenne, Northern Arapaho and Southern Cheyenne and Arapaho Nations, their tribal flags will be displayed on campus now and in the future alongside the flags of the United States, the State of Colorado and the University of Denver."[38] The MOU is in process, and provides a foundation for future collaborations between the University and the Northern Cheyenne, Northern Arapaho and Southern Cheyenne and Arapaho nations. Additionally, DU participates in the annual Sand Creek Healing Run/Walk, which begins at the site of the massacre and concludes on the steps of the Colorado State Capitol.

At the same time, the University's student body continues to push and agitate for change. The University's now-defunct mascot, "Denver Boone," a 1960s-era cartoon character drawn by a Walt Disney illustrator, as well as the nickname, "Pioneers," (sometimes shortened to "Pios") both continue to draw fire. On October 9, 2017, Indigenous Peoples

---

37. "DU Alumna and Staff Member Elevates Native American Outreach," *University of Denver Newsroom*, April 25, 2017, http://news.du.edu/du-alumna-and-staff-member-elevates-native-american-outreach/.

38. "Tribal Flags to Fly Over DU Campus," *University of Denver Newsroom*, March 28, 2018, http://news.du.edu/du-hosts-tribal-flag-raising-ceremony/.

Day, the Native Student Alliance (NSA) launched its #NoMorePios campaign.[39] On March 2, 2018, the DU Student Activists (DUSA) and NSA held a joint direct action at a DU home hockey game against University of Miami Ohio, holding a banner with a coonskin cap (a signature part of the "Boone" character) in a "no" sign that read "#NoMorePios—Pioneers Stole Indian Land and Killed Indian People."[40] These current students have set themselves up in direct opposition to a vocal portion of the largely white-identified, Baby Boomer-era generation alumni base, many of whom attended the University during the "Boone" era. The NSA also organized a protest in November 2016 in response to the University's College of Business's "Pipeline Leadership Conference," sponsored by Enbridge Energy Partners and Michels Corporation, two of the financial sponsors of the Dakota Access Pipeline, which the Standing Rock Sioux had been protesting for the past year.[41] The University's hesitation to address these concerns directly can be seen as an example of Tuck and Yang's "settler moves to innocence"—while DU is making many of the right "noises" in the public sphere, it has yet to directly address some of the more challenging requests of its student body and community members, especially since some of them may cost the university in financial resources and support from its alumni base.

Working within Existing Structures While Challenging for Change

Given all of the considerations, frameworks, and projects on which to model our approach to Native American name authorities, the authors decided to address the issue, within this specific context, in the following

39. "DU Native Student Alliance Launches #NoMorePios Campaign," *University of Denver Clarion*, October 16, 2017, https://duclarion.com/2017/10/du-native-student-alliance-launches-nomorepios-campaign/.

40. Twitter post with multiple images from University of Denver Native Student Alliance-affiliated student activist documenting protest, March 3, 2018.

41. Justin Cygan, "A Look Inside the #NoDAPL Protest," *University of Denver Clarion*, November 9, 2016, https://duclarion.com/2016/11/a-look-inside-the-nodapl-protest/.

ways. First, we decided to focus specifically on names within the communities and tribal nations most directly connected with the University —namely, the Cheyenne and Arapaho, as well as Native faculty or other published authors, scholars, or other individuals closely associated with the University and its history. This focus will allow us to build community and remain accountable to the peoples and nations with whom the University is developing an MOU. In addition, it will allow us to narrow our scope to a more manageable project, especially in its pilot stages.

Related, the University of Denver Libraries is involved with the Western Names Authority Project, which received a two-year planning grant from the IMLS in 2016 to develop a collaborative focusing on more robust local and regional name authorities through data sharing, cleanup, and cooperation. This project focuses broadly on regional name authorities and Linked Open Data, but not necessarily on Native American name authorities, provides several potential inroads to infuse the project with this data. While the University of Denver is not the principal investigator and as a result does not have access to in-depth information about the initial sources of local name authority lists for all partners, some of the presentations give clues – for example, the University of Utah utilized the "Daughters of Utah Pioneers" as one such list—that raise some questions.[42] First, while these lists of "pioneers" are admittedly a source of data that has already been compiled, we would ask if efforts have been made to pull in other sources of such data—for example, lists of names of individuals in Native American communities affected by events like the Sand Creek Massacre, or those who participated in the Battle of Julesburg, a battle precipitated by the violence of the Massacre, and unusual in that much of the information about it comes from Native American participants like George Bent, who was connected to both events.[43] This very well may have been

42. Anna Neatour and Jeremy Myntti, "The Western Name Authority File: Improving Access for Digital Collections and Archives." *Digital Matters: Digital Culture Studies at the University of Utah Symposium*, presentation at Digital Humanities Utah 2, February 11, 2017.

43. George Bent and George E. Hyde. *Life of George Bent, Written from His Letters* (Norman, OK: University of Oklahoma Press, 1968), 168.

taken into account during project development—again, we are not privy to all project information—but this is the kind of due diligence that is important for these types of name authority projects if they are to be inclusive of all individuals, organizations, and families significant to regional history. We look forward to future partnerships in this vein.

The authors looked at several individuals from the Cheyenne Nation who were personally impacted by the Sand Creek Massacre, or related in some way, to road test some of the approaches we might take. George Bent, the son of William Bent, a white trader, and Owl Woman, William Bent's first wife, has an LCNAF authority record, but it contains only one form of his name, not his Cheyenne name, Ho-my-ike, which translates as "Beaver."[44] There is no record in any authority file for Owl Woman, George Bent's mother and William Bent's first wife, despite her appearance in numerous written histories of territorial Colorado. These two examples provide proof of the need for name authority improvement efforts to include subject experts and community members, and to look at issues beyond the mere inclusion of all name forms, and flexibility in format. Short of re-cataloging all materials covering a particular indigenous nation and clans within those nations, it would take a certain amount of historical knowledge, analysis of existing authorities lists for gaps, and cultural sensitivity to know that individuals such like Owl Woman are missing from Library of Congress name authority records.

Ideally, an authority record, especially one like George Bent's, would include all variations outlined by Frank Exner, Little Bear: traditional, European, and mixed form, as well as complete name sets (the various names an individual can be known by simultaneously) and name sequences (the various names by which an individual may be known by over a period of time). Preferred forms of names would be thoroughly researched (or in the case of the living, asked of the person), and easy to change when called for. In an ideal world, the authority record would allow for multiple preferred forms, or at least a preferred form that

---

44. "Bent, George, 1843-1918," *VIAF: Virtual International Authority File*, https://viaf.org/viaf/56725635/.

acknowledged all parts of a name set. Library OPACs and discovery layers would be configured to search and retrieve on all of them, using a name/author/creator search scope. Locally managed authority files would be created to meet the specific needs of a collection, a system of knowledge organization, or user-base. Library staff would be allowed the time and space to become experts in the indigenous groups represented in their collection. Literary warrant would still hold as a general principle, but could be expanded to include epistemic warrant, allowing for different ways of knowing and searching than what might be found in the published literature.[45] In this vein, pronunciation of names would be included in the authority records, especially for names that have warrant via the existence of an oral history or object, but have not necessarily been written down except for the sake of metadata.

Unfortunately, many of these proposed changes would require structural changes to LCNAF and like name authorities lists and guidelines. The existing knowledge organization structures for name authorities predominantly used in the United States *do* include fields for various and limited name forms, and in theory, the records and preferred forms are well researched in their creation and update. However, these records call for a single preferred form of a name, failing to recognize all parts of a name set as simultaneously used by a person. These records often do not correctly identify components of a name sequence as such. Pronunciation is not included. The records are often created by non-subject specialists, and for a very wide-application. OPACs and discovery layers sometimes do not index all versions of a name, and even when indexed for retrieval, the name variations do not display. In practice, there are a number of barriers to timely, accurate, and culturally sensitive updates to authority files.

Taking a cue from writings that have addressed subject headings, one possible solution for improving authority records is not unlike that which Doyle presented as a "qualitative research project" for classification and

---

45. Daniel Martínez-Ávila, John M. Budd. "Epistemic Warrant for Categorizational Activities and the Development of Controlled Vocabularies," *Journal of Documentation* 73, no. 4 (2017): 711.

subject headings. Doyle's five-part process that starts with an inventory of existing Aboriginal terms and classifications, then interviews with the creators and users of these ontologies, followed by collaboration with the Aboriginal communities and reflection on design principles, and ending with a proof of concept case study.[46] Doyle's study involves working with communities, but not at every step; it does not place a great burden upon the Indigenous communities to do the legwork. While Doyle's project sought interview with a community that intended to describe collections from a non-Euro-centric perspective, the method need not be so library-centric. Jay Colbert suggests a methodology that seeks the natural language of researchers and encourages understanding how the interviewee places themselves in the world, and the relationships they naturally build between seemingly disparate concepts. Colbert took extra care to create an interview process and environment that eliminated (to the best of one's ability) any establishment of power that an interviewer may have over an interviewee. Although these "semi-structured" interviews were held with the intention of gathering terms and relationships for improved subject access, a similar process could be used for the improvement of name representation.[47]

Most institutions, including those with the subject expertise in and connections to particular tribal nations, may not have the ability to enhance national authority records (either lacking the actual memberships, training and access needed to do so, or simply lacking the staff time required for such resource-intensive endeavors). Action can be taken, however, beyond national authority work. In some systems, local maintenance of authority records is possible. Even when using a national authority file, the records can be imported into the local system and altered or enhanced. In the absence of the ability to enhance authority records either on a national or local level, there are other, more feasible

---

46. Doyle, 440.

47. Jessica L. Colbert, "Patron-Driven Subject Access: How Librarians Can Mitigate that 'Power to Name'," *In the Library with the Leadpipe* (November 2017). Colbert changed their first name to Jay after publication of "Patron-Driven Subject Access" and their works under both names are collocated at https://orcid.org/0000-0001-5733-5168.

methods that can be taken in the immediacy. Catalogers can also choose
to enhance bibliographic records to include name variations or forms
that are not found in the national authority record, which has been our
institutional approach. When added to free-text note fields, the names
become a searchable and visible part of the record (the visibility aspect
being an advantage that a linked authority record does not have, in our
and many other current Library Management Systems). While this is
specific to the system being used at the University of Denver, even in
a system that allows the users to view authority records, not all versions
of the name display in the bibliographic records—only the savviest of
researchers would know where to go to find the additional name forms.

Library systems are built upon standards and protocols that allow for
the exchange of bibliographic and related data; any individual library
challenge to standards and protocols could lead to the disruption of that
library's ability to share or exchange data. With the method of enhancing free-text note fields, the name form does not go into controlled
fields in an unauthorized form, therefore the records still conform
to the standards used by other institutions and it does not disrupt the
potential for shared or linked data. The drawbacks, of course, are that
enhancing the bibliographic records also does not *improve* any of the
fields that would be shared in a linked data environment, and that it
takes more time to enhance multiple bibliographic records than it does
a single authority record. Our current approach is for the DU catalogers
to look for any name variant as found on the piece, or through some
additional research, and add all found name variants to the free-text note.
These fields are also only keyword searchable, so their content is not
indexed as an author/creator scope. One such version of these notes
has been to create or enhance existing summary notes. For the book
Tribal Strength and Education, by Terry Huffman, the OCLC record used
by the DU libraries had no mention of Sitting Bull, despite repeated
references of him through the book, in the index and in the publisher's
description. The DU catalogers not only added a subject heading for
Sitting Bull, but also created a summary note that describes his influences as discussed in the book, and included in that summary note his

Lakota name, using the Lakota orthography. The Library of Congress authority record used for the subject heading Sitting Bull does contain thirteen name forms, but none using the Lakota diacritics.[48] The lack of diacritics in the LC authority record means that if a researcher were to search the DU catalog for the name form that uses the diacritics, they would not get any results. By adding this form to the free-text note, the user can now find works on Sitting Bull, using his Lakota name form, both with and without the use of the diacritics.

Additionally, none of these catalogers have subject expertise in this area, so there has been a learning curve. Those working with these materials in technical services have been trained on what to look for as a potential item that warrants this additional level of cataloging attention, and work with acquisitions to ensure new purchases are flagged as those that may qualify for this treatment. So, while it is far from the previously described ideal situation, and may not work at every institution, we have found this to be an immediate and actionable improvement that could be implemented while we advocate for longer-term solutions and structural changes to authority work, and arrange for cooperation with community members to develop lists of locally applied keywords and subject headings. It is a commitment of time and resources, both for the bibliographic work and in seeking authority solutions, but it is a commitment that the DU Libraries believes is worthwhile both morally and ethically, while serving as a proof of concept for other libraries with similar goals.

While the University of Denver's specific situation and approach may not be exactly applicable to other institutions, we hope that, much like some of the other project-based solutions mentioned earlier have been adapted and applied outside their immediate context, and ultimately in a more systemic or holistic way, that this will serves as a model, or at least a prompt, to other like institutions. The University of Denver's history with the Cheyenne and Arapaho nations is horrific, even when placed

---

48. "Sitting Bull, 1831-1890," Library of Congress Authorities, https://lccn.loc.gov/n50025199

in the context of the considerable brutality visited on Native nations by the United States. Many other institutions are just now grappling with their own histories with slavery, gentrification, and other forms of systemic oppression that have affected and continue to disproportionately affect marginalized communities. Similar steps, appropriate to the context and specificity of the situation at hand, and mindful of institutional potential to perpetuate the legacies of racism and settler colonialism, can and should be taken by institutions housing material that document the histories and cultures of indigenous peoples. Duarte and Belarde-Lewis' call for non-indigenous people to be "epistemic partners" and to "forge partnerships [with indigenous communities] for building systems that reflect, as appropriate, Indigenous epistemologies and local needs"[49] feels particularly salient for this project.

Conclusion

Despite the lack of solutions in the existing literature for indigenous, and specifically Native American, representation in name authority files, there are a number of ongoing projects we will look to as we move forward, many of which use methodological and ontological underpinnings that lend themselves to application in name authority files for Indigenous peoples. We also look forward to a more formal MOU and process for working directly with the Cheyenne and Arapaho nations in ways that respect tribal sovereignty and cultural traditions.

This project, as of the writing of this chapter, is in its beginnings. Working with name authorities in this way is necessarily iterative, and as with hooks' theorizing, our work is necessarily informed by community input and practice—something we've not yet fully embarked on. We will dive in, review, rewrite the framework from what we learn, change our process accordingly, dive back in, and repeat. This blended method, mentioned in part by hooks and by Doyle, Lawson and Dupont, "reflects the dynamic interrelationship between theory and practice we

---

49. Duarte & Belarde-Lewis, 679.

learn from our daily professional activities that in turn inform theoretical frameworks, including concepts, that are then tested in practice through an interactive cycle (Ranganathan) of applied research."[50] In some ways, the process is similar to the existing cycle of feedback on name authorities that librarians are already familiar with, except that the current situation is rooted in the authors' lack of direct experience with and knowledge about indigenous cultures—a cycle of "standard sources" that "by definition choose more of the same standard sources, creating a closed system."[51]

Also, as we acknowledged initially, the project is not ambitious enough to extend to the logical end goal of decolonization: the repatriation of land and restoration of full Native American sovereignty. Our goal is far more modest: to break down barriers, resulting in an open system that allows for recognition of Indigenous names for indexing, discovery and retrieval by all levels of scholarship and research. This is the beginning of our work on such a system, and we're eager to try, fail a bit, learn from our mistakes, and continue to move forward.

Acknowledgements

Thanks to Naomi Bishop for her thorough and thoughtful editorial comments.

Bibliography

"American Library Association Releases New Data to Update Diversity Counts Report." *Targeted News Service*, September 15, 2012.

"Bent, George, 1843-1918." *VIAF: Virtual International Authority File.* https://viaf.org/viaf/56725635/.

Bent, George Bent and George E. Hyde. *Life of George Bent, Written from His Letters.* Norman, OK: University of Oklahoma Press, 1968.

---

50. Dolye, Lawson & Dupont, 107.
51. Doyle, 438.

Bishop, Naomi, Jonathan Pringle, and Carissa Tsosie. "Connecting Cline Library with tribal communities: A case study." *Collection Management* 42, no. 3-4 (2017): 240-55.

Bowers, Jennifer, Katherine Crowe, and Peggy Keeran, "'If You Want the History of a White Man, You Go to the Library': Critiquing Our Legacy, Addressing Our Library Collections Gaps." *Collection Management* 42, no. 3-4 (2017): 159-79.

Brayboy, Bryan McKinley Jones, "Toward a Tribal Critical Race Theory in Education." *The Urban Review* 37, no. 5 (2005): 425-46.

Callison, Camille, Loriene Roy, and Gretchen Alice LeCheminant, *Indigenous Notions of Ownership and Libraries, Archives, and Museums*. Boston: IFLA Publications, 2016.

Cherry, Alissa and Keshav Mukunda. "A Case Study in Indigenous Classification: Revisiting and Reviving the Brian Deer Scheme." *Cataloging & Classification Quarterly* 53, no. 5-6 (2015): 543-67.

Colbert, Jessica L. "Patron-driven Subject Access: How Librarians Can Mitigate that 'Power to Name,'" *In the Library with the Leadpipe.* (November 2017). http://www.inthelibrarywiththeleadpipe.org/2017/patron-driven-subject-access-how-librarians-can-mitigate-that-power-to-name/.

Cygan, Justin. "A Look Inside the #NoDAPL Protest." *University of Denver Clarion,* November 9, 2016. https://duclarion.com/2016/11/a-look-inside-the-nodapl-protest/.

Doyle, Ann M. "Naming and Reclaiming Indigenous Knowledges in Public Institutions: Intersections of Landscapes and Experience." *Advances in Knowledge Organization* 10 (2006): 435-42.

Doyle, Ann M., Kimberley Lawson, and Sarah Dupont. "Indigenization of Knowledge Organization at the Xwi7xwa Library." *Journal of Library and Information Studies* 13, no. 2 (2015): 107-134.

"DU Alumna and Staff Member Elevates Native American Outreach." *University of Denver Newsroom,* April 25, 2017. http://news.du.edu/du-alumna-and-staff-member-elevates-native-american-outreach/.

Duarte, Marisa Elena, and Miranda Belarde-Lewis. "Imagining: Creating spaces for indigenous ontologies." *Cataloging & Classification Quarterly* 53, no. 5-6 (2015): 677-702. doi: 10.1080/01639374.2015.1018396.

"DU Native Student Alliance Launches #NoMorePios Campaign." *University of Denver Clarion*, October 16, 2017. https://duclarion. com/2017/10/du-native-student-alliance-launches-nomorepios- campaign/.

Frank Exner, Little Bear. "North American Indian Personal Names in National Bibliographies." In *Radical Cataloging*, edited by K.R. Roberto, 150-64. Jefferson, NC: McFarland, 2008.

Frank Exner, Little Bear. "Indexing Integrated Manual Sets at Northern Telecom." *Bulletin of the American Society for Information Science and Technology* 23, no. 4 (1997): 20-24.

Frank Exner, Little Bear. "North American Indians: Personal Names with Semantic Meaning," *Names* 55.1 (2007): 3-15.

hooks, bell. *Teaching to Transgress: Education as the Practice of Freedom*. New York: Routledge, 1994.

Jules, Bergis. "Confronting Our Failure of Care Around the Legacies of Marginalized People in the Archives." *Medium* (blog), November 11, 2016. https://medium.com/on-archivy/confronting-our- failure-of-care-around-the-legacies-of-marginalized-people-in-the- archives-dc4180397280.

Littletree, Sandra and Cheryl A. Metoyer. "Knowledge Organization from an Indigenous Perspective: The Mashantucket Pequot Thesaurus of American Indian Terminology Project." *Cataloging & Classification Quarterly* 53, no. 5-6 (2015): 640-57.

Lougheed, Brett, Ry Morgan, and Camille Callison. "Reconciliation through Description: Using Metadata to Realize the Vision of the National Research Centre for Truth and Reconciliation." *Cataloging & Classification Quarterly* 53, no. 5-6 (2015): 596-614.

Jacobs, Margaret D. *White Mother to a Dark Race: Settler Colonialism, Maternalism, and the Removal of Indigenous Children in the American West and Australia, 1880-1940*. Lincoln: University of Nebraska Press, 2009.

Library of Congress. "Sitting Bull, 1831-1890." Library of Congress Authorities. https://lccn.loc.gov/n50025199.

Littletree, Sandra and Cheryl A. Metoyer. "Knowledge Organization from an Indigenous Perspective: The Mashantucket Pequot Thesaurus of American Indian Terminology Project." *Cataloging & Classification Quarterly* 53, no. 5-6 (2015): 640-57.

Martinez-Ávila Daniel and John M. Budd. "Epistemic Warrant for Categorizational Activities and the Development of Controlled Vocabularies." *Journal of Documentation* 73, no. 4 (2017): 700-715.

Moorcroft, Heather. "The Construction of Silence." *Australian Library Journal* 42, no. 1 (1993): 27-32.

Neatour, Anna and Jeremy Myntti. "The Western Name Authority File: Improving Access for Digital Collections and Archives." *Digital Matters: Digital Culture Studies at the University of Utah Symposium*, presentation at Digital Humanities Utah 2, February 11, 2017.

Rich, Adrienne Cecile. *The Will to Change: Poems 1968-70*. London: Chatto & Windus, 1972.

Roberto, K.R., *Radical Cataloging: Essays at the Front*. Jefferson, NC: McFarland & Co., 2008.

Schlesselman-Tarango, Gina. "The Legacy of Lady Bountiful: White Women in the Library." *Library Trends* 64, no. 4 (2016): 667-686.

Tuck, Eve and K. Wayne Yang. "Decolonization is Not a Metaphor." *Decolonization: Indigeneity, Education & Society* 1, no. 1 (2012): 1-40.

Srinivasan, Ramesh, Alberto Pepe, and Marko A. Rodriguez. "A Clustering-Based Semi-Automated Technique to Build Cultural Ontologies." *Journal of the American Society for Information Science and Technology* 60, no. 3 (2009): 608-620.

Swanson, Raegan. "Adapting the Brian Deer Classification System for Aan-
ischaaukamikw Cree Cultural Institute." *Cataloging & Classification
Quarterly* 53, no. 5-6 (2015): 568-79.

"Tribal Flags to Fly Over DU Campus." *University of Denver Newsroom*, March
28, 2018. http://news.du.edu/du-hosts-tribal-flag-raising-ceremo-
ny/.

Truth and Reconciliation Commission of Canada. *The Survivors Speak: Report
of the Truth and Reconciliation Commission of Canada.* Ottawa: Truth
and Reconciliation Commission of Canada, 2015.

Twitter. Post with multiple images from anonymous University of Denver
Native Student Alliance-affiliated student activist documenting protest, March 3, 2018.

University of Denver John Evans Study Committee. *Report of the John Evans
Study Committee of the University of Denver.* Denver, CO: University
of Denver, 2014.

University of Denver Task Force on Native American Inclusivity. *Strategic
Recommendations of the Task Force on Native American Inclusivity for the
Sustainable Development of a Native American Community Presence at the
University of Denver.* Denver, CO: University of Denver, 2016.

Chapter 6

CATALOGING KURDISTAN: IMAGINING LIBERATED
GEOGRAPHIES

Heather K. Hughes

This essay examines how cataloging practices on Kurds and Kurdistan have reflected colonial subjecthood imposed on peoples living in majority-Kurdish areas of Iran, Iraq, Syria, and Turkey. This is exemplified in the current Library of Congress (LOC) subject headings, which situate Kurds within their occupying powers and erases Kurdistan and Kurdish geographies. The Kurds' plight as a stateless people suffering from repression and human rights abuses is widely known, that these violences fit into a larger pattern of colonial domination perhaps less so. Thinking about this issue in the framework of colonialism is helpful in critiquing how language, knowledge production and organization reify domination of Kurdish people and lands, and to initiate interventions into decolonizing the language of the catalog and avoid reproducing state violence. Dr. İsmail Beşikçi, a notable Turkish sociologist, writes about Kurdistan as an "international" or "interstate" colony, subject to imperialism from global powers and occupation by local states with the support of global powers.[1] The reproduction of occupying states' frames of knowledge on the Kurds are also shared and reproduced by the global powers supporting these nation-states; thus, geographic

---

1. İsmail Beşikçi, *International Colony Kurdistan* (Reading: Taderon Press, 2004).

terms, group descriptors, and language reinforce colonial realities for Kurdish peoples.

Over the course of the 20th and 21st centuries, Kurds have experienced various forms of ethnic cleansing through political and cultural violences, including the denial of their existence, renaming of Kurdish cities and people, and demographic engineering. Kurdish national and political movements have sought to counter this through protecting their culture and gaining political autonomy. While various movements and actors have had divergent political goals and tactics, the importance of the recognition and usage of "Kurdistan" as a geographical term, and the status of Kurdistan as an occupied territory, has featured prominently in Kurdish emancipatory discourses. The term is particularly politically charged in Turkey, where usage of the term has been criminalized at times, whereas in Iran and Iraq Kurdistan refers to political-administrative units even though these units do not include all Kurdish populated areas.

In critiquing and determining solutions concerning how library subject headings classify and describe Kurds and Kurdistan, it is helpful to consider the critical literature on cataloging and colonialism. The literature, discussions, and practices of decolonizing the catalog in North America have necessarily been focused on Native and Indigenous knowledge and representation. I believe that the critiques and solutions proposed within this literature have potential for wider application in decolonizing the catalog. Marisa Elena Duarte and Miranda Belarde-Lewis provide a helpful overview of colonization in the catalog: "When we understand how colonization works through techniques of reducing, mis-naming, particularizing, marginalizing, and ghettoizing, we can better appreciate practices that more accurately and precisely name, describe, and collocate historically subjugated knowledge."[2] They also identify the following practices as problematic:

"(1) misnaming, or using Western-centric terms to describe Indigenous

---

2. Marisa Elena Duarte and Miranda Belarde-Lewis, "Imagining: Creating Spaces for Indigenous Ontologies," *Cataloging & Classification Quarterly* 53, no. 5-6 (2015): 699, doi: 10.1080/01639374.2015.1018396.

phenomena; (2) using parts to describe a more holistic phenomena, or the reduction, removal, and de-linking of a piece of a knowledge system from a greater ontology; (3) emphasis on modern nationalist periodization, inclusive of a notion that history as it is written by the colonizers cannot be changed; and (4) emphasis on prohibiting changes to practices that would upset the efficiency of the existing standardized schema.[3]

These practices and processes are very much at work in describing and classifying other groups. Duarte and Belarde Lewis advocate for "imagining" as a technique to decolonize knowledge organization. They define imagining as "creating figurative and literal space for the work of building, analyzing, and experimenting with Indigenous knowledge organization."[4] I see "imagining" as vital to seeing beyond the colonial present, particularly in representing colonized geographies and peoples. Kurdistan is very much imagined and lived through various practices and discourses, despite state antagonism towards Kurdish culture and politics.

In addition to considering the important work done by librarians and activists to decolonize description of Indigenous people, the history of area studies and international collecting should also be considered in developing critical cataloging practices for Middle Eastern materials. Scholars have traced the history of area studies in the United States, and have discussed the strategic and national defense interests in international and area studies, and the accompanying library collections which were established to support such programs.[5] If such programs and library collections have been weaponized, it is difficult not to make assumptions about how the "user" of such collections might have been configured, and how this might have impacted the creation of subject headings and cataloging practices. These dynamics have been present in Kurdish

3. Duarte and Belarde-Lewis, "Imagining," 683-4.

4. Duarte and Belarde-Lewis, "Imagining," 687.

5. See Zachary Lockman, *Field Notes: The Making of Middle East Studies in the United States* (Stanford, CA: Stanford University Press, 2016); Timothy Mitchell, "The Middle East in the Past and Future of Social Science," in *The Politics of Knowledge: Area Knowledge and the Disciplines*, ed. David L. Szanton (Berkeley: University of California Press, 2010; David Hirsch, "From Parchment to Pixels: Middle Eastern Collection Development in Academic Libraries," in *Building Area Studies Collections*, eds. Dan Hazen and James Henry Spohrer (Wiesbaden: Harrassowitz Verlag, 2007), 81-107.

Studies, along with colonial cataloging practices which "misname" and "marginalize."

One way that LOC subject headings act to reinforce colonialism is to situate Kurdistan in the past. Although an LOC subject for Kurdistan exists, along with Kurdistān (Iraq) and Kurdistān (Iran : Province) which are political and administrative units, the Kurdistan heading is designated as encompassing "works on old Kurdistan which comprised southeast Turkey, northeast Iraq, and northwest Iran are entered under the subject heading Kurdistan."[6] This ahistorical description assumes Kurdistan to consist of parts of nation states that were not in existence during the Ottoman and Persian Empires, and reproduces a "methodological nationalism"[7] that naturalizes the category of nation-states as the main units of analysis. The vagueness of this description is compounded by the fact that Kurdistan has operated as a geographic term and not a political entity, so when this "old Kurdistan" begins and ends is not clear. We can guess that "old Kurdistan" ends with the breakup of the Ottoman and Persian Empires, which resulted in Kurdish populations being split amongst the borders of Iran, Iraq, Syria, and Turkey. The possibility of Kurdistan disappeared from the map, and Kurds experienced new periods of political subjugation. Furthermore, this subject heading also ignores the fact that Kurdish populations have continued to inhabit these areas.

While Kurdistan has been erased through colonial naming practices, the distinctiveness of the Kurdish region in Turkey is recognized and simultaneously misnamed through subject headings such as "Turkey, Eastern," or "Turkey, Southeastern." These terms work to identify a territory that has historically posed challenges to state authorities, from the Ottoman Empire to the modern-day Turkish Republic, due to ethnic minorities, tribal societies, rugged terrain, and economic marginalization.

---

6. "Kurdistān (Iraq)," Library of Congress Name Authority File, http://id.loc.gov/authorities/names/n86066772.html.

7. Andreas Wimmer and Nina Glick Schiller, "Methodological Nationalism, the Social Sciences, and the Study of Migration: An Essay in Historical Epistemology," *International Migration Review* 37, no. 3 (2003): 576-610.

Referring to this area as Turkey's southeast works both to isolate it as an area of distinction and a peripheral area within the Turkish nation, but also to contain it within the Turkish state. Interestingly, the more general heading "Turkey, Eastern" has been used to describe thousands of works, including works on Kurds, while "Turkey, Southeastern," is attached to a number of works on the Güneydoğu Anadolu Projesi, or GAP, a development project aimed at transforming the area through agricultural, economic, and social initiatives. Given the fact that modernization initiatives have had dual intentions of assimilating the populations of this area, it is difficult not to associate the term and subject heading of "Turkey, Southeastern" with state-sponsored efforts to subdue Kurdishness.

Issues of geographies and naming are further complicated by the renaming, or misnaming, of areas with Kurdish language names. Scholars have discussed the renaming or "Arabization" and "Turkification" of place names as methods of nation-building and rendering of different ethnic and religious groups invisible.[8] While authority records for Kurdish cities or towns generally include Kurdish names and perhaps Armenian or Assyrian names as alternate versions, official state names do not necessarily reflect how people refer to a place in everyday language. One such example is the city and province of Dersim, which has historically had a significant Alevi Zaza[9] population and was renamed Tunceli in 1935. Despite the official name change, the name Dersim continues to be widely used. Dersim was also the site of an uprising which was brutally suppressed in 1937-1938 in which approximately 10,000 people died and several thousand others were displaced. The

---

8. Jordi Tejel, *Syria's Kurds: History, Politics, and Society*, trans. Emily Welle and Jane Welle (London; New York: Routledge, 2011); Joost Jongerden, "Crafting Space, Making People: The Spatial Design of Nation in Modern Turkey," *European Journal of Turkish Studies* 10 (2009), https://journals.openedition.org/ejts/4014; Kerem Öktem, "The Nation's Imprint: Demographic Engineering and the Change of Toponymes in Republican Turkey," *European Journal of Turkish Studies* 7 (2008), https://journals.open edition.org/ejts/2243.

9. Alevism is a heterodox sect of Islam in Turkey, while Zazas are an ethnic group considered by many to be Kurds but also a distinct group.

renaming of Dersim and the subsequent military intervention are both attempts to order, control, and remake this space, and should not be viewed as discrete events. In popular discourse this event is referred to as the Dersim massacre, but according to LOC it exists as su:Dersim Revolt, Tunceli İli, Turkey, 1937-1938, thereby situating Dersim as the unruly past within state-defined history. The renaming of cities, the erasure of non-official languages, all reflect colonial occupation at work. This history also illustrates how a place might have multiple names, but an authority file will always privilege one name to the detriment of other groups.

With regards to cataloging practices describing Kurdish peoples, items can be classified under the subject heading "Kurds," which accommodates works on Kurds in general. This subject also subdivides geographically, so one can find relevant titles under headings such as "Kurds—Turkey" or "Kurds—Iraq." These headings are conducive to the classification and location of materials on Kurds, yet they reinforce colonial subjecthood and modern state boundaries through ignoring Kurdistan and situating Kurds as minorities. As Beşikçi writes, "The Kurds are not a minority. The Kurds live in Kurdistan."[10] Furthermore, the emphasis on states as geographical units ignores the movement and exchanges of people and ideas. Since Kurds in different regions have different languages, cultural practices, and political formations, categorizing all works on Kurds and Kurdish areas under "Kurdistan" might not be accurate or desirable, as a number of Kurds live outside Kurdish areas, and there is also a significant overlap between Kurdistan and Armenia. European cataloging systems, however, seems to offer possible solutions in decolonizing cataloging practices for this particular case. I am not certain as to why European cataloging systems better represent Kurdistan, but I suspect it is related to the political advocacy of the Kurdish diaspora in Europe, which has been mobilized around human-rights issues and Kurdish politics.

---

10. Beşikçi, 26.

The Bibliotheque Nationale Francaise (BNP, or French National Library), and the Deutsche Nationalbibliothek (DNB, or German Nation Library) present two possible models. The German National Library shows cataloging practices and subject headings that seem to best reflect Kurdish nationalist discourse, which asserts that the Kurdish areas make up a larger Kurdistan. Germany's category for Kurdistan subdivides geographically to include Kurdistan (Nord), Kurdistan (Nordwest), Kurdistan (Sud), and Kurdistan (Sudost). It is also worth noting that the subject heading for Kurdistan is used more flexibly than in the United States. Furthermore, DNB is the only cataloging system with a geographic term for Rojava, the autonomous region in Northern Syria where Kurdish groups have established self-governance in wake of the chaos following the Syrian Conflict. The subject heading "Föderation Nordsyrien—Rojava" is undoubtedly how those participating in this political process would prefer this territory be labeled, but it is also arguably the terminology that researchers might use to identify works on this geographic area and political movement.

While DNB subject headings best reflect Kurdish emancipatory discourse, they also render the colonial realities of Kurdistan less visible. BNF subject headings, on the other hand, label Kurdish territories as Kurdistan but situate them within their occupying powers. In addition to the subject heading "Kurdistan," works can also be categorized under Kurdistan (Irak), Kurdistan (Iran), Kurdistan (Syrie), and Kurdistan (Turquie). The presence of multiple Kurdistan headings are consistent with the realities of Kurds' regional differences and being occupied by different states, while countering colonial states that deny and oppress Kurdish peoples. Such headings would still accommodate researchers and scholars who situate their work in Kurdistan. I believe that both systems utilize imagining to decolonize subject headings, and I am not myself in a position to judge whether one is better or more ethical.

Determining ethical ways to name Kurdish peoples and geographies might involve consulting Kurdish scholarly groups such the Kurdish Studies Network, an international network of researchers and scholars. Such a group might not have a consensus on how to proceed, but input from Kurdish scholars is essential to addressing the ethics of Kurdish representation. Introducing Kurdistan more widely into authority terminology might cause additional confusion as Kurdish areas have historically been diverse areas. However, cataloging works in an ethical manner might necessitate complicating national boundaries and ownership, and deviating from practices that emphasize efficiency and practicality. This is definitely a challenge for catalogers and librarians dealing with high workloads and significant backlogs. There is also room for greater collaboration between subject librarians and cataloging librarians, including consulting the Middle East Librarians Association, a professional association of librarians with subject and language expertise whose responsibilities range from collecting to cataloging Middle Eastern materials. Through collaboration and "imagining" together, librarians can decolonize terminology and establish ethical practices.

Bibliography

Beşikçi, İsmail, *International Colony Kurdistan*. Reading: Taderon Press, 2004.

Duarte, Marisa Elena and Miranda Belarde-Lewis. "Imagining: Creating Spaces for Indigenous Ontologies." *Cataloging & Classification Quarterly* 53, no. 5-6 (2015): 677-702. doi:
10.1080/01639374.2015.1018396.

Hirsch, David. "From Parchment to Pixels: Middle Eastern Collection
Development in Academic Libraries." In *Building Area Studies Col-
lections*, edited by Dan Hazen and James Henry Spohrer, 81-107.
Wiesbaden: Harrassowitz Verlag, 2007.

Jongerden, Joost. "Crafting Space, Making People: The Spatial Design of
Nation in Modern Turkey." *European Journal of Turkish Studies* 10,
(2009). https://journals.openedition.org/ejts/4014.

Library of Congress Name Authority File. "Kurdistān (Iraq)." http://id.loc.
gov/authorities/names/n86066772.html.

Lockman, Zachary. *Field Notes: The Making of Middle East Studies in the United States.* Stanford, CA: Stanford University Press, 2016.

Mitchell, Timothy. "The Middle East in the Past and Future of Social Science." In *The Politics of Knowledge: Area Knowledge and the Disciplines,* edited by David L. Szanton. Berkeley: University of California Press, 2010.

Öktem, Kerem. "The Nation's Imprint: Demographic Engineering and the Change of Toponymes in Republican Turkey." *European Journal of Turkish Studies* 7, (2008). https://journals.openedition.org/ejts/2243.

Tejel, Jordi. *Syria's Kurds: History, Politics, and Society,* translated by Emily Welle and Jane Welle. London; New York: Routledge, 2011.

Wimmer, Andreas, and Nina Glick Schiller. "Methodological Nationalism, the Social Sciences, and the Study of Migration: An Essay in Historical Epistemology." *The International Migration Review* 37, no. 3 (2003): 576-610.

PART III:

GENDER VARIANCE AND

TRANSGENDER IDENTITIES

Chapter 7

Who Asked You? Consent, Self-Determination, and the Report of the PCC Ad Hoc Task Group on Gender in Name Authority Records

Kalani Adolpho

The original intention of name authority records (NARs) was to ensure consistency, both within and across library catalogs, by using a single standardized form of an author or creator's name, under which their respective works would be collocated. Established in 1999, the IFLA Functional Requirements and Numbering of Authority Records (FRANAR) Working Group sought to clarify and improve upon current authority work to, among other things, ensure catalog users can identify and disambiguate an entity, view relationships between works or entities, and to contextualize this information. Published a decade later, the Functional Requirements for Bibliographic Records (FRBR) and Functional Requirements for Authority Data (FRAD) expanded upon the type of information that should be included in authority records in order to identify, disambiguate, and contextualize. This includes where one was born or where they died, country, language used, profession or occupation, biography or history, and gender.[1] In 2013, Library of Congress implemented Resource Description &

---

1. Bob Thomas, "Name Disambiguation—Learning From User-Friendly Models," *Cataloging & Classification Quarterly* 49, no. 3 (2011): 229-30, doi: 10.1080 .01639374.2011.560834.

Access (RDA), which is based on both FRBR and FRAD. The specific rule to record gender is found in RDA rule 9.7 in Section 3.[2]

In "More Than a Name: A Content Analysis of Name Authority Records for Authors who Self-Identify as Trans," Kelly J. Thompson argues that "the inclusion of a gender field [in MARC 21] is meant to support the shifting purpose of the name authority record from a documented list of authorized name headings to be used in records, to a record of characteristics of the individual authors themselves."[3] This shift in the nature of authority work, from personal names to persons themselves, bestows an enormous amount of power on those engaged with the creation of NARs. Thompson demonstrated that the power to name and assign labels to individuals' gender identities in RDA 9.7 has resulted in the outing of self-identified transgender authors in 65% of NARs that they had examined.

The Program for Cooperative Cataloging (PCC) Ad Hoc Task Group on Gender in Name Authority Records formed in August 2016 in response to concerns raised by the Gay, Lesbian, Bisexual, and Transgender Round Table of the American Library Association, numerous authors, and the PCC membership. Two months later, they published their report (hereafter referred to as "the Report") detailing instructions on best practices for recording gender in MARC Authority Field 375.[4]

The main failings of the Task Group's proposed recommendations fall into two categories. The first is that they deny transgender and

---

2. Amber Billey, Emily Drabinksi, and K.R. Roberto, "What' Gender Got to Do with It? A Critique of RDA 9.7," *Cataloging & Classification Quarterly* 52, no. 4 (2014): 415-6, doi: 10.1080/01639374.2014.882465.

3. Kelly J. Thompson, "More Than a Name: A Content Analysis of Name Authority Records for Authors Who Self-Identify as Trans," *Library Resources and Technical Services* 60, no. 3 (2016): 142. http://dx.doi.org/10.5860/lrts.60n3.140.

4. Amber Billey, Matthew Haugen, John Hostage, Nancy Sack, and Adam L. Schiff, "Report of the PCC Ad Hoc Task Group on Gender in Name Authority Records," *Library of Congress*, October 4, 2016: 1, https://www.loc.gov/aba/pcc/documents/Gender_375%20field_RecommendationReport.pdf.

gender diverse people true agency over our identities. The second is that the recommendations are still situated from an outsider, privileged, Western, and fairly cisnormative understanding of gender. Most notably, the recommendations mark a profound misunderstanding of the boundaries and complexities involved with being "out," that identity is fluid and identification may be context-specific, that identity is deeply personal and individuals have different terminology and comfort levels to describe their gender history (and this language may change over time), and that the level of training and amount of direct communication with the subjects of NARs necessary to even approach ethically recording gender would be unsustainable.

Any ethical set of recommendations designed to be inclusive of transgender and gender diverse peoples must respect the privacy and agency of these people. This would, at minimum, necessitate recommendations written by us, for us, as well handing direct control over NARs to those that they represent. Although the work of the PCC Ad Hoc Task Group on Gender in Name Authority Records is a well-intentioned attempt to mitigate trans-exclusion in RDA 9.7, their overall report and proposed best practices are still rooted in Western-centric, cisnormative understandings of gender that deny gender diverse people both agency over our own identities and decision-making power over the frameworks that seek to include us.

The need to respect the agency of transgender and gender diverse people, as well as the importance of obtaining informed consent are central themes to my book chapter. For this reason, any transgender or gender diverse people who are explicitly named in this chapter have given consent to have their information shared in this context, and have personally reviewed and approved what was written about them. Portions of this chapter that had named individuals that I was not able to contact or obtain the informed consent of, were removed.

Terminology

In Western society, gender is assigned at birth on a socially constructed male/female binary, based off of the appearance of an infant's genitals.[5] The word *cisgender* (often shortened to cis) refers to individuals who do identify with the gender they were assigned at birth. The words *trans* and *transgender* are Western umbrella terms that refer to individuals who 1. do not identify, either wholly or in part, with the gender that they were assigned at birth, and 2. do identify as transgender.[6] In this chapter, I will use the terms *gender variant* and *gender diverse* rather than transgender in order to be more inclusive of non-Western gender identities.

Cisgender privilege is a system of visible and invisible advantages afforded to cisgender people in a society that normalizes the experiences and perceptions of the people who hold this identity.[7] *Cisnormativity* is the assumption that all people are cisgender. *Cissexism* is a set of acts and norms that enforce the gender binary and gender essentialism which

---

5. I, personally, do not distinguish between gender and sex, and will not do so in this chapter. Often, the concept of sex (or "biological sex") is used to misgender, delegitimize, and exclude trans and gender diverse people.

6. While gender diversity and gender fluidity have existed in cultures around the world for hundreds upon hundreds of years, not all cultures use the umbrella term "transgender." The cisgender/transgender binary is a Western construction and to classify gender diverse peoples of other cultures as transgender against their will would be a colonial imposition. This is why I include the caveat that in order to be transgender, one must also identify with that term. This will be discussed at greater length later in my chapter.; "What is Intersex?" *Intersex Society of North America*, accessed April 14, 2018, http://www.isna.org/faq/what_is_intersex. It is also worth noting that both the male/female gender binary and the transgender/cisgender binary routinely exclude the experiences of intersex people who are born with characteristics that do not conform to the social construction of the Western male/female binary, yet may or may not identify with the gender that they were (forcibly) assigned at birth. I use the term "forcibly" here to refer to the common practice of surgically altering an infant's genitals to conform to cisnormative binary ideals, without the consent of the intersex person.

7. Peggy McIntosh, "White Privilege: Unpacking the Invisible Knapsack," *The National SEED Project*, 1989, https://nationalseedproject.org/white-privilege-unpacking-the-invisible-knapsack. This definition is loosely based off of Peggy McIntosh's work on white privilege.

result in the oppression and exclusion of transgender and gender diverse people.

Gender diverse people *come out* when we voluntarily tell others about our gender identity.[8] It is important to note that coming out is not a single event and then, suddenly, a person's gender identity may be considered public information. Someone can be out in some aspects of their life, and to some people in their life, but not others. When an individual's gender identity is disclosed by another without their explicit consent to do so, it is called *outing*. *Misgendering* is the intentional or unintentional use of gendered language or incorrect pronouns, most generally tied to the gender one was assigned a birth. *Deadnaming* is using a gender diverse person's old/given name. Both misgendering and deadnaming result in outing. Beyond basic human decency and respecting the agency of others over their own identity, one reason why outing someone without their permission can be harmful is because of transphobia. *Transphobia* is a set of overt negative attitudes which include fear, revulsion, and hatred of transgender people. This contributes to elevated rates of homelessness and unemployment, as well as violence, assault, and murder.[9]

Gender as Legible Knowledge

The recommendations provided by the task group expand the original list of gender identities to include terminology from Library of Congress Demographic Group Terms (LCDGT), in addition to several term revisions and additions. Furthermore, they included a list of "Best

---

8. The fact that we even have to "come out" is cisnormative and heteronormative, meaning it is assumed everyone is cisgender and heterosexual and this will continue to be assumed about us until we tell people otherwise (and even after that).

9. Morgan Tilleman, "(Trans)forming the Provocation Defense," *Journal of Criminal Law & Criminology* 100, no. 4 (2010): 1668-9. An example of transphobia is the trans panic defense, which is only banned in California and Illinois. In all other states, perpetrators of assault and/or murder of trans people can blame the victim's gender identity for their "loss of self-control" in the hopes of lighter sentencing. In forty-eight states it is acceptable to argue that we are so repulsive that it is perfectly understandable that someone would react violently upon finding out we are trans.

Practices for Recording Information about Gender." What follows is an abbreviated list of these practices:

> Record information about gender as the person self-identifies and explicitly discloses, taking information from readily and publicly available sources such as:
> -Biographical information published on the resource
> -Biographical information provided by the publisher
> -Author's personal website or social media profiles
> -Direct communication with the author
> -For non-contemporary persons use works by the person as well as biographies, obituaries, articles, etc. about the person
>
> Record Males or Females in accordance with the term used by the person, or with gendered pronouns and/or inflected nouns used in the source
>
> -Do not assume gender identity based on pictures or names
> -Do not dig for given names or genders assigned at birth
>   […]
> -Take into account the following considerations:
> -"Is there potential for this information to harm the [person] through outing or violating the right to privacy?
> -Is there an indication that the [person] consents to having this information shared publicly?
> -Will including this information help a library user in the search process?"[10]

Although my concerns with the PCC Ad Hoc Task Group's recommendations are endless, for the purposes of this chapter I will focus on the following aspects of the report: the fixedness of gender, cisnormative and regressive understandings of gender, lack of discussion on currency of source material, imposition of Western gender classification on indigenous gender systems, and ignorance of the fact that most cataloguers do not possess the level of cultural competency that would be required to record gender in NARs.

---

10. Billey, Haugen, Hostage, Sack, and Schiff, "Report of the PCC Ad Hoc Task Group on Gender in Name Authority Records," 2.

Who Asked You? Consent, Self-Determination, and
the Report of the PCC Ad Hoc Task Group on
Gender in Name Authority Records

117

RDA rule 9.7 can only function if gender is a static identity that is both easily verified and capable of being contained within a few words. In "Information Systems and the Translation of Transgender," Jeffrey Alan Johnson uses James C. Scott's concept of "legible knowledge" to describe a "transformation of reality into standardized, aggregated, static facts that are capable of consistent documentation."[11] Both the original iteration of the rule and the proposed recommendations by the PCC Ad Hoc Task Group make and perpetuate gender as legible knowledge that can be selected from a controlled vocabulary and treated as "consistent." Johnson refers to this practice as "translation regime," or "a set of implicit or explicit principles, norms, rules, and decision-making procedures through which single, commensurable data sets are selected to represent conditions in the world."[12] RDA 9.7 continues the work of cisgender and Western hegemony by packaging complex and personal gender identities into static, discrete controlled vocabularies.

Gender identity is fluid, and many (but not all) gender diverse people will change the terminology that they use to describe their gender, and/or identify with different gender identities (or lack thereof) over time. The recommendations made by the PCC Ad Hoc Task Group are insufficient in acknowledging the fluidity of gender and our changing relationship(s) with our gender(s). The recommendations have not rectified the fact that recording gender at all will "freeze identities in time and universalize them," and, unfortunately, the main affirmation of gender fluidity involves recording dates associated with a gender for "well-known persons who publicly transition between male and female."[13] As Billey et al. state,

---

11. Jeffrey Alan Johnson, "Information Systems and the Translation of Transgender," *Transgender Studies Quarterly* 2, no. 1 (2015), 161, https://doi.org/10.1215/23289252-2848940.

12. Johnson, "Information Systems and the Translation of Transgender," 161.

13. Billey, Haugen, Hostage, Sack, and Schiff, "Report of the PCC Ad Hoc Task Group on Gender in Name Authority Records," 3; Billey, Drabinski, and Roberto, "What's Gender Got to Do with It?," 414.

The idea of being a single gender one year and then another the next does not conform to many trans people's narratives, and many transgender people do not fully identify with the gender that they were assigned at birth. The RDA requirement that changes in gender be marked by dates, while usefully acknowledging that gender can indeed shift, obscures the fact that changes in gender do not necessarily follow a linear path.[14]

The provided examples of NARs with multiple genders and their purportedly corresponding dates convey the gender history of binary trans people, from the gender they were assigned at birth to their actual gender. The demonstrated function of this feature, therefore, is to out binary trans people. For instance, nowhere in the report did an example include a NAR for someone who identified as a trans man in the past, but presently identifies as non-binary. It is also worth noting that the authors of the report do not mention *updating* an individual's NAR to change the recorded gender to the individual's actual gender if we later become aware an author identifies differently than we described. Nor does the report mention checking-in to see if it becomes necessary to update terminology when an individual begins to describe their gender history differently, or becomes uncomfortable with information that is or was publicly known or previously "comfortable" for them. To be clear, I am not advocating for the production of comprehensive gender histories in the NARs for all gender diverse people. Instead, I am hoping to illuminate both the fact that gender "history" does not only exist in the past (meaning, it may change after the creation of NARs) as well as the type of gender history that NARs creators seem interested in recording.

Gender History and Cited Sources

Rather than recording self-identification, recording gender assignation often reveals more about external interpretations of gender identity by the cisgender public than actual internal self-identification with gender for the person the NAR describes. In an example at the end of Appendix A: DCM-Z1 375 Draft, the following information from a *New York*

---

14. Billey, Drabinski, and Roberto, "What's Gender Got to Do with It?," 417.

Times article is provided as a source verifying the recorded gender of a trans woman: "For those who knew Dr. [Joan] Roughgarden well, and the many more who knew [her] only through [her] prolific production of scientific papers and books, it came as a much-discussed surprise when this Stanford professor, then fifty-two, announced on [her] Web Site that [she] was a transsexual, posting pictures of [herself] as Joan."[15] Because of this quote and a cisgender cultural preoccupation with knowing and sharing gender assignation at birth, Joan Roughgarden's 375 field records her as being male from 1946-1998. This is despite the fact that the article includes comments from Joan indicating that, before she was publicly out, she "emulate[d]" being male but did not identify with maleness. Her gender identification is made plain in statements such as "'Imagine as a woman if you'd set out to be a man, to learn how to live as a man. Could you do it? I couldn't. It's like asking a fish to fly,'" and, "Dr. Roughgarden, who […] has always identified herself as female…"[16] Lastly, it is worth mentioning that the article used she/her/hers to refer to Joan over ninety times, but the portion that the NAR creator selected included five out of the six instances that the article misgendered Joan via incorrect pronoun use.[17]

The *New York Times* article used in Joan Roughgarden's NAR was the second result when I Googled her name, right after her Wikipedia entry. The Report recommends people not "dig for given names or genders assigned at birth," but the line where one crosses over into "digging" is not only subjective, but assumes that easily accessible information that

---

15. Billey, Haugen, Hostage, Sack, and Schiff, "Report of the PCC Ad Hoc Task Group on Gender in Name Authority Records," 9. The original quote provided in the Report both deadnamed and misgendered Joan Roughgarden.

16. I removed "in her own mind" from this quotation as it was dismissive and cissexist. Gender identification is *always* in one's own mind, and yet it is only described that way by cisgender people when they are talking about gender diverse people.

17. Carol Kaesuk Yoon, "Scientist at Work: Joan Roughgarden; A Theorist With Personal Experience of the Divide Between the Sexes," *New York Times*, October 17 2000, https://www.nytimes.com/2000/10/17/science/scientist-work-joan-roughgarden-theorist-with-personal-experience-divide-between.html.

deadnames or outs people justifies doing so in NARs.[18] Furthermore, the quoted article on Joan Roughgarden was published 18 years ago, and nowhere within the recommendations do they discuss the currency of sources that may or ought to be used to record gender in NARs.

Beyond the possibility that an old source may contain information about an individual's gender identity that is no longer accurate, it may also contain language and terminology that the individual is no longer comfortable with. One might share their birth name, but later decide that information is private, or describe themselves as a "girl" as a child, but later use "boy" or another term. The ways that we describe our gender identity, our transitions, and our life prior to coming out changes over time. Especially early on in our transitions and after we first begin to come out (for those who do come out), we are still unlearning internalized cissexism and transphobia. Our public narratives are often constructed around and to a cis audience, and so it is unsurprising that public discourse on a gender diverse person's identity often reflects cisnormative understandings about gender. To put it plainly, an 18-year-old interview that was conducted shortly after someone transitioned ought not to be considered a credible source of information on someone's gender history and terminology.

Indigenous Genders and Ways of Being

Another difficulty with attempting to find reliable information about a person's gender identity through any avenue *other* than direct communication is that, often, transgender and gender diverse people identify (or are identified) differently in different situations. This is sometimes done for reasons related to safety and privacy if we are not out (at all or in specific contexts). In other cases, our gender identification changes (or is changed) to make our genders more intelligible to outsiders. In *Imagining Transgender: An Ethnography of a Category*, author David Valentine

---

18. Billey, Haugen, Hostage, Sack, and Schiff, "Report of the PCC Ad Hoc Task Group on Gender in Name Authority Records," 2.

argues, "On the one hand, [the term "transgender"] validates those
people who adopt transgender as a meaningful category of self-identity;
but it also draws attention to how people are identified by others as
being transgender even though they may not necessarily use this term
in talking about themselves."[19] This non-consensual identification is
commonly performed by cultural outsiders who author popular articles
and academic research on non-Western gender identities. The use of
Western understandings about gender to translate Indigenous genders
to the rest of the world strips gender of its cultural context.

The Report of the PCC Ad Hoc Task Group on Gender in NARs
acknowledges non-Western genders and identities, but not non-Western,
non-individualized understandings of these identities. In *Gender on the
Edge: Transgender, Gay, and Other Pacific Islanders*, Alexeyeff and Besnier
argue that "In contemporary Western ideologies, sexual identity (as
well as identity *tout court*) is understood as being a property of persons.
[…] One *is* male or female, and consequently one *is* a man or a woman
and performs these identities socially. […] In many other societies, sex
and gender are much more squarely matters of interpersonal relationships, of dispositions that enable and restrict social action."[20] Māhū is
a Native Hawaiian third way of being for those born "in the middle"
who embody both kāne (male) and wahine (female) spirits.[21] Westerners
often describe māhū as they would Western binary transgender people,

---

19. David Valentine, *Imagining Transgender: An Ethnography of a Category* (Durham, NC:
Duke University Press, 2007), 26.

20. Kalissa Alexeyeff and Niko Besnier, "Gender on the Edge: Identities, Politics,
Transformations," in Gender on the Edge Transgender, Gay and Other Pacific Islanders, eds. Niko Besnier and Kalissa Alexeyeff (Honolulu: University of Hawai'i Press,
2014), 5.

21. Andrew Matzner, "'Transgender, Queens, Mahu, Whatever': An Oral History
from Hawai'i," *Intersections: Gender, History and Culture in the Asian Context* no. 6 (2001),
http://intersections.anu.edu.au/issue6/matzner.html. Māhū predate colonialism and,
unfortunately, māhū people and the identity itself were attacked by missionaries following arrival. Since then, the term māhū has been used disparagingly by non-māhū.
While the term has been reclaimed by many, it is still not a term to use for someone
without their express permission.

with māhū who would have been assigned male at birth as trans women, and māhū who would have been assigned female at birth as trans men.

In "Beyond the Binary," Jade Snow explains the concept of le'a as "the pleasure principle from which a person not only determined fulfillment individually, but also as a member of the community." Snow goes further to explain "individuals were encouraged by this principle to fulfill their sexual and gender identities," describing this exploration not only as "healthy" but also "virtuous."[22] In this same article, a Native Hawaiian activist and performer states that "[māhū] is not a gender, it's not an orientation, it's not a sect, it's not a particular demographic and it's definitely not a race. It is simply an expression of the third person as it involves the individual. When you find that place in yourself to acknowledge both male and female aspects within and accept the capacity to embrace both ... that is where the māhū exists and true liberation happens."[23] Between the definitions for le´a and māhū, it is clear that gender in Hawai´i is less a static and discrete individual category, and more of a process and exploration between oneself and one's community. Subsuming Indigenous identities under Western categories and/or conflating them with Western genders is not only a misrepresentation, but also a perpetuation of colonialism.

Historically, many First Nations have acknowledged more than two genders, with some Nations having three, four, and six gender identities.[24] At the third annual Inter-Tribal Native American, First Nations Gay and Lesbian American Conference in 1990, the umbrella term "Two-Sprit" was coined to describe "a person whose body simultaneously houses a masculine spirit and a feminine spirit."[25] While the term is Pan-Indian,

---

22. Jade Snow, "Beyond the Binary" in *Mana: A Journal of Hawai'i*, ed. Christine Hitt (Honolulu: Watermark Publishing, 2015), 136.

23. Snow, "Beyond the Binary," 138.

24. "Two Spirit People: A talk by Harlen Pruden (First Nations Cree)," *AMS Sexual Assault Support Centre*, last modified January 16, 2015, http://amssasc.ca/two-spirit-people-a-talk-by-harlen-pruden-first-nations-cree/.

25. "Walking in Two Worlds: Understanding the Two-Spirit & LGBTQ Community," *Diné Equality*, accessed June 2, 2018. https://docs.wixstatic.com/ugd/881017_d2cd-153b68ab4c2188c555be511cb487.pdf.

not all nations have genders that fall under the Two-Spirit umbrella, but
for those who do, the specific name, roles and traditions associated with
Two-Spirit people vary between them. In a presentation at the University of British Colombia in October of 2016, Harlan Pruden describes
Two-Spirit as "an organizing strategy and not an identity."[26] Two-Spirit,
therefore, functions an umbrella term for these diverse gender identities
within nations native to Turtle Island (North America) rather than the
name of a specific gender identity. Some examples of specific genders
under the Two-Spirit umbrella include Winkté (Lakota), Nádleehí (Diné),
Mixu'ga (Omaha), and Hemaneh (Cheyenne).[27]

In Appendix C: Proposals for LCDGT Gender Terms of the PCC
Ad Hoc Task Group report, "Two-spirit people" is proposed as a new
gender term. Unfortunately, the source data defining the term is largely
situated from a Western viewpoint, using colonial, cisnormative, and dismissive language such as "a term used throughout many Native American
tribes and cultures that describes individuals who are neither men nor
women, but who are *believed* to possess both masculine and feminine
spirits. Two spirits are often *believed* to have special gifts…" [emphasis
mine].[28] While many of the definitions used in this report contain problematic and cisnormative language, nowhere else is a term described as
a gender that an individual is "believed" to have.

In this report, Western umbrella terms (such as non-binary and transgender) were further broken down to provide greater specificity, but
this was not done with Two-Spirit.[29] There was no acknowledgement of

---

26. Harlan Pruden, *UBC TEFA Talks Two Spirit with Harlan Pruden*, video, 56:01,
October 26, 2016, https://youtu.be/1Tb07GDNpow.

27. Pruden, *UBC TEFA Talks Two Spirit with Harlan Pruden*; Tony Enos, "8 Things
You Should Know About Two Spirit People," *Indian Country Today*, March 28, 2017,
https://indiancountrymedianetwork.com/culture/social-issues/8-misconceptions-things-know-two-spirit-people/; Duane Brayboy, "Two Spirits, One Heart, Five
Genders," *Indian Country Today*, September 7, 2017, https://indiancountrymedianetwork.com/news/opinions/two-spirits-one-heart-five-genders/.

28. Billey, Haugen, Hostage, Sack, and Schiff, "Report of the PCC Ad Hoc Task
Group on Gender in Name Authority Records," 12.

29. Billey, Haugen, Hostage, Sack, and Schiff, "Report of the PCC Ad Hoc Task
Group on Gender in Name Authority Records," 11-16. This is not to say that the other

nation-specific genders, although both Niizh manidoowag and Berdaches were included in the 450 field for Two-Spirit people.[30] Niizh Manidoowag is specifically an Ojibwe term that translates as "Two-Spirit," and is not the name of one of the nation's genders. Berdache, on the other hand, is a colonizer-imposed term of French origin which erased gender by conflating it with sexuality, a phenomena that Z. Nicolazzo terms "compulsory heterogenderism."[31] This misrepresentation and comparative lack of detail for indigenous issues is not uncommon in cataloging and classification, and there is a wealth of literature as this relates to Library of Congress Subject Headings, for instance.[32] The original iteration of RDA 9.7 erased Indigenous genders entirely, and while a goal of this Report was to rectify these earlier exclusions, what it delivers is legitimization and de-legitimization in the same breath.

Another example of Western, colonial understandings of gender can be found in the "other comments" section in Appendix C. Here, the authors discuss non-Western genders by asking, "should gender categories such as Two-Spirit people, Hijras, Kathoeys, Fa'afafine, etc. be constrained or related in some way to the ethnic groups which define them? [...and] are [Western gender and sexual orientation categories] applicable when describing people and works from other cultural and

---

terms were broken down well, however. In the areas that dealt with non-binary identities, many terms were conflated (such as genderqueer and non-binary, and neutois and agender) which are neither equivalent nor interchangeable.

30. Billey, Haugen, Hostage, Sack, and Schiff, "Report of the PCC Ad Hoc Task Group on Gender in Name Authority Records," 11.

31. Z. Nicolazzo. "Compulsory Heterogenderism: A Collective Case Study," *NASPA Journal About Women in Higher Education* 10, no. 4 (2017): 245-61. doi: 10.1080/19407882.2017.1351376. Specifically, *berdache* conflates gender with "passive" male homosexuality, or bottoming (which, by the way, is not inherently "passive").

32. See: Marisa Elena Duarte and Miranda Belarde-Lewis, "Imagining: Creating Space for Indigenous Ontologies," *Cataloging & Classification Quarterly* 53, no. 5-6 (2015): 677-702, doi: 10.1080/01639374.2015.1018396.; Michael Q. Dudley, "A Library Matter of Genocide: The Library of Congress and the Historiography of the Native American Holocaust," *International Indigenous Policy Journal* 8, no. 2 (2017): doi: 10.18584/iipj.2017.8.2.9.; Sandra Littletree and Cheryl A. Metoyer, "Knowledge Organization from an Indigenous Perspective: The Mashantucket Pequot Thesaurus of American Indian Terminology Project," *Cataloging & Classification Quarterly* 53, no. 5-6 (2015): 640-57, doi: 10.1080/01639374.2015.1010113.

historical contexts."[33] Gender is socially and culturally constructed and enacted. Gender identities which are attached to particular roles and historical contexts in a given society cannot be held by members outside of the relevant group. To do so would be a form of cultural appropriation.[34] This adds another dimension to the ethics of recording gender in NARs, namely, even if we allowed the subjects of NARs the agency to define their own genders, what happens if they select a non-Western gender? Would we investigate their ethnic background and right to identify as such? Would we ask individuals if they are indigenous (for instance), and if so, do we ask for proof? What counts as proof? Regardless of whether the policy would be to require "proof" or accept someone at their word, both options would perpetuate colonialism. The second part of their question has a less complicated answer: applying Western language to describe a non-Westerner's identity, when they themselves do not self-identify with those same terms, denies people agency over their own identities. When there is a history of genocide and forced assimilation tied to the gender identities that would be overwritten by Western language and classification, this becomes especially egregious.

Cultural Competency

Cultural competency is "the ability to understand, communicate with, and effectively interact with diverse populations, and it can be measured by awareness, attitude, knowledge, skills, behaviors, policies, procedures, and organizational systems."[35] Willy Wilkinson, a public health consultant who has extensively trained and advised others on providing equal access to LGBT populations, argues that "rather than

---

33. Billey, Haugen, Hostage, Sack, and Schiff, "Report of the PCC Ad Hoc Task Group on Gender in Name Authority Records," 20.

34. Enos, "8 Things You Should Know About Two Spirit People."; Kai Minosh, "Why Non-Natives Appropriating 'Two-Spirit' Hurts," *BDG Blog*, last modified July 21, 2016. https://www.bgdblog.org/2016/07/appropriating-two-spirit/.

35. Willy Wilkinson, "Cultural Competency," *Transgender Studies Quarterly* 1, nos. 1-2 (2014): 68, doi: 10.1215/23289252-2399641.

a body of knowledge that can be learned in an afternoon workshop, training series, or course, cultural competency is a lifelong process of engagement."[36] I have spent the past decade actively learning from and discussing gender with other gender diverse people; reading countless articles, books, tweets, and blogs; and negotiating my own identity as a non-binary person. Even with all of my background knowledge and personal experiences, I would not feel equipped to investigate, comfortably identify, and record the genders of others.

As it currently stands, only those libraries who participate in the Name Authority Cooperative Program (NACO) may create new NARs to be submitted to the Library of Congress.[37] The necessary training one must undertake consists of five afternoon workshops, only one of which is dedicated to identifying persons.[38] If one afternoon worth of training is not enough to become culturally competent in transgender and gender diverse identities, then one *portion* of an afternoon certainly is not either. The inclusion of gender in NARs marks a fundamental lack of cultural competency with transgender and gender diverse populations. And, although the recommendations made by the PCC Ad Hoc Task Group on Gender in Name Authority Records are far more inclusive of transgender and gender diverse identities than the original rule, they likewise perpetuate cissexist and Western conceptions about gender identity, and will result in outing and misgendering gender diverse people.

Conclusion

As a trans person, all the recommendations made in this Report, with a conditional exception of "direct communication with the author," have the potential to be problematic. Not only is there no mention that

36. Wilkinson, "Cultural Competency," 68.

37. "Authorities: Create Name Authority Records," OCLC Connexion Client Guides, March 2012: 5, https://www.oclc.org/content/dam/support/connexion/documentation/client/authorities/create/createauth.pdf.

38. "Five-day NACO Training Outline," Library of Congress, accessed April 5, 2018, https://www.loc.gov/aba/pcc/naco/outline.html.

sources must be as current as possible, but there seems to be a fundamental misunderstanding about how gender diverse people "explicitly
disclose" our gender identities. Each and every time that we choose to
come out or discuss our gender, we are only explicitly consenting to
do so in that specific context. I have named and discussed my gender
on social media, in zines, in meetings at work, in the classroom, etc.,
but that does not mean I would want that information shared in, say,
the library magazine on campus, without my approval.[39] Of the task
group's recommendations, the only guaranteed ethical way to record
information about someone's gender in their NAR would be after direct
communication in which an individual explicitly states their gender
and desired terminology, fully knowing where this information will be
recorded and used. Every other option contains the possibility of outing,
deadnaming, and misgendering transgender and gender diverse people.
Unless someone clearly states that information about their gender and
personal background with gender may be shared freely in all contexts,
it is unethical to record it in NARs.

Ethical name authority control necessitates understanding the implications our rules have on marginalized groups. The fact that RDA 9.7
excludes trans and gender diverse people is well known, and yet, I have
not found evidence of any coordinated efforts to solicit feedback and
recommendations from the communities the authors sought to represent
and include in this report. The provided recommendations, therefore, are
not supported by any research ascertaining preferences, best practices,
or frameworks developed by trans or gender diverse communities, as
they relate to this cataloging rule.

Unless trans and gender diverse people hold decision making power
over recommendations that seek to represent and include us, these recommendations cannot be considered ethical. Unless we (librarians) give
up our power to name and give authors absolute agency over the gender

---

39. It also does not mean I would be comfortable having my gender recorded in a
Name Authority Record, just to be clear.

field(s) in their respective NARs, this cataloging rule cannot be considered ethical. To borrow a slogan from the disability rights movement, there should be "nothing about us without us."[40] We must remember that name authority records describe people, and nothing should be privileged above the privacy, safety, and agency of marginalized people.

Bibliography

Alexeyeff, Kalissa, and Niko Besnier. "Gender on the Edge: Identities, Politics, Transformations." In *Gender on the Edge Transgender, Gay and Other Pacific Islanders,* edited by Niko Besnier and Kalissa Alexeyeff. Honolulu: University of Hawai'i Press, 2014.

"Authorities: Create Name Authority Records." OCLC Connexion Client Guides. March 2012. https://www.oclc.org/content/dam/support/connexion/documentation/client/authorities/create/create-auth.pdf.

Billey, Amber, Emily Drabinksi, and K.R. Roberto. "What' Gender Got to Do with It? A Critique of RDA 9.7." *Cataloging & Classification Quarterly* 52, no.4 (2014): 412-21. doi: 10.1080/01639374.2014.882465.

Billey, Amber, Matthew Haugen, John Hostage, Nancy Sack, and Adam L. Schiff. "Report of the PCC Ad Hoc Task Group on Gender in Name Authority Records." *Library of Congress*, October 4, 2016. https://www.loc.gov/aba/pcc/documents/Gender_375%20field_RecommendationReport.pdf.

Brayboy, Duane. "Two Spirits, One Heart, Five Genders." *Indian Country Today.* September 7, 2017. https://indiancountrymedianetwork.com/news/opinions/two-spirits-one-heart-five-genders/.

Charlton, James I. *Nothing About Us Without Us: Disability Oppression and Empowerment.* Berkeley: University of California Press, 2000.

Duarte, Marisa Elena, and Miranda Belarde-Lewis. "Imagining: Creating Space for Indigenous Ontologies." *Catalog-*

---

40. James I. Charlton, *Nothing About Us Without Us: Disability Oppression and Empowerment* (Berkeley: University of California Press, 2000).

ing & Classification Quarterly 53, no. 5-6 (2015): 677-702. doi:
10.1080/01639374.2015.1018396.

Dudley, Michael Q. "A Library Matter of Genocide: The Library of
Congress and the Historiography of the Native American Holocaust." *The International Indigenous Policy Journal* 8, no. 2 (2017): doi:
10.18584/iipj.2017.8.2.9.

Enos, Tony. "8 Things You Should Know About Two Spirit People." *Indian
Country Today.* March 28, 2017. https://indiancountrymedianet-
work.com/culture/social-issues/8-misconceptions-things-know-
two-spirit-people/.

"Five-day NACO Training Outline." Library of Congress. https://www.loc.
gov/aba/pcc/naco/outline.html.

Johnson, Jeffrey Alan. "Information Systems and the Translation of Transgender." *Transgender Studies Quarterly* 2, no. 1 (2015): 160-5. https://
doi.org/10.1215/23289252-2848940.

Kaesuk Yoon, Carol. "Scientist at Work: Joan Roughgarden; A Theorist With Personal Experience of the Divide Between the
Sexes." *New York Times*, October 17 2000. https://www.nytimes.
com/2000/10/17/science/scientist-work-joan-roughgarden-theo-
rist-with-personal-experience-divide-between.html.

Littletree, Sandra, and Cheryl A. Metoyer, "Knowledge Organization
from an Indigenous Perspective: The Mashantucket Pequot
Thesaurus of American Indian Terminology Project." *Cataloging & Classification Quarterly* 53, no. 5-6 (2015): 640-57. doi:
10.1080/01639374.2015.1010113.

Matzner, Andrew. "'Transgender, Queens, Mahu, Whatever': An Oral History from Hawai´i." *Intersections: Gender, History and Culture in the
Asian Context*, no. 6 (2001). http://intersections.anu.edu.au/issue6/
matzner.html.

Minosh, Kai. "Why Non-Natives Appropriating 'Two-Spirit' Hurts."
BDG Blog. Last modified July 21, 2016. https://www.bgdblog.
org/2016/07/appropriating-two-spirit/.

McIntosh, Peggy. "White Privilege: Unpacking the Invisible Knapsack." *The National SEED Project.* 1989. https://nationalseedproject.org/white-privilege-unpacking-the-invisible-knapsack.

Nicolazzo, Z. "Compulsory Heterogenderism: A Collective Case Study." *NASPA Journal About Women in Higher Education* 10, no. 4 (2017): 245-61. doi: 10.1080/19407882.2017.1351376.

Pruden, Harlan. *UBC TEFA Talks Two Spirit with Harlan Pruden.* Video. 56:01. October 26, 2016. https://youtu.be/1Tb07GDNpow.

Snow, Jade. "Beyond the Binary." In *Mana: A Journal of Hawai´i,* edited by Christine Hitt. Honolulu: Watermark Publishing, 2015.

Thomas, Bob. "Name Disambiguation—Learning From User-Friendly Models." *Cataloging & Classification Quarterly* 49, no. 3 (2011): 223-32. doi: 10.1080.01639374.2011.560834.

Thompson, Kelly J. "More Than a Name: A Content Analysis of Name Authority Records for Authors Who Self-Identify as Trans." *Library Resources and Technical Services* 60, no. 3 (2016). http://dx.doi.org/10.5860/lrts.60n3 140.

Tilleman, Morgan. "(Trans)forming the Provocation Defense." *Journal of Criminal Law & Criminology* 100, no. 4 (2010): 1659-88.

"Two Spirit People: A talk by Harlen Pruden (First Nations Cree)." *AMS Sexual Assault Support Centre.* Last modified January 16, 2015. http://amssasc.ca/two-spirit-people-a-talk-by-harlen-pruden-first-nations-cree/.

Valentine, David. *Imagining Transgender: An Ethnography of a Category.* Durham: Duke University Press, 2007.

"Walking in Two Worlds: Understanding the Two-Spirit & LGBTQ Community." *Diné Equality.* Accessed June 2, 2018. https://docs.wix-static.com/ugd/881017_d2cd153b68ab4c2188c555be511cb487.pdf.

"What is Intersex?" *Intersex Society of North America.* Accessed April 14, 2018. http://www.isna.org/faq/what_is_intersex.

Wilkinson, Willy. "Cultural Competency." *Transgender Studies Quarterly* 1, no. 1-2 (2014): 68-73. doi: 10.1215/23289252-2399641.

Chapter 8

FREE TO BE...ONLY HE OR SHE: OVERCOMING OBSTACLES TO ACCURATELY RECORDING GENDER IDENTITY IN A HIGHLY-GENDERED LANGUAGE

Ahava Cohen

There is no reliable estimate of the number of people in the world who identify outside the gender binary. One recent meta-analysis estimates that 390 U.S. adults out of 100,000 identify as a gender other than that assigned them at birth.[1] This estimate is problematic; it takes transgender-identifying persons as its baseline, thus leaving aside those outside the gender binary who do not identify as transgender.[2] It is not only fair to accurately represent the genders of agents, it is part of the long tradition of cataloging.

IFLA-LRM (Library Reference Model), which stands behind the newest iteration of RDA (Resource Description & Access), does not define gender as an attribute of the entity *person*. In contrast, RDA, in instruction 9.7 of the iteration most familiar to librarians, does specify gender as a non-core, identifying attribute of persons. This instruction

---

1. Esther L. Meerwijk and Jae M. Sevelius, "Transgender Population Size in the United States: A Meta-Regression of Population-Based Probability Samples," *American Journal of Public Health* 107, no. 2 (February 2017): e1–8, doi:10.2105/AJPH.2016.303578.

2. Nat Titman, "How Many People in the United Kingdom Are Nonbinary?," *Practical Androgyny*, 2014, https://practicalandrogyny.com/2014/12/16/how-many-people-in-the-uk-are-nonbinary/#tel-aviv-queering-gender.

has been criticized, particularly by those who understand gender through the filter of queer theory.[3]

Queering the PCC

Efforts to permit more accurate reporting of gender identification were two-pronged. A Fast Track proposal was submitted to the Joint Steering Committee of RDA (later the RDA Steering Committee) and the Program for Cooperative Cataloging (PCC) convened an ad hoc committee[4] charged with recommending best practices for recording gender within name authority records. The Fast Track request was not approved, but a different proposal led, in February 2016, to the deprecation of the controlled vocabulary in 9.7 and its replacement with the instruction to use "an appropriate term in a language preferred by the agency creating the data. Select a term from a standard list, if available."[5]

The ad hoc committee's work resulted in recommendations to be implemented in Library of Congress's DCM Z1, LC-PCC PS, and LCDGT. These recommendations include suggested sources of information and dos and don'ts for importing information found in those sources into authority records. The recommendations, if and when implemented, will inform cataloging policy in the US and abroad and will affect catalogers across language and national communities.

In fixing one wrong, the authors of the report perpetrated another by imposing a very specific, narrow point of view upon all those who use Library of Congress (LC) and PCC policy statements as the basis of their cataloging. The report perpetuates the very institutionalized entitlement it propounds to fight, enshrining the privileged place of the

3. Amber Billey, Emily Drabinski, and K. R. Roberto, "What's Gender Got to Do with It? A Critique of RDA 9.7," *Cataloging and Classification Quarterly* 52, no. 4 (April 24, 2014): 412–21, doi:10.1080/01639374.2014.882465.

4. Amber Billey et al., "Report of the PCC Ad Hoc Task Group on Gender in Name Authority Records" (Washington, D.C.: Library of Congress, 2016), https://www.loc.gov/aba/pcc/documents/Gender_375 field_RecommendationReport.pdf.

5. RDA Steering Committee, "RDA Toolkit," 2017, http://access.rdatoolkit.org/.

English language whilst ignoring the many languages used by agents
throughout the world to create and to embody their identities. The
Anglophone bias of the report is unabashed and unacknowledged while
the RDA instruction has lost its Anglophone bias in deprecating the
English-language controlled vocabulary.

It is disingenuous to say that LC and the PCC need concern themselves only with English. The LC collection is multi-lingual, as are the
collections of many PCC institutions. Non-English resources account
for 61% of WorldCat records.[6] The ad hoc committee's report does
ask whether "Western gender and sexual orientation categories already
reflected in the vocabulary [are] any less culture-specific[.] That is, are
they applicable when describing people and works from other cultural
and historical contexts?"[7] The open-ended question appears at the end
of the report, as though the earlier conclusions had not already assumed
the answer.

The Problem with English

> About pronouns and sex English leaves its options open
> in practice each I
> has all the options
> she is he when it's you
> I doesn't have a sex
> there's no difference between she-you and he-you
> and all things are it – not man not woman[8]

In a webinar devoted to the change in RDA 9.7, Amber Billey
stated that the instruction's controlled vocabulary othered those who

---

6. OCLC, "Inside WorldCat," 2018, https://www.oclc.org/en/worldcat/inside-worldcat.html.

7. Billey et al., "Report of the PCC Ad Hoc Task Group on Gender in Name Author-ity Records," 20.

8. Yona Wallach, "Hebrew," in *The Defiant Muse: Hebrew Feminist Poems from Antiquity to the Present: A Bilingual Anthology*, ed. Shirley Kaufman, Galit Hasan-Rokem, and Tamar Hess, trans. Lisa Katz (New York: The Feminist Press of the City University of New York, 1999), 189–91.

understand gender from a queer perspective and showed them "passive hostility."[9] The ad hoc committee's recommendations try to alleviate that injustice but fall into the trap of othering many languages and cultures throughout the world.

In choosing a controlled vocabulary the members of the committee acknowledged their Anglophone biases, but in the broader recommendations these biases remain unchecked. A particularly painful point is the second item on the list of recommended best practices: "Record Males or Females in accordance with the term used by the person, or with *gendered pronouns and/or inflected nouns used in the source.*"[10] The assumption that only pronouns and nouns carry gender information excludes languages which are more highly gendered than is English; catalogers who work with foreign language materials will lose valuable information found in verbs, adjectives, and possessive suffixes when following these recommendations.

> when every verb and verb group are marked
> [...]
> and what sign given to an object
> and to an abstract noun and particles[11]

The Anglophone bias runs very deep within the work of those seeking to make authority records more queer-friendly. During the webinar[12] Emily Drabinski stated, "I'm not sure it's necessary or what value there is" in recording gender in authority records. Billey added, "If a puppet can have gender, that draws questions as to what defines gender and how we apply gender in name authority records." These doubts are a product of Anglophone bias. In Hebrew and Arabic, puppets can and do have gender, both as characters and as objects called "puppets." All

---

9. Amber Billey and Emily Drabinski, "Cataloging, Gender, and RDA Rule 9.7," *ALCTS Exchange*, 2017, http://www.ala.org/alcts/confevents/upcoming/webinar/031517.

10. Billey et al., 2016, p. 2. Emphasis added.

11. Wallach, "Hebrew."

12. Billey and Drabinski, "Cataloging, Gender, and RDA Rule 9.7."

entities have gender. Books have gender, databases have gender, committees have gender. Language itself has gender. Genders are crucial grammatical information which informs the structure of any sentence referring to the entity. Gender information recorded in authority records is not only useful to the cataloger seeking to gather the works of one individual, but when turned into gender-marked relationship designators in the bibliographic record it also helps patrons to speak and write about those agents using preferred normative grammar.

Languages can, in general terms, be divided between natural gender languages and grammatical gender languages. In natural gender languages only entities which have, or which are perceived by that culture as having, gender will be referred to by gendered nouns and pronouns. In grammatical gender languages, all entities are sorted into male, female, or neutral genders and gender is reflected in nouns, pronouns, adjectives, verbs, adverbs, and sometimes even articles.[13]

The Problem of Hebrew

Hebrew is one instance of a highly gendered language. All nouns are either male or female, with a small number simultaneously both and another small number having switched genders from biblical to modern times. All parts of speech must match the grammatical gender of their related noun.

Most of these parts of speech would not fall under the rubric of best practices proposed by the ad hoc committee. The information conveyed by the statement of responsibility כתבה טל כהן, אייר טל כה ן "[feminine] written [by] Tal Cohen, [masculine] illustrated [by] Tal Cohen"—that we are dealing with two separate agents, one of whom is identified as female and the other as male – would fail the standard set by the committee; the gendered information is carried by verbs with nary a pronoun or inflected noun in sight. Similarly, a statement of responsibility found on

---

13. Levi C R Hord, "Bucking the Linguistic Binary : Gender Neutral Language in English, Swedish, French, and German," *Proceedings of Western Interdisciplinary Student Symposium on Language Research (WISSLR)* 3, no. 1 (2016).

a zine: דן החמוד ונועה המהממת מציגים "[masculine] sweet Dan and [feminine] amazing Noa [masculine unmarked plural] present" uses neither nouns nor pronouns to establish gender; the information is carried by gender-inflected adjectives.

There are over 4.4 million records for Hebrew resources in WorldCat[14] and the language is consistently in the top twenty languages cataloged in the international database. Other European and Middle Eastern languages also have a variety of parts of speech which can convey gender. It is unclear why the committee thought that rejecting this linguistic richness in favor of those parts of speech which carry gender marking in English was the best path to follow. A formulation such as "Record Males or Females in accordance with the term used by the person, or with *gendered parts of speech used in the source*" would have allowed information to be drawn in keeping with the language of the resource.

It must be borne in mind that each type of language has its own problems with gender. Natural languages tend to divide up what they do engender using the traditional male/female dichotomy and thus conflate biological sex with gender identity. Grammatical gender languages offer leeway in that the division of real world objects between male and female can feel arbitrary and thus the liminal territory between sex and gender is wider. On the other hand, grammatical gender languages often lack the vocabulary needed to envision and describe liminality.

Hebrew shows this lack in its pronouns, precisely the part of speech the ad hoc committee would have us look to as a source of gender information. There is no neutral gender; the closest Hebrew comes to a statement without gender marking is first-person singular past (הלכתי *halakhti* – I went) and first-person singular future (אלך *elekh* – I will go) which are the same for male and female.

Hebrew is among a handful of languages which has an official body creating new words and ruling on grammar and spelling. The Academy of the Hebrew Language's official stand is that Hebrew includes two

---

14. Lucia Shelton, "Searching WorldCat Efficiently" (San Juan: OCLC, 2016), https://www.oclc.org/content/dam/oclc/events/member-forums/PR_Searching-WorldCatEfficiently.pdf.

genders, the unmarked masculine and the usually-marked feminine.[15]
While the Academy dictates formal language, colloquial Hebrew develops
in more haphazard ways, showing strong trends towards foreign loan
words and towards neutralization. Gonen and Rubinstein[16] point out
that neutralization in informal Hebrew is achieved through incorrect
grammar.

In an opinion piece on the Academy website, the scientific secretary of
the Academy responded to those who sought formal inclusive language:

> What can we do if in our language (as in many other languages aside
> from English) everything has a grammatical gender […] Were we able
> to design the language as one designs a building or a legal system we
> certainly would have foregone gender categorization in many parts of the
> language […] Just when linguistic feminism has requested a greater pres-
> ence for women in Hebrew, there are those who approach the Academy
> with a new demand: give us a linguistic solution for those who cannot or
> do not wish to define their gender! What can we tell them? In Hebrew
> there is no way to avoid marking gender.[17]

Preferred gender pronouns can be specified in Hebrew, but all choices
will be bound to masculine or feminine forms. Non-binary or genderfluid
people have no choice within grammatical Hebrew; even plural pronouns
are gender-bound. Attempts have been made, in the name of gender
equality, to create portmanteau pronouns which combine the masculine
and feminine forms, but these terms sound artificial and generally are
used to refer to mixed-gender audiences in lieu of the generic masculine,
leaving the terms unavailable as gender-neutral choices.

---

15. The Academy of the Hebrew Language, "General Grammatical Background on Hebrew," accessed March 12, 2018, http://en.hebrew-academy.org.il/
hebrew-language/general-grammatical-background-on-hebrew/.

16. "Gender Neutralization in Hebrew: The Case of the Numerals in Colloquial
Hebrew," *Brill's Journal of Afroasiatic Languages and Linguistics* 7, no. 1 (2015): 1–29,
doi:10.1163/18776930-00701002.

17. Ronit Gadish, "haShivyon Hamigdari, haLashon haIvrit v'haAkademia
[Gender Equality, the Hebrew Language and the Academy]," The Academy
of the Hebrew Language, 2017, http://hebrew-academy.org.il/2017/10/23/
השוויון-המגדרי-הלשון-העברית-והאקדמיה/.

Gender in Hebrew and in Judaism

> Hebrew is a sex maniac
> and whatever you women say in a feminist complaint
> searching for stimulation outside the language
> with an intonation that gives meaning to things
> signs just of male or female in a sentence
> will change sexual relations, make them strange,
> mark every female, a different mark for men[18]

Many attempts have been made to work within the bounds of the Hebrew language and yet avoid giving the masculine the preferential position of being the unmarked gender. One attempt uses both masculine and feminine suffixes in a single word, creating a new, doubly marked form which includes both genders (though still excluding those neither masculine nor feminine). This attempt at inclusivity can fall apart in mid-sentence: Katri[19] uses the term א.נשים טרנסים [*a/ nashim transim*] to refer to trans*, but the first word, "wo/men," preserves the binary structure of gender and the second word reverts to the unmarked masculine form.

All people using Hebrew must align themselves with a gender. "Every author is considered biologically one of the two genders, and in our language there is nothing we can do but call him 'author' or 'authoress' in keeping with the binary thinking of the reigning patriarchal culture."[20] Conforming to a non-binary or fluid gender or to no gender at all is not an opinion in Israeli Hebrew discourse.[21] This is not necessarily

---

18. Wallach, "Hebrew."

19. "Lo Ovrot, Lo Nechmadot - haMa'avak haTransi v'Tactikot Shel Mishtur b'Hukei Isur Aflayah [Not Passing, Not Sweet - the Trans Struggle and Policing Tactics in Non-Discrimination Laws]," in *Sex Acher: Mivchar Mamarim b'Limudim Lahatabii'm u'Qveeru'im Yisraeli'im [Other Sex: A Selection of Essays on Israeli LGBT and Queer Studies]*, ed. Aeyal Gross, Amalia Ziv, and Raz Yosef (Tel Aviv: Resling, 2016), 615–56.

20. Hannah Naveh, "Leket, Peah V'shikacha: Hahaim Mechutz Lacanon [Gleanings, the Corners of the Field, and Forgotten Produce: Life Outside the Canon]," in *Sex Gender Politics: Women in Israel,* ed. Dafna N. Izraeli, et al. (Tel Aviv: Hakibbutz Hameuchad, 1999), 49.

21. Katri, "Lo Ovrot, Lo Nechmadot - haMa'avak haTransi v'Tactikot Shel Mishtur b'Hukei Isur Aflayah [Not Passing, Not Sweet - the Trans Struggle and Policing Tactics in Non-Discrimination Laws]."

experienced as oppressive by those who transverse the liminal spaces
between genders.

The Israeli legal system recognizes the rights of transgender persons,
but conditions these rights on conformation to gender norms. Men have
rights and women have rights; people who identify as a gender other than
that which they were assigned at birth have their rights acknowledged
when they conform to the gender opposite. Israeli LGTBQ activists
have stated that the structure of the Hebrew language is affirming for
transgender people; the language constantly and consistently affirms
and reinforces their preferred gender.[22]

Though Hebrew lacks the grammar to refer to genders other than
male and female, the tradition from which the language stems has long
acknowledged the lived experience of possibilities beyond the binary.
Classical Jewish literature describes the space between the male and the
female, but always based on physical sexual characteristics.[23]

The 12th century commentary of Ibn Ezra (on Leviticus 18:22)
quotes Rabbenu Chananel, an 11th century scholar, in a discussion of
whether sex between two men, one of whom has had a vagina surgically
created for him, constitutes a homosexual act.[24] In addition to discussions of transgendered persons, there are four distinct intersex genders
in Jewish tradition: *androgynous*, *tumtum*, *ay'lonit*, and *saris*.

Modern writing about people who identify as non-binary does not
use traditional terminology. In contemporary scholarship about intersex
people[25] interviewees choose to be identified using binary gender terminology. In a document prepared for distribution to the press during

22. Rachel Delia Benaim, "Does the Hebrew Language Have a Gender Problem?"
Forward, November 9, 2015, https://forward.com/sisterhood/324205/degendering
-hebrew/.

23. Elliot Kukla, "Terms for Gender Diversity in Classical Jewish Texts,"
TransTorah, 2006, http://www.transtorah.org/PDFs/Classical_Jewish_Terms_for_
Gender_Diversity.pdf.

24. Michael J. Broyde, "The Establishment of Maternity & Paternity in Jewish and
American Law," *National Jewish Law Review* III (1998): 117–52, http://www.jlaw.com/
Articles/maternity1.html.

25. Limor Meoded Danon, *What Kind of Body?: The Affects of the Sexing Process on Intersexed People's Lives* (Tel Aviv: Resling, 2014).

Pride Month 2018 Ma'avarim, a trans* advocacy group, explicitly states: "If it is unclear how a trans [unmarked/masculine] man wishes to be written about, the best thing is to simply ask him or her. If it is impossible to ask, choose the most reasonable option for self-identification; i.e., a trans woman should be addressed in female terms though she seems to have been born as a male baby, a trans man should be addressed in masculine terms though he was marked as female at birth."[26]

Those who do not wish to be identified as either gender may play with grammatical gender assignment by switching between the masculine and feminine or by trying to combine both forms into a single word, but they have no natural, consistent way to speak of themselves as cisgendered persons are privileged to do. The lack of grammatically valid ways to describe non-binary options in highly gendered languages may lead agents to "misgender…in order to be understood."[27] In an effort to be free of sexism women, too, may refer to themselves using masculine grammar.[28]

Even when preferred pronouns are known and used, the rules of Hebrew grammar may cause confusion for the unwary cataloger. Since the masculine is also the unmarked, the masculine form is used to describe mixed-gendered groups. Thus, אוצרים: רותם ישראלי והדר אברמס ([masculine] curators: Rotem Israeli and Hadar Abrams) may refer to two men or to one man and one woman. The masculine form is generic; the poet Lea Goldberg told an interviewer that she did not like being described as a poetess. "There is something which I do not [feminine] like in this whole women's section. The woman is a [masculine] author or not a [masculine] author. I will always be grateful to Yakov Ficman. When he wrote a review of my first book, in his words about me he

---

26. Ma'avarim, "Hamlazot l'sikur anashim transim" [Recommendations for coverage of trans people], May 2018, https://drive.google.com/file/d/1cQvzH8tP3oAGgsrae WLy2XVaKgmqUSMl/view.

27. Hord, "Bucking the Linguistic Binary: Gender Neutral Language in English, Swedish, French, and German."

28. Amalia Sa'ar, "Masculine Talk: On the Subconcious Use of Masculine Linguistic Forms among Hebrew- and Arabic-Speaking Women in Israel," *Signs* 32, no. 2 (2007): 405–29, doi:10.1086/676943.

called me 'a new [masculine] poet."[29] The poet's preferred grammatical
noun, used in isolation, might lead a cataloger to record a gender other
than that which Goldberg used to refer to herself in discourse.

Arabic is a problematic language for genderqueer people[30] for much
the same reasons as is Hebrew. There are no gender-neutral nouns in the
various forms of Arabic and pronouns are inherently gender-marked.[31]

Gender Clues

If nouns and pronouns are unreliable indicators of gender in Hebrew
(and Arabic), what can be used to help catalogers understand the gender
with which an agent identifies? Because of the textual bias in the ad hoc
committee report, no non-linguistic sources are allowed as best practice. Judith Butler wrote "I am not outside the language that structures
me, but neither am I determined by the language that makes this 'I'
possible."[32] Lived experience is not textual and the ways agents capture
and encode experience and creativity is not solely textual. Metadata is
moving away from literal strings as containers of information, but the
ad hoc committee's recommendations tie gender information to a very
small subset of literals.

Wilchins[33] states that Western cultures value language as a dominant
paradigm, to the extent that language can be seen as defining reality.
This preoccupation with language (as opposed to non-verbal expression) is not necessarily true of every language and culture catalogers
will encounter or live in.

---

29. Talma Alyagon, "Pegishah im Lea Goldberg," [Meeting with Lea Goldberg],
Ma'ariv - yamim ve-lelot, January 24, 1969, pg. 23.

30. Hannah Harris Green, "Translating Identity across the Language Barrier," *How
We Get to Next*, 2017, https://howwegettonext.com/translating-identity-across-the-
language-barrier-66a87163a8e1; Fatima Sadiqi, *Women, Gender and Language in Morocco*
(Leiden: Brill, 2003).

31. Ibid.

32. *Gender Trouble: Feminism and the Subversion of Identity*, 2nd ed. (New York: Routledge
Classics, 2006), xxvi.

33. Cited in Hord, 2016.

In a post-representationalist world which no longer believes in the unshatterable linkage between things and the words which describe them,[34] the primacy of language as a signifier of identity represents a confusion between language and discourse. Performing gender can take place through multiple forms of discourse, language being only one of the possible stages on which gender is performed. "It would be a mistake," Judith Butler wrote, "to think that received grammar is the best vehicle for expressing radical views, given the constraints that grammar imposes on thought, indeed upon the thinkable itself."[35]

> Each of us has a name
> given by God
> and given by our parents
>
> Each of us has a name
> given by our stature and our smile
> and given by what we wear
> [...]
> Each of us has a name
> given by our sins
> and given by our longing[36]

There are sources beyond the text which the ad hoc committee recommendations would deny us, though they can be powerful clues of performance which seeks to extend beyond grammatical limitations on who we can be. "Do not assume gender identity based on pictures or names," the report instructs.

But names are powerful things. The Reverend Dr. Paula Stone Williams has said that the start of reconciliation with her father happened when he called her by her chosen name, signaling a willingness to accept her transition, to see her as the daughter she is rather than as the son

---

34. Karen Barad, "Posthumanist Performativity: Toward an Understanding of How Matter Comes to Matter," *Signs* 23, no. 3 (2003): 801–31.

35. *Gender Trouble: Feminism and the Subversion of Identity*, xix.

36. Zelda, "Each of Us Has a Name," in *The Spectacular Difference: Selected Poems*, trans. Marcia Falk (Cincinnati: Hebrew Union College, 2004), 141.

she was thought to be.[37] Her son also cites accepting his father's chosen name as a moment of acceptance.[38] Names, the wizards once knew, have power we ignore at our own risk.

Of course names are messy and complicated. Therein lies their power. Of course names are not always indicative of a person's chosen gender or even of their gender assigned at birth. Even if the whole world were binary, names would not be enough to tell us definitely, in every single case, what gender an agent identifies with. Some names are used by multiple genders. Some names switch genders when they switch languages and national borders. Yet names can give powerful clues as to gender. Some cultures have strong traditions of gendered names. Some countries, such as Finland and Iceland (and Germany before 2008), have lists of names which may be assigned, based on gender, and few or no unisex names allowed by law. Some cultures use patronymics or matronymics with gender-based suffixes. In creating an authority record for an Icelandic agent, why is it more proper to determine gender from the sentence "She is the daughter of Jon" than from the name "Jonsdottir," which quite literally means the same thing?

Photographs of agents also present catalogers with important clues. Again, a photograph can be misleading and should never replace an explicit statement of gender on the part of an agent. But when agents are limited to the choice of one of two genders, as is the case in Hebrew, Arabic, and other non-English languages, choices of names and visual performance not complicit with "normative" gender standards can signal identification with genders beyond the binary and trigger further investigation on the part of the cataloger. Thus, a man with a name more typical for women can either use gendered language or can appear in a picture wearing male religious vestments. In the first case the cataloger would record the male gender in the authority record. In the second, the

---

37. Paula Stone Williams, "I've Lived as a Man & a Woman—Here's What I Learned," 2017, https://www.youtube.com/watch?v=lrYx7HaUlMY.

38. John Leland, "Faith and Family, in Transition," *New York Times*, 2017, https://www.nytimes.com/2017/06/16/nyregion/forefront-pastors-father-became-a-woman.html.

mismatch between the name and the picture would prompt the cataloger to search sources external to the resource-in-hand for authoritative gender information. In audiovisual materials voice can also signify the need to research gender identification.[39]

The Israeli Experience

in the singular chances are equal
who says it's a lost case[40]

The National Library of Israel (NLI) maintains and administers NNL10, a multilingual, multiscript national authority database containing nearly 1.5 million personal name authority records.[41] Over twenty academic libraries, as well as the national union catalog, use this database and NNL10 is publicly available through the Israeli union catalog and in the Community Zone of Ex Libris's Alma integrated library system. NNL10's primary advantage, besides cooperative authority work, is that it allows a single search across multiple scripts to produce results. Thus, a search for any of

Dickens, Charles, 1812-1870

Диккенс, Чарлз, 1812-1870

דיקנס, צ'ארלס, 1812-1870

ديكنز, چارلز

will each present the reader with the same list of results, covering all languages in an NNL10 library's collection.

In creating policies statements, NLI began with PCC policies: NLI is a NACO library and in doing NACO work PCC policies are adhered

---

39. Gilad Padva, "Hey, Man, You're My Girlfriend! Poetic Genderfuck and Queer Hebrew in Eran Zur's Performance of Yona Wallach's Lyrics," in *Queering the Popular Pitch*, ed. Sheila Whiteley and Jennifer Rycenga (New York: Routledge, 2006), 101–14.

40. Wallach, "Hebrew."

41. Ahava Cohen, "Each of Us Has a Name: Creating a Multilingual, Multiscript National Authority Database," *Catalogue and Index* 186 (2017): 15–19, https://www.cilip.org.uk/sites/default/files/media/document/2017/ci186cohen_ahava._each_of_us_has_name_creating_a_multilingual_multis.pdf.

to strictly. PCC policy was adapted for NNL10 authority work in accordance with the needs of our core collections and language bases. NACO authority records created under PCC policy are copied into NNL10 and revised to conform to Israeli policy.

These differing policies are most evident in our understanding of gender. Performativity is emphasized as a means of acknowledging the non-linguistic ways in which agents subvert the binary paradigm to signify the binary and non-binary genders of their bibliographic lives. In determining gender for NNL10 work we follow the revised RDA 9.7.1.2 ("Take information on gender from *any source*" – emphasis added).

NNL10 member libraries collect materials from a variety of published and unpublished sources, including graduate work, personal narratives, oral histories, photojournalism, and self-published religious and secular works. The database's policy mandates that all agents given access points have authority records created for them, but names often repeat themselves and catalogers must decide if a particular string represents one or more agents.

Theses and dissertations rarely carry significant personal information and the level of self-disclosure in self-published material is often low. Given the highly gendered nature of the language, gender information is often unintentionally disclosed and becomes a primary method of distinguishing between agents with identical names. If in one publication an agent named Tal Segal writes "I [masculine] say" while in another an agent named Tal Segal identifies as a "[feminine] registered [feminine] nurse" it is enough to signal to the cataloger that separate authority records must be maintained for each of these agents.

Due to the NNL10 policy of anticipating a future need for disambiguation in names of Israeli, Hebraica, and Judaica authors, Israeli catalogers attempt to glean information about alternate names, timespans, gender, affiliation, professions, and areas of interest and record sources of all information for all agents. Where available we also add the names of the agent's parents to assist in future disambiguation. If all needed information is not available in the resource in hand we attempt to find it in publicly available information.

Gender of agents is sought from a variety of sources:

- Information in the resource in hand
- (For contemporary agents) Self-identification on social media platforms and personal or official websites associated with the agent
- (For deceased agents) Publicly available photographs of tombstones
- Scholarship about the agent
- Names and photographs in coordination with cultural knowledge of the era or milieu of the agent (for example, persons using the name *Daniyel* [Daniel] prior to the twentieth century and who have left bibliographic traces were performing the male gender)
- Titles and works associated with an agent in coordination with cultural knowledge of the era or milieu of the agent (for example, persons serving as rabbis or imams prior to the twentieth century and who have left bibliographic traces were, with a few known exceptions, performing the male gender)
- Direct contact with the agent by phone or e-mail, including completion of a "creative agent" form. As the NNL10 network increases in size and staffing, this channel is increasingly preferred.

We take advantage of the low power distance in Israeli society[42] to directly contact many agents. When contact information is readily available, as it is in many self-published books, a phone call or email actually takes less time than does searching online for information. In addition, we have cultivated relationships with publishers and with subject experts who will, upon request, provide catalogers with agent contact information. NLI has created forms in Arabic, English, and Hebrew to guide agents in providing all the information necessary to build a full authority record. The issue of gender, despite the binary bias in Hebrew and Arabic, is presented as an open question—"Gender:", thus avoiding

---

42. Gerte Hofstede, "Israel," *The Hofstede Center*, 2016, https://geert-hofstede.com/israel.html.

prejudicing answers with any grammatical markings. To date, not a single respondent has replied with anything but male or female. As opposed to the experience of Billey, Drabinski & Roberto,[43] the only confusion Israeli authors express about encoding gender in the authority record is about the question itself, stating that they thought their gender was obvious given their name, photograph, or the field in which they work.

An advantage to contacting agents directly is the opportunity to collaborate with them in building not only our authority database, but also our collections. Before asking for information we explain why authority control is important and how the national database works. We also inform agents about the country's mandatory deposit laws and ask for a list of publications with which they have been involved; this list, along with contact details, is passed to the Mandatory Deposit department at NLI.

After completing the authority form agents are invited to proof their record as it appears in our catalog and to share information about NNL10 with other creative agents. Thus we are contacted several times a week by agents and their families with new information for our authority records and with the deposit of new materials into our national collection. Information received either directly or from within resources is analyzed and appropriate action is taken within the authority file. For example, a change in gender identification may trigger a change in preferred name and additional gender information fields—if under the new name the agent claims works created under previous names—or trigger the creation of a separate authority record if the agent does not claim those previous works or if the agent contacts us and asks to have the identities separated. Connection between the two authority records would, again, depend on the stated preferences of the agent.

Collaboration, we have found, is key to creating precise and representative records for contemporary authors. Our care in seeking information and hearing what our creative agents are saying (and what they are

---

43. Billey, Drabinski, and Roberto, "What's Gender Got to Do with It? A Critique of RDA 9.7."

expressing in non-verbal ways) serves as an excellent public relations tool for all members of the national database, enhancing the libraries' prestige and patronage.

Opening a Window onto Unfamiliar Worlds

Though Billey has said that "deprecating the entire vocabulary helped support internationalization of RDA because different cataloging communities and different countries will then have the ability to define gender based on how that cataloging community in that country or that region understands gender,"[44] the ad hoc committee's report is still bound to the Anglophone experience. The authors do not acknowledge "the challenge that non-Western speech communities present to their theories."[45] With a few minor changes the recommendations could be far more inclusive than they are now.

Perhaps, as the RDA Steering Committee has learned to its advantage, the time has come to include representatives of other cultures into groups making decisions. It is important, in a world growing ever more connected, to climb out of the trap of Anglophone privilege and see creative agents throughout the world through the lens of their own lived experiences. In letting them speak their truth through our catalogs we all will win.

Bibliography

Alyagon, Talma, "Pegishah im Lea Goldberg," [Meeting with Lea Goldberg], *Ma'ariv - yamim ve-lelot*, January 24, 1969, pg. 23.

Barad, Karen. "Posthumanist Performativity: Toward an Understanding of How Matter Comes to Matter." *Signs* 23, no. 3 (2003): 801–31.

---

44. "Cataloging, Gender, and RDA Rule 9.7."
45. Sadiqi, *Women, Gender and Language in Morocco*, xvi.

Benaim, Rachel Delia. "Does the Hebrew Language Have a Gender Problem?" *Forward*, November 9, 2015. https://forward.com/sister-
hood/324205/degendering-hebrew/.

Billey, Amber, and Emily Drabinski. "Cataloging, Gender, and RDA Rule
9.7." *ALCTS Exchange*, 2017. http://www.ala.org/alcts/confe-
vents/upcoming/webinar/031517.

Billey, Amber, Emily Drabinski, and K. R. Roberto. "What's Gender Got
to Do with It? A Critique of RDA 9.7." *Cataloging and Classification
Quarterly* 52, no. 4 (April 24, 2014): 412–21. doi:10.1080/01639374
.2014.882465.

Billey, Amber, Matthew Haugen, John Hostage, Nancy Sack, and Adam L.
Schiff. "Report of the PCC Ad Hoc Task Group on Gender in
Name Authority Records." Washington, D.C.: Library of Congress,
2016. https://www.loc.gov/aba/pcc/documents/Gender_375
field_RecommendationReport.pdf.

Broyde, Michael J. "The Establishment of Maternity & Paternity in Jewish
and American Law." *National Jewish Law Review* III (1998): 117–52.
http://www.jlaw.com/Articles/maternity1.html.

Butler, Judith. *Gender Trouble: Feminism and the Subversion of Identity*. 2nd ed.
New York: Routledge Classics, 2006.

Cohen, Ahava. "Each of Us Has a Name: Creating a Multilingual, Multiscript National Authority Database." *Catalogue and Index* 186
(2017): 15–19. https://www.cilip.org.uk/sites/default/files/media/
document/2017/ci186cohen_ahava._each_of_us_has_name_
creating_a_multilingual_multis.pdf.

Danon, Limor Meoded. *What Kind of Body? The Affects of the Sexing Process on
Intersexed People's Lives*. Tel Aviv: Resling, 2014.

Gadish, Ronit. "haShivyon Hamigdari, haLashon haIvrit v'haAkademia
[Gender Equality, the Hebrew Language and the Academy]." *The
Academy of the Hebrew Language*, 2017. http://hebrew-academy.org.
il/2017/10/23/הימדקאהו-תירבעה-ןושלה-ירדגמה-ןויוושה/.

Gonen, Einat, and Doron Rubinstein. "Gender Neutralization in Hebrew: The Case of the Numerals in Colloquial Hebrew." *Brill's
Journal of Afroasiatic Languages and Linguistics* 7, no. 1 (2015): 1–29.
doi:10.1163/18776930-00701002.

Harris Green, Hannah. "Translating Identity across the Language Barrier."
How We Get to Next, 2017. https://howwegettonext.com/translat-
ing-identity-across-the-language-barrier-66a87163a8e1.

Hofstede, Gerte. "Israel." *The Hofstede Center*, 2016. https://geert-hofstede.
com/israel.html.

Hord, Levi C R. "Bucking the Linguistic Binary: Gender Neutral Language
in English, Swedish, French, and German." *Proceedings of Western
Interdisciplinary Student Symposium on Language Research (WISSLR)* 3,
no. 1 (2016).

Katri, Ido. "Lo Ovrot, Lo Nechmadot - haMa'avak haTransi v'Tactikot
Shel Mishtur b'Hukei Isur Aflayah [Not Passing, Not Sweet - the
Trans Struggle and Policing Tactics in Non-Discrimination Laws]."
In *Sex Acher : Mivchar Mamarim b'Limudim Lahatabii'm u'Qveeru'im
Yisraeli'im [Other Sex : A Selection of Essays on Israeli LGBT and Queer
Studies]*, edited by Aeyal Gross, Amalia Ziv, and Raz Yosef, 615–56.
Tel Aviv: Resling, 2016.

Kukla, Elliot. "Terms for Gender Diversity in Classical Jewish Texts."
TransTorah, 2006. http://www.transtorah.org/PDFs/Classical_Jew-
ish_Terms_for_Gender_Diversity.pdf.

Leland, John. "Faith and Family, in Transition." *The New York Times*. 2017.
https://www.nytimes.com/2017/06/16/nyregion/forefront-pas-
tors-father-became-a-woman.html.

Ma'avarim, "Hamlazot l'sikur anashim transim" [Recommendations for
coverage of trans people], May 2018. https://drive.google.com/
file/d/1cQvzH8tP3oAGgsraeWLy2XVaKgmqUSMl/view.

Meerwijk, Esther L., and Jae M. Sevelius. "Transgender Population Size in
the United States: A Meta-Regression of Population-Based Probability Samples." *American Journal of Public Health* 107, no. 2 (February 2017): e1–8. doi:10.2105/AJPH.2016.303578.

Naveh, Hannah. "Leket, Peah V'shikacha: Hahaim Mechutz Lacanon
    [Gleanings, the Corners of the Field, and Forgotten Produce: Life
    Outside the Canon]." In *Sex Gender Politics: Women in Israel*, edited
    by Dafna N. Izraeli, Ariella Friedman, Henriette Dahan-Kalev,
    Fogiel-Bijaoui, Hanna Herzog, Manar Hasan, and Hannah Naveh,
    49–106. Tel Aviv: Hakibbutz Hameuchad, 1999.

OCLC. "Inside WorldCat," 2018. https://www.oclc.org/en/worldcat/
    inside-worldcat.html.

Padva, Gilad. "Hey, Man, You're My Girlfriend!: Poetic Genderfuck and
    Queer Hebrew in Eran Zur's Performance of Yona Wallach's
    Lyrics." In *Queering the Popular Pitch*, edited by Sheila Whiteley and
    Jennifer Rycenga, 101–14. New York: Routledge, 2006.

RDA Steering Committee. "RDA Toolkit," 2017. http://access.rdatoolkit.
    org/.

Sa'ar, Amalia. "Masculine Talk: On the Subconcious Use of Masculine
    Linguistic Forms among Hebrew- and Arabic-Speaking Women in
    Israel." *Signs* 32, no. 2 (2007): 405–29. doi:10.1086/676943.

Sadiqi, Fatima. *Women, Gender and Language in Morocco*. Leiden: Brill, 2003.

Shelton, Lucia. "Searching WorldCat Efficiently." San Juan: OCLC, 2016.
    https://www.oclc.org/content/dam/oclc/events/member-fo-
    rums/PR_SearchingWorldCatEfficiently.pdf.

The Academy of the Hebrew Language. "General Grammatical Background
    on Hebrew." Accessed March 12, 2018. http://en.hebrew-academy.
    org.il/hebrew-language/general-grammatical-background-on-
    hebrew/.

Titman, Nat. "How Many People in the United Kingdom Are Nonbi-
    nary?" *Practical Androgyny*, 2014. https://practicalandrogyny.
    com/2014/12/16/how-many-people-in-the-uk-are-nonbinary/.

Wallach, Yona. "Hebrew." In *The Defiant Muse: Hebrew Feminist Poems from An-
    tiquity to the Present: A Bilingual Anthology*, edited by Shirley Kaufman,
    Galit Hasan-Rokem, and Tamar Hess, translated by Lisa Katz,
    189–91. New York: The Feminist Press of the City University of
    New York, 1999.

Williams, Paula Stone. "I've lived as a man & a woman—here's what I learned." YouTube video, 15:24. Posted December 2017. https://www.youtube.com/watch?v=lrYx7HaUlMY.

Zelda. "Each of Us Has a Name." In *The Spectacular Difference: Selected Poems*, translated by Marcia Falk, 141–44. Cincinnati: Hebrew Union College, 2004.

Chapter 9

VIOLENT CIS-TEMS: IDENTIFYING TRANSPHOBIA IN
LIBRARY OF CONGRESS NAME AUTHORITY RECORDS

Hale Polebaum-Freeman

CANDACE TOWNS | STEPHANIE MONTEZ | ALLY LEE
STEINFELD | DERRICKA BANNER | KASHMIRE NAZIER
REDD | KIWI HERRING | GWYNEVERE RIVER SONG |
TEETEE DANGERFIELD | EBONY MORGAN | AVA LE'RAY
BARRIN | KENDRA MARIE ADAMS | KENNE MCFADDEN
| SHERRELL FAULKNER | KENNETH BOSTICK | CHAY
REED | ALPHONZA WATSON | JAQUARRIUS HOLLAND |
CHYNA GIBSON | CIARA MCELVEEN | MESHA CALDWELL
| JAMIE LEE WOUNDED ARROW | TIARA RICHMOND |
JOJO STRIKER | SEAN HAKE | JAYLOW MCGLORY | SCOUT
SCHULTZ | BROOKLYN BREYANNA STEVENSON | BRANDI
SEALS | RHIANNON LAYENDECKER

These are the names of the twenty-nine transgender people who were
killed in the U.S. in 2017.[1] This is after 2016 closed as the deadliest year
for transgender and gender nonconforming Americans, with twenty-
four homicides, an increase from 2015's twenty-two homicides. The
majority of the lives taken were those of queer transgender women
and femmes of color.[2] In the face of this epidemic, many activists find

1. Human Rights Campaign, "Violence Against the Transgender Community in
2017," *Resources*, January, 2018, accessed November 11, 2018, https://www.hrc.org/
resources/violence-against-the-transgender-community-in-2017

2. Hilton Dresden, "7 Trans Women of Color Have Been Murdered in 2017,"
Out, March 6, 2017, accessed March 21, 2017, https://www.out.com/news

themselves staring down problems that seem insurmountable, deep-seated social issues such as racism, class inequality, homophobia, sexism, and transphobia.[3] Systemic social issues thrive in systemic administrative environments, many of which have been crafted to support, disseminate, and reinforce the hierarchies of race and gender. The categories of race and gender are then used to reinforce the norms of society.[4] This "nation-making activity" is carried out through everyday interactions with administrative systems,[5] the same systems that proliferate library environments.

We live in times where more transgender women and femmes of color are losing their lives to transphobic violence every year. In response to this appalling phenomenon, this chapter uses an inspection of Library of Congress Name Authority Records (LC NARs) created as representations of transgender authors to elucidate the ways LC catalogers have made purposeful, transphobic decisions about the nature of the metadata selected for inclusion in the authority records of transgender people. This metadata not only influences how transgender identities are communicated throughout their authority records, but also interprets the lives of transgender authors in a way which upholds binary, essentialist, and ultimately transmisogynistic ideals. Essentialist views shape many American's beliefs about the body, limiting the understanding of transgender individuals and their decisions about physically transitioning. In regards to gender, essentialism is the belief that one's membership (or inclusion) in a social identity category is intrinsically linked to biologically determined portions of that same identity. At its most basic transphobia can be defined as "societal discrimination and stigma of individuals

-opinion/2017/3/06/7-trans-women-color-have-been-murdered-2017.

3. Diana Tourjee, "How Society Let This Happen: The Transgender People Killed in 2016," *Broadly*, November 20, 2016, accessed March 21, 2017, https://broadly.vice.com/en_us/article/a3wgvz/how-society-let-this-happen-the-transgender-people-killed-in-2016.

4. Dean Spade, *Normal Life* (New York: South End Press, 2011), 78-9.

5. Spade, *Normal Life*, 78-9.

who do not conform to traditional norms of sex and gender."[6] Taken
together, these ideals encourage increasing violence against transgender
bodies of color, echoing the same logic that is used to justify the trans
panic defense; a legal strategy used to reduce the sentence of a perpetrator of violence against transgender individuals.

This chapter uses transgender theory to expand the complexities of
gender. Transgender theory expands upon society's normative spectrum
of gender to include gender identities that combine or fall outside of the
binary designations of male/female. The act of growing into a transgender identity must be understood as not merely a single movement
from one binary gender to the other (through the act of transitioning),
but also as a movement that transgresses binary gender. Transgender
theory breaks apart the simple, binary understanding of gender and
instead brings attention to the fact that gender is not only fluid within
and beyond the spectrum of the male/female binary, but also intersects
with other identities (like sexuality and race). Transgender theory leaves
room for individuals who exist in a space between embracing affinity
within an identity and not wanting to be defined by a singular collective identity.[7]

The utilization of a transgender theory lens creates room to develop
an understanding of the rationale that motivates LC catalogers to over
justify the decisions they make in the process of classifying transgender
authors. At the same time, transgender theory makes clear the reasons
why this strategy of over justification is unethical. Additionally, the
application of transgender theory to this issue steers catalogers toward
direct action they might take to combat the continued seeping of transmisogyny into the Library of Congress' administrative systems.

---

6. Eiko Sugano, Tooru Nemoto, and Don Operario, "The Impact of Exposure to
Transphobia on HIV Risk Behavior in a Sample of Transgendered Women of Color
in San Francisco," *AIDS and Behavior* 10, no. 2 (March, 2006): 217.

7. Julie L. Nagoshi, Craig T. Nagoshi, and Stephan/ie Brzuzy, *Gender and Sexual Identity: Transcending Feminist and Queer Theory* (New York, Springer, 2014), 76.

Cataloging Gender

The introduction of RDA instruction 9.7 fully manifested the description of gender in the catalog. Developed to incorporate the tasks outlined by the Functional Requirements for Authority Description (FRAD), particularly the new additions of contextualization and justification, RDA 9.7 was added as an additional means to organize and disambiguate between persons described in the LC NARs.[8] The original instructions found at RDA 9.7, written in 2011, advise cataloguers to "record the gender of the person using an appropriate term from the list below." Included in the list of terms are "male," "female," and "not known." While the instructions at RDA 9.7 do concede that these three terms may not be "appropriate or sufficiently specific," the terms that they offer as potential alternatives, "intersex" and "transsexual woman," problematically conflate gender and sex. Many catalogers and librarians[9] protested not only the binary controlled vocabulary suggested in RDA 9.7, but also the inclusion of gender as a descriptive category. While RDA instruction 9.7 was updated to remove LC's binary controlled vocabulary, LC catalogers are still given the opportunity to record gender in the MARC21 environment, an opportunity that many seize with reckless abandon.

Even with the option of using a somewhat more inclusive set of terminology,[10] the attitudes that justified imposing a vocabulary based in a binary system of gender still reverberate throughout the NARs of transgender individuals, extending beyond MARC21 field 375. Transphobia has migrated into other areas of the NARs for transgender people,

8. Amber Billey and Emily Drabinski, "Cataloging Gender & RDA Instruction 9.7" (Webinar, ALCTS Exchange, March 15, 2017), 15:34, 31:25.

9. Including Drabinski, Amber Billey, Kelly Thompson, and others cited in this chapter.

10. While the Library of Congress Demographic Group Vocabulary (LCDGT) includes a wide variety of language to represent gender identities and expressions, the term nonbinary (among many others) is absent from the list. Find these terms at: http://netanelganin.com/projects/lcdgt/lcdgtType.html#gdr

most notably the 670 field designated as a container for "source data found." The contents of the 670 field of MARC21 are governed by the instructions found at the end of RDA 9.7. This instruction points catalogers to "Indicate the source from which the information on the gender of the person was derived applying the instructions given under 8.12." RDA 8.12 covers the recording of sources consulted, with the "source citation" listed in subfield a and "information found" listed in subfield b.[11] While the Library of Congress reminds catalogers that name authority records are not intended to serve as a complete biographical representation of an author, and to use judgement to assemble a 670 field that is "cogent and concise yet complete,"[12] Kelly J. Thompson notes that it is general cataloging practice to use this field to "justify" the contents of other fields."[13] While, generally, the use of this field is limited to recording where variant forms of a name are found, in the case of NARs for transgender authors information provided to justify one's gender identity is often included at this location. This information is never included in NARs for cisgender authors.[14]

Essentialism and Classification

The NAR for Kate Bornstein, a nonbinary author, is an example of how the damage done to transgender individuals extends beyond the information recorded in MARC21 field 375.[15] In the 670 field of

---

11. Library of Congress, "670 – Source Data Found (R)," https://www.loc.gov/marc/authority/ad670.html.

12. Library of Congress, "FAQ on the 670 (Source Data Found) Field in Name Authority Records (NARs) for NACO," https://www.loc.gov/aba/pcc/naco/670faq.html#3.

13. Kelly J. Thompson, "More Than a Name: A Content Analysis of Name Authority Records for Authors Who Self-Identify as Trans," *Library Resources and Technical Services* 60, no. 3 (2016): 148-9, doi: 10.5860/lrts.60n3.

14. Ibid.: Thompson also notes here "Further research is needed to compare the amount of information, especially that of a personal nature, that has been provided in name authority records for authors who are trans versus those who are cisgender."

15. The author has made a conscious choice to not recreate the privacy violating entries in this paper. To do so in both cases would only further exacerbate the problem created by the disclosure of personal information.

Bornstein's NAR there is an overdisclosure of personal information relating to hir gender-related surgical history.[16] This information is offered by the LC cataloger as proof that Bornstein qualifies as transgender. The inclusion of this type of personal medical information is not only disrespectful to an author's right to privacy,[17] it also renders invisible the lived experience of transgender individuals who cannot or choose not to pursue medical intervention as part of their transition.[18] One would think that Bornstein's word should be enough to confirm hir transgender identity, and yet an LC cataloger thought it more important to justify their designation of Bornstein as "transgender people" by sharing extremely personal information. This need smacks of essentialism.

By using surgical history as a qualification of an individual's transgender identity, LC catalogers uphold a system that inordinately values transgender efforts to align themselves physically in an essentialist gender binary. Surgery and other medical methods of transitioning are central to the construction of gender identity for many transgender people.[19] However, to insist that transgender individuals are not transgender unless they have had or desire medical intervention in the course of their transition is to deeply misunderstand what it means to be transgender in favor of a more essentialist understanding of gender, one that favors societal norms over the lived experiences of transgender individuals.[20] In turn, this devalues the existence of transgender individuals who do not want or are unable to pursue treatments that would more physically align them with either gender party in the biologically determinate binary system. To imply that the only 'real' trans individuals are those

---

16. Billey and Drabinski, "Cataloging Gender," 23:50.

17. Both Billey and Drabinski ("Cataloging Gender") and Thompson make reference to laws that guide the ethical sharing of personal information, most notably those protections that make up the foundation for HIPPA.

18. Thompson, "More Than a Name," 152.

19. Susan Stryker, "My Words to Victor Frankenstein Above the Village of Chamounix: Performing Transgender Rage," *GLQ* 1 (1994): 238.

20. Rachel McKinnon, "Stereotype Threat and Attributional Ambiguity for Trans Women," *Hypatia* 29, no. 4 (2014): 858-9.

who medically alter their bodies to better fit within the essential, binary
construction of socially acceptable gender is to say that without surgery
a transgender person is not truly the gender they claim, and additionally that all trans individuals who medically transition wish to embody
a binary gender identity. This is simply untrue: trans women and trans
men are still women and men without surgery, and many nonbinary trans
people choose to medically transition and yet not identify as a member
of a binary gender group. This includes Kate Bornstein, who reflects
"I never did feel like a girl or a woman; rather it was my unshakeable
conviction that I was not a boy or a man. It was the absence of feeling,
rather than its presence, that convinced me to change my gender."[21]
Essentialist thinking privileges the biological aspects of gender over
social aspects, even though gender is primarily understood by social
theorists to be a socially constructed identity.[22]

Ascribing unchanging characteristics to members of a gender category
(or any identity category) is a strategy used to enable a system to render
all members of said category as alike, allowing for many generalizations
to be made.[23] Some of these generalizations might be that all women
like pink (a traditionally feminine trait), and dislike sports (a traditionally
masculine trait).[24] Society teaches us these "archetypes of proper being,"
and each individual is expected to play their assigned part, despite the
reality that ever achieving the ideal gender is an impossibility.[25] This sort
of evaluation of abilities and preferences based on gender is distinctly
anti-feminist, and is limiting for people of all genders, trans and cis alike.

---

21. Kate Bornstein, *Gender Outlaw: On Men, Women, and the Rest of Us* (New York:
Vintage Books, 1994), 24.

22. McKinnon, "Stereotype threat," 858-9.

23. Nick Haslam and Sheri R. Levy, "Essentialist Beliefs About Homosexuality:
Structure and Implications for Prejudice," *Personality and Social Psychology Bulletin* 32,
no. 4 (2006): 471.

24. Boby Ho-Hong Ching and Jason Teng Xu, "The Effects of Gender Neuroessen-
tialism on Transprejudice: An Experimental Study," *Sex Roles* 78 (2018): 229.

25. Spade, *Normal Life*, 53.

Essentialist thinking highlights the differences between social categories, legitimizing and naturalizing social inequality while offering protection to dominant social identities.[26] Gender classification happens for many in utero, assigned to us before any other marker of our identity. Genitals[27] are a key element in this classification, a required attribute to be seen within a binary, mandatory system that assigns social characteristics to sexed anatomy.[28] The societal correlation between genitals and gender assignment is plainly illustrated in an instructional webinar released by the Library of Congress in 2013. In this session the LC trainer explains to catalogers how to make the distinction between gender and sexual orientation, saying "we're interested in knowing what your gender is—you know, what's your physical equipment? Not who you go to bed with."[29] This initial classification is only the first step in how gender is reinforced through societal norms. After genitalia-based-gender is assigned to the human body, society uses this information to socialize individuals in a manner consistent with essentialism.[30] Society uses a myriad of methods[31] of positive and negative reinforcement throughout an individual's lifetime to reinforce essentialist, binary gender roles.[32] However, for the purpose of daily functioning on an interpersonal level, external genitalia is, socially, the least relevant element for determining gender.[33] Instead, perception of gender is based on a combination of several

---

26. Haslam & Levy, "Essentialist Beliefs," 472.

27. Stryker notes that the only plausible explanation of the importance assigned to genitalia in gender classification is due to the way these body parts signal "future reproductive potential" (249).

28. Nagoshi et al., 16.

29. Library of Congress, "Module 2.d: MARC21 in NACO RDA Authority Records: Old Fields, New Fields and How We Are Using Them," 10 min., MPEG, available on iTunes, accessed March 1, 2017: 7:14:02.

30. Thompson, "More Than a Name," 141.

31. Nagoshi, et al. list legal, religious, and cultural practices (16).

32. Nagoshi, et al., *Gender and Sexual Identity*, 16.

33. Morgan Tilleman, "(Trans)forming the Provocation Defense." *Journal of Criminal Law & Criminology* 100, no. 4 (2010): 1684.

elements, including visual,[34] auditory,[35] and cultural cues.[36] If more of these cues indicate masculinity than femininity it is generally assumed that an individual is male, while a majority of feminine cues leads to the assumption that an individual is female.[37] Any discord between one's genitalia and the gendered cues that one communicates often produces discomfort, for both cisgender members of society as well as for the trans and gender nonconforming individuals themselves. However, it is important to understand that this discomfort is not a problem with the gender identity of transgender people, but rather a problem that stems from a society that demands conformity to socially constructed definitions of gender identities to which transgender individuals do not fit properly.[38] Further discomfort stems from the fact that gender classification is not consensual: as Stryker notes, "Gender attribution is compulsory; it codes and deploys our bodies in ways that materially affect us, yet we choose neither our marks nor the meanings they carry."[39]

Non-consensual gender classification rears its head in the Library of Congress NARs as well. This is the case with the LC NAR of Ivan E. Coyote. The authorized access point for Coyote includes an unnecessary disclosure of the author's middle name which, as a feminine name, effectively outs the masculine Coyote as transgender. As Ivan E. Coyote has never published under a name that included their full middle name, this information with no literary warrant has been widely shared with the public without Coyote's consent. This information is revealed by a simple catalog search for Coyote's name in an author list, a disturbing occurrence with implications that transcend the controlled environment of a NAR: Coyote is outed to every catalog user who wishes to find their work. The ability to control the disclosure of information about

---

34. Gait, body, and facial characteristics, body language, and dress.

35. Voice and vocabulary.

36. Interpersonal style, profession, job title, social status, and economic status.

37. Jillian Todd Weiss, "The Gender Caste System: Identity, Privacy, and Heteronormativity," *Law & Sexuality* 10 (2001): 179.

38. Nagoshi et al., *Gender and Sexual Identity*, 131-2.

39. Stryker, "My Words to Victor Frankenstein," 249.

oneself is critical to those who self-identify with a social identity that carries with it the possibility of discrimination or violence. The rules of disclosing gender sensitive information in the NAR of a transgender author is unethical unless the cataloger is certain the individual has publicly shared said information with the intent of informing others.[40] Some cataloguers might argue that the inclusion of Coyote's feminine middle name is a crucial element for disambiguation. However, the instructions found at RDA 9.5 state "A fuller form of name is a core element when needed to distinguish a person from another person with the same name." As there is only one author by the name of Ivan E. Coyote in the NAF, additional qualifiers in the heading, including Coyote's middle name are unnecessary. Issues of name disclosure and consent concerning transgender authors seem to be particularly difficult for catalogers to comprehend. Another transgender author, Justin Vivian Bond, has a similar combination of contrastingly gendered names. Even though Bond has published under this name, v's NAR doesn't reflect this consensual disclosure as the primary entry for v's name.

By continuing to hold space for gender classification, name authority records uphold society's essentialist, binary system of gender, one which practically demands that catalogers find a way to fit the subjects they are describing into this limiting system. Transgender theory argues that a binary system of gender values the alignment of sex characteristics with those of gender as "natural" and therefore more fully human.[41] By following society's expectations for gender classification, NARs contribute to the pressure transgender individuals feel to conform, potentially through medical intervention. Including gender as a form of classification centers gender as an essential element of what makes a person human. This aids in the exclusion and dehumanization of many transgender people who do not fit into the man-woman binary. This

---

40. Thompson, "More Than a Name," 141.

41. Patrice Diquinzio, "Exclusion and Essentialism in Feminist Theory: The Problem of Mothering," *Hypatia* 8, no. 3 (August 1993): 2-3.

loss of gender privilege is often matched by a loss of personhood and accompanied by violence.[42]

Unjustified Justification

A common theme that resonates through Kate Bornstein and Ivan E. Coyote's name authority records, as well as the records for several other transgender authors, is the tendency of LC catalogers to add extra, unjustified information. This is not done with cisgender authors[43]—the question is why? Amber Billey and Emily Drabinski point to ignorance, stigma, and transphobia as causes for these inconsistencies between cisgender and transgender NARs.[44] Article V of the Library Bill of Rights claims that a library won't limit or refuse access to any person because of their age, origin, background, or views.[45] Under this mandate, users of any sex, gender identity, gender expression, or sexual orientation are granted access to services, materials, and programs offered by their library. As transgender authors are "members of the communities that cataloging is meant to serve" it would make sense for catalogers to do their best to distance themselves, and the metadata they produce, from attitudes that oppress the transgender community.[46] Unfortunately, as evidenced by the NARs of Bornstein and Coyote, and countless other transgender authors represented by LC, it seems that many catalogers do not take this commitment to their transgender community members seriously. This lack of attention stems from the fact that it is considered socially acceptable to try to "solve" the gender of a transgender person.[47]

42. Linda Heidenreich, "Learning from the Death of Gwen Araujo: Transphobic Racial Subordination and Queer Latina Survival in the Twenty-First Century," *Chicana/Latina Studies* 6, no. 1 (2006): 60.

43. Billey and Drabinski make this assertion in "Cataloging Gender," 26:28. Thompson, however believes more research on cisgender authors is necessary (see note 21).

44. Billey and Drabinski, "Cataloging Gender," 26:28.

45. "Library Bill of Rights," *American Library Association*, accessed March 22, 2017, http://www.ala.org/advocacy/intfreedom/librarybill.

46. Thompson, "More Than a Name," 144.

47. Spade, *Normal Life*, 75-6.

As the majority of catalogers are cisgender, and benefit from cisgender privilege, the current standards for recording gender are comfortable. As Billey et. al observe, "For LC, gender is easy: to know about oneself, to determine on behalf of others, and to codify in a MARC authority record."[48] Transgender theory challenges this comfort, demanding that "cataloging professionals…decline to adopt standards that reinforce hierarchies of privilege," hierarchies that further exclude transgender communities.[49] As Thompson points to, "gender identity is a protected class in many states, and should be given the full weight of respect afforded to other legally protected identity groups."[50]

As creators of LC authority records, catalogers hold administrative control over the communities they strive to represent. Trans activist, writer, and teacher Dean Spade recognizes how, while the use of gender categories is something neutral and obvious to administrators, it is also a "potential vector of vulnerability" that can decrease the "life chances and life spans" of transgender individuals.[51] Systems that classify their subjects according to gender have the potential to contribute to gender misclassification, which when combined with other factors[52] "produce[s] conditions of exacerbated poverty, criminalization, and violence for trans populations."[53] Dean Spade marks population-level institutional programs, like the LC authority records, as especially implicated in the ways transgender communities struggle with "purportedly banal and innocuous daily administrati[ve tasks]."[54] While seen as neutral, innocu-

---

48. Thompson, "More Than a Name," 143-4.

49. Amber Billey, Emily Drabinski and K.R. Roberto, "What's Gender Got to Do with It? A Critique of RDA 9.7," *Cataloging and Classification Quarterly* 52, no. 4 (2014): 413, doi: 10.1080/01639374.2014.882465.

50. Thompson, "More Than a Name," 153: Here Thompson asks catalogers to "… imagine the response if RDA suggested the addition of a race or religion category to the name authority record"—an interesting thought project.

51. Spade, *Normal Life*, 84.

52. Spade lists "widespread family rejection and routinized stigmatization" among the factors that produce conditions that are harmful to transgender communities.

53. Ibid., 84.

54. Ibid., 73-5.

ous information, gender becomes ubiquitous to immeasurable levels
when utilized by government and other administrative agencies. This
integration of gender into government systems begins with the sex
recorded on one's birth certificate, a designation that follows people
through life. As a government organization, it is unsurprising that the
Library of Congress has found gender a difficult obstacle to overcome
in the creation of NARs. However, catalogers are not governments, but
rather individual people making individual decisions. A community can
be a place of great power and potential, as it is community organizing
and resource sharing that have been the most effective strategies for
effecting structural change in a way that makes an authentic difference
for transgender people.[55] When LC NARs are the population-level
program, catalogers are the entities who have the ability to protect and
cultivate the life chances of transgender users.

Systems of Harm

The impact that administrative systems have on the life chances of
transgender individuals manifests itself in a variety of ways. Direct
contact with offensive material in NARs is easily identified as a micro-
aggression to transgender individuals. Microaggressions are defined by
Sue et al. as:

> brief and commonplace daily verbal, behavioral and environmental indig-
> nities, whether intentional or unintentional, that communicate hostile,
> derogatory or negative racial slights and insults that potentially have
> harmful or unpleasant psychological impact on the target person or
> group.[56]

Daily experiences with both overt and subtle discrimination has been
correlated to high rates of suicide, substance abuse, and depression

---

55. Heidenreich, "Learning from…Gwen Araujo," 76.

56. D. W. Sue, C.M. Capodilupo, G. C. Torino, J. M. Bucceri, A. M. B. Holder, K. L.
Nadal, and M. Esquilin, "Racial Microaggressions in Everyday life: Implications for
Clinical Practice," *American Psychologist* 62, no.4 (2007): 271

experienced by members of the transgender community.[57] It is in these ways that systems like LC authorities contribute to the harm of transgender bodies. As a population-level program of mass transgender identification,[58] LC authorities are responsible for developing cultural understandings of transgender persons. Activist catalogers resist the ignorant, stigmatizing, and transphobic attitudes found in LC NARs because they "perpetuate the notion of trans* [individuals] as deceptive, as criminals, as less than human, and as disposable people."[59] The urge LC catalogers feel to include extra justification in the NARs of transgender individuals is not only symptomatic of these attitudes, but also insidiously presents this metadata to catalog users as neutral and necessary. This "general feeling of disgust or revulsion" toward transgender individuals is a causative element in cases of transphobic violence.[60]

This correlation is especially impactful to transgender women and femmes of color, who experience violence at rates much higher than any other marginalized population in the United States.[61] Gender identity is only one facet of an individual's identity, and it is important to understand how factors like race, ethnicity, and class are always entangled with sex, gender, and gender identity.[62] By not considering the way that multiple axes of oppression interact, one is presuming that all women are White, all people of color are male, and everyone identifies

---

57. Tiffany K. Chang and Y. Barry Chung, "Transgender Microaggressions: Complexity of the Heterogeneity of Transgender Identities," *Journal of LGBT Issues in Counseling* 9, no. 3 (2015): 219.

58. Billey et al., "What's Gender…?," 419.

59. Aimee Wodda and Vanessa R. Panfil, "'Don't talk to me about deception: the necessary erosion of the trans* panic defense," *Albany Law Review* 78, no. 3 (2014-15): 958.

60. Wodda and Panfil, "Trans* panic defense," 931-2.

61. Ibid., 929-31: Wodda & Panfil report here "…according to the most recently released National Coalition of Anti-Violence Programs' hate violence report, LGBTQ people of color represented fifty-three percent of total reported victims and survivors of all hate crimes in the United States in 2012 and comprised 73.1% of LGBTQ homicide victims. A shocking ninety-eight percent of incidents perpetrated against trans* folk are suffered by those occupying the male-to-female spectrum."

62. Tilleman, "(Trans)forming the Provocation Defense," 1671 (footnote).

as heterosexual and cisgender.[63] The impact of intersectional identities
is easily illustrated by the fact that the vast majority of trans authors
described within the Library of Congress' name authority records are
White. While these trans authors are subject to transphobia, as seen
through their NARs, the race and class privilege they possess gives them
access to opportunities, like formal representation in the publishing
industry, that are not as readily available to transgender individuals of
color. We often only learn about the lives of transgender women and
femmes of color through the media coverage of their deaths.

Race and gender are both visible identities, an attribute that links the
two identity categories. This visibility influences the ideological claims
that race and gender are categories that are constructed only through
biology, as well as the belief that violence toward transgender women
and femmes of color is reasonable due to the human fear of things that
look different. As visible identities, race and gender are instrumental in
structuring the roles and relationships encountered by an individual in
their lifetime. To have a body, and to be seen, is to live a racialized and
gendered existence.[64] If transmisogyny is defined as the "policing of
femininity on bodies it is understood to not belong to," then all people
of color can be understood to experience transmisogyny.[65] Race and
gender can't be read off of people like book dust jackets. There is infi-
nitely more to a person's existence than can be surmised from the level
of interaction that exists between authority record catalogers and the
subjects they are describing in NARs. The classification of the visible
identities of race and gender is used as a metric to determine where an
individual should be placed in the social order.

In the United States and across the globe, this hierarchy and the dominant ideologies of race and gender are maintained through "symbolic, yet

---

63. Nagoshi, et al., *Gender and Sexual Identity*, 19.

64. Linda Martín Alcoff, *Visible Identities: Race, Gender, and the Self* (Oxford: Oxford
University Press, 2006), 103.

65 Elías Cosenza Krell, "Is Transmisogyny Killing Trans Women of Color? Black
Trans Feminisms and the Exigencies of White Femininity," *TSQ: Transgender Studies
Quarterly* 4, no. 2 (2017): 237.

very real acts of violence."[66] As Linda Heidenreich notices, "Persons who cannot be identified as either male or female are subjected to violence. Men who perform femininity and women who perform masculinity face similar violence."[67] While a White, heterosexual, cisgender male has the least need to be justified, the need for justification increases as identities descend down the social hierarchy. Library organizational systems have mimicked this hierarchy since their creation. Hope Olson notes that "topics relating to women and minorities [are] subsumed under mainstream topics," revealing the way LCSH centers the lived experience of White, straight, cisgender males.[68] In society and library organizational systems alike, the combination of visible identities embodied by transgender women and femmes of color place these individuals at the intersection of multiple layers of oppression, rendering individuals who find themselves at this identity intersection particularly vulnerable to violence. As Angelica Ross writes, "Being trans comes at a high cost, but being black and trans can cost you your life."[69]

The Trans Panic Defense

LC's tendency to over-justify the trans-ness of authors in their NAR is disturbingly reminiscent of the logic that has been used to craft a trans panic defense.[70] The basic legal claim that is the foundation of a

---

66. Heidenreich, "Learning from...Gwen Araujo," 65.

67. Ibid., 60-1.

68. Hope Olson, "How We Construct Subjects," *Library Trends* 56, no. 2 (2007): 520: While Olson specifically mentions the fact that there are subject headings for "Mentally ill women," "Mentally ill children," and "Mentally ill older people," but not "Mentally ill men" and "Sexual ethics for women," "Sexual ethics for teenagers," "Sexual ethics for youth," but not "Sexual ethics for men," this centering of the White, hetero, cis, male experience proliferates the LCSH.

69. Angelica Ross, "Call Me Caitlyn. Sincerely, Miss Ross," Black Voices (blog), *Huffington Post*, September 4, 2015, https://www.huffingtonpost.com/angelica-ross/i-am-not-cait_b_8039492.html.

70. Wodda and Panfil clarify on p. 933: "There is no official, freestanding gay or trans panic defense that exists within the legal sphere as a recognized affirmative defense. However, claims of gay panic or trans* panic are typically presented within

trans panic defense is closely related to that of the homosexual panic defense: that being so infuriated and offended by a nonviolent, non-heteronormative sexual advance that one is driven to harm or kill an individual is the behavior of a "reasonable" person.[71] The trans panic defense only works if the typical American juror is indeed so influenced by the transphobia and ciscentrism of American society that they react to the transgender victim with similar, potentially deadly feelings of fury and offense.[72] The attacker who invokes the trans panic defense hopes to convince the jury that their hateful, violent emotional response to the victim was the only response that the average American citizen could "reasonably" make.[73] Catalogers who create NARs for the Library of Congress are products of this same society, and so have been socialized to find many of the transphobic details of American society and the negative reactions these details provoke "reasonable." Thus it may seem "reasonable" to the typical NAR creator to treat the transgender subject as if they necessitate extra explanation. The over justification found in the NARs of transgender authors implies that the gender identities of transgender people are more difficult to understand than cisgender people's gender identities, while at the same time penalizing transgender authors by diminishing their humanity and the empathy felt toward them as subjects.[74]

Authority record catalogers consider transgender authors puzzles that need solving. Again, this is reminiscent of another claim made by the trans panic defense: the assertion that the victim purposefully misled their attacker.[75] This reasoning was central to how the alleged killer, Mark Daniel Lewis, was charged in June 2017 murder of Kenne McFadden, a Black trans woman. Lewis admitted pushing McFadden into the San

the context of an existing criminal law defense, such as temporary insanity, provocation, or self-defense."

71. Tilleman, "(Trans)forming the Provocation Defense," 1667.

72. Ibid.

73. Tilleman, "(Trans)forming the Provocation Defense," 1667.

74. Ibid., 1670-1.

75. Ibid., 1668-9.

Antonio river, where she drowned, after McFadden touched his buttocks. Lewis claimed he was acting in self-defense. Despite Lewis' admission of guilt, he was never brought to trial for the killing of McFadden. This decision, made by Judge Joey Contreras, was ostensibly motivated by lack of sufficiently compelling evidence, despite the fact that the court was presented with a video tape of Lewis' confession. As Judge Contreras is known to be particularly tough on crime, this dismissal of evidence is confusing unless something else, like transphobia, was at play. Importantly, the trans panic defense is still legal in Texas, where this decision was made.[76] Kenne McFadden is not the only case of a trans woman and/or femme of color murdered in 2017 where the legal aftermath doesn't seem to fit the circumstances of the crime. Despite the excessively hateful circumstances of many of the deaths, none of them were classified as hate crimes. Similar to both Judge Contreras and the jurors with whom the trans panic defense resonates, it seems plausible that catalogers who include justification of the existence of transgender authors in the authority records they create hold similar biases about transgender individuals.[77] This unreasonable claim that the transgender identity is inherently puzzling and deceitful, when transgender individuals have done nothing to provoke such a claim except have sex and gender that contrast, must be disallowed if transgender people are to survive in American society.[78]

The trans panic defense normalizes lethal rage and violence, turning the focus away from the perpetrator's actions and toward the incongruous gender and sex of the victim.[79] Just like many LC NARs for transgender individuals, the trans panic defense relies heavily on essentialism. As Aimee Wodda and Vanessa R. Panfil clarify, "[t]he victim's 'true'

---

76. Eli Erlick, "Man Who Admitted To Pushing Trans Woman In San Antonio River Will Not Go To Trial For Her Murder," *Into*, 13 March 2018, https://into-more.com/impact/man-who-admitted-to-pushing-trans-woman-in-san-antonio-river-will-not-go-to-trial-for-her-murder/ff8a311ec1d74d89.

77. Tilleman, "(Trans)forming the Provocation Defense," 1670-1.

78. Ibid., 1673 (footnote).

79. Wodda and Panfil, "Trans* panic defense," 936.

sex is what trans* panic is about—the defendants perceive 'real women' to be anatomically female, no matter how they present."[80] No matter where transphobic behaviors manifest on the spectrum of violence between lower-impact harm (e.g., LC NARs for transgender authors) and lethal force (e.g., the murder of twenty-nine transgender women and femmes of color in 2017), the impression given is "…that LGBTQ lives are worth less than other lives, that their victimization will not be taken seriously."[81] When normalized, as they are within the LC NARS, transphobic attitudes may even "…encourage anti-LGBTQ violence by sending these messages, as well as promulgating antigay and anti-trans* sentiments and stereotypes."[82]

Conclusion: Realignment through Reflection

There is no room in libraries for transphobia. And yet, in the LC Name Authority Records, it persists. Catalogers must focus on creating or adapting classification systems into structures that minimize harm to transgender communities.[83] While activist catalogers and library scholars have argued for the removal of gender designations from the NAR environment, gender endures as a way to organize and identify individuals. By continuing to incorporate this information in their cataloging practices, catalogers are revealing their own, and reinforcing society's, implicit transphobic attitudes. These harmful attitudes resonate throughout the catalog, further marginalizing the already violently impacted transgender community. Catalogers, especially those who work for the Library of Congress, are in a unique position to modify how they interact with the harmful classification structures currently in use, creating humane and consensual systems that return agency to marginalized communities.[84]

---

80. Ibid., 937.
81. Wodda and Panfil, "Trans* panic defense," 932, 962.
82. Ibid., 962.
83. Ibid., 969.
84. Thompson, "More Than a Name," 153.

By recognizing the privilege and power they possess, catalogers have the ability to realign themselves with transgender user communities, and in turn reinforce a more just cultural perception of the transgender community.

There are many ways that catalogers can begin the work of realigning themselves to create authority records that minimize harm to the transgender community. Catalogers must first recognize the ways the catalog inherently upholds a "traditional cissexist binary" under which the majority of them possess cisgender privilege, and how it may come through in their cataloging practices.[85] Librarians must avoid objectifying transgender individuals as subjects whose existence must be explained. As human beings, the lived experience of a transgender individual is much more complex than can be captured within a name authority record. Accepting this reality is central to understanding the infinite possibilities of the interaction between gender and sex that occur in an individual's lifetime.[86] Cataloguers must work to center the lived experiences of transgender women and femmes of color in their professional activities. While, ideally, this centering would be a result of leadership from trans women and femmes of color, the overwhelming Whiteness and cisgender-ness of librarianship are obstacles in this regard. Nonetheless, the lived experiences of those most affected by transphobic violence must be the motivating factor for changes in cataloging practice.[87] The experience of being classified is uncomfortable, and often dangerous for many transgender individuals. Many of us have spent years of our lives not fitting in the categories to which we have been assigned. The thought of having another category assigned can bring back, or amplify, those feelings of discomfort and vulnerability. By attempting to better understand the lived experience of transgender individuals, catalogers may begin to embrace the understanding that every identity

85. Thompson, "More Than a Name," 153; Billey & Drabinski, "Cataloging Gender," 26-8.

86. Nagoshi, et al., *Gender and Sexual Identity*, 88.

87. Spade, *Normal Life*, 109.

is intersectional, embodied, and socially embedded; an understanding seminal to the process of building empathy.[88] Empathy is built on self-reflection and an "appreciation of the narratives of lived experiences" of both oneself and those different than oneself (i.e., the typically heteronormative, cisgender cataloger and the non-heteronormative, transgender subject being described).[89] Catalogers must engage in critical, reflective practices that will help them to inspect their own intersecting identities and how those identities position them in the social hierarchies in which they function. Transgender individuals are well practiced at this sort of self-reflexivity. As Susan Stryker challenges, "I call upon you to investigate your nature as I have been compelled to confront mine. I challenge you to risk abjection and flourish as well as have I. Heed my words, and you may well discover the seams and sutures in yourself."[90] We are all human, and the more catalogers can embrace that truth perhaps the less likely they will be to objectify identity groups to which they don't belong.

Catalogers who are willing to confront their own nature possess the potential to reduce the violence experienced by transgender individuals. Catalogers, indeed librarians of all stripes, must realize that cataloging systems, including authority records, are tools of the patriarchy. It is in the interest of the patriarchy to enlist women, femmes, and queer individuals of greater privilege in the work of oppressing those with less privilege. Importantly, just because NARs aren't actively oppressing the average authority record creator doesn't mean that they are not tools of oppression.[91] As Lorde wrote, "To imply…that all women suffer the same oppression simply because we are women, is to lose sight of the many varied tools of patriarchy. It is to ignore how those tools are used by women without awareness against each other."[92] Name authority

---

88. Nagoshi, et al., *Gender and Sexual Identity*, 89.

89. Ibid., 127.

90. Stryker, "My Words to Victor Frankenstein," 240-1.

91. Krell, "Is Transmisogyny Killing Trans Women of Color?," 238.

92. Audre Lorde, "An Open Letter to Mary Daly," *This Bridge Called My Back: Writings*

record creators must transcend this ignorance, becoming fully aware of the position they hold in the fight to transform society and save the lives of transgender women and femmes of color.

Bibliography

Alcoff, Linda Martín. *Visible Identities: Race, Gender, and the Self.* Oxford: Oxford University Press, 2006.

Billey, Amber and Emily Drabinski. "Cataloging Gender & RDA Instruction 9.7." Webinar, ALCTS Exchange, March 15, 2017.

Billey, Amber, Emily Drabinski and K.R. Roberto. "What's Gender Got to Do with It? A Critique of RDA 9.7." *Cataloging and Classification Quarterly* 52, no. 4 (2014): 412-21. doi: 10.1080/01639374.2014.882465.

Bornstein, Kate. *Gender Outlaw: On Men, Women, and the Rest of Us.* New York: Vintage Books, 1994.

Chang, Tiffany K. and Y. Barry Chung, "Transgender Microaggressions: Complexity of the Heterogeneity of Transgender Identities," *Journal of LGBT Issues in Counseling* 9, no. 3 (2015).

Ching, Boby Ho-Hong and Jason Teng Xu. "The Effects of Gender Neuro-essentialism on Transprejudice: An Experimental Study." *Sex Roles* 78 (2018): 228-41.

Diquinzio, Patrice. "Exclusion and Essentialism in Feminist Theory: The Problem of Mothering." *Hypatia* 8, no. 3 (August 1993): 1-20.

Erlick, Eli. "Man Who Admitted To Pushing Trans Woman In San Antonio River Will Not Go To Trial For Her Murder." *Into*, 13 March 2018. https://bit.ly/2xNw4RQ (accessed July 13, 2018).

---

by Radical Women of Color, edited by Cherríe Moraga and Gloria Anzaldúa (Watertown, MA: Persephone Press, Inc., 1981): 95.

Dresden, Hilton. "7 Trans Women of Color Have Been Murdered in 2017." *Out*, March 6, 2017. https://www.out.com/news-opinion/2017/3/06/7-trans-women-color-have-been-murdered-2017 (accessed July 13, 2018).

Haslam, Nick and Sheri R. Levy. "Essentialist Beliefs About Homosexuality: Structure and Implications for Prejudice." *Personality and Social Psychology Bulletin* 32, no. 4 (2006): 471-85.

Heidenreich, Linda. "Learning from the Death of Gwen Araujo: Transphobic Racial Subordination and Queer Latina Survival in the Twenty-First Century." *Chicana/Latina Studies* 6, no. 1 (2006): 50-86.

Human Rights Campaign. "Violence Against the Transgender Community in 2017." Resources. January, 2018. Accessed November 11, 2018. https://www.hrc.org/resources/violence-against-the-transgender-community-in-2017.

Krell, Elías Cosenza. "Is Transmisogyny Killing Trans Women of Color? Black Trans Feminisms and the Exigencies of White Femininity." *TSQ: Transgender Studies Quarterly* 4, no. 2 (2017): 226-42.

"Library Bill of Rights." *American Library Association*, accessed July 13, 2018, http://www.ala.org/advocacy/intfreedom/librarybill.

Library of Congress. "670 – Source Data Found (R)." Accessed July 13, 2018, https://www.loc.gov/marc/authority/ad670.html.

Library of Congress, "FAQ on the 670 (Source Data Found) Field in Name Authority Records (NARs) for NACO." Accessed July 13, 2018, https://www.loc.gov/aba/pcc/naco/670faq.html#3.

Library of Congress, "Module 2.d: MARC21 in NACO RDA Authority Records: Old Fields, New Fields and How We Are Using Them," 10 min., MPEG, available on iTunes, accessed March 1, 2017.

Lorde, Audre. "An Open Letter to Mary Daly." *This Bridge Called My Back: Writings by Radical Women of Color*, Edited by Cherríe Moraga and Gloria Anzaldúa (Watertown, Massachusetts: Persephone Press, Inc., 1981): 94-7.

McKinnon, Rachel. "Stereotype Threat and Attributional Ambiguity for Trans Women." *Hypatia* 29, no. 4 (2014): 857-72.

Nagoshi, Julie L., Craig T. Nagoshi, and Stephan/ie Brzuzy. *Gender and Sexual Identity: Transcending Feminist and Queer Theory*. New York: Springer, 2014.

Olson, Hope. "How We Construct Subjects: A Feminist Analysis." *Library Trends* 56, no. 2 (2007): 509-41.

Ross, Angelica. "Call Me Caitlyn. Sincerely, Miss Ross." *Black Voices* (Blog). *Huffington Post*, September 4, 2015. https://www.huffingtonpost.com/angelica-ross/i-am-not-cait_b_8039492.html.

Spade, Dean. *Normal Life*. New York: South End Press, 2011.

Steinberg, Victoria L. "A Heat of Passion Offense: Emotions and Bias in 'Trans Panic' Mitigation Claims." *Boston College Third World Law Journal* 25, no. 499 (2005): 499-524.

Stryker, Susan. "My Words to Victor Frankenstein Above the Village of Chamounix: Performing Transgender Rage." *GLQ* 1 (1994): 237-54.

Sue, D. W., C. M. Capodilupo, G. C. Torino, J. M. Bucceri, A. M. B. Holder, K. L. Nadal, and M. Esquilin. "Racial Microaggressions in Everyday Life: Implications for Clinical Practice," *American Psychologist* 62, no.4 (2007): 271-86.

Sugano, Eiko, Tooru Nemoto, and Don Operario. "The Impact of Exposure to Transphobia on HIV Risk Behavior in a Sample of Transgendered Women of Color in San Francisco." *AIDS and Behavior* 10, no. 2 (March, 2006): 217-25.

Thompson, Kelly J. "More Than a Name: A Content Analysis of Name Authority Records for Authors Who Self-Identify as Trans." *Library Resources and Technical Services* 60, no. 3 (2016): 140-55. doi: 10.5860/lrts.60n3.

Tilleman, Morgan. "(Trans)forming the Provocation Defense." *The Journal of Criminal Law & Criminology* 100, no. 4 (2010): 1659-88.

Tourjee, Diana. "How Society Let This Happen: The Transgender People Killed in 2016." *Broadly*, November 20, 2016. https://broadly.vice.com/en_us/article/a3wgvz/how-society-let-this-happen-the-transgender-people-killed-in-2016 (accessed July 13, 2018).

Weiss, Jillian Todd. "The Gender Caste System: Identity, Privacy, and Heteronormativity." *Law & Sexuality* 10 (2001): 123-86.

Wodda, Aimee and Vanessa R. Panfil. "'Don't talk to me about deception: the necessary erosion of the trans* panic defense." *Albany Law Review* 78, no. 3 (2014-15): 927-71.

Chapter 10

ACCURACY OF IDENTITY INFORMATION AND NAME AUTHORITY RECORDS

Naomi Shiraishi

Introduction

For those who have used library catalogs, the importance of name authority control is quite obvious. Without name authority control, searching a library catalog would be much more difficult and inefficient; library users would have difficulty finding resources since different works by the same author may be under different forms of the name, and users could easily confuse different authors with the same name. Disambiguating information for the purpose of collocation is one of the primary goals for name authority files. In most cases, authority records are useful for organizing information about authors with multiple names or the same names used by different authors. Pre-RDA name authority records offered enough information for disambiguating names, but RDA name authority records offer significantly richer information that is expected to improve library users' search experience much more. With linked data, information contained in name authority records will be shared beyond the library community.

Diligent catalogers may search as much as they can to collect detailed information about a person. Catalogers place much importance on the accuracy of the records they create. But what exactly is "accurate information" about a person's identity? Is it (a) as close as possible to how society as a whole perceives that person? Or is it (b) as close as possible to the role that person plays in the specific literary or academic community? Or is it (c) as close as possible to how one perceives one-self (or how one requests the society to perceive oneself)? (a) could be further divided as (i) what appears on the person's official records and (ii) how the person is frequently viewed by other individuals. How do catalogers know if there is a discrepancy between their description of a person and that person's self-identification? Significant problems may arise when these different levels of identity are confused.

If name authority files are to be used to organize information for library users, then what they primarily deal with is one's "bibliographic" identity that makes the most sense within the context of the bibliographic community, and is not necessarily how a person self identifies. But, of course, this does not mean that library professionals can invade a person's privacy or misrepresent their view of their identity in order to broaden a library user's search experience. So far it is up to each cataloger to decide how much personal information can be included in name authority records. But it would be nice to have some kind of criteria as to what catalogers should or need not include in authority records. To have such criteria, we need to think about what roles names play in the information world and how much impact that catalogers could make by creating or adding information to name authority records.

Recording more accurate and detailed information about a person means more aspects of that person get revealed. A person as a whole can be sliced up in many different ways by society, culture, and the lin-guistic communities to which that person belongs. Sometimes an aspect that is "accurate" by one definition may not be "true" by another. As a primary example of this, gender information will be discussed later in this chapter.

To understand the problem, this chapter will review related theo-retical literature: philosophy of language that deals with the meaning of names and identity; and feminism and queer theory's views of the fluid nature of gender identity. By doing so, it offers both theoretical and practical aspects of the identity issues name authority records may contain. Catalogers need to understand how complex issues regarding personal names and one's "identity" are and recognize that the ethical responsibilities and the magnitude of influence they have in creating name authority records are greater than ever.

Philosophy of Language Approach to Name Authority Records

To understand what impact name authority records potentially have, it may help to consider what kind of information personal names carry and why organizing names in the bibliographic world is important and at the same time contains sensitive issues.

Disambiguating information regarding names is not as simple as it may seem if personal names are more than mere tags or signs. Some philosophers of language have explored the meaning of names and their views may help us understand what information names carry.

The simplest and most intuitive view of the meaning of personal names is that what personal names mean is the people who are called by those names. In this view, names are mere tags and nothing else. Some philosophers hold this view and argue that names are arbitrarily attached to things and their meanings are what they denote or refer to.[1]

But there are some philosophers who think differently. For example, Gottlob Frege, a logician and philosopher of language (1848-1925) wondered why an identity statement between two names would carry any information.[2] If names are arbitrary tags, then "a = a" and "a = b" should mean the same when "a" and "b" are names of the same thing. But they seem to offer different information. For example, "Clark Kent is Clark Kent" is a mere tautology, but "Clark Kent is Superman" surprises

---

1. John Stuart Mill, *A System of Logic: Ratiocinative and Inductive*, 8th ed. (New York and London: Longmans, 1965); For direct reference theory that drew upon the work of Mill, also see: Hilary Putnam, *Mind, Language and Reality* (New York: Cambridge University Press, 1975) and Saul A. Kripke, *Naming and Necessity* (Cambridge, MA: Harvard University Press, 1980).

2. Gottlob Frege, "On Sense and Meaning," in *Translations from the Philosophical Writings of Gottlob Frege*, ed. Peter Geach and Max Black (Oxford: Blackwell, 1980) 56-78.

Lois Lane because she clearly acquires new information from it. According to Frege, when multiple names denote or refer to the same thing, they share the same meaning (a person, in this case). But they may have different "senses." A sense is a "mode of presentation" of a meaning. It can be interpreted as a piece of information about that person that people grasp and share associated with a particular name used for that person. So according to Frege's view, "Clark Kent" and "Superman" refer to the same person, but have different senses. The sense of "Clark Kent" may be something like "a mild-mannered journalist" and the sense of "Superman" may be "a powerful superhero." Then, the information that the identity statement "Clark Kent is Superman" carries is "a mild-mannered journalist is the same person as a powerful superhero." No wonder the statement surprises Lois.

Now consider organizing the information of the same author under different names. "Lewis Carrol = Charles Lutwidge Dodgson" conveys that a sense associated with the former name refers to the same person as the sense associated with the latter. In the bibliographic world, a sense that is associated with a personal name is mostly the bibliographic history recorded under that name. Therefore, the identity statement shows that an author of enigmatic children's fiction is identified to be the same person who is an author of mathematical books, conveying new information about that author.

In some cases, senses associated with names in name authority records potentially contain more personal information, and revealing identity between names may lead to a greater social impact. Consider an example of names that are associated with different genders. "George Eliot = Mary Anne Evans" carries more information than that the real name of the author of *Middlemarch* is Mary Anne Evans. When different gender information is associated with each name, the identity statement does more than combining two sets of bibliographic records since gender information is loaded with stereotypes. In the case of George Eliot, the author herself revealed her identity. But there are authors who want to keep their gender identity intact. There are female writers who use male pseudonyms to avoid prejudices associated with female authors, or male writers who use female pseudonyms to attract female readers. For them, revealing their real names has a great impact on their career as writers. There is no justifiable reason for catalogers to find out and reveal the "true gender" of those authors by adding their real names to their name authority records.

When it comes to transgender people, what information should be included in their name authority records carries even more serious ethical questions regarding their identity. Name authority records often include authors' other names including their legal and previous names. But including the birth names of transgender authors would contain "outing" information that may harm them and put them in dangerous situations. Such a risk would far outweigh the potential usefulness of that added information.[3]

If Fregean senses of names are re-interpreted as information contained in name authority records, it is easy to see that each name authority record may carry social perceptions associated with any personal information included in the record as well as bibliographic information under the name as an access point. Such information should not be treated lightly.

Gender in Name Authority Records

As the philosophy of language interpretation of name authority information shows, adding personal information to a name authority record could have an impact that is highly controversial. One good example for this is gender. Ever since RDA name authority control has been introduced, many concerns and critiques have been raised

---

3. One thing this chapter does not discuss is a deceased person's identity. Adding a new "sense" to a deceased person's name authority record would not affect their ongoing career or put them in imminent danger. But there is an ethical issue if a cataloger deviates from what a deceased person self-identified with by adding new information to their name authority record which the author could not possibly contest. There also is a separate question of whether or not it is appropriate to categorize a person belonging to a different era according to the current societal practices. This would require a separate discussion.

about the way the gender field (375) is included. This section reviews the criticism of the gender field and the PCC's response to these concerns by examining different definitions of "gender" including who determines one's gender, and the purpose of adding the gender field to name authority records.

"Gender" is one of the attributes of a person in name authority records. Some attributes (such as date of birth) never change, but other attributes (such as affiliation) may change over time. Whether or not the attribute "gender" changes depends on its definition. If, as in the Art and Architecture Thesaurus,[4] "male" and "female" are defined as biological characteristics, then this attribute is not likely to change over time. When RDA authority records were first introduced, LC's recommendation for the 375 field was to enter one of the two controlled terms: males or females, or "not known."[5] It was clearly assumed that "gender" is biological, binary and objective.

Critiques of the 375 field primarily come from the view, as represented by queer theory, that gender is socially constructed and fluid.[6] It is most often assumed that a person who is assigned a female sex at birth will have a female gender and most likely perform "feminine" gender roles that are perceived in society as appropriate for the female gender. But according to social constructionists, gender roles are forms of behavior constructed through social negotiation in relation to specific historical and cultural contexts and not something universal.[7] This view correlates

4. "Art and Architecture Thesaurus." accessed March 3, 2018, http://www.getty.edu/research/tools/vocabularies/aat

5. This is how LC instructed NACO catalogers during the training. See: Amber Billey, Emily Drabinski, and K. R. Roberto, "What's Gender Got to Do with It? A Critique of RDA 9.7," *Cataloging & Classification Quarterly* 52, no. 4 (2014): 412-21, doi: 10.1080/01639374.2014.882465.

6. Ibid.; Kelly J. Thompson, "More Than a Name: A Content Analysis of Name Authority Records for Authors Who Self-Identify as Trans," *Library Resources & Technical Services* 60, no. 3 (2016): 140-156, doi: 10.5860/lrts.60n3.

7. Jeanne Marecek, Mary Crawford, and Danielle Popp, "On the Construction of Gender, Sex, and Sexualities." in *The Psychology of Gender*, ed. Alice H. Eagly, Anne E Beall and Robert J. Sternberg (New York: Guilford Press, 2004), 192–216; Julie L. Nagoshi, Craig T. Nagoshi, Stephen/ie Brzuzy, "Feminist and Queer Theories: The Response to the Social Construction of Gender," in *Gender and Sexual Identity: Transcending Feminist and Queer Theory* (New York: Springer, 2014), 15-29.

with the idea advanced by the feminist philosopher Judith Butler who argues that gender is "performative."[8] From this perspective, when biological sex is considered synonymous with gender, there is a leap of assumption that what is determined based on one's physical appearance will be attached with socially and culturally constructed roles. Further, when gender is understood as socially constructed and separated from what is biological,[9] its binary system is also questioned.

In addition, there were no clear guidelines about how to determine one's gender. Catalogers often make their judgment based on unreliable "evidence" such as names and photos of people. IFLA defines "gender" as "a gender by which the person is identified."[10] This definition is ambiguous in that it is not clear who identifies a person's gender. RDA9.7 defines "gender" as "a gender with which a person identifies," thus indicating that a person self-identifies their gender(s). It is important to make clear how this attribute is defined before determining how it should be entered in a record.

The contrast between biological sex and socially constructed gender is similar to the mutually exclusive views of biological race and socially constructed race. RDA name authority records do not have a specific field for a race/ethnic group, perhaps because it could be highly controversial; although, such information can be added in the 368 field and there have been discussions over how such an option should be implemented.[11] Some critics of 375 fields suggest that RDA remove the gender field altogether just as there is no race/ethnic group field.[12]

8. Judith Butler, *Gender Trouble: Feminism and the Subversion of Identity*.

9. Many who hold gender constructionist views also consider biological sex as socially constructed. Judith Butler, *Undoing Gender* (New York: Routledge, 2004)9-10; Marecek, Crawford, and Popp, "On Construction of Gender, Sex, and Sexualities," 205-207; Ash, "Not Your Mom's Trans101," *Tranarchism* (blog), http://www.tranarchism.com/2010/11/26/not-your-moms-trans-101/index.html.

10. IFLA Working Group on Functional Requirements and Numbering of Authority Records (FRANAR), "Functional Requirements for Authority Data: A Conceptual Model, https://www.ifla.org/files/assets/cataloguing/frad/frad_2013.pdf.

11. For example, it was discussed on PCC listserv: October 11-17, 2017.

12. Billey, Drabinski, and Roberto. "What's Gender Got to Do with It? A Critique of RDA 9.7."

In response to this criticism, the PCC Ad Hoc Task Group on Gender in Name Authority Records was formed and issued their report in October, 2016.[13] The report includes recommendations on new vocabularies and best practices, offers more options of terms, and makes clear that gender information is "what the person self-identifies and explicitly discloses."[14] It also instructs to "[r]ecord dates associated with a particular gender identity in subfield $s and $t only when the person explicitly provides them."[15]

The Task Group's suggestions are a vast improvement from the previous instructions. But they also open doors to complex issues such as understanding the fluid nature of gender identity and what counts as "explicit disclosure" when it comes to dates of gender transition.

In reality, it is rather rare for a transgender person to have a specific date of transition since many of them go through hormone therapies and multiple surgeries over the course of many years. But suppose there could be a specific date that a person publicly reveals. The report repeatedly mentions one's self identification and explicit disclosure as if they were essentially the same factor that determines one's identity. Of course, there is no way for catalogers to learn about what gender (or no gender) with which a person identifies unless it is publicly disclosed by that person. However, there may be discrepancies between what a person self-identifies with and what that person publicly discloses. One may self-identify as male for his entire life and start performing masculine gender roles far before his "public transition," but make his gender affirmation surgery date (assuming he only had one surgery) open to the public. Does "physical change" such as a surgery mark the time for a start of transition? Or does a social or legal recognition of a new gender marker such as what appears in official documents, e.g.,

---

13. Amber Billey, Matthew Haugen, John Hostage, Nancy Sack, Adam L. Schiff, "Report of the PCC Ad Hoc Task Group on Gender in Name Authority Records," last modified October 4, 2016. https://www.loc.gov/aba/pcc/documents/Gender_375% 20field_RecommendationReport.pdf.

14. Ibid., 2.

15. Ibid., 2.

one's passport, driver's license, or birth certificate determine the date of transition if the person explicitly discloses such dates? Just because a person has a surgery or has had their gender marker changed in official documents, that does not mean their identification as a certain gender starts at that point. Gender identity is extremely complex and each person has different levels of recognition as to what gender(s) they identify with. Transgender people's lived experience of their transitions vary, but few express a clear transitional point in terms of their self-perception. Some point out a gradual change of how others view them and the discrepancy between that and the change in how they perceive themselves,[16] and some express different modes of self-perception they go through during their transitional period.[17]

Adding gender information is particularly difficult when it comes to non-binary or genderqueer people. These are the people who do not conform to the idea of two genders. Some of them do not have a gender at all and some of them identify with both genders, and there are yet others who move between two genders back and forth.[18] These people clearly consider gender as a non-fixed characteristic that can change in a fluid manner. If it is publicly stated that a person is non-binary, umbrella terms such as "gender minorities" or "transgender people" can be applied in a name authority record. But it is easily imaginable that in some cases, a non-binary person is recorded as either male or female because the information about the gender(s) with which this person identifies is not included in available sources. Because of this

---

16. Max Wolf Valerio, *The Testosterone Files: My Hormonal and Social Transformation from Female to Male* (Emeryville, CA : Seal Press, 2006).

17. Julia Serano, *Whipping Girl: A Transsexual Woman on Sexism and the Scapegoating of Femininity* (Emeryville, CA : Seal Press, 2007), 217.

18. Christina Richards, Walter Pierre Bouman, Leighton Seal, Meg John Barker, Timo O. Nieder and Guy T'Sjoen, "Non-binary or Genderqueer Genders," *International Review of Psychiatry* 28, no. 1 (2016); Some of them identify with entirely new genders by creating new words that describe their genders. See: "Understanding Gender," *Gender Spectrum*, accessed April 3, 2018. https://www.genderspectrum.org/quick-links/understanding-gender/.

possibility, perhaps it is a good idea to instruct *not* to record one's gender unless it is clearly stated in reliable sources.

It may help to consider the purpose of adding gender information in name authority records. IFLA maps attributes to corresponding user tasks (find, identify, contextualize, justify) and "gender" is mapped to "identify."[19] In other words, gender information is needed to identify a person for the purpose of collocation. If so, in an extreme case, gender information should only be needed in a name authority record when there are two people with exactly the same name, birthday, and any other possible qualifiers and attributes, and gender information is the only thing that could separate them. But it seems that disambiguation of names is no longer the only purpose for adding more attributes. In a linked-data environment, name authority records contain rich biographical information that could be linked to other pieces of information. Adding another attribute such as gender will enable researchers to retrieve a list of works organized by that attribute.[20] In such an environment, it is easy to lose sight of what type of identity information is needed in the bibliographic world.

To understand how gender information may be interpreted differently depending on what type of identity information is desired, let us go back to the different levels of identity information mentioned in the beginning of this chapter: (a) how society as a whole perceives a person; (i) what appears on the person's official records and (ii) how the person is frequently viewed by other individuals, (b) the role a person plays in the specific literary or academic community, (c) how one perceives oneself. If a transgender person explicitly discloses a date when their gender marker is officially changed and that date is recorded as the date of transition regardless of how that person self-identifies (at

---

19. FRANAR, "Functional Requirement for Authority Data: A Conceptual Model," 47.

20. Billey, Drabinski, and Roberto. "What's Gender Got to Do with It? A Critique of RDA 9.7."419-420.

different times), then the record falls under category (a)(i). Such a name authority record, although accurate in this specific category of identity information, could be accused of being disrespectful to a person's self-identity. Gender information from (a) (ii) comes from the way a person is viewed and treated by most people (based on their appearance?) and such information would be both unreliable and hard to evaluate, not to mention it does not correlate with what gender a person self-identifies. If the identity information that name authority records should include is category (b), then in most cases, gender information is not necessary unless it is highly relevant to a person's works. It is extremely difficult to achieve the accuracy of category (c) unless a person clearly and explicitly discloses this information (and not just the dates of public changes) or catalogers directly contact authors about their identities.[21]

What this chapter points out is that identity information in name authority records should not be based on vague definitions and what is assumed to be a common understanding. To organize information, it should be first made clear what type of information is sought after and for what purpose. It is dangerous to start including personal information without first carefully considering and thoroughly discussing these fundamental issues.

In sum, recording highly personal information such as gender is a very difficult undertaking that may require both a great deal of effort and a high degree of sensitivity from catalogers. Technical service professionals need to pay attention to the kinds of critiques referenced here and give these issues the due concern they deserve. The Task Group's contribution to this issue has been of great utility, but to accommodate the problems posed by gender, endless further revisions may be necessary and it is questionable if doing so is worth such time and effort.

---

21. Amelia Bowen Koford, "Engaging an Author in a Critical Reading of Subject Headings," *Journal of Critical Library and Information Studies* 1, no. 1 (2017). DOI: 10.24242/jclis.c1i1.20. In this article, Koford encourages librarians to communicate with authors about their library records.

Conclusion

Name authority records with rich information are helpful both to users who search for specific authors' works and also to catalogers who organize bibliographic information and try to avoid creating duplicate or ambiguous records. The more attributes are added to a record, the fuller and more useful that record becomes. But adding more attributes could create new problems because a name authority record is not just a bundle of descriptions assigned to an access point; it contains personal information some of which is crucial to a person's identity. When gender was introduced as a new attribute of a person, some catalogers felt uncomfortable with the idea while others thought it was just adding another piece of information to records believing that more information would only be beneficial. These different perceptions come from different interpretations of what "gender" is. It should have been discussed and made clear from the beginning how this new attribute is defined and what consequences could follow when used in a certain way. This is not to suggest that the library community should decide on one definition of gender and stick to it no matter what (even if that may potentially harm some people). A record with "accurate" information (in relation to a certain definition of an attribute) about a person is good only if it does not forcibly out or harm the person in the record.

Everyone would agree that ideal library records should be error free and contain accurate information. But accuracy of information may be relative to a type of information required in a specific context. Consideration of different levels of identity information may shed light on how certain information should or should not be included in name authority records. Philosophy of language interpretation of name authority records shows that information attached to a name is correlated with public knowledge and social perception of the person associated to that name and therefore, adding a new piece of information to the record potentially has a great social impact both on that person and society. Catalogers who create and edit name authority records therefore have tremendous responsibilities. This chapter aims to emphasize such potential social impacts name authority records carry and warns that there could always be different views and definitions that are important to the lives of some people and thus it is crucial for library professionals to engage in thorough discussions and reviews before implementing any personal information in name authority records.

Bibliography

Billey, Amber, Emily Drabinski, and K. R. Roberto. "What's Gender Got to Do with It?" *Cataloging & Classification Quarterly* 52, no. 4 (2014): 412–21. doi: 10.1080/01639374.2014.882465.

Billley, Amber, Matthew Haugen, John Hostage, Nancy Sack, and Adam L. Schiff. "Report of the PCC Ad Hoc Task Group on Gender in Name Authority Records." Library of Congress, October 2016. https://www.loc.gov/aba/pcc/documents/Gender_375%20field_RecommendationReport.pdf.

Butler, Judith. *Gender Trouble: Feminism and the Subversion of Identity*. New York and London: Routledge, 1999.

Butler, Judith. *Undoing Gender*. New York: Routledge, 2004.

Eagly, Alice H., Anne E. Beall, and Robert J. Sternberg. *The Psychology of Gender*. 2nd ed. New York: Guilford Press, 2004.

Frege, Gottlob. *Translations from the Philosophical Writings of Gottlob Frege*. Edited by Peter Geach and Max Black. Oxford: Blackwell, 1980.

IFLA Working Group on Functional Requirement and Numbering of Authority Records (FRANAR). "Functional Requirement for Authority Data: A Conceptual Model," July 2013. https://www.ifla.org/files/assets/cataloguing/frad/frad_2013.pdf.

Koford, Amelia Bowen. "Engaging an Author in a Critical Reading of Subject Headings." *Journal of Critical Library and Information Studies* 1, no. 1 (2017). doi:10.24242/jclis.v1i1.20.

Kripke, Saul A. *Naming and Necessity*. Cambridge, MA: Harvard University Press, 1980.

Marecek, Jeanne, Mary Crawford, and Danielle Popp. "On the Construction of Gender, Sex, and Sexualities." In *The Psychology of Gender*, ed. Alice H. Eagly, Anne E Beall, and Robert J. Sternberg, 2nd ed., 192–216. New York: Guilford Press, 2004.

Mill, John Stuart. *A System of Logic: Ratiocinative and Inductive*. 8th ed. New York and London: Longmans, 1965.

Nagoshi, Julie L., Craig T. Nagoshi, and Stephen/ie Brzuzy. *Gender and Sexual Identity: Transcending Feminist and Queer Theory*. New York: Springer, 2014.

Putnam, Hilary. *Mind, Language and Reality*. New York: Cambridge University Press, 1975.

Richards, Christina, Walter Pierre Bouman, Leighton Seal, Meg John Barker, Timo O. Nieder, and Guy T'Sjoen. "Non-Binary or Genderqueer Genders." *International Review of Psychiatry* vol. 28, no. 1 (2016): 95–102.

Serano, Julia. *Whipping Girl: A Transsexual Woman on Sexism and the Scapegoating of Femininity*. Emeryville, CA: Seal Press, 2007.

Thompson, Kelly J. "More Than a Name: A Content Analysis of Name Authority Records for Authors Who Self-Identify as Trans." *Library Resources & Technical Services* 60, no. 3 (July 2016): 140–55. doi: 10.5860/lrts.60n3.

"Understanding Gender," *Gender Spectrum*, accessed April 3, 2018. https://www.genderspectrum.org/quick-links/understanding-gender/.

Valerio, Max Wolf. *The Testosterone Files: My Hormonal and Social Transformation from Female to Male*. Emeryville, CA: Seal Press, 2006.

Chapter 11

FINDING "MISS BETTY" JOE CARSTAIRS: THE ETHICS OF UNPACKING MISNAMING IN CATALOGING AND BIOGRAPHICAL PRACTICES

Travis L. Wagner

Introduction

A camera lingers on a person smoking a cigarette on a cruise ship. They are wearing a beret, a shirt with a clipped tie, and an ankle-long skirt. The person smiles and talks though nothing is heard as the recording is done on filmstrips without sound. A cut brings viewers to the same person walking towards camera. Uneventfully the camera changes to a scene of two men jovially talking on the boat.[1] In only a minute, viewers see silent, moving images of Marion Barbara Carstairs who preferred to go by the name Joe. The film strip, part of a series of outtakes within the Fox Movietone Newsreel Collection, is one of a handful of clips depicting Joe, who was a prolific speedboat racer during much of the 1920s. The description for this particular video is produced by the Moving Image Research Collections at The University of South Carolina, as interpreted by notes provided by camera operator's which give historical context to what is seen. The record currently reads "Joe Carstairs (Miss

---

1. *Arrivals on SS/RMS Berengaria--outtakes. 1929-08-02.* Directed by Mike Prusch (1929; New York, NY: Fox Movietone News), Digital Video.

Betty Carstairs) smoking a cigarette and walking towards camera."[2] The presence of Betty as a name proves baffling as it is not a name ever preferred by the boat racer. Kate Summerscale, however, observes that upon their arrival in America "the press in North America insisted on referring to Joe as 'Betty,' a nickname Joe vehemently despised, but one that nonetheless stuck.[3] The clip described above is one such journalistic encounter and its retention of the name Betty speaks to the reliance on original contextual records to describe the people within historical materials. Imagine a cataloger were to encounter Joe in an archival moment. Without knowledge about who Joe was, the cataloger might seek out such contexts and if the cataloger did not have the resources, time, or foresight to attend to the potentials that Betty Carstairs is not the name of the person, then it is quite feasible that this encounter with Joe would have been irretrievable within search queries in any database holding the item.

Joe Carstairs is a fascinating figure. Kate Summerscale's biography on Joe, titled *The Queen of Whale Cay: The Eccentric Story of "Joe" Carstairs, Fastest Woman on Water*, observes Carstairs had a proclivity for carrying a wooden doll around, lived on an island called Whale Cay which they purchased for $40,000 and on occasion hosted the actress Marlene Dietrich who made passes at Carstairs while staying with them.[4] As Summerscale's biography on Carstairs and many descriptions of the historical figure of Carstairs suggest, they were an 'eccentric' figure. If one uses their imagination and the descriptions of Carstairs thus far, it is easy to know what was meant by the term *eccentric*. Carstairs was likely queer. Thus, the threat of losing their identity to a cross-historical misnaming enacts not a theoretical silencing of queer bodies in an archive, but potentially an actual one. Misnaming Joe's presence within this moment would be to deny voice to Joe. However, expanding on

---

2. *Arrivals on SS/RMS Berengaria--outtakes. 1929-08-02*

3. Kate Summerscale, *The Queen of Whale Cay: The Eccentric Story of "Joe" Carstairs, Fastest Woman on Water* (New York, NY: Bloomsbury, 2012), 84.

4. Summerscale, *The Queen of Whale Cay*, 162.

Joe's identity the naming conventions of Joe's queerness become further
complicated and (un)naming Joe results in confronting the actualities
of enacting queer historiography within and against queer knowledges.
Summerscale codifies Joe, rather justifiably, as "a cross-dressing lesbian."[5]
There was no confusion over Joe's preference for women during their
lifetime and their fondness of Dietrich is one of many historical markers.
Yet, throughout the entirety of Summercale's biography (to include its
most edition from 2012) no mention is made as to how Joe might have
been engaging in more than just cross-dressing. Summerscale, assumes
the choice to be one emergent of "practical reasons," and Carstairs
also had considerable bit of wealth which allowed them the ability to
exist in their gender in a non-normative way. Can there be other ways
of asking about Joe's identity though? What would it mean to say that
Joe was a cross-dressing lesbian, but also possibly trans, or possibly
gender non-conforming?

This chapter aims to explore the implications of naming and unnam-
ing queerness within both cataloging and biographical practices. While it
is difficult, and ethically challenging, to take Joe's life and claim it as one
that is trans or gender non-conforming, a question as to the way they
might have been identified or could still be identified is worth exploring.
Yet both the limitations of cataloging and the biographical record place
rigidity on any of Joe's queer (but more distinctly gendered) potentials.
Moreover, it is not simply a matter of reconstituting one biographical
record or one cataloging line to address Joe's unique case. As noted, Joe
appears at multiple times throughout the Fox Movietone Newsreel Collection, however, each original description titled them as "Miss Betty"
and each cataloging record required a line nuancing that naming. It
proves that such changes have to arise out of a more systemic change,
one that imagines seeing figures for their queer potentialities, even when
the records might block such sites of seeing. The further irony of this
particular iteration of overlooking is that Joe almost remained entirely
overlooked within the collection, despite the Library of Congress having

---

5. Summerscale, *The Queen of Whale Cay*, 2.

an authority record for Joe Carstairs, which is itself redirected from a previous record for Marion Barbara Carstairs. This change shows that renaming can be suggested and even made 'authoritative' but, nonetheless, remains at odds with a larger cultural knowledge of what is correct, or perhaps even possible. Much like this limitation, the chapter analyzes the implications of seeing beyond historical naming and biographical representation when it comes to figures with queer potentiality. Having already noted the disservices done by singularly considering the historical narrative concerning Joe's identity, prominently their rejection of female identifying language, the chapter also asks how Joe's gender might be better understood in an era far less reliant on essentialized male and female binaries. Ultimately, this chapter advocates for not simply reconfiguring naming authorities to avoid issues which might relate to historically emerging trans and gender non-conforming figures, but a complete reframing of how gender is *seen* and *described* within the bibliographic record. The chapter concludes by focusing on other potentially queer figures within the Fox Movietone Collection who do not possess Carstair's celebrity and asks how misnaming or overlooking these figures might run counter to a more queered historiography.

Queering Up the Dust on the Window of Gendered Histories: Re/Recording the Queer Biographical History

The very endeavor to make a past of queerness(es) necessitates a navigation of what it means to make a past queer. In her germinal work *Feeling Backward: Loss and The Politics of Queer History*, Heather Love takes on the embodied traumas of locating queerness throughout history. Love sees the locating of queer figures as allowing "queer readers to see [them]selves as reaching back toward isolated figures in the queer past in order to rescue and save them" and each of these turns have "layered historical and personal contexts."[6] Making queer histories, as

---

6. Heather Love, *Feeling Backward: Loss and the Politics of Queer History* (Cambridge, MA: Harvard University Press, 2007), 8-15.

the subtitle of Love's work reminds readers, is one with personal and political investment. Queer folks look to historical figures to make sense of their contemporary moment often using these figures to make the contemporary landscape seem better. Yet Love's project is not one of simply locating the historical queer figure and bringing them into the present, but, more crucially, noting that not all queer historical figures can be, nor want to be, saved. Love asserts that even as subjects in the past say "don't touch me" there still exists an unfilled desire to do so because their presence in the past serves to verify the queer "existence in the present.[7] Simply, the act of creating queer figures in history (regardless of their actual presence) is one inextricably committed to making queer figures in the present. Seemingly then, the locating of joyful, successful queer figures who emerge within history that lived and thrived would presume to be an act with wholly positive consequences. However, queerness, while a term deployed to cover many people within the LGBTQ+ identity spectrum, is not a term that erases the nuanced identities located within daily lived experiences. Further, it cannot always correctly attend to all the potential for identities in a figure like Joe, especially if their queer historical potential is one worth interrogating.

As Jack Halberstam notes in his exhaustive exploration of butch lesbian identities and FTM trans narratives titled *Female Masculinities*, locating either a historically butch feminity or a distinctly trans male identity is difficult as he notes that "it is true that transgender and transsexual (sic) men have been wrongly folded into lesbian history, it is also true that the distinctions between some transexual identities and some lesbian identities may at times become quite blurry."[8] Much like Halberstam who wrote *Female Masculinity* at a time when he identified as a butch lesbian, bodies can change and can be in the process of becoming. Yet, bodies do not always have the contemporary power to name themselves into history and are thus subject to being claimed or

---

7. Love, *Feeling Backward*, 40.

8. Judith Halberstam, *Female Masculinity* (Durham, NC: Duke University Press, 1998), 150.

'wrongly folded' into a history. Joe may well be a figure wholly of lesbian butch identity, but what might it mean to unfold their identity more to allow it a moment of multiplicity? Yet, even with a firm knowledge of one's identity as transgender, the historical refusal to acknowledge such identities remains. As Margaret Deidre O'Hartigan shows in their brilliant, albeit disconcerting, piece on the historic memory of Dr. Alan Hart, the identity politics of queer figures can result in amplified animosity when the figure moves to prominence. Fixating on the repeated deadnaming and misgendering of the late Hart, O'Hartigan observes that his memory became one so contested and misremembered that it hindered his ability "finally be allowed to rest in peace."[9] Residing within the complexities provided by the aforementioned authors is the challenge of knowing, naming, and getting others to not only change their understandings, but agree that such changes are right or even possible. While a figure like Alan Hart evokes frustration given his clear claims to his male identity, figures like Joe remain categorically amorphous. Joe is decidedly a body in the past, but their presence deeply informs and echoes how queerness is seen in the contemporary.

As Rosemary Henessey asserts: "recent gay visibility [is] aimed at producing new and potentially lucrative markets" of exploitation without the promise of "liberation."[10] In her cautionary approach to the economics of visibility, Henessey asks us to think about who benefits from visibility and how any moment of 'acceptance' might itself be catalyst for further exploitation and violence. Visibility can also prove literally dangerous regarding queer bodies, specifically trans bodies. Dean Spade observes that with the heightened acknowledgement of trans populations and increased visibility comes an exponential growth in "economic marginalization and criminalization" on trans bodies. Yet success is denied them as other members of the queer community (read

---

9. Margaret Deidre O'Hartigan, "Alan Hart," in *The Phallus Palace: Female To Male Transsexuals*, ed. William E. Parker (Los Angeles, CA: Turnaround Publisher Services Ltd., 2002), 164.

10. Rosemary Henessey, *Profit and Pleasure: Sexual Identities in Late Capitalism* (New York: Routledge, 2000), 112.

cisgender gays and lesbians) favor personal (read normative political) gains over the lives of others. Spade asserts not a model of identification, but of "resistance for trans bodies."[11] However, even as caution against the deceptive power of visibility exists, the reality of seeing and embracing trans folks is present and necessary now more than ever. Indeed, contemporary research suggests positive psychological outcomes when trans and gender non-conforming individuals are accepted, approved of, and correctly named within social space.[12] Moreover, the political implications of trans and gender nonconforming persons entering into spaces and making their voices heard and bodies seen has political power, evidenced by the powerful images of trans and gender nonconforming persons and their allies amassing to lay claim to their social presence recently during the international Trans Day of Visibility. In the words of activists, as 2018 witnesses a heightened violence against trans bodies, it is important to be seen "as more than our oppressions."[13] This cross-temporal and cross-spatial notion of visibility matters, because when returning to Joe's presence in archival encounters, naming them and making them more visibly queer can invite generative ways to transcend the oppression-only understanding of queerness as visible.

As already established within the LGBTQ+ community there is a political and theoretical battle that has occurred and continues to occur when defining transness or other forms of queerness within a past historical moment. Yet, the debate is not one concerned with anachronism, but instead a fear of losing a finite amount of visible representations. The problem here, however, is that what lacks is an imagination of infinite possibilities of representation, a way of thinking about potentialities versus limitations. Thinking of queer history building, such work is

11. Dean Spade, *Normal Life: Administrative Violence, Critical Trans Politics, and the Limits of the Law* (Durham, NC: Duke University Press, 2015), 14.

12. Samanta R. Pflum, Rylan J. Testa, Kimberly F. Balsam, Peter B. Goldblum, Bruce Bongar, "Social Support, Trans Community Connectedness, and Mental Health Symptoms Among Transgender and Gender Nonconforming Adults," *Psychology of Sexual Orientation and Gender Diversity* 2, no. 3 (2015): 281.

13. Grace Lisa Scott, "Trans Day of Visibility: Activists Explain What It Means to 'Be Seen' in 2018" *Inverse*, March 28, 2018.

already occurring. Take for example a guest post on the blog *A Gender Variance Who's Who*, wherein Charlotte Goiar advocates for considering Joe as a trans man, going so far as to use masculine pronouns when discussing Joe's life.[14] Similarly, a recent (albeit unsuccessful) crowdsourced fundraiser attempted to make a musical about Joe in which it posits their life as a pioneering trans narrative.[15] Both of these approaches to Joe's identity remain marginalized as they do not replicate the authoritative research of Summerscale's biography and become subject to being questionable in their knowledgeability. Yet by redefining the argument of how authority and knowledge look in a "networked era" as Henry Jenkins, Mizuko Ito, and danah boyd advocate, one can see that both the blog and the use of crowdsourcing as a "way of thinking creatively about possible alternatives."[16] Moreover, these alternatives tend to link up with a young generation's use of technology. This means naming Joe's identities becomes a project invested within use of both older generations logics of naming, as well as potential future logics of naming. The biographical work of Joe's queerness must attend to both histories and this reimagining of how history might look is conceptually fruitful. Perhaps unsurprisingly, this challenge syncs up with the endeavors of cataloging queerness in equally complicated ways to how biography can and cannot name queerness.

Noting the Limits of Cataloging Queerness and Imagining the Possibilities of More Inclusive Record Keeping

As was already acknowledged, Joe Carstairs possesses a subject heading within the Library of Congress, one that tracks their name given at

---

14. Charlotte Goair, "Joe Carstairs (1900 - 1993): Part III: Lord of the Island," *A Gender Variance Who's Who* (blog), August 13, 2015.

15. Phoebe Legere, "SPEED QUEEN," Pink Start (Crowdsourcing project), December 10, 2017.

16. Henry Jenkins, Mizuko Ito, and danah body, *Participatory Culture in a Networked Era: A Conversation on Youth, Learning, Commerce, and Politics* (Cambridge, UK: Polity Press, 2016), 133.

birth as a past iteration in regards to their preferred identity. Again, it is currently impossible to say that Joe represents a trans figure in history, but it might be an accidental attempt to avoid deadnaming Joe which is surprisingly radical for the Library of Congress, an institution not known for its turn towards including marginalized and oppressed populations. Sanford Berman asserts that the information organization system like the Library of Congress "can only "satisfy" parochial, jingoistic, Europeans and North Americans, white-hued, at least nominally Christian (and preferably Protestant) in faith."[17] In Berman's larger treatise he also locates the failures of such standards to represent sexualities and genders, while also noting his own attempts (often unsuccessfully) to advocate for the changing of outdated terminologies. Pulling outward, to the actual incorporation of systems themselves, Hope Olson argues that aforementioned subject headings deploy logics of unspoken privilege that name difference as a means to distinguish it from what has been made to be 'normal' (ie. locating women, but not men or notating persons for being black, but not acknowledging whiteness).[18] Returning to sexualties and trans or gender nonconforming individuals, much like raced bodies, they are marked for their differences. Yet, unlike many of the other identities, their historical location with deviances result in their naming being associated with the paraphilic and the perverse, which as Melissa Adler suggests, "serves to discipline sex and sexualities through the act of naming."[19] This linkage is most realized in many libraries, and specifically within Adler's own library at her home university, with the shelving of books on transgender identity alongside books of pedophilia.

It is easy to disavow the problems of such organization standards by locating them onto traditional methods of cataloging and information organization, or as relative to older ways of thinking about the materiality of information. Yet, as standards evolve so come with them the

---

17. Sanford Berman, *Prejudices and Antipathies: A Tract on the LC Subject Headings Concerning People* (Metuchen, NJ: The Scarecrow Press, 1971), ix.

18. Hope A. Olson, *The Power to Name: Locating the Limits of Subject Representation in Libraries* (Dordrecht, Holland: Springer, 2002), 16.

19. Melissa Adler, *Cruising the Library: Perversities in the Organization of Knowledge* (New York: Fordham University Press, 2017), 30.

biases built into them. Information organization is a technology and technologies come with their own affordances which tend to favor those who created them. The creators build environments and models in ways that reflect their comforts and the unlikelihood of "collision" with "obstacles" to borrow from Gibson's social psychology idea of affordance.[20] Bodies and identities in places of marginalization still face silences and exclusion and more crucially they are aware of the barriers or as Sara Ahmed describes it they exist in a constant state of "disorientation" always being aware of needing to make themselves fit into a space.[21] An unfortunate result of these affordances and privileged orientations is the reality that it remains then the work of folks who are done a disservice by information organization systems to locate and speak up when problems emerge. Take for example the work done by Amber Billey, Emily Drabinski, and K.R. Roberto to push back on implementations of information organization standards like Resource Description & Access (RDA) for their oversimplification and hyper essentialization of gender within cataloging standards as something that only exists as a binary between cisgender male and cisgender female. This logic calls attention to the reality that "binary gender is a central organizing feature of contemporary life" which manifests itself in cataloging practices though the authors note that such logics need not be permanent.[22] The critical work done by Billey, Drabinski, and Roberto resulted in an expansion of RDA's deployment of gender to be based on information provided by the subjects whose gender is in need of description. Alongside this shift was an emphasis that catalogers could transcribe things based on their own perceptions. As I have shown, even with these expansions there still rest presumptions on clarity and

---

20. James J. Gibson. *The Ecological Approach to Visual Perception*, Classic Ed. (New York: Psychology Press, 2014), 31.

21. Sara Ahmed, *Queer Phenomenology: Orientations, Objects, Others* (Durham, NC: Duke University Press, 2006), 157.

22. Amber Billey, Emily Drabinski, and K.R. Roberto, "What's Gender Got to Do With It? A Critique of RDA 9.7," *Cataloging & Classification Quarterly* 52, no. 4 (2014), 420, doi: 10.1080/01639374.2014.882465.

simplicity in how a person identifies with a gender, especially one that is complicated when a person has a historical record that crosses through their own shift in queerness, or when their being (much like Joe) is contested by multiple viewers. I note that in the cases of potentially trans or non-gender-conforming persons within visual materials that a person transitioning "could exist liminally between male or female" and "should not be presumed to be an eventual transition between one or other, indeed, it could be either or both simultaneously."[23] In the above examples cataloging relies on the necessity of limitations and the only way to attend to the complexities of queerness is to afford the potential for malleability. To catalog queer identities with multiplicities of possible identities cannot be a discussion of this *or* that identity. It has to embrace the possibility of this *and* that *but also maybe even* this identity. This ambiguity is necessary and it means looking to cataloging and authority as a far less fixed process.

Cataloging Queer Horizons: Teaching, Knowing, and Seeing Queerness in the Catalog

The late queer theorist Jose Esteban Muñoz wrote about the need to treat queerness as a horizon for which we always long for and look towards, stating that: "queerness is not yet here. Queerness is an ideality. Put another way, we are not yet queer."[24] While an immediate reaction to the declaration of Muñoz might be one of pessimism, he is offering something far more radical, the idea that queerness can always be more. Queerness can grow and expand. Queerness can always be in a state of wanting to be more queer. Joe is a figure who is proving to be an epitome of being more queer. While they are contested as

---

23. Travis L. Wagner, "Transcribe as Seen: Challenging RDA Regarding Gender in Moving Image Materials," in *Organization, Representation, and Description Through the Digital Age: Information in Libraries, Archives, and Museums*, ed. Christine M. Angel and Caroline Fuchs (Berlin, Germany: De Gruyter, 2018), 184.

24. Jose Esteban Muñoz, *Cruising Utopia: The Then and There of Queer Futurity* (New York, NY: New York University Press, 2009), 1.

being either a figure of butch lesbianism or a pioneering trans man, there exists hesitancy that they might well be both and that they could well be more than those two things in the future. Joe's presence in an archive asks catalogers and information professionals to do more with the profession to see how it might be possible to not simply catalog beyond rigid binaries, but even beyond the concrete notions of space and time. One of the obvious answers to how we might talk through Joe's many possible identities resides in the very fact that information organization does little to engage with users and/or patrons and looks only insularly towards what is and needs to be done to be a 'good' cataloger. Emphasizing the importance of dialoguing through both the limitations of cataloging standards and the way they are beholden to power structures larger than libraries themselves, Emily Drabinski advocates for "teaching the radical catalog" wherein reference librarians and even catalogers talk with patrons about how identities might be compromised within a system of power and how acknowledging this while locating hidden materials can be generative.[25] In Drabinski's vision of cataloging and queer potentialities, it is the affective labor of discussion that can give Joe their other identities, she argues that we do not need to name them within the catalog. Indeed, naming has proved to always be an act that is too late and inevitably wrong. Drabinski rightly locates the reference desk as a space to generate new knowledges that can make the library one of intimacies that show physical embodiment to be much more impactful than textual affirmation. Joe can be multiply queer in the moment where a cataloger and a patron share in that potential and perhaps this is enough to make sense. It allows the two discussants and those who join in the conversation to "impress upon a space the objects" of queerness, even if they are not show in a record.[26] For Drabinski the idea of naming new potentials in a space impactfully changes that space. Acknowledging Joe's many queer potentials have

---

25. Emily Drabinski, "Teaching the Radical Catalog," in *Radical Cataloging: Essays at the Front*, ed. K.R. Roberto (Jefferson, NC: McFarland & Company, 2008).

26. Sara Ahmed, *The Cultural Politics of Emotion* (Edinburgh, Scotland: Routledge, 2004), 6.

tangible in-the-moment results here. In a divergent strand of thinking Reed Garber-Pearson looks through the lens of both queer theory and indigenous knowledges to see information organization as a space for "dreaming" new ways of organizing knowledge. How might we label things to speak not for the future, but of a future that is already in the now? Garber-Pearson initiates a potential that we might be able to say things about a catalog record before we know them to be 'certain,' but more radically still we might be able to lay claim to the record's representation even if we do not yet have the words to say exactly what the representation means.[27] For Garber-Pearson, it is not simply that we need to talk through how cataloging is failing to represent Joe's multiple queer potentials, but instead that we might imagine in the moment of cataloging an encounter with Joe that accounts for the ways that they could be queer into futurity. Ideally, attending to queer historiography and its relationship to cataloging would necessitate attending to both these approaches, but practicing this requires examples, even if said examples would be contingent on one's respective time and place.

How Does a Queerly Historiographic Catalog Record Look: A Reluctant Case Study

Joe's story is but one of many moments in but one of many archives. Each story and bodily encounter could be expanded outward to think of queer potentialities. The discussion of yet another moving image, also from the Fox Movietone News Collection at The University of South Carolina's Moving Image Research Collections, is an attempt to attend to these complexities. This thought experiment will serve as a conclusion to this chapter, but it is by no means intended to be the definitive answer to the questions raised here. Alternatively, it only

---

27. Reed Garber-Pearson, "Personal and Institutional Decolonization Practices—Exploring Intersections of Indigenous Knowledge Formations and Queer Epistemologies to Disrupt the Scholarly Canon" at the 2nd Bi-Annual Gender and Sexuality in Information Studies Colloquium, Simon Fraser University, Vancouver, British Columbia, April, 2016.

hopes to invite a new way of thinking about queer visibilities and queer histories in the archive (visual or otherwise). The hope of this chapter is that folks will take to heart the slippages of identity whether they be gendered, sexed, raced, classed or any other informative identity. In these slippages, the hope is to push towards an expansion, as opposed to a reduction as the outcome. No catalog record can ever be perfect, but the hope is that information professionals can begin to think more queerly about things like perfection. What if perfection were a thing always on the horizon, always to be sought but never achieved. Much like Jack Halberstam wants to imagine queer failure as a moment of constant generative possibility, how might a striving for an unrelenting hope for almost perfect be useful?[28] Admitting that this very question is one that closes off the possibility of fixity and an attempt at a 'right' answer will nonetheless be made.

Jazz wedding--outtakes is described within the current catalog record as involving the following even: "Girls of Brenau College hold a jazz wedding to depict the spirit of modern times."[29] What is seen is a group of individuals some femme presenting and others masculine presenting lined up around a stone staircase outside. The group of "girls" as defined by the catalog description are promenading through a walkway with the masculine presenting individuals crossing arms with the feminine presenting individuals. Crucially the masculine presenting folks are wearing tuxedos while the feminine presenting folks are donning bridal garb. The group comes together under the gaze of another 'girl' presenting as a priest of sorts. In silence, viewers watch a recreation of a wedding ceremony. Both the "groomsmen" a term actually placed within quotations in the description and the brides are shown dancing in syncopation as a group. After the dancing the groomsmen and the brides begin to kiss, concluding with one particularly tender kiss between a couple. This kiss is important as it is a kiss that was deployed during the credits for

---

28. Judith Halberstam, *The Queer Art of Failure* (Durham, NC: Duke University Press, 2011), 105.

29. *Jazz wedding--outtakes*. Directed by A. Chereton (1928; Gainesville, GA: Fox Movietone News), Digital Video.

the second season of the show *Transparent*, one that claims emphatically
trans identity as part of its narrative. The clip itself has already been
used as part of a queer imagined historiography. Yet to attend to the
precautions of rigidity within cataloging, alongside the hesitancies of
queer communities to share queer figures between one another might
mean ignoring such historical turns were it not for *Transparent*. Cataloging this moment and giving it a name remains dictated by what can and
cannot be authoritatively said about the figures being viewed. However,
if one were to see the record as serving a myriad of possible queernesses,
then naming conventions would not be the primary concern. Instead,
concern would focus on giving ethical consideration to how it might
be taken up in both legitimized spaces of queer interrogation, as well
as 'non-authoritative' ones. If Joe's moving image materials were to go
beyond the very simple (though almost overlooked) task of not violently
calling them Betty and moving to call them lesbian *and* trans *and* gender
nonconforming *and* the promise of an eventual queer liberation what
might it do for the encounter with a catalog record? Joe would no longer
be an accidentally encountered body in the past, but one who shows that
the brightness of queer visibility in the future is tangible because said
visibility already exists. Were this the case it would then be possible to
say, with cautious optimism, that trans bodies existed in the past, exist
in the present, and must, in turn, exist on into the future. The fact that
Jazz wedding--outtakes already does this through being remediated within
cultural productions cannot be overlooked. If a television show can
offer up queer potentialities for a century old piece of film, is it not
time for us to demand that cataloging do the same?

Bibliography

Ahmed, Sara. *The Cultural Politics of Emotion*. Edinburgh: Routledge, 2004.

Ahmed, Sara. *Queer Phenomenology: Orientations, Objects, Others*. Durham, NC:
    Duke University Press, 2006.

Adler, Melissa. *Cruising the Library: Perversities in the Organization of Knowledge*.
    New York: Fordham University Press, 2017.

Berman, Sanford. *Prejudices and Antipathies: A Tract on the LC Subject Headings Concerning People.* Metuchen, NJ: The Scarecrow Press, 1971.

Billey, Amber, Emily Drabinski, and K.R. Roberto. "What's Gender Got to Do with It? A Critique of RDA 9.7." *Cataloging & Classification Quarterly* 52, no. 4 (2014): 412-21. doi: 10.1080 /01639374.2014.882465.

Chereton, A. dir. *Jazz wedding--outtakes.* 1928; Gainesville, GA: Fox Movietone News. Digital Video.

Drabinski, Emily. "Teaching the Radical Catalog." In *Radical Cataloging: Essays at the Front,* edited by K.R. Roberto, 198-205. Jefferson, NC: McFarland & Company, 2008.

Garber-Pearson, Reed. "Personal and Institutional Decolonization Practices—Exploring Intersections of Indigenous Knowledge Formations and Queer Epistemologies to Disrupt the Scholarly Canon" at the 2nd Bi-Annual Gender and Sexuality in Information Studies Colloquium. Simon Fraser University, Vancouver, British Columbia, April, 2016.

Gibson, James J. *The Ecological Approach to Visual Perception.* Classic Ed. New York: Psychology Press, 2014.

Goair, Charlotte. "Joe Carstairs (1900 - 1993): Part III: Lord of the Island." *A Gender Variance Who's Who* (blog), August 13, 2015. https://zagria.blogspot.com/2015/08/joe-carstairs-1900-1993-part-iii-lord. html#.WtDRcxiZOu4.

Halberstam, Judith. *The Queer Art of Failure.* Durham, NC: Duke University Press, 2011.

Halberstam, Judith. *Female Masculinity.* Durham, NC: Duke University Press, 1998.

Henessey, Rosemary. *Profit and Pleasure: Sexual Identities in Late Capitalism.* New York: Routledge, 2000.

Jenkins, Henry, Ito, Mizuko, and danah boyd. *Participatory Culture in a Networked Era: A Conversation on Youth, Learning, Commerce, and Politics.* Cambridge, UK: Polity Press, 2016.

Legere, Phoebe. "SPEED QUEEN." Pink Start (Crowdsourcing project). December 10, 2017. Accessed April 4, 2018. http://www.pinkstart. me/en/speedqueen.

Love, Heather. *Feeling Backward: Loss and the Politics of Queer History.* Cambridge, MA: Harvard University Press, 2007.

Muñoz, Jose Esteban. *Cruising Utopia: The Then and There of Queer Futurity.* New York: New York University Press, 2009.

O'Hartigan, Margaret Deidre. "Alan Hart." In *The Phallus Palace: Female To Male Transsexuals*, edited by William E. Park, 157-66. Los Angeles: Turnaround Publisher Services Ltd., 2002.

Olson, Hope A. *The Power to Name: Locating the Limits of Subject Representation in Libraries* (Dordrecht, Holland: Springer, 2002).

Pflum, Samantha R., Rylan J. Testa, Kimberly F. Balsam, Peter B. Goldblum, Bruce Bongar. "Social Support, Trans Community Connectedness, and Mental Health Symptoms Among Transgender and Gender Nonconforming Adults," *Psychology of Sexual Orientation and Gender Diversity* 2, no. 3 (2015): 281-6.

Prusch, Mike, dir. *Arrivals on SS/RMS Berengaria--outtakes. 1929-08-02.* 1929; New York, NY: Fox Movietone News. Digital Video.

Scott, Grace Lisa. "Trans Day of Visibility: Activists Explain What It Means to 'Be Seen' in 2018." *Inverse*, March 28, 2018. https://www.inverse. com/article/42541-transgender-day-of-visibility-raquel-willis-activists

Spade, Dean. *Normal Life: Administrative Violence, Critical Trans Politics, and the Limits of the Law.* Durham, NC: Duke University Press, 2015.

Summerscale, Heather. *The Queen of Whale Cay: The Eccentric Story of "Joe" Carstairs, Fastest Woman on Water.* New York: Bloomsbury, 2012.

Wagner, Travis L. "Transcribe as Seen: Challenging RDA Regarding Gender in Moving Image Materials." In *Organization, Representation, and Description Through the Digital Age: Information in Libraries, Archives, and Museums*, edited by Christine M. Angel and Caroline Fuchs, 177-188. Berlin, Germany: De Gruyter, 2018.

PART IV:

CHALLENGES TO THE DIGITAL

SCHOLARLY RECORD

Chapter 12

From Personal to Corporate and from Names to Titles: The Challenges of Iranian Scholars with Scientific Publications

Sholeh Arastoopoor and Fatemeh Ahmadinasab[1]

> When you tell a lie, you steal someone's right to the truth...
> —Khaled Hosseini, *The Kite Runner*

Introduction

Authority control has always been considered as an approach which helps about collocating names, titles, and subjects in information retrieval systems. Choosing one preferred form of recording an attribute of an entity over others develops a family of different forms of the same attribute of that entity which benefit the system through searching any member of the family and finding all others in one session. Any bibliographic record consists of different parts such as access points, bibliographic description and location or the link to the document online.[2] Users find records through them, thus

1.Author affiliations: Sholeh Arastoopoor: PhD. In Library and Information studies / Ferdowsi University of Mashhad, Iran / arastoopoor@ferdowsi.um.ac.ir. Fatemeh Ahmadinasab: PhD. in Linguistics / Shahid Chamran University of Ahvaz, Iran / f.ahmadinasab@scu.ac.ir.

2. Michael Gorman, "Authority Control in the Context of Bibliographic Control in the Electronic Environment," *Cataloging & Classification Quarterly* 38, no. 3-4 (2004): 12.

any access point could or should be subjected to some sort of control;[3] otherwise, the discrepancy of recording these names, titles or subjects pose a major challenge for users in their search of desired documents.[4]

All the information professionals have to make sure that their collection is represented in such a way that users can easily find, identify, select and obtain the required materials. Thus as Bair[5] puts it, information professionals have the absolute power in libraries and information systems, since they control the access point and they have the responsibility of naming them.[6] Their decisions form the information space of a library or information system in the first place, but due to the increased use of web and the number of web-users, they name the entities for the whole world.[7] In other words, the result of authority control in a specific information system or catalog might be used by anybody across the globe; and this puts a great responsibility on information professionals. In order to meet these responsibilities, they have to act ethically and provide the information about the documents with sufficient accuracy. Their job is providing the truth about each information resource and, in this context, truth could be defined as conformity and agreement with facts and reality.[8] Due to this power and responsibility, information professionals must maintain specificity and cultural values based on information access equity and ethical values. Therefore, adhering to a principle or set of principles, called

---

3. Tom Delsey, "Authority Control in an International Context," *Cataloging & Classification Quarterly* 9, no. 3 (1989):15-16.

4. Gorman, "Authority Control in the Context," 12-15; Arlene G. Taylor, *The Organization of Information* (Englewood, CO: Libraries Unlimited, 1999); Barbara B. Tillett, "Authority Control: State of the Art and New Perspectives," *Cataloging & Classification Quarterly* 38, no. 3-4 (2004): 29.

5. Sheila A. Bair, "Toward a Code of Ethics for Cataloging," *Technical Services Quarterly* 23 no. 1 (2005): 15.

6. Hope A. Olson, *The Power to Name: Locating the Limits of Subject Representation in Libraries* (Boston: Kluwer Academic Publishers, 2002), 4.

7. Hope A. Olson, "The Ethics of Naming and the Discourse of Globalization" in *Libraries: Global Reach—Local Touch*, edited by K. McCook, B.J. Ford, and K. Lippincott (Chicago: American Library Association, 1998), 210.

8. Bair, "Toward a Code of Ethics for Cataloging," 17.

professional code of ethics, which represent the noted values is imperative for them.[9] But since authority control itself has different dimensions
such as subject, title or name control, these values also differ in nature.
Thus, it is not surprising that the ethical codes one is required to adhere
to for subject access control would be different from those dealing with
name (personal or corporate) and titles. This necessitates that our codes
of ethics consider such differences and make clear distinction between
authority control and the name control aspects.

Library associations of over sixty countries along with IFLA have
prepared their national professional codes of ethics and most of them
focus on broad principles such as:

1. Access to information
2. Responsibilities toward the users
3. Privacy and transparency
4. Safeguarding the copyright, open access and intellectual property
5. Neutrality, personal integrity and skills
6. Relationships with colleagues or employers

Although they are different in wording or in the number of their
principles, the essence of most of these codes is more or less the same.
Currently, there are sixty-two professional codes of ethics for librarians
available through FAIFE from different countries.[10] A simple content
analysis of these codes reveals that most of them do not mention
any direct relation with name authority control, and only a few such
as codes of Belgium, Portugal, Ukraine, and IFLA have stressed the
importance of accuracy in representing bibliographic information in
general. In contrast, Spanish Federation of Associations of Archivists,
Librarians, Archaeologists, Museologists and Documentalists under its
fourth category named copyright and intellectual property, mandates

---

9. Bair, "Toward a Code of Ethics for Cataloging," 22; Elizabeth A. Buchanan, "An
Overview of Information Ethics Issues in a World-Wide Context," *Ethics and Information Technology* 1, no. 3 (1999): 199; Elizabeth A. Buchanan, "Ethical Considerations for
the Information Professions" in *Readings in Cyberethics*, edited by R.A. Spinello and H.T.
Tavani (Boston: Jones and Bartlett Publishers, 2004).

10. From https://www.ifla.org/faife/professional-codes-of-ethics-for-librarians#na
tionalcodes; the search was conducted on 25-3-2018.

professionals to "identify and clearly indicate the author of the original source of information provided."[11] This means that neither IFLA's nor other national codes of ethics have allocated sufficient articles directly associated with the name authority control aspect, although experts such as Bierbaum,[12] Buchanan,[13] Britz, Olson,[14] and Bair[15] have insisted on the necessity of developing such a code of ethics. One can argue that such a code would at least mention these two articles Bair previously mentioned:[16]

> 4) We are honest and truthful in the representation of resources in regards to its subject area, the identity of those responsible for the intellectual content and its accurate description.
> 5) We keep authority files up-to-date, accurately reflecting the intellectual efforts of authors. We avoid cultural bias and preserve cultural specificity in name headings.

Authority Control and Indexing Databases

Although authority control is a central point of concern in library profession and it has had a rather long tradition, as Gorman[17] puts it, there still remain a large number of libraries that have literally no authority control in cataloging processes. Therefore, it is not surprising to see indexing databases always paying less attention to authority

---

11. Spanish Association for Documentation and Information (SEDIC), SPAIN: CODE OF ETHICS FOR LIBRARIANS AND INFORMATION PROFESSIONALS, L. Spanish Federation of Societies of Archivists, Documentalists and Museology, (Toledo: Spanish Federation of Societies of Archivists, Librarians, Documentalists and Museology, 2013).

12. Esther G. Bierbaum, "Searching for the Human Good," *Technical Services Quarterly* 11, no. 3 (1994): 2-3.

13. Buchanan, "An Overview of Information Ethics Issues," 199.

14. Olson, "The Power to Name," 226.

15. Sheila A. Bair, "Toward a Code of Ethics for Cataloging": 23.

16. Ibid.

17. Jonathan Gorman, "Respect My Authority," in *Cataloging and Indexing: Challenges and Solutions*, edited by J. McIntosh (Oakville, ON: Apple Academic Press, 2011), 292-293.

control than library catalogs. This means that these databases mostly rely on the users' ability to perform a more sophisticated search; and due to the fact that users might not always have enough information regarding different variations of author names or the impact of testing these variations during the search sessions, most of the retrieved results are prone to inaccuracy or incompleteness.[18]

As mentioned above, the authority control is a challenge for information professionals even with long experience of working with authority files. Yet this process is far more challenging to indexing databases.[19] These challenges could be divided into six categories:

1. Documents and Publishers

Indexing databases usually act as an aggregator, and this means that they receive the information which has been previously created by the authors or publishers. Some publishers still require their authors to write their names with initials, whereas others have different instructions regarding recording the names and their affiliations. Thus, indexing databases might not have enough information to gather required data for developing an authority file.

2. Authors

Authors may also record their names in different forms, sometimes due to changes in names, or even change in how they prefer to record it, and sometimes due to the fact that people might inadvertently make typographical errors. This makes the job of authority control more sophisticated or even impossible. The indexing database has to establish

---

18. Shahrbanu Sadeghi Gouraji, Aliakbar Pourahmad, Mohsen Hajizeinolabedini & Soraya Ziaii, "Evaluation of the Effectiveness of Google Scholar in Authors' Information Retrieval," *Journal of Theoretical and Applied Research in Knowledge and Information Science* 5, no.1 (2015): 218.

19. Denise B. Bennett and Priscilla Williams, "Name Authority Challenges for Indexing and Abstracting Databases" in *Cataloging and Indexing: Challenges and Solutions*, edited by J. McIntosh, (Oakville, ON: Apple Academic Press, 2011), 38.

a large authority control unit and allocate reasonable number of experienced information professionals to develop such a file. Needless to say, it is rather hard to accomplish this task automatically since the original data received may not have the required quality.

3. Information about Authors

Authors' affiliations are constantly subject to change as they offer their services to different institutions throughout their academic life. This problem multiplied by the name variations would cause major issues in collocating all works of the same author.

4. Users

Users of indexing databases usually have seen a certain form of the name of an author and they believe that the name of the author of a particular paper is as it has been written on the document itself.[20] It is possible for users to search for a certain name variation of an author and finding other variants might confuse them or even make them assume that the search engine of the database is not functioning well. This issue is so important that in a fairly similar situation RDA 1.7.9, 2.3.1.4 in dealing with typographical mistakes insists on transcribing an element as it appears on the source of information and record the corrected version in another field only if it is necessary.

5. Citing and Being Found

Oftentimes, we as users export citation data or simply copy the metadata provided by the database in order to cite papers. Whenever name variation control is present in a database, it is possible to copy or export the preferred variant of the name, but the name as it appears on the

20. Dorothea Salo, "Name Authority Control in Institutional Repositories," *Cataloging & Classification Quarterly* 47, no. 3-4 (2009): 250.

paper might not conform to it. Then finding the references of this type might be hard for users and it makes the whole process of finding and identifying a lot more confusing.

6. Time and Labor Force

Not only in indexing databases but also in any setting other than library catalogs such as institutional repositories, authority control and name authority control in particular are not completely feasible due to the fact that they are really time and labor consuming.[21] Day by day, a large number of papers are added to different large-scale general data-bases covering different subject areas. It seems no other option except automatic name authority control is the solution. Yet due to the fact that most of the contents of these fields are not provided by professionals,[22] pure automatic procedures do not completely resolve the problem.

Although challenging, some databases have tried to tackle authority control issue either through automated methods (like Scopus) or through maintaining manual/semi manual authority files (like Mathscinet). As for the Mathscinet, the whole process of author identification is carried out in four steps:[23] The first step is extracting bibliographic information from documents and also from their publishers. In the second step, the subject category of the work is identified since most of the mathematicians tend to focus on narrow subject areas. After setting-up the bibliographic information of the paper in the third step, catalogers start the process of author identification through which the authority record for an author is created or updated if necessary. Scopus author identification uses

21. Heather Moulaison Sandy and Felicity Dykas, "High-Quality Metadata and Repository Staffing: Perceptions of United States–Based Open DOAR Participants," *Cataloging & Classification Quarterly* 54, no. 2 (2016): 105.

22. Gorman, "Authority Control in the Context," 16; Carl Lagoze et al., "Meta-data Aggregation and "Automated Digital Libraries": A Retrospective on the NSDL Experience" in *Proceedings of the 6th ACM/IEEE-CS Joint Conference on Digital Libraries.* (Chapel Hill, NC: ACM, 2006), 231.

23. Norman Richert, "Authors in the Mathematical Reviews/MathSciNet Database," *Cataloging & Classification Quarterly* 49, no. 6 (2011): 524-525.

an automated procedure. It assigns any author a unique ID-number and identifies the authors using an algorithm matching author names based on their affiliation address, subject area, source title, dates of publications, citations, and co-authors. In order to further validate this procedure, Scopus provides two other options called "Request to merge authors" and "Request author detail corrections," giving the authors the chance to check and edit their profiles[24] themselves.

The challenges of authority control for indexing databases are not limited to the categories mentioned above. As Buchanan mentions, publishers, vendors, and all the major gatekeepers of scientific literature are dominated by English language materials.[25] Thus, a large number of other scientists for whom English is not the native language and who use languages requiring non-Roman alphabets have to publish their work in English. Such authors therefore not only have to transcribe their names in roman alphabets but they also translate their affiliation into English. Literature has shown that this translation/transcription of names worsens the issue of variant names.

The Challenge of Romanizing Names from an Ethical Perspective

Transcription of personal and corporate names from/to different languages with different cultural backgrounds poses various problems to scholars and scientific community respectively, particularly where source and target orthography is not the same. Yet addressing this issue is not straightforward, nor completely achievable, due to the natural differences among languages, arising from linguistic features. Discrepancies in recording one's name, because of shifting between languages, impose at least three challenges; one for their whole scientific community and the other two for authors. Delsey[26] highlights this problem in

24. Scopus, "What is the Scopus Author Identifier?" 2018, https://service.elsevier. com/app/answers/detail/a_id/11212/supporthub/scopus/

25. Buchanan, "An Overview of Information Ethics Issues," 198.

26. Delsey, "Authority Control," 16.

catalogs and states that at a national level, name authority control is rather straightforward, but the problem arises when foreign names are merged. Nowadays, all the information we produce is somehow accessible on the web; therefore, people from around the world are now considered potential users. The language traditions of the authors along with the dominant users of the system and the potential users searching the web come to a crossroad where delicate decisions must be made and each decision might deprive a group from finding the required information.

This problem is doubled considering the scholarly journals and indexing databases, since most of the renowned databases and international publishers are publishing papers mostly in English languages. For instance, in Scopus or WOS, indexed materials have to have references in Roman script and English language abstracts and titles. This requirement is common among many other indexing databases and this is a major challenge for authors and publishers whose language is not English. Publishers have to develop extra regulations for translating or transcribing their references, author names, affiliations and addresses, etc.

Persian writing system is a consonant heavy inventory of letters with a low presentation of short vowels. The script is cursive, meaning that in a word, some letters are connected together and unlike many writing systems, Persian script direction is right to left. Since it is originated from Arabic, the system also has some letters without any corresponding phonemes in Persian phonology. For example, four letters of "ز", "ظ", "ذ" and "ض", presenting four different phonemes in Arabic, stand just for one single phoneme, /z/ in Persian. These unique features of Persian orthography have brought inconsistency and multiplicity of word spellings both in Persianization and Romanization of proper names.

Skimming the literature published about challenges of Persian language shows that there is a fair amount of published studies stressing the prevalent problem of not having a common framework for transcription into English. Literature has also addressed the reasons for lack of such a framework.[27] For instance, the name "Hawthorn" is likely to be

___

27. Mohamadreza Falahati Qadimi Fumani, "Frequency-Based Analysis: A Method to Rank Persian Equivalents of Non-Iranian Author Names" in *The Second National*

recorded in at least five forms in Persian: "هاتّورن", "هاسورن", "هاتورن,"
"هاوتورن", and "هاوثّورن". Again, some might think that the first and the
last variants are more accurate but actually they are not, since in Persian,
unlike Arabic, "ث" and "س" are identical phonemes.

Another reason for proper name transcription is rooted in linguistic
and cultural background of names, which affects the way a name is written from one language into another. The familiarity of the transcriber
of the name with a specific linguistic and cultural background also
affects the transcription process. For instance, the name "Joseph" is
written exactly the same in German and French but they are pronounced
completely different. The best variation for transcribing "Joseph" from
English to Persian is "جوزف", while in the case of French, the preferred
form is "ژوزف" and if the source language is German "يوزف" is the
correct form. This discrepancy is multiplied when a transcriber decides
to translate "Joseph" in to Persian and record it as "يوسف" pronounced
/Yusef/.

Ethical Issues of Name Variations in Citation Databases

It is estimated that the number of English language journals is
much higher than the journals publishing scholarly materials in other
languages and these journals are usually considered to constitute
the mainstream of the scholarly publications.[28] Salager-Meyer analyzed different reports in this regard, and found the following facts:

* In 2001, the United States of America, the European Union
  (then made up of fifteen members only), and Japan, some of the
  world's wealthiest countries, collectively accounted for 78.3% of
  the world's published scientific research.

Conference on Farsi Language Teaching and Linguistics, 2013: Shiraz: 2.

28. Cenyu Shen, "Open Access Scholarly Journal Publishing in Chinese," Publications 5, no. 4 (2017): 1; Politimi E. Valkimadi et al., "Increasing Dominance of English
in Publications Archived by PubMed," *Scientometrics* 81, no. 1 (2009): 219.

- Thirty-one nations only (out of a total of 191) contribute 98% of the volume of citations to scientific research. Among them US ranked first and the UK came second, but the European Union was overall second. Then followed Germany, Japan, Canada, France and Italy.
- 90% of important scientific research is published in 10% of journals, and while developing countries comprise 80% of the world's population, only 2% of indexed scientific publications come from these parts of the world.
- There is a strong association between scientific research output and national wealth distribution across the world.[29]

Although writing in English might be quite difficult for them,[30] scholars around the world strive to publish their papers in international English journals especially those which are being indexed in citation databases such as WOS or Scopus, since it brings them popularity, prestige, academic royalties and rewards. Consequently, there are more people who are Romanizing their names or the names of those who have been cited in their papers. Furthermore, almost all English journals require the papers to have Romanized references, and since the non-English authors are likely to cite documents in their own language, but they cite Persian documents in their preferred ways; some translate, and some transcribe the reference parts such as titles or source titles and as for transcription of the names, they adhere to no specific standard, which adds to the name discrepancies. The situation is rather problematic since these transcribed names provided in references are delivered not by the name bearers themselves but by those who cite them. This means that other people are deciding how people are represented as an author. This raises serious ethical questions.

29. Francoise Salager-Meyer, "Scientific Publishing in Developing Countries: Challenges for the Future," *Journal of English for Academic Purposes* 7, no. 2 (2008): 122.

30. Irene López-Navarro et al., "Why Do I Publish Research Articles in English Instead of My Own Language? Differences in Spanish Researchers' Motivations across Scientific Domains," *Scientometrics* 103, no. 3 (2015): 220.

As previously mentioned, whenever personal names are recorded in an inconsistent way, scientific community might not be able to track all the achievements of a certain scholar. As for the Iranian scholars whose papers are being published in English-language journals and thus their names are being transcribed, the challenge of not collocating all their scientific products especially in information retrieval systems or citation databases such as WOS or Scopus, sometimes takes the form of a threat to their lifelong academic achievements. The same problem affects the reputation of Iranian scholars' affiliated bodies which has been now considered as a hazard for these institutions since their names are also recorded in different forms. It eventually leads to the diffusion of their scientific products under different names and this means getting lower points in international ranking systems. For instance, thirteen different forms for Ferdowsi University of Mashhad have been detected in a 2006 to 2016 search results from WOS; as for the Scopus this number is reduced to six and all of these six name variants have a different ID-number. Similarly, Goltaji and Alinejad Chemazketi's research showed that some universities even had up to 183 name variants.[31] This has been so important for Iranian universities thus some internal regulations were passed in order to unify the way a university's name is recorded in the published papers. They also devised some penalties for those authors who recorded their affiliation in a way other than the approved one. In Iran, policy makers of the Ministry of Science, Research and Technology (MSRT) have considered WOS as an important index and the papers included in this database get the highest points in evaluating profiles of academicians. Such policies put the pressure on the researchers to do publish their research in journals indexed in WOS or Scopus. Although some sort of automatic name authority control is in place, Clarivate

---

31. Marzieh Goltaji & Fatemeh Alinejad Chemazketi. *A Study of Name Variants of MSRT Universities in Thomson Reuters and Unifying Them* (Shiraz: Takh-e-Jamshid: Islamic World Science Citation Center, 2011).

WOS has no control over the names and since the product captures
names exactly as they appear in the source publication, one should
search for names by using various forms of the name. This means that
researchers could only have rough estimations of one's scientific output
and an institution's impact in general.

Taxonomy of Name Transcription Inconsistencies

As previously mentioned, automated procedures would benefit the
situation in indexing databases, especially citation ones; and to tackle
this problem we must at first examine the reasons behind these discrepancies. Thus, a comprehensive search was conducted for documents
authored by Iranians and indexed in WOS and Scopus during 2006 to
2016 and also for transcribed names from other languages into Persian
based on a search from 2006 to 2016 in National Bibliography of Iran.
To this end, samples of personal/corporate names of 542,265 search
results from WOS and Scopus along with 42,726 search results from
National Bibliography of Iran were selected (1000 names from each
year). After data analysis, taxonomies of the inconsistencies were offered
for Roman and Persian transcription. Using such taxonomy, there would
be a possibility for automatic detection of possible variations of each
name using machine learning in order to develop a new approach for
an automatic authority control.

To attain the goals of present study, and to find the origins and reasons for the diversity of Roman transcription of Persian proper names
and corporate titles, they are analyzed based on the records extracted
from Scopus and WOS. In addition, to inspect Persianization of non-
Persian names, bibliographic records' main entries of the National
Library of the Islamic Republic of Iran were collected. According to
the data, the observed variations are due to a number of linguistic as
well as nonlinguistic reasons which are as follows:

1. Romanization[32]

1-1) Vowels

Persian vowels are categorized in three groups: short /a, e, o/, long /ä, ï, ü/, and a diphthong /ow/. Of course, it should be noted that linguists do not agree on the existence and the number of diphthongs in Persian. Based on the data analysis, Iranian scholars have benefited all possible (sequences of) English letters to represent Persian vowels as: ea, ei, ee, e, y, ie for / ï/; a, aa for /ä/; o, ou, u, oo for /ü/; and e, a, i for /e/. The variations of Yasuj/ Yasouj/ Yasoj/ Yasooj in the affiliated organization of Yasouj University (the form publicized in the university website) are rooted in scholars' partial freedom of selecting every possible sequence of vowels to display a certain vowel.

1-2) Consonants

Five Persian consonants are troublesome in Roman transcription, because they have no equivalents in English. They are /ʒ/, /q/, /x/, /ɣ/, /ʔ/. J and zh are used to represent /ʒ/; qh, q and rarely k for /q/; kh, k and even x for /x/; gh and q for /ɣ/; and finally a, aa, and ' to represent /ʔ/. Sometimes /ʔ/ is not displayed at all. /ʔ/ has a unique situation in Persian phonology. The phonological value of /ʔ/ is disputed by many linguists and its behavior varies depending on its position in the word and the surrounding phonemes. For example, at the beginning of the word it is often hardly audible, but after the short vowels /a/ and /e/ and before /ü/ is stronger. Ahmadinezhad/ Ahmadinejad, A'lami/ Aalami/Alami, University of Ghom/Qom, and Allameh Tabataba'i/ Allameh Tabatabaii University are variations originated from the absence of /ʒ/, /q/ and /ʔ/ in English.

1-3) Consonant clusters

Persian syllable structure is CVCC. It means that a consonant cluster is not acceptable at the beginning of Persian words. Hence Romanization of two Persian surnames "فریدونی" and "فروتن" and the University of

---

32. Here for the ease of discussion, the strict and narrow sense of linguistic definitions and symbols are put aside and we applied broad definitions and symbols.

Isfahan in the form of "fridoni," "frootan," and "University of Sfahan" violate the syllable structure rules of Persian language.

1-4) Words boundary

In Iran, personal names, both given names and surnames can be made of two or more names. For example, from the combination of three popular independent male names "Ali," "Reza," and "Mohammad", four other popular names "Alireza," "Alimohammad," "Mohammadali," and "Mohammadreza" are derived. Except for Alireza, the Roman transcriptions of the other three are long and hence difficult to read. This answers the reason for other variations "Ali Reza," "Ali Mohammad," "Mohammad Ali," and Mohammad Reza." The recent varieties also cause ambiguity. The inspection of the data revealed the cases in which, the second part of the given name was wrongly considered the first part of the surname. For example, "Ali Mohammad Amini" has two possible readings, "Ali Mohammad" as the given name and "Amini" as the surname or "Ali" as the given name and "Mohammad Amini" as the surname.

1-5) Persian honorofics:

In Persian, there are some honorofic terms that convey respect and esteem. They are "seyyed" at the beginning of male names, "seyyedeh" before female names and "sadat" after female names. These terms show that the bearers are descendants of holy prophet of Islam, Mohammad. The honorofics are registered in the birth certificate and are officially considered an integral part of the names. However, many people consider them an optional part of their names and assume they are not required to be written, whether in Persian or Latin transcriptions. This has also led to more variations. This explains the casual absence of "Shahid" (meaning: martyr) in corporate title "Shahid Chamran University of Ahvaz."

1-6) Different possible pronunciations for a single name

A number of Persian names have different pronunciations for historical reasons, the influence of regional accents, as well as the absence of short vowels. The duals of "Mehrad/ Mahrad," "Siavosh/ Siavash", "Mehdi/ Mahdi," and "Ozari/ Ezari" root in this fact.

1-7) Silent h

In Persian orthography, some words and personal names end in h. This final h represents no consonant and is not pronounced. This also gave rise to more variations of names as seen in duals of "Fatemeh/ Fateme," "Alizadeh/ Alizade," because some authors prefer to transcribe based on pronunciation rather than the spelling.

1-8) Surname suffixes

There are some meaningful suffixes in a number of Persian names such as "zadeh," "pour," "nejad," "nasab," "niya." They express a range of meanings such as "descendent of," "son of," "originated from." In some cases, these suffixes were transcribed as independent names and hence created different forms. This fact explains why Lotfi Aliaskerzadeh (the father of fuzzy logic) is known as Zadeh in Western World, because his name was transcribed as "Lotfi Aliasker Zadeh."

1-9) Cross-linguistic effect

Other languages and dialects than Persian are spoken as the first language in different provinces of Iran. A few to mention are Arabic in Khuzestan, Baluchi in Sistan and Baluchestan, Turkish in West and East Azarbijan, Kurdish in Kordestan and Kermanshah. In our data, two personal names of Wahedi and Lowaimi and corporate title of Shahid Chamran University of Ahwaz are clearly transcribed under the effect of Arabic language. Persian speakers transcribe these names as Vahedi, Lovaimi and Ahvaz since /w/ is not a Persian consonant. Surprisingly, some names like Najafi, Jamshidi and Gorji are transcribed Nadjafi, Djamshidi and Gordji under the influence of French.

1-10) Over-heavy-letter names

Cursive nature of Persian orthography and low presentation of short vowels have caused Persian words to have short appearance. When transcribing into Roman, they will turn into very long words like Eshti-aghhosseini (اشتیاق‌حسینی) and Mohammadhosseinzadeh (محمدحسین‌زاده) which are not aesthetically beautiful and disturb eyes. They are also difficult to read. This is why variations Eshtiagh Hosseini for the former and Mohammad Hosseinzadeh and Mohammad Hossein zadeh for the latter exist. However recent variations cause problems in identifying the given name and surname of the author because the first part of both surnames could be mistakenly considered as the second part of the given name.

1-11) Translation of names

In some cases, Persian names are very close in meaning or pronunciation to non-Persian names by accident or since they have risen from the same origin. Some authors have transcribed their names into forms that do not reveal their Iranian origin and Persian pronunciation. The relevant examples are Syrus for Siroos, Daniel for Danyal, Susan for Soosan and Rose for Roz. They can be assumed examples of translation rather than transcription of proper names.

1-12) Transcription to common nouns

Some Persian names are transcribed into forms identical with common nouns in English such as "Salary" for "Salari," "Imam" for "Emam," and "Cobra" for "Kobra." Such transcriptions should be avoided.

1-13) Kasreh ezafeh

Kasreh ezafeh is a grammatical morpheme /e/, added to the first word in a sequence of every two words in Persian NPs. This morpheme is not usually represented in orthography, but sometimes it is displayed in Romanization of corporate titles. It is never displayed in personal names. However, in our data, a rare case of "Shariyare Ahmadi" was found. "Shahriyar" is a Persian male given name and "Ahmadi" a very popular surname. As a routine, it should be transcribed as "Shahriyar Ahmadi." However, Kasreh Ezafeh is preserved in a few corporate titles like "Vali-e-Asr university of Rafsanjan," although "Vali Asr" and "Valiye Asr" are other variations.

1-14) Gemination

Gemination is a phonological term referring to the pronunciation of a consonant for a longer period of time. In Persian it is called Tashdid. Tashdid happens in a number of Persian loanwords from Arabic.

In the transcription of Persian names, Iranian scholars had three different approaches to gemination, displaying the gemination for example by the sequence of "rr" in "Tarbiyat Modarres University," ignoring the gemination in such cases as "Tarbiyat Modares University" and finally wrongly displaying gemination where there is no gemination at all, such as in two given names "Hossein" and "Hassan." These given names are pronounced "Hosein" and "Hasan" by Persian speakers.

1-15) Word order

Analysing the data, it is evident that word order is another source of inconsistency in transcribing and translating of corporate titles. For example, "Arak University" and "University of Arak" are two variants to refer to a single university. "Shahid Chamran University of Ahvaz" and "Ahvaz University of Shahid Chamran" are another example of varieties driven from word order.

Figure 1 depicts the taxonomy of sources of current variations in names including personal names and corporate titles during the Romanization process.

2. Persianization

The afore-mentioned peculiarities of Persian language also have given rise to variations in Persianization of non- Persian names. They are as follows:

2-1) Cursiveness

The cursive nature of Persian gives scholars the opportunity to freely transcribe names into different forms especially in longer names. "زانی" "نی" and "زانینی" for "Zanini" and "سپولودا" and "سپول ودا" for "Sepulveda" are two examples of variations rooted in cursiveness of Persian orthography.

2-2) Consonants

Four consonants of /θ/, /ð/, /ŋ/ and /w/ do not exist in the phonology of Persian. Iranian scholars undisputedly transcribe /ŋ/ and /w/ by two letters of گ and و but they approached /θ/ and /ð/ more flexibly by transcribing /θ/ to ث, س and even ت and /ð/ to ذ, د, ز and س. "Smith" has turned into "اسمیت" and "اسمیث"; "Roth" into "راس" and "راث"; and "Then" (surname) into "ذن" and "دن".

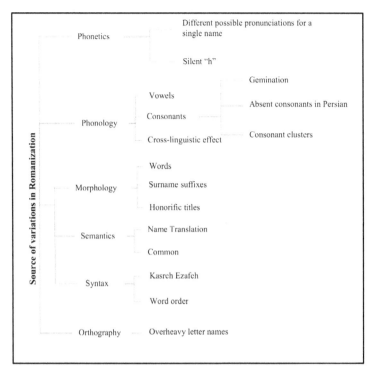

Figure 1. The Taxonomy of Name Romanization
in Scholarly Publications

2-3) Middle initials

In some cultures, there are middle names including maiden and mater-nal surnames. They are usually abbreviated to middle initials. Middle initials have been subjected to four different approaches: transcription of the middle initial into corresponding Persian letter like "م" for "M"; transcription in the way it is pronounced in the alphabet of the source language such as in case of "اِف" for F pronounced /ef/; transcription in the way it is pronounced in the alphabet of target language such as in case of "جیم" for "J" pronounced /jïm/. Finally, the middle name may be completely ignored in the transcription of the name.

2-4) Imposing English phonology over non-English names

The dominant foreign language in Iran is English and Iranian scholars have proved that they sometimes transcribe names under the influence of

English, regardless of the nationality of the bearers. This fact explains the variations of "بئاتریس برگرو" and "بئاتریچه برجه رو" for "Beatrice Bergero." The former transcription was carried out under the influence of English pronunciation and the latter according to the Italian phonology. To stop producing such variations, scholars are recommended to pay attention to the phonological and orthographical rules of the language of name bearers.

2-5) Adherence to the SL pronunciation

It is often a common practice to transcribe proper names with faithfulness to its pronunciation in the source language, and at the same time bringing them closer to the pronunciation in the target language. The variations of "تامس" and "توماس" for "Thomas" and "جکلین" and "ژاکلین" for "Jacqueline" root in this point. The first transcriptions in every case are close to their English pronunciation and the second are closer to their Persianized pronunciation.

2-6) Transcription to common nouns

Transcription of non-Persian names to Persian sometimes leads into forms identical with common nouns in Persian. In the absence of short vowels in Persian orthography, it even results in homography which in turn causes ambiguity in correct pronunciation of the transcribed names. "آستین" for "Austen" (meaning sleeve), "شوم" for "Schuam" (meaning ominus) and "برده" for "Bordet" (meaning taken or slave) are good examples supporting the point.

2-7) Taboo words

The transcription of a very few names leads to the creation of words that are considered taboo, and hence many scholars and translators modify the transcriptions in order to prevent them. "Ngozi," "Cosetti," and "Kiran" are a few examples that (a part of) their transcriptions into Persian are taboo words (vulgar terms for flatus, female and male sex organs).

2-8) Transliteration instead of transcription

Although there were not many such cases in the data, but some names were transliterated rather than transcribed. It means that the scholars had turned the letters into Persian regardless of the fact that they are not pronounced in the source language. An example is "هاگز" pronounced /hagz/ instead of "هیوز" for "Hughs."

2-9) Translation of names

Whatever is mentioned about the translation of Persian names is true about the translation of non-Persian names into Persian. The variant of "اسحاق نیوتن" for "Isaac Newton" is rooted in the translation of the given name into Persian. "اسحاق" is a Persian name originated from Arabic. "ایزاک نیوتن" is the correct Persian transcription of "Isaac Newton."

2-10) In-word boundaries

Number of non-Persian names are composed of two or more meaningful parts. While Persianizing, Iranian scholars may not recognize the boundaries and hence transcribe names to the forms that are wrongly fragmented. The cursive nature of Persian will highlight the problem and gives rise to incorrect pronunciation of the names. As an example, "Bishopsgate" as a surname is transcribed to "بیشاب اسگیت" in Persian. It means that the transcriber fragmented the name into "bishop.sgate" while the correct fragmentation is "bishops.gate" and accordingly "بیشابس گیت" is the acceptable transcription.

Figure 2 depicts the taxonomy of sources of current variations in names during the Persianization process. As we see from this figure, when translating or transcribing personal/corporate names from or into Persian, a lot of inconsistencies lend their origin to syntactic, semantic, phonological, morphological and orthographical differences. In general, analyzing this corpus of personal/corporate names suggests that recorded inconsistencies in names could be categorized into broad areas of syntactic, semantic, phonological, morphological and orthographical; each of which has its own subcategories. These categories form two small taxonomies of name-discrepancy roots both in Persian and Roman transcription of names. The taxonomies still need further tests, but give a clear, organized and scientific view towards the common problems of names shifting between languages.

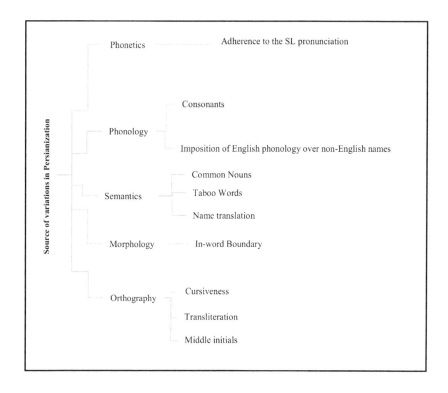

Figure 2. The Taxonomy of Name Persianization
in Scholarly Publications

Concluding Remarks

Smiraglia[33] in his paper regarding two groundbreaking conferences on ethical issues of knowledge organization in 2009 and 2013, conducts a thematical analysis regarding the contents of the presented papers. By skimming the keywords and terms he identified, one can assume that a small number of papers focused directly on the ethical issues regarding name authority control. In this chapter we addressed the problematic nature of the process of Persianizing or Romanizing names with a

33. Richard P. Smiraglia, "Ethics in Knowledge Organization: Two Conferences Point to a New Core in the Domain," *Encontros Bibli: revista eletrônica de biblioteconomia e ciência da informação* 20, no. 1 (2015).

slanted view towards scientific community's problems and the ethical issues which rise due to these discrepancies. The different types of name inconsistencies identified in Romanization section shows how variably these names are being recorded and therefore indexed in citation databases. These names are transcribed not only by the authors themselves but also by those who cite their papers. When a person is being cited, the information helps their affiliated bodies to evaluate their impact for instance through finding their h-index. This means that how getting cited is not completely in the authors' hands.

Affiliating bodies of authors sometimes encourage their academicians to publish their research in international journals with higher impact through offering rewards or royalties. This multiplied by the fact that the number of English language international journals is higher, and in some languages or fields of studies there is no renowned journal, has made authors prefer having international publications. The scientific publishing community in different countries, developed or developing, seems to move toward a monopolism in which authors have to publish their works internationally to preserve their academic carrier on one hand and they have to do it in the way western journals designate in order to get published and in this process the systems fail to control names for the purpose of collocation. These trends gradually speed up the accumulation of variants of the same name in citation databases and without any authority control the following issues rise:

1. Authors' publications scatter under different name variants of the same author.
2. Publications of different authors who might have same name variants might falsely be collocated during information retrieval.
3. Authors citing publications in their national language (except for English) have to transcribe authors' names of these publications during the process of Romanizing references, as it is required by publishers and journals.
4. Affiliations of these authors go under transcription and at the same time translation. The reason lies in this fact that at least

one word of the institutions' titles is a general word like "university," "industry," and "teacher." Maybe the large number of the observed variations can be attributed to the different processes that an author had to take care of during Romanizing their affiliated institutions. The situation was still worsened due to the authors' failure to follow the same rules. For example, there is no logical explanation why "دانشگاه تربیت معلم" is translated into "Teacher Training University," but "دانشگاه تربیت مدرس" is only transcribed into "Tarbiat Modares University," while both have close meaning, the former means "teacher training university" and the latter means "lecturer training university." Fortunately, in recent years, institutions required their affiliated scholars to use a standard surface form in their publications. This form is approved by the authorities and violation will lead to losing credits.

As mentioned before, each of these issues poses serious ethical considerations for the scientific community and most of the responsibility relies on the citation databases. Due to the problems that these databases face in order to perform an authority control effectively, it is advisable to resolve the issue through automatic procedures. Scopus currently does such control, yet there still remain problems with some names previously mentioned in the taxonomy section of this chapter. A global approach such as VIAF could be considered as a solution or a model to localize in citation databases, but currently some countries or regions like Iran for instance, fail to provide data for these projects. This failure is due to the fact that the authority files in these countries are not standard or complete in their own right.[34] Unique identifiers such as researcher ID and ORCID can be used for the purpose of authority control, since they have the same premise but due to the fact that these identifiers are still optional for authors and they provide it upon

---

34. Nosrat RiahiNia & Masoumeh Niknia, "The Obstacles facing Iran's Authority File Being Shared with VIAF," *National Studies on Librarianship and Information Organization* 27 no. 3 (2016): 64-65.

the request of the publisher, they can't be the sole tool for authority control in citation databases.

It seems that with the aid of a dictionary of names and their variations, the authority control would generate more satisfying results. But as mentioned before, developing such file manually would be time consuming and labor-intensive. On the contrary, using an automatically generated dictionary of name variants would reduce the costs of authority control, and to this end studies such as the current one and developing or enriching taxonomies like what have been presented in **Figure 1** and **Figure 2** would be beneficial in this matter.

Bibliography

Bair, Sheila A. "Toward a Code of Ethics for Cataloging." *Technical Services Quarterly* 23, no. 1 (2005): 13-26.

Bennett, Denise B. and Priscilla Williams. "Name Authority Challenges for Indexing and Abstracting Databases." In *Cataloging and Indexing: Challenges and Solutions*, edited by J. McIntosh, 25-47. Oakville, ON: Apple Academic Press, 2011.

Bierbaum, Esther G. "Searching for the Human Good." *Technical Services Quarterly* 11, no. 3 (1994): 1-18.

Buchanan, Elizabeth A. "An Overview of Information Ethics Issues in a World-Wide context." *Ethics and Information Technology* 1, no. 3 (1999): 193-201.

Buchanan, Elizabeth A. "Ethical Considerations for the Information Professions." In *Readings in Cyberethics*, edited by R.A. Spinello and H.T. Tavani, 613-624. Boston: Jones and Bartlett Publishers, 2004.

Delsey, Tom. "Authority Control in an International Context." *Cataloging & Classification Quarterly* 9, no. 3 (1989): 13-28.

Falahati Qadimi Fumani, Mohamadreza. "Frequency-Based Analysis: A Method to Rank Persian Equivalents of Non-Iranian Author Names." In *The Second National Conference on Farsi Language Teaching and Linguistics*. 2013: Shiraz.

Goltaji, Marzieh, and Fatemeh Alinejad Chemazketi. *A Study of Name Variants of MSRT Universities in Thomson Reuters and Unifying Them*. Shiraz: Takh-e-Jamshid: Islamic World Science Citation Center, 2011.

Gorman, Jonathan. "Respect My Authority." In *Cataloging and Indexing: Challenges and Solutions*, edited by J. McIntosh, 277-295. Oakville, ON: Apple Academic Press, 2011.

Gorman, Michael. "Authority Control in the Context of Bibliographic Control in the Electronic Environment." *Cataloging & Classification Quarterly*. 38, no. 3-4 (2004): 11-22.

Lagoze, Carl, et al., "Metadata Aggregation and "Automated Digital Libraries": A Retrospective on the NSDL Experience." In *Proceedings of the 6th ACM/IEEE-CS Joint Conference on Digital Libraries*, 230-9. Chapel Hill, NC: ACM, 2006.

López-Navarro, Irene, et al., "Why Do I Publish Research Articles in English Instead of my Own Language? Differences in Spanish Researchers' Motivations across Scientific Domains." *Scientometrics* 103, no. 3 (2015): 939-76.

Moulaison Sandy, Heather and Felicity Dykas. "High-Quality Metadata and Repository Staffing: Perceptions of United States–Based Open-DOAR Participants." *Cataloging & Classification Quarterly* 54, no. 2 (2016): 101-16.

Olson, Hope A. "The Ethics of Naming and the Discourse of Globalization." In *Libraries: Global Reach—Local Touch*, edited by K. McCook, B.J. Ford, and K. Lippincott, 210-18. Chicago: American Library Association, 1998.

Olson, Hope A. *The Power to Name: Locating the Limits of Subject Representation in Libraries*. Boston: Kluwer Academic Publishers, 2002.

RiahiNia, Nosrat and Masoumeh Niknia. "The Obstacles Facing Iran's Authority File Being Shared with VIAF." *National Studies on Librarianship and Information Organization* 27, no. 3 (2016).

Richert, Norman. "Authors in the Mathematical Reviews/MathSciNet Database." *Cataloging & Classification Quarterly* 49, no. 6 (2011): 521-7.

Sadeghi Gouraji, Shahrbanu; Aliakbar Pourahmad; Mohsen Hajizeinolabedini and Soraya Ziaii. "Evaluation of the Effectiveness of Google Scholar in Authors' Information Retrieval." *Journal of Theoretical and Applied Research in Knowledge and Information Science* 5, no.1 (2015): 205-20.

Salager-Meyer, Francoise. "Scientific Publishing in Developing Countries: Challenges for the Future." *Journal of English for Academic Purposes* 7, no. 2 (2008).

Salo, Dorothea. "Name Authority Control in Institutional Repositories." *Cataloging & Classification Quarterly* 47, no. 3-4 (2009): 249-61.

Scopus. *What is the Scopus Author Identifier?* 2018 Available from: https://service.elsevier.com/app/answers/detail/a_id/11212/supporthub/scopus/

Shen, Cenyu. "Open Access Scholarly Journal Publishing in Chinese." *Publications* 5, no. 4 (2017).

Smiraglia, Richard P. "Ethics in Knowledge Organization: Two Conferences Point to a New Core in the Domain." *Encontros Bibli: revista eletrônica de biblioteconomia e ciência da informação* 20, no. 1 (2015): 1-18.

Spanish Association for Documentation and Information (SEDIC). *SPAIN: CODE OF ETHICS FOR LIBRARIANS AND INFORMATION PROFESSIONALS*, L. Spanish Federation of Societies of Archivists, Documentalists and Museology. Toledo: Spanish Federation of Societies of Archivists, Librarians, Documentalists and Museology, 2013.

Taylor, Arlene G. *The Organization of Information*. Englewood, CO: Libraries Unlimited, 1999.

Tillett, Barbara B. "Authority Control: State of the Art and New Perspectives." *Cataloging & Classification Quarterly* 38, no. 3-4 (2004): 23-41.

Valkimadi, Politimi E. et al., "Increasing Dominance of English in Publications Archived by PubMed." *Scientometrics* 81, no.1 (2009): 219-23.

Chapter 13

BARRIERS TO ETHICAL NAME MODELING IN CURRENT LINKED DATA ENCODING PRACTICES

Ruth Kitchin Tillman

When confronting the nuances—both political and personal—of reforming naming practices in authority work, linked data appears a tantalizing option.[1] By allowing anyone to say anything about any topic,[2] and easily publish it for harvesting and reuse, linked data offers an alternative vision of decentralized authority work, where proposals don't have to make their way through months or years of review or contend with entrenched practice. Indeed, linked data undermines and expands

---

1. For those only minimally familiar with linked data, a suitable definition for understanding this chapter might be: data structured using URIs (Uniform Resource Identifiers). URIs are the links in linked data, often URLs. This data is generally represented in 3-part statements (RDF triples) in which the first part is the Thing being described (as URI), the second part is the properties being applied to it (as URI), and the third part is the value of the property. The third part may or may not be a URI, but should be if it can. These will be represented in the chapter as Turtle (an RDF shorthand, see footnote 4). An example would be:

  `lcnaf:n87816063 madsrdf:occupation lcsh:sh85077231`

Translated: The person represented by the LC Name Authority File "n87816063" had the occupation (as occupation is defined in MADS RDF) of the LC Subject Heading "sh85077231" (Linguists). The information is meant to be gathered and interpreted by machines, then translated for humans or used as a source for searches.

2. Dean Allemang and James Hendler, *Semantic Web for the Working Ontologist* (Waltham, MA: Morgan Kaufmann, 2011), 6.

ideas of authority, as anyone could create records describing individuals and publish them.[3]

Yet adopting names from alternative sources need not require one to break entirely with current practices. Linked data allows for a multiplicity of perspectives. It assumes the inherent incompleteness of any record, that no one can know everything about everything. And no one thing (including a Person[4]), need have only one representative record. Any system which supports linked data must allow for linking—multiple URIs representing multiple aspects of an entity's existence. These might be encoded as a series of parallel statements, assertions that a person was represented by a Library of Congress URI as well as a URI to an independent source. They might rely on inferencing—Library of Congress records include URI assertions tying them to references in VIAF (the OCLC-run Virtual International International Authority File), from which one might traverse a network of relationships to both national authority systems and Wikidata, and from Wikidata perhaps onward to other representations.

With linked data, we could include communities outside of the world of libraries, archives, and museums, incorporating their own self-published self-naming into our systems. And, because of possibilities for modeling, we could even find new ways to express our own records with an extensibility not present in traditional MARC formats. We might

----

3. Working within the constraints of word count limits and from the desire to represent the possibilities in a way which does not require in-depth understandings of linked data, I was unable to address several areas I had initially wished to treat. First, the differences in an authority record and an LC Agent record and how these may complicate and provide additional barriers merits more than the gloss it receives in Barrier 1 later in this chapter, but could be its own chapter. And second, the question of "authority" is dealt with elsewhere in this book, and while technologies may offer possible mechanisms for challenging a controlling hegemony, they are only a tool and should be regarded with appropriate scrutiny.

4. Classes of things are capitalized when expressed as RDF. This chapter retains that practice, when generalizing a class which appears in many ontologies such as "Agent" or "Person." When referring to a class or property within a specific ontology, its most common prefix-representation (such as foaf: or skos: will be used). For more on the function of these prefixes, see https://www.w3.org/TR/turtle/#prefixed-name.

create records to represent names following multiple standards and community practices, and identifying each representation as falling within a particular scheme.

While this chapter proposes to address various barriers which exist to a large scale practice of using linked data to better address ethical questions in name authority work, there is nothing to stop an individual, institution, or cooperative from beginning the work.

Possibilities of Linked Data

Before exploring the barriers that exist within the current environment of linked data implementations for authorities at scale, let us explore in greater depth some of the potential of RDF modeling (see footnote 1) and linked data environments. First, there is the opportunity of encoding[5] with more than just a library context—engaging diverse standards and recommending how the system should act on data encoded. Next, there is the multiplicity of representation, the idea that no one body or even type of body (such as national authorities) could monopolize representation. And finally, there is inferencing, or how one might move between one's own encoding and multiple representations.

---

5. This chapter frequently uses the word "encode." A working definition might be "to represent information in a standardized way so that computers (and other humans familiar with the encoding process) understand clear statements about the information." Information in each line of a MARC record is encoded. Choice of field number, indicators, and subfield communicate information about that information, how it should be understood—which should affect searching and display. While Library of Congress authority record encoding is done entirely as MARC, when working in linked data one must not only make choices comparable to field, subfield, and indicators, but also make choices about the ontology (see following footnote) in which one encodes data. One must consider the community which created and supports it, the kinds of description it does and doesn't support, and more, when choosing an ontology. Fortunately, one is not locked into a single choice when choosing an ontology, as the standards for encoding linked data support the use of multiple ontologies. However, such choices should be made with care.

Encoding with Context

Much as MARC indicators allow an encoder to represent certain characteristics of a field (e.g. encoding a 1 as the first indicator of a 100 field to indicate that the field's layout will follow a Surname format), various ontologies[6] through which data can be expressed as RDF[7] allow one to encode that data with additional, flexible context. Some of this context may be represented through the ontologies that one chooses when encoding the information. Other aspects would be the implementation choices of such ontologies.

For example, if using labels in SKOS and SKOS-XL[8] to express names, one might choose to use hidden labels when a name should not be displayed for some reason but sufficient (and ethical) reasons existed to associate that name with that person in order to get a searcher to materials. One might apply the property skos:inScheme to each instance of a label in order to express that this particular name belongs to a particular standard, that it came from the Library of Congress's names, that it was formulated in accordance with NACO standards, or that it was created according to the practices laid out by another community. Unlike the more general declarations of the 040, 042, and 008/10 MARC fields, such encoding could occur label-by-label or be applied to a set of statements within the record.

The aggregate representations of entities in VIAF combine representations which exist in participating authority bodies, as well as VIAF's own representation of the entity's name and a relationship to Wikidata. Each of these representations remains in its own grouping, as expressed

---

6. A collection of concepts and terms attempting to describe specific aspects of the world. The terms "vocabulary" and "ontology" overlap to some degree in linked data. https://www.w3.org/standards/semanticweb/ontology.

7. Data expressed as RDF is not necessarily linked data, however discussions of RDF encoding in this chapter will assume that linked data is being expressed and not attempt to address the nuances.

8. Alistair Miles and Sean Bechhofer, "SKOS Simple Knowledge Organization System eXtension for Labels (SKOS-XL) Namespace Document - HTML Variant" (2009) https://www.w3.org/TR/skos-reference/skos-xl.html.

by a single external entity, with a skos:inScheme reference pointing to VIAF's own scheme of URIs which represent the partner entities.

The above is just one example of how such context might be encoded and grouped using one of many existing ontologies, although wide adoption of SKOS in authority work makes it an excellent candidate for further exploration.[9] Those encoding authorities might choose to follow diverse standards and practices, indicating that some statements in their name authorities come from one institution and follow its standards while others follow alternative practices. Or, an entity might choose to explicitly name itself and its standards in the publication of data according to one standard. For example, the Library of Congress's linked data service declares that its name authorities are skos:inScheme http://id.loc. gov/authorities/names. Anyone harvesting such records need not rely on deduction about the scheme to which the RDF statements belong.

Choosing to encode with context should make one more mindful in necessarily naming each source and considering its appropriateness for the material. Who do we consider the authorities on how a person should be named? Whom else might we consult? Engaging the context of our choices reminds us that we can engage with those beyond our centralizing organizations. There is benefit and risk in this. As Duarte and Belard-Lewis remind us, the Mashantucket Pequot Thesaurus, an indigenous project to provide a descriptive source is exactly that, a thesaurus for the Mashantucket Pequot. They note the hundreds of other peoples whose knowledge might be similarly represented.[10] To name things, ourselves or the world, is both personal and communal. As we seek out other communities and engage other representations, we must be mindful that we do not simply substitute one perceived authority for another—the Mashantucket Pequot do not speak for the Diné.

---

9. Besides exploring other ontologies for representation, one might choose to express data as N-Quads https://www.w3.org/TR/n-quads/ rather than RDF triples. The fourth part of such statements may represent provenance for the triple or indicate how it should be grouped with like triples.

10. Marisa Elena Duarte and Miranda Belarde-Lewis, "Imagining: Creating Spaces for Indigenous Ontologies," *Cataloging & Classification Quarterly* 53, no. 5-6 (2015): 698, doi: 10.1080/01639374.2015.1018396

Multiplicity of Representation

As touched on above, one of the greatest possibilities for ethical work in name authority which exists within linked data is multiplicity of representation, this engagement with other communities. Anyone can say anything about anything and express it in similar ways for their own use or for distribution. Although being able to create and distribute such statements requires certain levels of technological aptitude, funding, and support, an individual or community which had sufficient resources could choose to publish their own self-naming and description. They choose to address and present a counter-description to some existing authority system, or simply publish it for the sake of creating and sharing such self-description.

Such representations might focus on properties or characteristics which the creator considered fundamental aspects of records intended to represent them (for example, choosing to self-describe using terms established in the Homosaurus[11]). They might publish such description in a counter-narrative to how they or those they represent were described in another authority file. In early 2018, for example, Chaz Bono's sole "field of activity" in the Library of Congress was "Transgenderism."[12] They might publish such a description because no "authority" about them existed (or yet existed).

Sometimes this multiplicity of representation may reflect the work with standardized name forms for local researchers (in systems such as VIVO)[13] or local collections (such as archival collections). Such work may at times seem banal, such as finding the appropriate form of a librarian whose name may be displayed as Tillman, Ruth Kitchin, R.K. Tillman, R. Tillman, and Kitchin Tillman, Ruth by different systems generating citation metadata, but even this work contributes to a representation

---

11. http://homosaurus.org/

12. https://id.loc.gov/authorities/names/n98035961.html

13. A combination of software and ontology intended to create a linked web of scholarship. http://www.vivoweb.org/.

of that person being published in the world. If the statement is being made by an institution, it carries additional weight and care should be given to choices and modeling which best express how that name ought to be formed.

Inferencing

The true power within linked data comes from the ability its creators have to make linking statements about any particular thing and have those statements systematically discovered and processed. This is what makes linked data more than just another method of encoding information. Inferencing, programmatically drawing conclusions from these links, allows one to work with data from more than one set of statement or source. For example, if one could do a cross-web search for all records which could be inferenced as skos:exactMatch (or owl:sameAs, more on this below) for record A, one might discover multiple forms of the name as expressed in record A, perhaps using different ontologies or vocabularies, perhaps created automatically by one system or with great care by an individual doing a study of that individual.

Inferencing strings together records which may not explicitly reference record A but which can be connected through logic. For example, if a record on LC is the skos:exactMatch of a record on VIAF, and that VIAF record uses the same predicate, or property, to link its record to a Wikidata record, and a digital humanist also declares their project has statements about a person who is the skos:exactMatch of the Wikidata person, all of those records and their statements could be collected and treated as a set—filling gaps in information, making different and even contradictory assertions, and representing many views of the same person.[14]

If names or name authority records are encoded with care for their representation and the variety of ethical challenges which arise; if there

---

14. This kind of work is one place where challenges in relating representations of name authorities compared to Agents will be explored in Barrier 1.

are a multiplicity of representations, particularly when major authorities insist on getting it wrong; and if one may inference to bring all these representations together and develop protocols for working with and displaying such data, then there is great promise in what could be done with linked data and name authority work. And yet, nothing yet exists at a scaled or sustainable level which reflects most of these possibilities. The remainder of this chapter identifies and examines some of the current barriers to such work.

And the Barriers

As with the possibilities above, the barriers may be to aspects of linked data in general. However, this section focuses on the impacts of each barrier on the possibilities within linked data to reflect re-envisioned name authorities in new ethical frameworks. It begins with the challenges to encoding, both in lack of shared practices and the systemic ties of large linked data authorities to standards which do not allow for the implementation of such flexibility. It notes some of the risks and challenges of multiplicity in representation. And finally, it gives an overview of the infrastructural challenges, a critical barrier if such work is to succeed.

Barrier 1:
Varieties of Encoding Practice and System Dependencies

Although flexibility of encoding practice within linked data is one of its appealing features, implementing linked data from multiple sources requires an understanding of how encoding practices might compare to each other. Setting up a system which could use this data would require developing an understanding of how a FOAF (Friend of a Friend)[15]

---

15. Dan Brickley and Libby Miller, "FOAF Vocabulary Specification 0.99," (2014). http://xmlns.com/foaf/spec/.

name might differ from a SKOS-XL label might differ from a SKOS label and how the system should interpret each of these.

Another complication arises in interrelating these things. When describing how two things are essentially representations of the same thing, the predicates skos:exactMatch and owl:sameAs operate under different constraints. Should one infer that if A skos:exactMatch B owl:sameAs C, A and C should be considered essentially but not quite the same? Was the choice of ontology an intentional attempt to convey the specific qualities of the properties used, or did the person encoding employ one based on a personal preference? The ways in which similar types of records can interrelate only grows more complex as one branches out into additional ontologies.

With increased complexity, one must also consider the types of Thing being described. If I describe myself on my website as a Real World Object (RWO),[16] using the classs foaf:Agent, and a schema:Person, that record is of a fundamentally different type than a record of my name authority, which is more likely to be a Concept which is *about* a RWO. This difference between record types and what they attempt to represent led to the addition of the subfield 1 to the MARC standard as a place to record URIs for RWOs.[17]

When the two things are not the same, determining how to appropriately use their data in a shared environment becomes difficult. While at some level, it may seem straightforward to simply combine and mix assertions which have something to do with the same thing, there's a difference between saying that a name authority record should be labeled "Bell, Sarah J." and that a person should be. The Metadata Authority Description Schema in RDF 1.0 (MADS/RDF) includes a predicate to tie such records together mads:identifiesRWO. But that predicate as that predicate belongs to a schema developed for library and cultural heritage data work, and one should not expect to encounter it often elsewhere.

---

16. PCC Task Group on URIs in MARC, "MARC PROPOSAL NO. 2017-08" (Washington, DC: Library of Congress, 2017), https://www.loc.gov/marc/mac/2017/2017-08.html

17. Ibid.

Beyond all these ways of expressing data, an additional barrier for encoding may be imposed by the system requirements of that data's management. The Library of Congress's linked data service still publishes name authorities based on MARC records. The work of creating, updating, and maintaining these records is all done as MARC. Therefore, it a concept, idea, or relationship is not something which could be expressed through MARC encoding, it cannot be reflected in the linked data. Name authorities are encoded as SKOS and MADS/RDF, but cannot take full advantage of such properties as skos:hiddenLabel, because the concept of a "hidden label" does not exist in MARC. Although one might analyze and propose minor changes to the MARC standard to support linked data,[18] this is not a viable long-term effort, nor does it have any particular liberatory potential.

Barrier 2: Multiplicities of Representation

Despite the potential it offers for incorporating unheard voices, a multiplicity of representation or viewpoints does not inherently lead to ethical behavior or the prioritization of voices which have been excluded by white supremacist, patriarchal practices. If we wish to use linked data for name authorities as a tool to promote ethics and justice, we cannot expect the technology to be any less vulnerable to exploitation than others.[19] While there may be some protection in the comparatively arcane

---

18. In the process of writing this chapter, the author has engaged in many such thought exercises.

19. For example, white supremacists unhappy that white male actors did not dominate the popular films *Star Wars: The Force Awakens* (2015) and *Black Panther* (2018) mobilized in an attempt to overwhelm rating systems and influence public opinion and ticket sales. Emily Gaudette "'Black Panther' Targeted by Alt-Right Trolls Who also Tried to Tank 'Last Jedi'," *Newsweek* (February 2, 2018). http://www.newsweek.com/black-panther-reviews-fanboys-rotten-tomatoes-boycott-798445 Although such efforts are particularly clear examples of attempts to uphold white supremacy and patriarchy, one cannot discount the effects of data created by those attempting to uphold a status quo and enforce one culture's norms on another, as exemplified in statements on the Program for Cooperative Cataloging Listserv hypothesizing what Mexican cartoonist El Fisgón would call himself if he had been born in the United States with English as his first language https://listserv.loc.gov/cgi-bin/wa?A2=i

nature of library authority work practices, publishing disinformation or harmful statements is nearly as easy to do as linked data as it is as HTML. The idea that anyone can say anything about anything brings with it as much threat as promise. Website owners can and do easily publish statements in schema.org to be harvested by Google.

As one example of the harm which could be done, a person attempting to endanger or attack a transgender person might publish RDF statements asserting that they, with their current name and website, also have the dead name[20] which they shed long before they started publishing. Indeed, such behavior already happens online, in tweets, forum postings, blogs, comments, and elsewhere. Beyond the affront to dignity that is calling a person by a name they to not wish to be called, outing a person as transgender, rather than leaving that decision to the person, inherently endangers them.[21] Choosing to publish such information may cause cascading harm as it is reused and referenced elsewhere.

Librarians doing authority work are not innocent of such choices or behaviors. Thompson provides the compelling example of the treatment of writer Ivan E. Coyote.[22] Coyote changed their name to Ivan E. Coyote before becoming a writer. And yet, academics and catalogers have fixated on uncovering Coyote's "birth name" (Coyote's term). Thompson includes an excerpt from a 2012 newspaper piece in which Coyote describes feeling "frustrated[, ...] violated, and worried" after a

nd1709&L=PCCLIST&P=R24497. This, too, affects existing data and influences perception.

20. Amanda Armstrong, "Certificates of Live Birth and Dead Names: On the Subject of Recent Anti-Trans Legislation," *South Atlantic Quarterly* 116 no. 3 (2017): 623-625.

21. Per the report *Lesbian, Gay, Bisexual, Transgender, Queer, and HIV-Affected Hate Violence in 2016*, "Transgender and gender non-conforming survivors [of hate violence] were 2.8 times more likely to experience violence via the internet or by phone than cisgender survivors." It should be noted that this number is in relation to cisgender survivors who already experience gender, orientation, and HIV-status hate violence, not cisgender people as a group. National Coalition of Anti-Violence Programs (NCAVP), *Lesbian, Gay, Bisexual, Transgender, Queer, and HIV-Affected Hate Violence in 2016* (New York: NY, Emily Waters, 2016): 32

22. Kelly J. Thompson, "More Than a Name: A Content Analysis of Name Authority Records for Authors Who Self-Identify as Trans" *Library Resources & Technical Services* 60 no. 3 (2016): 141-142, doi: 10.5860/lrts.60n3.140.

college professor assigned students to find that name. The piece's subtitle contains their request; "Call us what we wish to be called."

Despite its irrelevance to their published work, to their everyday life (as they outline in the piece), and their stated wishes, Ivan E. Coyote's established name authority displays that birth name in a parenthetical. It is not even buried in the record, but is in the MARC 100 and skos:prefLabel of the MARC and RDF authorities respectively. With no other Ivan E. Coyotes in the Library of Congress catalog, let alone any who share the same birth year, Thompson points out the lack of necessity to add this "fuller form" for purposes of disambiguation. The justifications for this choice recorded in 670s all appear to be that Canada's Cataloging-in-Publication (not the author) used the name on the title page verso of a 2001 book (with no context of how it was obtained or how the writer responded) and that a blurb about Coyote from a festival which mentions it. Does a public discussion of one's complex name give catalogers license to ignore expressed wishes and display it in every catalog record of one's work forever?

When bringing in any data from external sources, we must be aware of its potential for harm as well as for fuller representation. Should we break through the barriers described below, we must engage all naming work with care. We should also be mindful that everything published as linked data could be harvested and used, whether by those who will examine and question it or by those putting faith in automated systems and the strength of its perceived authority, and exercise care in its creation and publication. If we wish to represent our own data as something worth sharing, we must do better.[23]

---

23. Coyote's authority record includes justifications in references to places this fuller form was found, but does not inquire whether its addition was necessary, wise, or ethical. Names and their use are complex. With such a strong published statement on record, one cannot presume that in airing the name in a particular context Coyote intended to rescind their position on being referred to by that name in the way something like a published retraction might indicate.

Barrier 3: Infrastructure, Scale, and Searching the Open Web

Even if one were to resolve the two previous barriers, there still remains the lack of reliable, systemic support for linked data. SPARQL, a language for querying RDF, runs notoriously slowly on single datasets, let alone when attempting cross-server inferencing. And those managing the servers may actively discourage such uses. As Christina Harlow pointed out in her 2017 Code4Lib keynote, the Library of Congress's Linked Open Data service hub requests that users make "no more than 1 HTTP request per 3 seconds." As she assesses, "this doesn't support production work…"[24] Moreover, while one may batch download data from this and other sites to support faster querying, this does not live out the vision of the semantic web. Rather than engage with an ever-growing web, we recreate an approximation on our own servers, if we are well-financed enough to have our own servers, and explore or query in the data equivalent of a backyard or community pool, not an ocean.

OCLC's VIAF offers one example of what combining varieties of linked data might look like by harvesting and combining subsets of linked data (or data translated to linked data) about the names. At the time of writing, these subsets only include SKOS preferred and alternate (not hidden) labels, as represented by the source and linking back to the source. But rather than host the entire contents of each contributing authority source as linked data, along with their own statements as they attempt to cluster records for the same entity, and make these open to queries as a kind of public sandbox, or community pool, the hosts at VIAF first perform the matching work and present it as a kind of unified whole, open to APIs calls, but not to SPARQL queries.

These methods, described above, also rely on knowledge of where one's data sites exist and following or discovering new links out from these known entities. If, for example, one follows a Library of Congress

---

24. Christina Harlow, "Resistance is Fertile," (keynote, Code4Lib, Los Angeles, CA, March 9, 2017).

record's relationship to the VIAF record over to the Wikidata representation, one may discover a new site linked to *by* Wikidata. But one does not discover the reverse use case--a new community project or community's webpage linking back to that Wikidata representation (or even back to that Library of Congress record). Although the two are linked, there is no mechanism for crawling, identifying, and acting on that link in a fashion one might aspire to on the semantic web. We end up relying, therefore, on aggregators such as VIAF or Wikidata to publish these relationships, which only occurs when their source carries sufficient respectability and has the resources and people to do this work.

The hope that we might use linked data's inferencing potential to query for alternative sites of naming and at least evaluate them for use within our own systems dashes itself on questions of scale, of sustainability and maintenance (whether of something as large as a Library of Congress endpoint or as small as a professor's project which evaporates with her netspace account when she moves on), and of discovery. Some of these could be resolved with sufficient care and resources, but only once those funding the work decide to support it at such scale. If such support were granted, whose data and voices would then be heard?

Conscientious Encoding, Sustainable Commitments

So what, then, to say to you—the person who has read other chapters in these books and identified linked data encoding as one possible way to address the various ways in which humans choose to name themselves and wish to be represented by others? Should these barriers discourage you from such a course of action? Perhaps. This conclusion, rather than offering a concrete solution, instead offers recommendations drawn from the possibilities and barriers you encounter when you undertake any such work with appropriate care and realistic expectations.

In doing such encoding work you should use relatively mainstream ontologies where possible and document your choices, to assist others in using this data in their own systems. Did you choose a particular predicate to encode a relationship because of its definition? Was your choice based on attempting to use as few ontologies as possible? Did you choose skos:exactMatch because the Library of Congress and French SUDOC both use it? Did you prefer owl:sameAs because you plan to relate it to DBpedia and wish to parallel how DBpedia links to other entities? Did you choose to use as much schema.org in order to make your data appealing to search engines? Identify and contextualize each of these choices, along with the ethical challenge you attempted to solve. For example, if you chose to prioritize the chosen names of women religious, while maintaining their former names as hiddenLabel for entity resolution purposes, explain your choice to those who might use your service for their own work. They may have a similar desire to display the woman's religious name but work with data sources which use either.

In considering your own work as a source now providing linked data, focus on how you will address ethical questions in your name work and what you will describe and also consider your engagements with external work. Which thesauri will you use? Who creates them and for what purpose? What inferred statements might be made? If you interrelate your record with other representations of the same person, do you believe you are still responsibly responding to ethical concerns which may have driven the record's creation in creating that association? Consider what you plan to do with it and why that relationship should or shouldn't exist. Are you the person to make that decision?

And finally, how can you commit to the sustainable publication and sharing of this data (as appropriate, again within the realm of ethical work)? The library world and web at large are filled with prototypes or abandoned projects, from journals to digital humanities to ontologies. A 2013 study by researchers at Harvard Law found that 50% of the URLs within Supreme Court Opinions either do not resolve or do not resolve to materials cited in that opinion.[25] If your resources might allow you to support SPARQL querying temporarily, but you do not anticipate that

---

25. Jonathan L. Zittrain, Kendra Albert, and Lawrence Lessig, "Perma: Scoping and Addressing the Problem of Link and Reference Rot in Legal Citations," *Harvard Public Law Working Paper No. 13-42* (2013): 172, 176. Available at SSRN: http://dx.doi.org/10.2139/ssrn.2329161

your own means, funding, and community group or affiliated institution will support this in the long term, scale your work to something you can support in the longer term. Again, document what you can and cannot make available, whether and how any updates would be handled, and whether you plan to store the information in additional locations, such as GitHub or a data repository.

The current linked data ecosystem around name authorities does not provide a robust support for those approaching it with goals of either making or finding and using their own alternatives. Yet ontologies used by more than one community and which can be published as more than local XML provide some appeal for those doing work which they intend to share. While maintaining awareness of the barriers which exist does not alleviate their presence, it may result in a sustainable project which respects the community whose needs it is intended to address and serves those in whose systems it can be used.

Acknowledgements

The author wishes to acknowledge the comments and support provided by Allana Mayer and Katy Rawdon. Without them, this chapter would not have been completed.

Bibliography

Allemang, Dean, and James Hendler. *Semantic Web for the Working Ontologist*. Waltham, MA: Morgan Kaufmann, 2011.

Armstrong, Amanda. "Certificates of Live Birth and Dead Names: On the Subject of Recent Anti-Trans Legislation." *South Atlantic Quarterly* 116, no. 3 (2017).

Brickley, Dan and Libby Miller. "FOAF Vocabulary Specification 0.99." 2014. http://xmlns.com/foaf/spec/.

Duarte, Marisa Elena and Miranda Belarde-Lewis. "Imagining: Creating Spaces for Indigenous Ontologies." *Cataloging & Classification Quarterly* 53, no. 5-6 (2015): 677-702. doi: 10.1080/01639374 .2015.1018396

Gaudette, Emily. "'Black Panther' Targeted by Alt-Right Trolls Who also Tried to Tank 'Last Jedi'." *Newsweek* (February 2, 2018). http:// www.newsweek.com/black-panther-reviews-fanboys-rotten-toma-toes-boycott-798445.

Harlow, Christina. "Resistance is Fertile." Code4Lib 2017. Keynote, Los Angeles, CA. March 9, 2017.

Miles, Alistair and Sean Bechhofer, "SKOS Simple Knowledge Organization System eXtension for Labels (SKOS-XL) Namespace Document - HTML Variant." 2009. https://www.w3.org/TR/skos-reference/ skos-xl.html.

National Coalition of Anti-Violence Programs (NCAVP). *Lesbian, Gay, Bisexual, Transgender, Queer, and HIV-Affected Hate Violence in 2016.* New York, NY: Emily Waters, 2016.

Program for Cooperative Cataloging Listserv, September 2017. https://list-serv.loc.gov/cgi-bin/wa?A2=ind1709&L=PCCLIST&P=R24497

PCC Task Group on URIs in MARC. "MARC PROPOSAL NO. 2017-08." Washington, DC: Library of Congress., 2017. https://www.loc. gov/marc/mac/2017/2017-08.html

Thompson, Kelly J. "More Than a Name: A Content Analysis of Name Au-thority Records for Authors Who Self-Identify as Trans." *Library Resources & Technical Services* 60, no. 3 (2016): 140-155. doi: 10.5860/ lrts.60n3.140.

Zittrain, Jonathan L., Kendra Albert, and Lawrence Lessig. "Perma: Scoping and Addressing the Problem of Link and Reference Rot in Legal Citations." *Harvard Public Law Working Paper. No. 13-42* (2013). doi: 10.2139/ssrn.2329161,

Chapter 14

THE TALE OF THREE SERVICE TYPES FOR RESEARCHER IDENTIFIERS AND THE ETHICAL IMPLICATION ON ACCESS TO INFORMATION AND REPRESENTATION OF AUTHORS

Anchalee Panigabutra-Roberts

Abstract

As the American Library Association's *Code of Professional Ethics for Librarians* emphasizes equitable access to information, the author analyzes the ethical implication of access to information and representation of researchers in three types of services in researcher identifier systems; self-registered service, for-profit professional service and non-profit professional service. In her analysis, the author draws upon her pilot study of the faculty at American University in Cairo in 2015, inspired by OCLC's research on researcher identifiers, with the addition of other popular researcher identifier systems. She further discusses the advantages and disadvantages of these services from the perspectives of open access and linked open data and how researchers are represented in these systems. Based on their popular and common usage among researchers and library professionals, the following systems are selected for the analysis; ORCID, ResearchGate and Google Scholar for the self-registered services; SCOPUS and ResearcherID for the for-profit professional services; and Library of Congress Linked Data Service, Virtual International Authority File (VIAF) and International Standard

Name Identifier (ISNI) for the non-profit professional services. The author concludes with the positive developments from the Library of Congress's Program for Cooperative Cataloging and a proposed solution to create the information flow to provide better access in bibliographic records for authors of book chapters and/or authors of papers in conference proceedings.

Authority Control and Identity Management: The Context

While the concept of researcher profiles on the web is a recent phenomenon, the concept of name authority in the library computer system dates back to the MARC Authority format created by the Library of Congress in 1970s.[1] And it is tied to the cataloging principles for uniform headings and disambiguation of authors' names addressed in the Paris Principles (guideline number 8 for single personal author) in 1961.[2] Cataloging codes, such as the Paris Principles, tie authors to their publications as the guiding principle to organize and provide the access to the library collection via the card catalog. Over time, this principle continues to provide the core of system design for the organization and access of library physical, electronic and digital collections. Thus, the concept of name authority control and disambiguation is still relevant in a shifting context as challenged by the growing numbers of researcher identifier systems.[3]

---

1. Library of Congress. Network Development and MARC Standards Office, *Understanding MARC Authority Records* (Washington, D.C.: Network Development and MARC Standards Office, Library of Congress, 2004), part II, http://www.loc.gov/marc/uma/pt1-7.html#pt2.

2. International Conference on Cataloguing Principles, *Statement of Principles: Adopted by the International Conference on Cataloguing Principles, Paris, October 1961* ([London]: [International Federation of Library Associations], 1961), guideline no. 8. Single Personal Author, https://www.ifla.org/files/assets/cataloguing/IMEICC/IMEICC1/statement_principles_paris_1961.pdf.

3. Karen Smith-Yoshimura et al., *Registering Researchers in Authority Files* (Dublin, Ohio: OCLC Research, 2014), https://www.oclc.org/content/dam/research/publications/library/2014/oclcresearch-registering-researchers-2014-a4.pdf; Clara Y. Tran and Jennifer A. Lyon, "Faculty Use of Author Identifiers and Researcher Networking Tools," *College & Research Libraries* 78, no. 2 (2017): 171-182; Carol Tenopir et al., "No Scholar

Per the Library of Congress (LC) Authorities website, the function of authority records is integral to library cataloging systems.[4] According to LC:

> An authority record is a tool used by librarians to establish forms of names (for persons, places, meetings, and organizations), titles, subjects, and genres and forms used on bibliographic records. Authority records enable librarians to provide uniform access to materials in library catalogs and to provide clear identification of authors and subject headings. … Authority records also provide cross references to lead users to the headings used in the catalog.[5]

Members from institutions participating in the Library of Congress's Program for Cooperative Cataloging's (LC PCC) Name Authority Cooperative (NACO) Program contribute authority records for personal, corporate, and jurisdictional names, uniform titles, and series to the LC/NACO Authority File.[6] Authority records made it possible for the design of online public catalogs to redirect library users from the variant names to the authorized names to discover all of an author's works in the catalog. While modern-day library search engines may or may not use this reference feature from the authority records, the uniform authors' names still function as the gathering point for an author/creator's unique name and the gathering tool for all of one's works.

Is an Island: The Impact of Sharing in the Work Life of Scholars," *Learned Publishing* 30, no. 1 (2017): 5–17 ; Library of Congress. Program for Cooperative Cataloging (PCC). Task Group on Identity Management, *Charge for PCC Task Group on Identity Management in NACO* (Washington, D.C.: LC, 2016), https://www.loc.gov/aba/pcc/documents/Identity-management-NACO-PCC-TG.pdf.

4. Library of Congress, "About Library of Congress Authorities," last updated on December 4, 2015, http://authorities.loc.gov/help/contents.htm

5. Library of Congress, *Understanding MARC Authority Records* (Washington: Cataloging Distribution Service, Library of Congress, 2004), part I, "What Is an Authority Record?" http://authorities.loc.gov/help/auth-faq.htm#1.

6. Library of Congress. Program for Cooperative Cataloging. Name Authority Cooperative Program (NACO), "What Is NACO?", accessed March 31, 2018, https://www.loc.gov/aba/pcc/naco/about.html.

The Shift from Authority Control to Identity Management

This classic function of authority records is now challenged by the availability of new researcher identifier systems that have proliferated over the past ten years. For example, ResearchGate and Academia.edu were both founded in 2008,[7] followed by ORCID in 2010 and ISNI as ISO 27729:2012, first published in 2012.[8] Millions of users created their own profiles in self-registered systems, such as Academia, ResearchGate and ORCID, in the past ten years, compared to 10 million LC authority records created by library professionals since 1970s (**Table 1** and **Figure 1**).

Researcher ID Systems	Year Created	Number of Users/Records	Growth Rate of Users/Records Per Year (Approx.)
*Academia	2008	61,013,528 users	6,100,000
*ResearchGate	2008	14,000,000+ users	1,400,00
ISNI	2012	9,140,000 records of individuals (of which 2,860,000 are researchers)	1,520,000
LC Name Authority File	1977	10,000,000 records	250,000
*ORCID	2010	4,597,632 users	574,704

*Self-registered researchers ID systems.

Table 1. Numbers of Users/Records Compared Among Five Researcher Identifier Systems (as of March 31, 2018)[9]

7. ResearchGate GmbH, "About Us," accessed March 31, 2018, https://www.researchgate.net/about; Wikipedia, *Academia.edu*, https://en.wikipedia.org/wiki/Academia.edu.

8. ORCID, Inc., "Certificate of Incorporation", accessed March 31, 2018, https://orcid.org/document/certificate-incorporationrevised-november-2015; International Organization for Standardization, ISO 27729:2012: *Information and documentation -- International standard name identifier (ISNI)*, https://www.iso.org/standard/44292.html.

9. *Academia*, https://www.academia.edu/; ResearchGate GmbH, "About Us," , https://www.researchgate.net/about; ISNI, "Key Statistics", accessed March 31, 2018, http://www.isni.org/; Doris H. Clack, Authority Control: Principles, Applications and Instructions (Chicago: American Library Association, 1990), 21; Paul Frank, Coordinator, NACO and SACO Programs, Library of Congress, e-mail message to author, June 18, 2018; ORCID, Inc., "ORCID Statistics", accessed March 31, 2018, https://orcid.org/statistics.

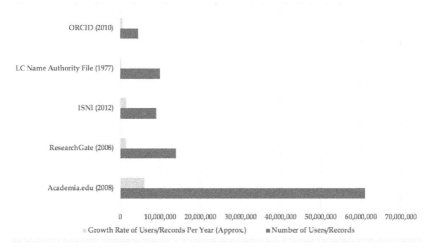

Figure 1. Numbers of Users/Records Compared Among
Five Researcher Identifier Systems (as of March 31, 2018)

The arrival of ORCID and ISNI, used to assign identifiers to individuals using the same identifier format,[10] impacts how name authority records have been created. A MARC proposal to encode the International Standard Name Identifier (ISNI) in the MARC 21 Bibliographic and Authority Formats was approved in 2010 with the addition of subfield $0 in MARC fields for names in bibliographic records.[11] This opened up the ability to include other name identifiers in bibliographic and authority records. ORCID and other researcher identifiers can be included in the MARC 024 field in authority records[12] and in subfield $0 in the MARC 100, 600, 700 and 800 for name entries in bibliographic

10. ORCID, Inc., "ORCID and ISNI Issue Joint Statement on Interoperation, April 2013," https://orcid.org/blog/2013/04/22/orcid-and-isni-issue-joint -statement-interoperation-april-2013.

11. American Library Association (ALA). Machine-Readable Bibliographic Information (MARBI) Committee, *MARC Proposal NO. 2010-06: Encoding the International Standard Name Identifier (ISNI) in the MARC 21 Bibliographic and Authority Formats*, last update August 26, 2010, https://www.loc.gov/marc/marbi/2010/2010-06.html

12. Library of Congress. Network Development and MARC Standards Office, MARC21 Format for Authority Data (Washington, D.C.: Library of Congress, 2013), MARC 024 - Other Standard Identifier, https://www.loc.gov/marc/authority/ad024. html

records.[13] ORCID identifiers are commonly used and required by many institutions. And ORCID institution membership continues to grow around the world.[14] Resource Description & Access (RDA) includes the guideline on identifying persons. It includes metadata elements and attributes of persons, from field of activity, address, biographical information such as place of birth and residence, profession to affiliated organization.[15] For an example, see the author's name authority record in **Figure 2**.

LC control no.: no2018028483
LCCN Permalink: https://lccn.loc.gov/no2018028483
Descriptive conventions: rda
Personal name heading: Anchalee Panigabutra-Roberts
Variant(s): Anchalee P. Roberts
Roberts, Anchalee P.
Panigabutra-Roberts, Anchalee
Roberts, Anchalee Panigabutra-
Other standard no.: 0000-0002-9333-1102 orcid
Located: Thailand United States Nebraska
Place of birth: Thailand
Field of activity: Library science
Women's studies
Affiliation: University of Nebraska--Lincoln
Profession or occupation: Academic librarians
Found in: Panigabutra-Roberts, Anchalee. Diversity and sensitivity in the workplace: understanding Asian Pacific American staff. In Workplace culture in academic libraries, 2013: page 125 (Anchalee Panigabutra-Roberts)
Journal of Southeast Asian American Education and Advancement, 2011, viewed on March 4, 2018: volume 6, issue 1, article 25, title page (Anchalee P. Roberts) page 1 (Anchalee Panigabutra-Roberts, University of Nebraska--Lincoln) about the author, page 3 (She was born and raised in Thailand. ... She is currently an assistant professor at the University of Nebraska-Lincoln Libraries, responsible for metadata and multicultural services, and is also the subject specialist in Women's and Gender Studies) https://docs.lib.purdue.edu/jsaaea/vol6/iss1/25
Associated language: eng

Figure 2. The Author's Name Authority Record[16]

Even with these changes, the effort to create name authorities by trained professionals are labor-intensive and limited only to the Library of Congress's staff and NACO members. As found in the author's

---

13. Library of Congress. Network Development and MARC Standards Office, *MARC21 Format for Bibliographic Data* (Washington, D.C.: Library of Congress, 2018), accessed May 2, 2018, X00 - Personal Names-General Information, https://www.loc.gov/marc/bibliographic/bdx00.html; Appendix A -- Control Subfields, https://www.loc.gov/marc/bibliographic/ecbdcntf.html.

14. As of March 31, 2018, there are currently 883 ORCID member organizations (*ORCID, Inc.*, "ORCID Member Organizations," https://orcid.org/members).

15. Joint Steering Committee for Development of RDA (JSC), *Resource Description & Access: RDA : 2013 Revision, Includes Changes and Updates Through July 2013* (Chicago: American Library Association, 2013), Section 3: Recording Attributes of Agents, 9: Identifying Persons.

16. Library of Congress. *Library of Congress Authorities*, "Anchalee Panigabutra-Roberts," https://lccn.loc.gov/no2018028483.

The Tale of Three Service Types for Researcher Identifiers
and the Ethical Implication on Access to Information
and Representation of Authors   267

pilot study of the faculty at American University in Cairo in 2015,[17] the way we currently create name authority records hinders the presence of early-career faculty and researchers in LC Authority File and VIAF. Their works are likely to be in the form of book chapters, journal articles, and conference papers: the types of publications that are listed in catalog records' content notes or not included in the records at all. This finding challenged our code of professional ethics of providing equal access and representation of information.[18] The author's study placed LC's practice in the context of researcher identity management as inspired by the work of OCLC Research on this topic.[19] Different types of services for researcher identifiers also emerged from this study.

The next section briefly reviews OCLC's research on researcher identifiers and its influence on the author's pilot study and findings. Then the author will explore the service categories that emerged from these findings: professional and self-registered services. The final section includes positive developments from LC PCC and the author's proposed solution to create the information flow to provide better access in bibliographic records for authors of book chapters and/or conference papers. For identity management of authors of journal articles, it is beyond the scope of this chapter whose main concern is for bibliographic records. Besides, Sandberg and Jin already proposed a solution using BIBFRAME linked data and a combination of identifiers, i.e. ISNI, ORCID, Scopus and VIAF, in providing identity management for the authors of journal articles.[20]

17. Anchalee Panigabutra-Roberts, "Researcher Identity Management in the 21st Century Networked World: A Pilot Study of American University in Cairo Faculty" (presentation, Semantic Web in Libraries Conference, Hamburg, Germany, November 24, 2015), http://swib.org/swib15/slides/panigabutra_researchers.pdf.

18. American Library Association, ALA Policy Manual: Section B.1.2. *Code of Professional Ethics for Librarians* (Chicago, IL: ALA, 2013), http://www.ala.org/aboutala/governance/policymanual/updatedpolicymanual/tableofcontents#section2

19. Smith-Yoshimura et al., *Registering Researchers in Authority Files.*

20. Jane Sandberg and Qiang Jin, "How Should Catalogers Provide Authority Control for Journal Article Authors? Name Identifiers in the Linked Data World," *Cataloging & Classification Quarterly* 54, no. 8 (2016): 537-552.

Background Studies

While name authority control as a concept in library and information science has existed for over forty years, the systems that allow researchers to create their own research profiles have emerged only in the past decade. As such platforms proliferated, managing them and trying to integrate them into the current information systems has become more complicated and gained attention among academic and research libraries. In 2014 OCLC Research Registering Researchers in Authority Files Task Group published the report, *Registering Researchers in Authority Files.*[21] The report presented functional requirements and recommendations for six stakeholders: researchers, funders, university administrators, librarians, identity management systems, and aggregators (including publishers). The task group selected twenty out of one hundred research networking and identifier systems and mapped each of the twenty systems to the functional requirements. The selected systems profiled are arXiv, AuthorClaim, Community of Scholars, Digital Author Identifier (DAI), Google Scholar, International Standard Name Identifier (ISNI), Lattes Platform, Library of Congress/NACO Authority File, LinkedIn, Mendeley, Names Project, nanoHUB, NARCIS (National Academic Research and Collaborations Information System), ORCID, ResearcherID, SciENcv, Symplectic Elements, Virtual International Authority File (VIAF), VIVO and Wikipedia. Among the key recommendations, the report addressed how funders and publishers prefer researcher identifiers and encouraged research institutions and libraries to adopt persistent identifiers to link scholars with their output. Funders also prefer researcher identifiers to track the research projects throughout their life cycles. The task group found overlaps among researcher identifier systems but they are not inclusive of all researchers, thus communication among these systems are crucial. Not all systems are interoperable, so there needs to be a third-party system to provide reconciliation or resolution services. Scholars might have published under many variations of their names,

---

21. Smith-Yoshimura et al., *Registering Researchers in Authority Files.*

especially in abbreviated given names used in journal articles and are generally absent from national authority files. And authors that publish only journal articles may not be represented in authority files at all.

Based on this OCLC Research, the author conducted a pilot study on how the faculty at the American University in Cairo (AUC) distributed and shared their scholarly and creative works and how their names were identified in various author identifier systems and/or on the Web.[22] The names of two hundred and sixty-one faculty members and administrators listed in AUC's *Faculty Publications 2012*[23] were searched in four author identifier systems: Library of Congress Name Authority File (LCNAF), Virtual International Authority File (VIAF), International Standard Name Identifier (ISNI), ResearchGate, and Google Scholar, to find if they were registered and/or self-registered in these systems; and whether their names were consistent or with variants and how the variants were handled. For the purpose of this book chapter on the professional ethics, the discussion to follow will focus on the findings related to LCNAF. Based on this study, the disciplinary difference is a major factor for the representation of these academic authors in LCNAF. The foci on the analyses are on two major schools represented in the AUC's publication which are School of Humanities and Social Sciences (HUSS) and School of Sciences and Engineering (SSE). Among the total of two hundred and sixty-one faculty members and administrators who published in 2012, seventy-nine faculty members (thirty percent) are from HUSS and eighty-six faculty members (thirty-three percent) are from SSE. In general, HUSS faculty were better represented than SSE faculty in LCNAF. Details of the findings are as follows:

- Eighty-nine AUC faculty members were in LCNAF, including HUSS faculty with the high rate of fifty-seven per cent (51/89)

22. Panigabutra-Roberts, "Researcher Identity Management in the 21st Century Networked World: A Pilot Study of American University in Cairo Faculty."

23. American University in Cairo. Office of the Associate Provost for Research Administration, *Faculty Publications 2012 Calendar Year* (New Cairo, Egypt: AUC, 2012), https://goo.gl/i48ktj.

of faculty with LCNAF in comparison to SSE faculty with only eleven per cent (10/89) of faculty with LCNAF (**Figure 3**).

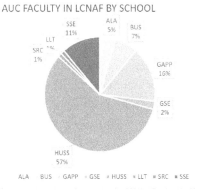

Figure 3. AUC faculty in LCNAF by school; Academy of the Liberal Arts (ALA), School of Business (BUS), School of Global Affairs & Public Policy (GAPP), Graduate School of Education (GSE), School of Humanities and Social Sciences (HUSS), School of Libraries and Learning Technologies (LLT), School of Sciences and Engineering (SSE) and Social Research Center (SRC)

- In contrast, SSE faculty had the high percentage of those without LCNAF (66/14 = 47 per cent) compared to HUSS (21/141 = 15 per cent) (**Figure 4**).

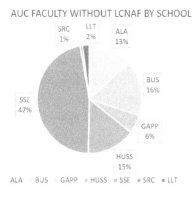

Figure 4. AUC Faculty Without Records in LCNAF by School

The Tale of Three Service Types for Researcher Identifiers
and the Ethical Implication on Access to Information
and Representation of Authors   271

- An additional analysis of publication patterns of the faculty in these two schools showed that HUSS faculty members published their works mostly as books and journal articles. In contrast, SSE faculty published their works mostly as conference papers and journal articles (**Table 2**).

AUC School	Books	Articles in Refereed Journals	Papers in Conference Proceedings
HUSS	9	66	7
SSE	2	114	162

Table 2. AUC's HUSS and SSE Faculty's Publication Types in 2012[24]

With papers in conference proceedings cataloged as articles in serials or as book chapters, SSE faculty who published in these formats are less likely to have their names listed in MARC 1xx or 7xx field, thus the low percentage of SSE faculty in LCNAF. In general, LCNAF and VIAF are better for creators of whole books than for authors of book chapters. Authors of book chapters are likely to be listed only in the content note area of catalog records (for AACR2R and RDA-based cataloging with MARC21), not as added authors with their own metadata in MARC 7xx fields (**Figure 5**).

In summary, the author's pilot study added the new dimension on disciplinary difference to OCLC's research (2014), that is the faculty in the humanities and the social sciences are more likely to have their names in LCNAF than those in sciences and engineering. It also raised the ethical concern about the dominance of authors of monographs in LCNAF and the limitation to provide access to authors of book chapters and conference papers in catalog records and its impact on their absence in LCNAF.

---

24. American University in Cairo. Office of the Associate Provost for Research Administration, 9-10.

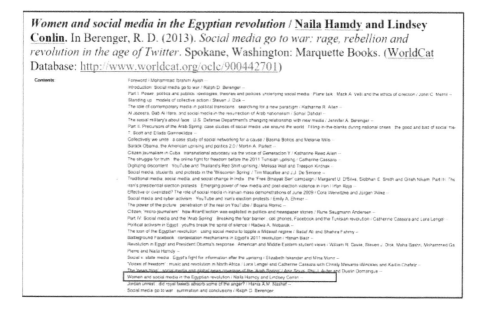

Figure 5. An example of an author of a book chapter listed in a catalog record's content note. Naila Hamdy, an AUC professor, is one of thirty-nine contributors of this book.

Researcher Identifiers as Augmentation to Name Authority Records

As discussed in the introduction, authority records can be created to include ORCID and other researcher identifiers in the MARC 024 field and other name entries using subfield $0. Aforementioned, RDA chapter nine on identifying persons also includes rich metadata elements and attributes about the persons. However, the problem still remains in providing access to authors of book chapters and conference papers in the bibliographic records and the lack of their profiles in the LC Name Authority File (LCNAF). Creating name authority records in LCNAF is still a labor-intensive practice limited to trained professionals (Library of Congress staff and NACO members) and limited output in comparison to other researcher identifier systems with the data input by the researchers themselves (**Figure 1**). With the availability of self-registered services

The Tale of Three Service Types for Researcher Identifiers
and the Ethical Implication on Access to Information
and Representation of Authors 273

(e.g. ORCID, ResearchGate and Google Scholar) that allow researchers and academic authors to create their own author profiles to generate identifiers, it is an ideal solution to fill in the gap of authority control for researchers and academic authors absent in LCNAF. As a caveat, these services are not the panacea. There are advantages and disadvantages for the self-registered services in comparison to professional (for-profit and non-profit) services.

The Tales of Three Service Types for Researcher Identifiers

The author's conference presentation in 2015 identified the service type as a major variable to analyze researcher identifier systems based on the sources of data and data creation process. The major types of services are self-registered and professional services. The self-registered service is used to describe the systems that allow researchers to create their own profiles and to have identifiers assigned to them via online systems with guidelines for data creation. For example, ORCID, ResearchGate and Google Scholar are considered to be self-registered services.

The second category, the professional service, is used to describe author and/or researcher identifier systems which trained professionals use to create researcher identifiers and profiles based on standards and best practices created by the professional communities, with a minimal input from the researchers themselves. These systems are Library of Congress Name Authority File (LCNAF), Virtual International Authority File (VIAF) and International Standard Name Identifier (ISNI). In the context of academic libraries, researchers are likely to have other identifiers for their publications from SCOPUS (SCOPUS I.D.) and Web of Science (ResearcherID), the major databases used by academic and research libraries and with integration with ORCID identifiers. Since catalogers can add SCOPUS and/or ResearcherID numbers in MARC 024 field in authority records and in MARC bibliographic records in subfield $0 for name entries, these IDs are included in the professional services, but with a warrant of their own category as for-profit services. As a result, the professional services are divided into two subcategories: for-profit professional services (SCOPUS I.D. and ResearcherID) and non-profit professional services (LCNAF, VIAF and ISNI). To sum it up, this analytical framework covers three types of services in researcher identifier systems: self-registered service, for-profit professional service, and non-profit professional service (**Table 3**). And the comparison among the three service types will help us weigh the advantages and disadvantages of these services to find the best approach to maximize the benefits of these services for our users.

Table 3. The Three Service Types in Researcher Identifier Systems and Examples

I. Self-Registered Services (e.g., ORCID, ResearchGate and Google Scholar)

In general, self-registered researcher profiles vary in data quality; from minimal data (as required in ORCID) to more robust than the data created by the non-profit professional services such as LCNAF. Thus, we need to weigh both advantages and disadvantages in using these self-registered services for researcher identifiers (**Table 4**).

a. Advantages of self-registered services

The advantages of using these services, such as ORCID, Research-Gate and Google Scholar are:

The Tale of Three Service Types for Researcher Identifiers
and the Ethical Implication on Access to Information
and Representation of Authors 275

- **Researchers' control of their profiles' information..**
  Researchers/authors have better control on what information are included in their own profiles and with privacy-control

Advantages	Disadvantages
• Researchers' control of their profiles' information • Ease of use • Automatic updates for new publications and the API's integration with other systems • Authors can receive e-mail updates on usage statistics and citation activities • Usage reports and charts • Free-of-charge for individual users • Semi-open systems • Social networking and collaboration features • Citation linkage to works citing and cited by each work	• Limited language options • Incomplete data and/or publication lists • With morbidity or mobility factors, the profiles may not be created or updated by their owners over time

Table 4. The Advantages and Disadvantages of Self-Registered Services
for Researcher Identifiers

settings lacking in the professional services (LCNAF, VIAF and ISNI). For example, in ORCID, one has several choices of names to include along with the ability to control visibility settings.[25] ORCID's knowledge base also includes step-by-step guidelines on how to build one's ORCID record and how to connect one's ORCID I.D. with other systems.[26]

---

25. ORCID offers three choices of visibility preferences: 'everyone', 'trusted parties', or 'only me' (*ORCID, Inc.*, "Account settings – Visibility preferences," accessed July 1, 2018, https://support.orcid.org/knowledgebase/articles/1807657).

26. ORCID, Inc., "Building your ORCID record and connecting your iD," accessed July 1, 2018, https://support.orcid.org/knowledgebase/articles/1804786

- **Ease of use**. Connection with other systems allows the automatic population of field data especially for publication data from other databases or researcher I.D. systems (e.g. with Crossref, ResearcherID or SCOPUS). Some provide form-based data fields and drop-down menus of terms to choose from (e.g., Resesarch-Gate for degree names and institutions).

- **Automatic updates for new publications** (Google Scholar and ResearchGate) and the **API's integration with other systems** (ORCID's integration with CrossRef, ResearcherID and SCOPUS, for example).

- **Authors can receive e-mail updates on usage statistics and citation activities** among other notifications. However, one can get inundated with too many e-mail notifications, such as from ResearchGate.

- **Usage reports and charts** (not available in ORCID), such as in publications' usage statistics and charts in ResearchGate (**Figure 6**) and publications' usage statistics, citation metrics and charts in Google Scholar (**Figure 7**).

- **Free-of-charge for individual users** (except for ORCID which offers both free individual accounts and for-fee institutional memberships and accounts).

- **Semi-open systems**. These systems provide some privacy of personal data for the users; researchers can control how much information they share with the public and/or which data are available for other users.

- **Social networking and collaboration features**. In Google Scholar, there are options to 'follow' and to link to coauthors. ResearchGate also offers special features such as following/ followers, read by, questions to other researchers and messages, skills endorsement by peers, suggestions of other publications to read and researchers to follow. Each publication has 'recommend,' 'follow,' and 'share' with other researchers one knows in

The Tale of Three Service Types for Researcher Identifiers
and the Ethical Implication on Access to Information
and Representation of Authors

277

the network. Other users can also download the publications and datasets shared by peer users in ResearchGate.

- **Citation linkage to works citing and cited by each work** (Google Scholar and ResearchGate).

With special features especially self-registered, citation ranking and linkages, ease of use, automatic updates and integration of data,

Figure 6. ResearchGate's Publications' Usage Statistics and Charts.

Figure 7. Google Scholar's Publications' Usage Statistics,
Citation Metrics and Charts.

social networking, and collaboration features, this type of service has been popular among researchers.[27]

b. Disadvantages of Self-registered Services

- **Limited language options.** Google Scholar has options for (web)pages written in these languages: Chinese (simplified or traditional), Dutch, English, French, German, Italian, Japanese, Korean, Polish, Portuguese, Spanish and Turkish.[28] Although one can search in Google Scholar in other languages (e.g. searching for the author's name 'Anchalee' in Thai 'อัญชลี'), one will get only Google's search results without Google Scholar's features. ResearchGate offers any language of input.[29] While ORCID does offer non-Roman languages, it has less options for language display than ResearchGate but better than Google Scholar: from Arabic, Czech, English, Spanish, French, Italian, Japanese, Korean, Portuguese, Russian and Chinese (two options).[30]
- **Incomplete data and/or publication lists** (especially for the individual accounts). However, they are likely to be better than the professional services such as LCNAF. When creating LC's authority records, one is not required to list all publications or works associated with the persons; only works acquired by the institutions and directly related to the persons are cited in their authority records. In contrast, the self-registered services (such as ORCID, ResearchGate, and Google Scholar) are built to establish researchers' scholarly records of publications and profiles

27. Tran and Lyon, "Faculty Use of Author Identifiers and Researcher Networking Tools."

28. Google LLC, "Settings/Languages," *Google Scholar*, accessed March 31, 2018, https://scholar.google.com/scholar_settings?hl=en#1.

29. ResearchGate GmbH, "How to Add Research," *ResearchGate*, accessed March 31, 2018, https://explore.researchgate.net/display/support/How+to+add+research.

30. ORCID, Inc., "Language display preferences," *ORCID*, accessed March 31, 2018, https://support.orcid.org/knowledgebase/articles/921666-language-display-pre ferences.

The Tale of Three Service Types for Researcher Identifiers
and the Ethical Implication on Access to Information
and Representation of Authors   279

to share and promote their works, and to establish their unique researcher identifiers. Therefore, their data are more comprehensive. Panigabutra-Roberts' profiles illustrate such contrasts (**Figure 8** and **Figure 9**).

LC control no.:	no2018028483
LCCN Permalink:	https://lccn.loc.gov/no2018028483
Descriptive conventions:	rda
Personal name heading:	Anchalee Panigabutra-Roberts
Variant(s):	Anchalee P. Roberts
	Roberts, Anchalee P.
	Panigabutra-Roberts, Anchalee
	Roberts, Anchalee Panigabutra-
Other standard no.:	0000-0002-9333-1102 orcid
Located:	Thailand United States Nebraska
Place of birth:	Thailand
Field of activity:	Library science
	Women's studies
Affiliation:	University of Nebraska--Lincoln
Profession or occupation:	Academic librarians
Found in:	Panigabutra-Roberts, Anchalee. Diversity and sensitivity in the workplace: understanding Asian Pacific American staff. In Workplace culture in academic libraries, 2013: page 125 (Anchalee Panigabutra-Roberts)
	Journal of Southeast Asian American Education and Advancement, 2011, viewed on March 4, 2018: volume 6, issue 1, article 25, title page (Anchalee P. Roberts) page 1 (Anchalee Panigabutra-Roberts, University of Nebraska--Lincoln) about the author, page 3 (She was born and raised in Thailand. ... She is currently an assistant professor at the University of Nebraska-Lincoln Libraries, responsible for metadata and multicultural services, and is also the subject specialist in Women's and Gender Studies) https://docs.lib.purdue.edu/jsaaea/vol6/iss1/25
Associated language:	eng

Figure 8. Name Authority Record for Anchalee Panigabutra-Roberts

- **With morbidity or mobility factors, the profiles may not be created or updated by their owners over time.** In self-registered services, the data creation and updates depend on the data owners to be living persons and their willingness to create, maintain and update their own data. With deaths of authors or their relocation to different institutions, their profiles may not be created nor updated over time.

Overall, the ease of use and the ability to control one's information with special features, such as citation and usage metrics and integration with other identifier systems, outweigh the shortcomings in self-registered services. With institutions or funders requiring authors to submit their ORCID IDs with their research publications and data, we can expect to see the increase in ORCID users and other self-registered ID users (as shown in **Table 1** and **Figure 1**).

Figure 9. ORCID I.D. for Anchalee Panigabutra-Roberts (Public Version)

librarians to inform researchers at their institutions of this special feature in ORCID. Similar to the self-registered services, there are both advantages and disadvantages in using for-profit professional services for researcher identifiers such as SCOPUS and ResearcherID identifiers (as compared in **Table 5**).

Advantages	Disadvantages
• System-supplied information and identifiers • Added features for citation metrics, h-index and citation data visualization • Ability to integrate with other identifier systems • Inclusion of collaborators' information and the ability to identify new collaborators.	• For-fee services • Limited control by the researchers • Content from each platform may vary per each researcher • Closed data

Table 5. The Advantages and Disadvantages of For-Profit Professional Services for Researcher Identifiers

a. Advantages of for-profit professional services

- **System-supplied information and identifiers.** For SCOPUS, authors are automatically assigned SCOPUS Author IDs, when they publish in journals indexed by SCOPUS.[31] Similarly, authors can register for free or as subscribers of Web of Science for unique ResearcherIDs, which are alphanumeric identifiers, to manage their publication lists.[32]
- **Added features for citation metrics, h-index and citation data visualization.** Both SCOPUS and ResearcherID profiles provide citation counts and linking for cited works and references. The systems also calculate and display h-index and its visual data.

31. Elsevier, "What is the SCOPUS Author Identifier?" *Scopus: Access and Use Support Center*, https://service.elsevier.com/app/answers/detail/a_id/11212/supporthub/scopus/

32. Thomson Reuters, "ResearcherID Help" copyright 2014, http://www.researcherid.com/resources/html/dsy5769-TRS.html

- **Ability to integrate with other identifier systems**. ORCID can be integrated with ResearcherID. ResearcherID is also integrated with Web of Science and ORCID compliant. Both identifiers can be added to LCNAF, VIAF and ISNI name entries.
- **Inclusion of collaborators' information and the ability to identify new collaborators**.

b. Disadvantages of for-profit professional services

- **For-fee services**. Researchers can take advantage of these services, but their institutions need to have subscriptions to these databases: SCOPUS and Web of Science.
- **Limited control by the researchers**. The profiles are created automatically by the systems, not by the researchers. SCOPUS assigns unique numbers to groups of documents written by the same authors using an algorithm based on a set of criteria.[33]
- **Content from each platform may vary per each researcher.** Researchers may not have all of their works indexed by the same database vendors, thus they may have to register in more than one service to cover all of their publications.
- **Closed data**. Since these are commercial products, their data are proprietary. Their content is not open and only integrated among other vendors and/or trusted partners they have agreements with.

Researchers benefit from many features provided by these for-profit services, from citation metrics, h-index, citation data visualization, system-supplied identifiers, and integration with other identifier systems and with collaborators' information. On the other hand, the disadvantages of using these services are their closed and proprietary data and integration only among trusted parties with agreements. And each database vendor may not have indexed all the publications by individual authors, thus each author needs to register in more than one service.

---

33. Elsevier, "What is the SCOPUS Author Identifier?"

The Tale of Three Service Types for Researcher Identifiers
and the Ethical Implication on Access to Information
and Representation of Authors   283

III. Non-Profit Professional Services
(LCNAF, VIAF and ISNI)

Traditionally, librarians and archivists have been at the forefront of the professional service for name authorities and identity management. This legacy non-profit professional service continues to be essential in library and archival practices and has expanded its role and resources over the years, from the Library of Congress's NACO to VIAF and ISNI. While other types of identity management services have surfaced, these non-profit professional services will continue to have their role and will continue to provide added values for our information content and access into the future. Nonetheless, these non-profit professional services also have their own advantages and disadvantages (as compared in **Table 6**).

Advantages	Disadvantages
• Free-of-charge for users • Metadata guidelines as shared best practices • Cooperative venture by member institutions worldwide • Robust language options including non-Roman scripts • Structured as linked open data • Fill in the gap of identity data created by morbidity or mobility factors	• Limit data creation to trained professionals • Labor-intensive • Based on literary warrant and name disambiguation • Authors' lack of ownership of their data • Limited listing of scholarly and creative works • Lack special features offered by other types of services • Not inclusive of authors of book chapters or authors of papers in conference proceedings

Table 6. The Advantages and Disadvantages of Non-Profit
Professional Services for Researcher Identifiers

a. **Advantages of non-profit professional services**

- **Free-of-charge for the users.** LC Authorities Services,[34] VIAF[35] and ISNI[36] can be accessed on the Web for free. However, to access and contribute authority records to the databases, libraries needs to subscribe to OCLC services. ISNI also offers fee-based memberships.[37]

- **Metadata guidelines as shared best practices.** LC staff and NACO members create authority records based on Resource Description & Access, Library of Congress's Descriptive Cataloging Manual: Z1: Name and Series Authority Records and other shared documents.[38] VIAF and ISNI are built upon contributions of multiple authority files and databases from around the world.

- **Cooperative venture by member institutions worldwide.** Aforementioned, LC Authority File is created and updated by LC staff and NACO members. VIAF's sixty contributors include LC/NACO, ISNI, national libraries, cultural agencies and other major institutions from more than thirty countries around the world.[39] ISNI database's contributors are from different domains (including VIAF and PCC NACO), from libraries authority files, rights management societies, researchers' databases, music industry to book supply chain and more.[40] Although the ISNI

---

34. Library of Congress, "Frequently Asked Questions," *Library of Congress Authorities*, May 18, 2016, https://authorities.loc.gov/help/auth-faq.htm#2

35. OCLC, Inc., "Data Source License," *Virtual International Authority File*, copyright 2010-2016, http://viaf.org/viaf/data/

36. ISNI International Agency, "How ISNI Works," http://www.isni.org/how-isni-works

37. ISNI International Agency, "ISNI Members," http://www.isni.org/content/isni-members

38. Library of Congress. Program for Cooperative Cataloging. Name Authority Cooperative Program (LC PCC NACO), "NACO Documentation & Updates," https://www.loc.gov/aba/pcc/naco/doc-updates.html

39. OCLC, Inc., "VIAF Contributors," *Virtual International Authority File*, http://viaf.org/

40. ISNI International Agency, "ISNI Data Contributors," http://www.isni.org/content/data-contributors

International Agency is a non-profit organization, it offers fee-based membership.[41] All three services are hosted by OCLC, a non-profit global library cooperative.

- **Robust language options including non-Roman scripts.** MARC21 Authority Format for LCNAF is based on the Unicode character sets that cover most of the world's writing systems in 139 modern and historic scripts.[42] Moreover, LCNAF extends its value as a multilingual database because it contributes data to VIAF and ISNI which also have data contributors worldwide. For an example, Eugene Garfield's VIAF record in **Figure 10** shows his variant names in different languages including non-Roman scripts.

- **Structured as linked open data.** The three non-profit services provide their data as linked open data, thus making them the most accessible types of services. LC provides name authority data and other controlled vocabularies via their Linked Data Services.[43] OCLC publishes VIAF data as linked data (as RDF and other formats).[44] And ISNI provides access to its data as linked open data via URIs and with its core metadata available in html and xml.[45]

---

41. ISNI International Agency is a non-profit organization registered as a private company limited by guarantee in England and Wales under the British Law (ISNI International Agency, "About the ISNI International Agency," http://www.isni.org/about).

42. Library of Congress. Network Development and MARC Standards Office, "MARC 21 Specifications for Record Structure, Character Sets, and Exchange Media, Character Sets and Encoding Options: Part 3, Unicode Encoding Environment," last update December 2007, http://www.loc.gov/marc/specifications/speccharucs.html

43. Library of Congress Linked Data Service, "About," accessed July 3, 2018, http://id.loc.gov/about/; "Library of Congress Names," http://id.loc.gov/authorities/names.html

44. OCLC, Inc. Developer Network, "OCLC Linked Data," last update 2017, https://www.oclc.org/developer/develop/linked-data.en.html

45. ISNI International Agency, "How ISNI Works—Linked Data," http://www.isni.org/how-isni-works#HowItWorks_LinkedData

Figure 10: Eugene Garfield's VIAF Record with Multi-Lingual Variant Names

- **Fill in the gap of identity data created by morbidity or mobility factors.** In self-registered services, the data creation and updates depend on the data owners and their willingness to create, maintain and update their own data. With the passing of researchers or their relocation to different institutions, their profiles may not be created or updated. Professional services can fill in this gap of identity data to create researcher profiles for those who passed away and to curate and update the profiles for

The Tale of Three Service Types for Researcher Identifiers
and the Ethical Implication on Access to Information
and Representation of Authors   287

those who relocated to other institutions. These actions adhere to their professional ethics and commitment to the equitable access and stewardship of information.

b. Disadvantages of non-profit professional services

- **Limit data creation to trained professionals.** While other identity services allow the authors to input and/or update their own data, these services use only trained professionals (LC staff and NACO members) to create and modify the authority records with occasional phone calls or e-mails to the living authors.[46]

- **Labor-intensive.** To be able to create records to contribute to LC Name Authority Files, one needs to be trained by LC for one month followed by a reviewing period before one can become an independent NACO contributor. To create a name authority record, each librarian needs to do some research about the person from the item in hand, websites, or archives, or to verify facts via e-mails or phone calls.

- **Based on literary warrant and name disambiguation.** Data creators in professional services do not always create or update the authority records. The creation and updates of authority records are based on 'literary warrant' or when new works are added to the local metadata systems. Name authority records are mostly created for non-unique names for disambiguation or based on local guidelines, if member libraries wish to create authority records for all affiliates at their institution whose works are present in both physical and digital collections. Thus, not all authors have authority records.

---

46. "LC staff members and libraries participating in the Name Authority Cooperative (NACO) component of the Program for Cooperative Cataloging (PCC) contribute records to the authority file." (Library of Congress. Policy and Standards Division, *Descriptive Cataloging Manual (DCM) Z1: Name and Series Authority Records*, updated October 2017, page 1, https://www.loc.gov/catdir/cpso/dcmz1.pdf)

- **Authors' lack of ownership of their data.** While the records are free to users,[47] the authors have neither ownership nor direct access to modify their own authority records as they can in the self-registered and some of the for-profit professional services. In most cases, they may not be aware that their name authorities have been created in the authority files, since there is no notification system to alert the authors automatically in the current system setting. However, W3C's Linked Data Notifications protocol is available and can be applied in the linked data services for name authorities in the future.[48]

- **Limited listing of scholarly and creative works.** In the authority records, only limited numbers of publications or creative works are used to verify information and sources used to establish name authorities, their variants and other metadata elements. Thus, these authority records are not meant to provide a full listing of publications or the creative outputs of their creators as in other identity service types. For an example, Eugene Garfield's VIAF record includes forty-four publications in VIAF in comparison to his ResearcherID's listing of 1,538 publications as shown in **Figure 11**).

- **Lack special features offered by other types of services**, such as citation metrics and visualization, social network functions to connect with other authors and e-mail notification services.

- **Authority records rarely include authors of book chapters or conference papers.** Based on RDA and Library of Congress's PCC Policy, book chapters' information is recorded in the content note area of catalog records as

---

47. Library of Congress, "Frequently Asked Questions 2) Are authority records available free of charge?" *Library of Congress Authorities*, https://authorities.loc.gov/help/auth-faq.htm#2

48. *Linked Data Notifications: W3C Recommendations 2 May 2017*, eds. Sarven Capadisli and Amy Guy (Cambridge, MA: World Wide Web Consortium, 2017), https://www.w3.org/TR/ldn/

The Tale of Three Service Types for Researcher Identifiers
and the Ethical Implication on Access to Information
and Representation of Authors

289

Figure 11. Eugene Garfield's VIAF's Record in Comparison to
His ResearcherID Record

MARC21 505, but conference papers are not included.[49] Analytical access points for authors/titles in the content note are not required. As a result, authors of book chapters may not have access points created for them, while authors of conference papers are not recorded in the content note. As for the creation of authority records for these authors, while LC's *Descriptive Cataloging Manual: Z1 Name and Series Authority Records* does not prohibit the creation of authority records for authors of book chapters (see **Figure 12**), its reliance on access points in the bibliographic records to create authority records limits the creation of authority records for these authors in the LC Authority File, nor VIAF and ISNI, the recipients of LC Authority data.

Summary: The Three Types of Identity Management Services

From the researchers' point of view, having the identity profiles and identifiers created, updated and maintained for them is less work and

---

49. Library of Congress-Program for Cooperative Cataloging's *Policy Statements (LC-PCC PS) 25.1. Related Work* instructs catalogers to add related works in a work in MARC 505 content note, with no limit on the number of works in the contents note "unless burdensome." For compilation of works (as for book chapters and their authors) it also suggests giving an analytical authorized access point for the predominant or first work in the compilation "when it represents a substantial part of the resource." The policy is also not to apply this guideline to conference proceedings (Library of Congress. Program for Cooperative Cataloging, "Policy Statements (LC-PCC PS). 25.1. Related Work" (In *RDA Toolkit* (Chicago IL: American Library Association, 2012; this section's last update March 2017), https://access.rdatoolkit.org/).

Per the *LC-PCC PS* for RDA 0.0 to determine the mode of issuance for conference publications, conference proceedings can be cataloged as serials or monographs per the criteria addressed in this statement. However, even when the proceedings are cataloged as monographs, *LC PCC PS 25.1. Related Work* guideline aforementioned suggests not to give analytical authorized access point for the works included in each conference paper. Thus, the authors of conference proceedings are less likely to have their own analytical entries in the bibliographic records that would facilitate the creation of their name authority records. (Library of Congress. Program for Cooperative Cataloging. "Policy Statements for Chapter 0: Introduction. Determining Mode of Issuance. Situations Requiring Further Consideration, C. LC Practice: Conference Publications." In *RDA Toolkit* (Chicago IL: American Library Association, 2012; this section's last update April 11, 2017), https://access.rdatoolkit.org/)..

The Tale of Three Service Types for Researcher Identifiers
and the Ethical Implication on Access to Information
and Representation of Authors   291

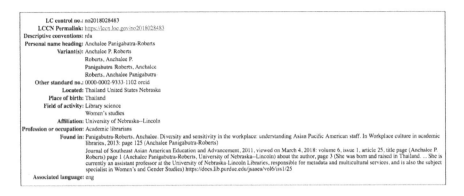

Figure 12. The Catalog Record with the Author's Book Chapter
and the LC Authority Record Created by the Author

more convenient. But they lack control over the content in its extent, types of data, privacy of their information and completeness of their scholarly records. The self-registered services can provide them with better control of the content's completeness and the privacy of their data. They can choose to list all types of their publications and creative works, educational background and work experience. Some services such as ResearchGate and Google Scholar provide special functions such as publications' usage statistics, citation metrics and charts. ResearchGate provides sharing of publications and data and collaboration opportunities, and Google Scholar links one's publications to her collaborators. And while SCOPUS and ResearcherID are free to the users, connection to the content in their associated databases is not free. Researchers have to rely on their current institutions to subscribe to SCOPUS and Web of Science databases to access the content. ORCID also offers a fee-based institutional membership. Thus, researchers' data are deemed proprietary, although ORCID IDs are persistent identifiers.[50] The creation, updates and maintenance of the data also depend on researchers. Their morbidity (their passing) and mobility (relocation to other institutions) will impact the long-term stewardship of their identity data. Most of all, some of these services' data are not open as linked data, thus applying linked data model to connect with these services may or may not be possible in the future.

All in all, non-profit professional services may not offer a comprehensive listing of researchers' publications and creative works (especially for book chapters, conference papers and journal articles), or special features other services offer (such as social networking, data sharing, and citation metrics). However, their professional commitment to provide access to name authorities in multiple languages and scripts, as linked open data and shared metadata practices, outweighs their shortcomings. Ongoing developments at the Library of Congress, such as Linked Data Services and the PCC's strategic plan 2018-21, underpin the vital role LC PCC, NACO and other professional organizations will continue to play in the future of researcher identity management.

---

50. ORCID, Inc., "Persistent Identifiers (PIDs)," https://support.orcid.org/knowledgebase/articles/1807774-persistent-identifiers-pids.

The Tale of Three Service Types for Researcher Identifiers
and the Ethical Implication on Access to Information
and Representation of Authors   293

Positive Developments

In 2016 the Library of Congress's Program for Cooperative Cataloging (LC PCC) established the Task Group on Identity Management and shifted its strategic planning from authority control to identity management.[51] For the non-profit professional services, there are new and positive developments in the U.S. research library communities.

- PCC-ISNI Pilot[52] and NACO Lite. PCC has a pilot with ISNI and the concept of NACO Lite may open up opportunities for more professionals to contribute to the LC Name Authority File.
- LC PCC's strategic plan 2018-21 includes all the above (LC PCC. Strategic Directions January 2018-December 2021, 2018).
- The addition of MARC subfields $0 and $1 to accommodate URIs in MARC21 formats.

These are positive signs for the better support of researcher identity management, particularly for the better support for linked data with the addition of MARC21 subfields '0' and '1'.

Recommended Workflow for Identity Management of Authors of Book Chapters and Conference Papers

As ORCID continues to grow its membership, its future plan to expand data elements in response to its members' wish list and to use persistent IDs would increase its status as the de facto researcher identifier.[53] As authors create their own ORCID IDs, it is ideal to link the

51. Library of Congress. Program for Cooperative Cataloging. Task Group on Identity Management, *Charge for PCC Task Group on Identity Management in NACO*, last update March 31, 2016, https://www.loc.gov/aba/pcc/documents/Identity-management-NACO-PCC-TG.pdf

52. Library of Congress. Program for Cooperative Cataloging, *PCC ISNI Pilot*, last modified on June 20, 2018, https://wiki.duraspace.org/display/PCCISNI/PCC+ISNI+Pilot+Home

53. "…Employment, education, qualifications, invited-position, distinctions, membership, service, projects, project proposals, funding, and research resources are just

ORCID IDs of authors of book chapters and conference papers to their bibliographic records using MARC subfield '0' with this workflow (**Figure 13**).

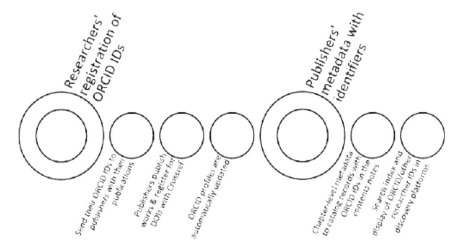

Figure 13. A Recommended Workflow for Identity Management of Authors of Book Chapters and Conference Papers (Monographs)

As illustrated above, researchers should create and supply their ORCID IDs in their publications when submitting them to the publishers. Once their works are published, the publishers register their works for DOIs with Crossref and Crossref automatically updates the authors' ORCID profiles (with the authors' permission).[54] Then the publishers create metadata for the book chapters and/or conference proceedings and add their metadata to the catalog records' content notes including

---

a short list of items that researchers and members want to connect to ORCID iDs." – (Robert Peters, *Why We Need to Explore Blockchain Technology to Connect Researchers and Research*, submitted by the author March 7, 2018, https://orcid.org/blog/2018/03/07/why-we-need-explore-blockchain-technology-connect-researchers-and-research)

54. "Enter once, when you submit a paper, then watch as your ORCID record is automatically updated as your work is published, registered with Crossref, and enters the global citation network," (Crossref, "ORCID Auto-update," last update May 29, 2018, https://www.crossref.org/community/orcid/)

titles, authors and their ORCID IDs. The catalog and discovery services can provide search index and display of ORCID and other researcher identifiers accordingly.

As mentioned above, MARC21 subfield '0' or '1' can be used to add identifiers for personal names such as ORCID or ISNI. However, subfield '0' or '1' is currently applicable only to the MARC fields 100, 600, 700 and 800 for personal names.[55] Based on the recommended workflow, the author proposes that subfield '0' or '1' be applicable to *MARC21 505 00 Enhanced Formatted Contents Note*, after subfield $r for the statement of responsibility. The following example is a use case for a book chapter written by the author:

> 505 00 $t Diversity and sensitivity in the workplace: understanding Asian Pacific American staff / $r Anchalee Panigabutra-Roberts. $0 (orcid)0000-0002-9333-1102.

Or
> 505 00 $t Diversity and sensitivity in the workplace: understanding Asian Pacific American staff / $r Anchalee Panigabutra-Roberts. $1 https://orcid.org/0000-0002-9333-1102.[56]

Automatic generation of the author's authority record, or a macro, is possible by using this MARC 505 00 field's data.

55. Library of Congress. Network Development and MARC Standards Office, *MARC21 Bibliographic Format. X00 - Personal Names- General Information*, last update December 2017, http://www.loc.gov/marc/bibliographic/bdx00.html.

56. Library of Congress. Program for Cooperative Cataloging Task Group on URIs in MARC, *Formulating and Obtaining URIs: A Guide to Commonly Used Vocabularies and Reference Sources*, contributors, (alphabetical order) Corine Deliot, Steven Folsom, MJ Han, Nancy Lorimer, Terry Reese, Adam Schiff, version date: 2018-02-14 (Washington, D.C.: Library of Congress, 2018), 57-58, https://www.loc.gov/aba/pcc/bibframe/TaskGroups/formulate_obtain_URI_guide.pdf

Conclusion

The author's pilot study of the American University in Cairo faculty in 2015 compared and contrasted the professional and self-registered services for researcher identifiers. Her findings raised ethical concerns regarding the dominance of authors of monographs in LCNAF and the limitation to provide access to authors of book chapters and conference papers in catalog records and its impact on their absence in LCNAF. By comparing the advantages and disadvantages of three types of researcher identity services, ORCID and non-profit professional services, such as LCNAF, emerged as a winning combination of services that library professionals can use to better serve the research community. The author proposes a workflow to interconnect the two services and a recommendation to enhance MARC21 metadata in 505 00 with subfield '0' for ORCID and other researcher identifiers to make this interconnection possible. With the inclusion of ORCID and/or other researcher identifiers in the catalog records' enhanced contents note, non-profit professional services, i.e. librarians, can provide better access and authority control for authors of book chapters and conference papers in catalog records. This is a short-term solution while the transition to the linked data in libraries is still in development.

Bibliography

Academia accessed March 31, 2018. https://www.academia.edu/

American Library Association. *ALA Policy Manual: Section B.1.2. Code of Professional Ethics for Librarians.* Chicago, IL: ALA, 2013. http://www.ala.org/aboutala/governance/policymanual/updatedpolicymanual/tableofcontents#section2

American Library Association. Machine-Readable Bibliographic Information Committee. *MARC Proposal NO. 2010-06: Encoding the International Standard Name Identifier (ISNI) in the MARC 21 Bibliographic and Authority Formats* last update August 26, 2010. https://www.loc.gov/marc/marbi/2010/2010-06.html

American University in Cairo. Office of the Associate Provost for Research Administration. *Faculty Publications 2012 Calendar Year*. New Cairo, Egypt: AUC, 2012. https://goo.gl/i48ktj

Clack, Doris H. *Authority Control: Principles, Applications and Instructions*. Chicago: American Library Association, 1990.

Crossref. "ORCID Auto-update" last update May 29, 2018. https://www.crossref.org/community/orcid/

Elsevier. "What is the SCOPUS Author Identifier?" *Scopus: Access and Use Support Center*. https://service.elsevier.com/app/answers/detail/a_id/11212/supporthub/scopus/

Google LLC. "Settings/Languages." *Google Scholar*. https://scholar.google.com/scholar_settings?hl=en#1

International Conference on Cataloguing Principles. *Statement of Principles: Adopted by the International Conference on Cataloguing Principles, Paris, October 1961*. [London]: [International Federation of Library Associations], 1961. https://www.ifla.org/files/assets/cataloguing/IMEICC/IMEICC1/statement_principles_paris_1961.pdf

International Organization for Standardization. *ISO 27729:2012: Information and documentation—International standard name identifier (ISNI)*. https://www.iso.org/standard/44292.html

ISNI International Agency. "About the ISNI International Agency." http://www.isni.org/about

ISNI International Agency. "How ISNI Works." http://www.isni.org/how-isni-works

ISNI International Agency. "How ISNI Works—Linked Data" accessed July 3, 2018. http://www.isni.org/how-isni-works#HowItWorks_LinkedData

ISNI International Agency. "ISNI Data Contributors." http://www.isni.org/content/data-contributors

ISNI International Agency. "ISNI Members." http://www.isni.org/content/isni-members

ISNI International Agency. "Key Statistics." http://www.isni.org/

Joint Steering Committee for Development of RDA. *Resource Description & Access. Section 3: Recording Attributes of Agents, 9: Identifying* Persons. 2013 revision, includes changes and updates through July 2013. Chicago: American Library Association, 2013.

Library of Congress. "About Library of Congress Authorities" last update December 4, 2015. http://authorities.loc.gov/help/contents.htm

Library of Congress. "Anchalee Panigabutra-Roberts." *Library of Congress Authorities.* https://lccn.loc.gov/no2018028483

Library of Congress. "Frequently Asked Questions." *Library of Congress Authorities.* https://authorities.loc.gov/help/auth-faq.htm

Library of Congress Linked Data Service. "About." http://id.loc.gov/about/

Library of Congress Linked Data Service. "Library of Congress Names." http://id.loc.gov/authorities/names.html

Library of Congress. Network Development and MARC Standards Office. *MARC21 Format for Authority Data. MARC 024 - Other Standard Identifier.* Washington, D.C.: Library of Congress, 2013. https://www.loc.gov/marc/authority/ad024.html

Library of Congress. Network Development and MARC Standards Office. *MARC21 Format for Bibliographic Data.* Washington, D.C.: Library of Congress, 2018. https://www.loc.gov/marc/bibliographic/

Library of Congress. Network Development and MARC Standards Office. "MARC 21 Specifications for Record Structure, Character Sets, and Exchange Media, Character Sets and Encoding Options: Part 3, Unicode Encoding Environment" last update December 2007. http://www.loc.gov/marc/specifications/speccharucs.html

Library of Congress. Network Development and MARC Standards Office. *Understanding MARC Authority Records.* Washington, D.C.: Network Development and MARC Standards Office, Library of Congress, 2004. http://www.loc.gov/marc/uma/index.html

The Tale of Three Service Types for Researcher Identifiers
and the Ethical Implication on Access to Information
and Representation of Authors   299

Library of Congress. Policy and Standards Division. *Descriptive Cataloging Manual (DCM) Z1: Name and Series Authority Records.* Updated October 2017. Washington, D.C.: Library of Congress, 2017. https://www.loc.gov/catdir/cpso/dcmz1.pdf

Library of Congress. Program for Cooperative Cataloging. *PCC ISNI Pilot,* last modified on June 20, 2018. https://wiki.duraspace.org/display/PCCISNI/PCC+ISNI+Pilot+Home

Library of Congress. Program for Cooperative Cataloging. "Policy Statements. 25.1. Related Work," this section last updated March 2017. In *RDA Toolkit.* Chicago IL: American Library Association, 2012. https://access.rdatoolkit.org/

Library of Congress. Program for Cooperative Cataloging. "Policy Statements for Chapter 0: Introduction. Determining Mode of Issuance. Situations Requiring Further Consideration, C. LC Practice: Conference Publications," last updated April 11, 2017. In *RDA Toolkit.* Chicago IL: American Library Association, 2012. https://access.rdatoolkit.org/

Library of Congress. Program for Cooperative Cataloging. Name Authority Cooperative Program. "NACO Documentation & Updates." https://www.loc.gov/aba/pcc/naco/doc-updates.html

Library of Congress. Program for Cooperative Cataloging. Name Authority Cooperative Program. "What Is NACO?" https://www.loc.gov/aba/pcc/naco/about.html.

Library of Congress. Program for Cooperative Cataloging. Task Group on Identity Management. *Charge for PCC Task Group on Identity Management in NACO.* Last update March 31, 2016. Washington, D.C.: Library of Congress, 2016. https://www.loc.gov/aba/pcc/documents/Identity-management-NACO-PCC-TG.pdf

Library of Congress. Program for Cooperative Cataloging. Task Group on URIs in MARC. *Formulating and Obtaining URIs: A Guide to Commonly Used Vocabularies and Reference Sources.* Contributors, (alphabetical order) Corine Deliot, Steven Folsom, MJ Han, Nancy Lorimer, Terry Reese, Adam Schiff. Version date: 2018-02-14. Washington, D.C.: Library of Congress, 2018. https://www.loc.gov/aba/pcc/bibframe/TaskGroups/formulate_obtain_URI_guide.pdf

Linked Data Notifications: W3C Recommendations 2 May 2017. Edited by Sarven Capadisli and Amy Guy. Cambridge, MA: World Wide Web Consortium, 2017. https://www.w3.org/TR/ldn/

OCLC. "Data Source License." *Virtual International Authority File,* copyright 2010-2016. http://viaf.org/viaf/data/

OCLC. "VIAF Contributors." *Virtual International Authority File.* http://viaf.org/

OCLC Developer Network. "OCLC Linked Data," last update 2017. https://www.oclc.org/developer/develop/linked-data.en.html

ORCID. "Account settings—Visibility preferences." https://support.orcid.org/knowledgebase/articles/1807657

ORCID. "Building your ORCID record and connecting your iD." https://support.orcid.org/knowledgebase/articles/1804786-building-your-orcid-record-and-connecting-your-id

ORCID. "Certificate of Incorporation." https://orcid.org/document/certificate-incorporationrevised-november-2015

ORCID. "Language display preferences." https://support.orcid.org/knowledgebase/articles/921666-language-display-preferences

ORCID. "ORCID and ISNI Issue Joint Statement on Interoperation, April 2013." https://orcid.org/blog/2013/04/22/orcid-and-isni-issue-joint-statement-interoperation-april-2013

ORCID, "ORCID Member Organizations." https://orcid.org/members

ORCID. "ORCID Statistics." https://orcid.org/statistics.

ORCID. "Persistent Identifiers (PIDs)." https://support.orcid.org/knowledgebase/articles/1807774-persistent-identifiers-pids

Panigabutra-Roberts, Anchalee. "Researcher Identity Management in the 21st Century Networked World: A Pilot Study of American University in Cairo Faculty." Presentation, Semantic Web in Libraries Conference, Hamburg, Germany, November 24, 2015. http://swib.org/swib15/slides/panigabutra_researchers.pdf

Peters, Robert. "Why We Need to Explore Blockchain Technology to Connect Researchers and Research" submitted by the author March 7,
2018. https://orcid.org/blog/2018/03/07/why-we-need-explore-
blockchain-technology-connect-researchers-and-research.

ResearchGate GmbH. "How to Add Research." https://explore.research-
gate.net/display/support/How+to+add+research

ResearchGate GmbH. "About Us." https://www.researchgate.net/about

Sandberg, Jane and Qiang Jin. "How Should Catalogers Provide Authority Control for Journal Article Authors? Name Identifiers in the
Linked Data World." *Cataloging & Classification Quarterly* 54, no. 8
(2016): 537-552.

Smith-Yoshimura, Karen et al. *Registering Researchers in Authority Files*. Dublin,
Ohio: OCLC Research, 2014. https://www.oclc.org/content/
dam/research/publications/library/2014/oclcresearch-registering-
researchers-2014-a4.pdf

Tenopir, Carol et al. "No Scholar Is an Island: The Impact of Sharing in the
Work Life of Scholars." *Learned Publishing* 30, no. 1 (2017): 5–17.

Thomson Reuters. "ResearcherID Help," copyright 2014. http://www.
researcherid.com/resources/html/dsy5769-TRS.html

Tran, Clara Y. and Jennifer A. Lyon. "Faculty Use of Author Identifiers and
Researcher Networking Tools." *College & Research Libraries* 78, no. 2
(2017): 171-182.

Wikipedia. *Academia.edu.* https://en.wikipedia.org/wiki/Academia.edu.

Image credits

Figure 5. "*Social Media Go to War: Rage, Rebellion and Revolution in the Age of Twitter*, edited by Ralph D. Berenger. Spokane, Wash: Marquette Books, 2013." *WorldCat.org*. Dublin, Ohio: OCLC, Inc. http://www. worldcat.org/oclc/900442701

Figure 6. "Anchalee Panigabutra-Roberts." *ResearchGate.net*. Berlin, Germany: ResearchGate GmbH. https://www.researchgate.net/profile/ Anchalee_Panigabutra-Roberts/stats. With the permission to use this information granted to the author by ResearchGate GmbH on July 9, 2018.

Figure 7. "Anchalee Panigabutra-Roberts." *Google Scholar*. Mountain View, CA: Google LLC accessed April 29, 2018. https://scholar.google. com/citations?user=zH7SxhQAAAAJ&hl=en. With the permission to use the information granted to the author by Google LLC on July 2, 2018.

Figure 9. "Anchalee Panigabutra-Roberts" (public version) last modified June 16, 2018. Bethesda, MD: ORCID, Inc. https://orcid.org/0000-0002-9333-1102 The author's use of this information per ORCID's Creative Commons CC0 Universal 1.0 Public Domain Dedication License.

Figures 10 & 11. "Eugene Garfield." *Virtual International Authority File*. Dublin, Ohio: OCLC, Inc. http://viaf.org/viaf/79414870

Figure 11. "Eugene Garfield." *ResearcherID.com*. Philadelphia, PA: Clarivate Analytics. http://www.researcherid.com/rid/A-1009-2008. The ResearcherID™ record is reproduced with permission from Clarivate Analytics © Clarivate Analytics 2018. ResearcherID™, Clarivate Analytics™ and the Clarivate Analytics logo are trademarks of Clarivate Analytics and its affiliated companies and are shown with permission. All rights reserved.

Figure 12. "*Workplace Culture in Academic Libraries: The Early 21st Century,*
edited by Kelly Blessinger and Paul L. Hrycaj. Oxford, UK : Chandos,
2013." *WorldCat.org.* Dublin, Ohio: OCLC, Inc. http://www.worldcat.
org/oclc/864899076

PART V:

EMANCIPATORY COLLABORATIONS

Chapter 15

WHAT'S IN A NAME? ARCHIVES FOR BLACK LIVES IN PHILADELPHIA AND THE IMPACT OF NAMES AND NAME AUTHORITIES IN ARCHIVAL DESCRIPTION

Alexis A. Antracoli and Katy Rawdon

Introduction

Archivists, working within a profession that is 87.7% white, have historically been focused on the description and naming of mostly white, male records creators and subjects.[1] This is largely a reflection of collecting practices that privilege the history of those who wield power in society. Describing and naming Black people and other marginalized groups, whether as creators or subjects of records, has often been an afterthought and sometimes has been undertaken without the appropriate respect and consideration for the communities who created or are described in the records. Practically speaking, the sheer volume of legacy finding aids describing primary source collections written over the course of many decades, and held in nearly every paper-based and electronic form imaginable, leads to difficult-to-access descriptive language. For this reason, remediating outdated language or pulling names for further analysis or authority work are rarely undertaken. Meanwhile,

---

1. A*CENSUS, Society of American Archivists, 2005, https://www2.archivists.org/initiatives/acensus-archival-census-education-needs-survey-in-the-united-states.

practices in archival collecting, processing, and description continue to generate oppressive language.

Specifically, the ability to perform name authority control within archival description is hampered by one or more factors: insufficient name information in archival collections; lack of established names in national authority databases for those found within a collection; lack of training or ability among archivists to establish name authority records; and the privileging of certain creators and subjects by processing archivists because of archival practice or their own personal biases. The lack of name description and name authority work for Black people represented in archival collections hampers research access, creates false silences by obscuring the names—and by extension, the existences—of Black people, and ultimately leads to the ongoing erasure and dehumanization of Black lives in our society's cultural memory and conscience.

Archives for Black Lives in Philadelphia (A4BLiP) is a loose association of about fifty archivists (primarily white and female) from the Philadelphia area, united by a concern for issues raised by the Black Lives Matter movement and a desire to contribute to professional conversations and actions related to combating racism in archives. In particular, A4BLiP approaches this work from the standpoint that it is white people's responsibility to fix the problems that they have created, and white archivists' responsibility to create an inclusive, equitable, and non-oppressive approach to archival work. The group has recently undertaken a racism audit project to provide guidance to white archivists on remediating harmful legacy description and creating inclusive, respectful, and equitable description moving forward. The authors of this article are two white women, both from the United States, who are members of A4BLiP. We attempt here to suggest an approach to name description that other archivists could use in making naming practices more equitable and inclusive.

This chapter begins with a literature review that explores the relationship between the archives and library professions' centering of whiteness and their implementation of description practices, including subject access, classification, and name authorities. It then introduces the A4BLiP group and its past and current projects, and describes the major challenges to implementing inclusive and ethical name description and name authority work in archival description. It concludes with preliminary proposals for implementing an anti-racist approach to name authorities and name access, taken from A4BLiP's draft recommendations for anti-racist archival description.

Literature Review

Recent scholarship in both archival and library science has addressed the concept of whiteness and how it has shaped the profession in ways that are relevant to the issue of names in archival description. However, the bulk of the literature on library work focuses on issues of subject headings and classification, with fewer addressing issues of naming, while literature on archival work has all but ignored names and name authorities altogether.

April Hathcock defines whiteness as "the socio-cultural differential of power and privilege that results from categories of race and ethnicity; it also stands as a marker for the privilege and power that acts to reinforce itself through hegemonic cultural practice that excludes all who are different."[2] Scholars and professionals in the field have examined the role of whiteness in shaping all aspects of the profession from how and why we acquire collections to the way we describe and provide access to them. Their critiques focus on the overwhelmingly white demographics of the archival and library professions, the lack of empathy for patrons who are people of color, the invisibility of people of color in our collections, and the traditional focus on ownership and acquisition by primarily white institutions over collaboration and partnership with communities of color. The most salient point of these critiques is that libraries and archives are far from being neutral spaces; instead they

---

2. April Hathcock, "White Librarianship in Blackface: Diversity Initiatives in LIS," *In the Library with the Lead Pipe*, October 2015, http://www.inthelibrarywiththeleadpipe.org/2015/lis-diversity.

usually support and center whiteness as the default identity, thereby marginalizing all other communities.[3]

The largest body of literature on the effect of whiteness on metadata and descriptive language focuses on the role of classification and subject analysis in library cataloging, and to a lesser extent in archival description. This exploration goes back at least to Sanford Berman's early criticism of Library of Congress Subject Headings in 1971.[4] More recent efforts to ameliorate the harmful legacy of practices influenced by colonialism and whiteness are the product of the years of ensuing research and practice to uncover structural racism in description and cataloging. Subject headings, in particular, continue to be problematic, not only because changes in outdated language are slow to appear,

---

3. Chris Bourg, "Debating y/our humanity, or Are Libraries Neutral?" *Feral Librarian* (blog), February 11, 2018, https://chrisbourg.wordpress.com/2018/02/11/debating-y-our-humanity-or-are-libraries-neutral/; Michelle Caswell, "Teaching to Dismantle White Supremacy in Archives," *Library Quarterly* 87, no. 3 (July 2017): 222-235, doi: 10.1086/692299; nina de jesus, "Locating the Library in Institutional Oppression," *In the Library with the Lead Pipe*, September, 2014, http://www.inthelibrary-withtheleadpipe.org/2014/locating-the-library-in-institutional-oppression/; Anthony W. Dunbar, "Introducing Critical Race Theory to Archival Discourse: Getting the Conversation Started," *Archival Science* 6, no. 1 (March 2006): 109–129; Livia Iacovino, "Rethinking Archival, Ethical and Legal Frameworks for records of Indigenous Australian Communities: A Participant Relationship Model of Rights and Responsibilities," *Archival Science* 10, no. 4 (December 2010): 353–372, doi: 10.1007/s10502-010-9120-3; Anna B. Loewenthal, "Comparing Representations of Race in Finding Aids Over Time" (master's thesis, University of North Carolina at Chapel Hill, 2015; Safiya Umoja Noble, "Google Search: Hyper-visibility as a Means of Rendering Black Women and Girls Invisible," *InVisible Culture* 19 (2013), http://ivc.lib.rochester.edu/google-search-hyper-visibility-as-a-means-of-rendering-black-women-and-girls-invisible/; Nicole Pagowsky and Niamh Wallace, "Black Lives Matter! Shedding Library Neutrality Rhetoric for Social Justice," *College & Research Libraries News* 76, no. 4 (2015): 196–214, http://crln.acrl.org/index.php/crlnews/article/view/9293/10373; Mario H. Ramirez, "Being Assumed Not to Be: A Critique of Whiteness as an Archival Imperative," *American Archivist* 78, no. 2 (Fall/Winter 2015): 339–356. doi: 10.17723/0360-9081.78.2.339; Carrie Wade, "Whiteness and the Myth of Neutrality," *Library Barbarian* (blog), February 13, 2018; Kellee E. Warren, "We Need These Bodies, But Not Their Knowledge: Black Women in the Archival Science Professions and Their Connection to the Archives of Enslaved Black Women in the French Antilles," *Library Trends* 64, no. 4 (2016): 776–794, doi: 10.1353/lib.2016.0012.

4. Sanford Berman, *Prejudices and Antipathies: A Tract on the LC Subject Heads Concerning People* (Metuchen, N.J.: Scarecrow Press, 1971).

but because the headings themselves appear to many as universal and unbiased.[5]

The literature on bias in subject classification generally focuses on the experiences of a single group or demographic, exploring the ways in which descriptive practices have "othered" people of color and other marginalized groups, and pushing for librarians and archivists to be explicit in their framing to dispel the myth of neutrality in the profession, make room for resources from outside the dominant culture, and create more inclusive description.[6]

---

5. Hope A. Olson, "The Power to Name: Representation in Library Catalogs," *Signs* 26, no. 3 (Spring 2001): 639–668.

6. Melissa Adler, "Case for Taxonomic Reparations," *Knowledge Organization* 43, no. 8 (2016): 630–640; Melissa Adler, "Classification Along the Color Line: Excavating Racism in the Stacks," *Journal of Critical Library and Information Studies* 1, no. 1 (2017): 1–32, doi: 10.24242/jclis.v1i1.17; Elvia Arroyo-Ramírez, "Invisible Defaults and Perceived Limitations: Processing the Juan Gelman Files," *On Archivy*, October 30, 2016, 2018, https://medium.com/on-archivy/invisible-defaults-and-perceived-limitations-processing-the-juan-gelman-files-4187fdd36759; Dorothy Berry, "Lost in Aggregation: Towards Inclusive Metadata and Descriptive Practices in Digital Collections" (working session at DPLA Fest, Chicago, Ill., April 21, 2017); Marisa Duarte and Miranda Belarde-Lewis, "Imagining: Creating Spaces for Indigenous Ontologies," *Cataloging and Classification Quarterly* 53, no. 5-6 (2015): 77–702, doi:10.1080/01639374.2015.1018396; Sharon Farnel, Sheila Laroque, Ian Bigelow, Denise Koufogiannakis, Anne Carr-Wiggin, Debbie Feisst, and Kayla Lar-Son, "Decolonizing Description: Changing Metadata in Response to the Truth and Reconciliation Commission" (presentation at Netspeed Library Technologies Conference, Edmonton, Alberta, Canada, October 3, 2017), doi: 10.7939/R3MS3KF68; Sharon Farnel, Sheila Laroque, Ian Bigelow, Denise Koufogiannakis, Anne Carr-Wiggin, Debbie Feisst, and Kayla Lar-Son. "Unsettling Our Practices: Decolonizing Description at the University of Alberta Libraries" (poster at Diversity by Design Symposium in Toronto, Ontario, Canada, September 14, 2017), doi: 10.7939/R3794175M; Iacovino, "Rethinking Archival, Ethical and Legal Frameworks for Records of Indigenous Australian Communities"; Sandra Littletree and Cheryl A. Metoyer, "Knowledge Organization from an Indigenous Perspective: The Mashantucket Pequot Thesaurus of American Indian Terminology Project," *Cataloging & Classification Quarterly* 53 (2015): 640–657; Kara Long, Santi Thompson, Sarah Potvin, and Monica Rivero, "The "Wicked Problem" of Neutral Description: Toward a Documentation Approach to Metadata Standards," *Cataloging & Classification Quarterly* 55, no. 3 (2017): 107–128, doi: 10.1080/01639374.2016.1278419; Mx A. Matienzo, "To Hell With Good Intentions: Linked Data, Community and the Power to Name," Mark A. Matienzo (website), February 11, 2016, http://matienzo.org/2016/to-hell-with-good-intentions/; K. J. Rawson, "Accessing Transgender // Desiring Queer(er?) Archival Logics," *Archivaria* 68 (Fall 2009): 123–140, https://archivaria.ca/index.php/archivaria/article/view/13234/14552; K. R. Roberto, "Inflexible Bodies: Metadata for Transgender

The past decade has seen increasingly active attempts to approach descriptive metadata in a non-oppressive fashion and to remediate legacy description. Anthony Dunbar was one of the earliest professionals to introduce critical race theory to the literature and to advocate for institutional policies that center trust and transparency and remedy past abuses.[7] Many efforts to introduce critical race theory to library practice since then have followed a collaborative model. Jon Newman describes a project in the United Kingdom focused on the possibility that "the single, neutral, authoritative and unattributed voice of the archive catalogue might be expanded, amplified and interpenetrated with a range of other, attributed voices."[8] The collaborative and participatory approach has found success as a way to produce more inclusive description of Indigenous communities.[9] Another approach is to create alternative taxonomies for classifying materials created by and about people of color, while the use of an intersectional approach has proved successful at the University of Texas at Austin.[10]

Identities," *Journal of Information Ethics* 20, no. 2 (2011): 56–64; Catelynne Sahadath, "Classifying the Margins: Using Alternative Classification Schemes to Empower Diverse and Marginalized Users," *Feliciter* 59, no. 3 (2013): 15.

7. Anthony Dunbar, "Introducing Critical Race Theory to Archival Discourse: Getting the Conversation Started," *Archival Science* 6, no. 1 (2006): 109–129.

8. Jon Newman, "Revisiting Archive Collections: Developing Models for Participatory Cataloguing," *Journal of the Society of Archivists* 33, no. 1 (2012): 58.

9. Iacovino, "Rethinking Archival, Ethical and Legal Frameworks for Records of Indigenous Australian Communities," Littletree and Metoyer, "Knowledge Organization from an Indigenous Perspective," Duarte and Belarde-Lewis, "Imagining: Creating Spaces for Indigenous Ontologies, "Decolonizing Descriptions: Finding, Naming and Changing the Relationship between Indigenous People, Libraries and Archives," OCLC webinar, November 6, 2017, https://www.youtube.com/watch?v=w4HGdWx2WY8, Farnel, Laroque, Bigelow, Koufogiannakis, Carr-Wiggin, Feisst, and Lar-Son, "Decolonizing Description"; Farnel, Laroque, Bigelow, Koufogiannakis, Carr-Wiggin, Feisst, and Lar-Son. "Unsettling Our Practices."; Raegan Swanson, "Adapting the Brian Deer Classification System for Aanischaaukamikw Cree Cultural Institute," *Cataloging & Classification Quarterly* 53, no. 5–6: *Indigenous Knowledge Organization* (2015): 568–579, doi: 10.1080/01639374.2015.009669

10. Molly O'Hagan Hardy, "The Practice of Everyday Cataloging: 'Blacks as Authors' and the Early American Bibliographic Record," *Past is Present* (American Antiquarian Society blog), June 29, 2017, http://pastispresent.org/2017/good-sources/the-practice-of-everyday-cataloging-black-bibliography-and-the-early-american-bibli-

While the issues of classification systems and subject analysis dominate most of the literature on how whiteness has shaped descriptive metadata in archives and libraries, the problem of naming in particular has also been explored. This body of literature, while smaller and more recent, has prompted LIS professionals to begin examining how name authorities can also center whiteness and "otherize" various marginalized communities. Heather Lea Moulaison describes a study examining a group of authority records to see which records contain the expanded attributes allowed and/or required under Resource Description & Access (RDA) rules—additional information such as gender, occupation, associated place, and language. She found that in fact few records made use of the RDA attributes, and those that did include expanded identity description tended to be records for "English-speakers, males, and those associated with universities in some way."[11] Frank Exner, Little Bear examines North American Indian names, which often follow multiple naming conventions and often do not follow the Western naming format conventions most used in the Library of Congress Name Authority File (LCNAF); he notes that "North American Indian personal names require special attention in authority control and cataloging because they do not necessarily follow rules developed for European names."[12]

As in general librarianship, archival work has traditionally viewed itself as ideally neutral and unbiased. Recent professional discussion has, however, thoroughly questioned the neutrality of archives and

---

ographic-record/, ALCTS Metadata Interest Group, "Diverse and Inclusive Metadata: Developing Cultural Competencies in Descriptive Practices" (presentation at the American Library Association Annual Conference, Orlando, Florida, June 2016), Kristen Hogan, "'Breaking Secrets' in the Catalog: Proposing the Black Queer Studies Collection at the University of Texas at Austin," *Progressive Librarian* 34 (Fall 2010): 50–57, http://www.progressivelibrariansguild.org/PL/PL34_35.pdf.Adler, "Case for Taxonomic Reparations," 632; Hogan, "'Breaking Secrets' in the Catalog."

11. Heather Lea Moulaison, "Authors and Authorities in Post-RDA Library Systems: A Case Study," (paper presented at IFLA WLIC 2014, Lyon, France, August 16–22, 2014), http://codabox.org/147/2/086-moulaison-en.pdf.

12. Frank Exner, Little Bear, "North American Indian Personal Names in National Bibliographies," in *Radical Cataloging: Essays at the Front*, ed. K. R. Roberto (Jefferson, N.C.: McFarland, April 2008), 150-164.

archivists. The works of Terry Cook, Wendy Duff and Verne Harris, Bergis Jules, Stacie Williams, Sam Winn, and Jennifer Douglas, among many others, have explored the ways in which records creation, acquisition, appraisal, and description are anything but neutral. Tradition is difficult to overcome, however, and the ideals of the unchanged archival collection left in its original order, objectively reflecting the recordkeeping practices of the creator, as well as the myth of the objective archivist whose work simply exposes records without impacting them, pervade much of archival work.

Sam Winn asserts the impossibility of neutrality in archival work, as archivists are unable—as all people are—to escape the societal biases in which they are steeped. The danger, she says, is when we leave these biases unexamined, and unquestioningly accept the hegemonic default.[13] Sharon Larade and Johanne Pelletier raised the issue of the conscious use of language in archival description, exploring archivists' reluctance to change their practices, including linguistic practices—again, leaning heavily on the specter of neutrality—while recognizing the importance of non-exclusionary language.[14]

Bergis Jules explicitly links the whiteness of archival work to physical violence against Black people: "The work we do as archivists, as librarians, as digital preservationists, have [sic] real consequences for marginalized people because who is remembered and how they're remembered dictates who gets violence perpetrated against them. Black bodies are either erased from the historical record or distorted in the historical record before we're shot in the street like Rekia Boyd and Trayvon Martin. That's partly what makes it ok to a large segment of the American public. That erasure from records, cultural spaces, and mass media are partly what allow people to accept absurd justifications

---

13. Sam Winn, "The Hubris of Neutrality in Archives," *On Archivy,* April 24, 2017, https://medium.com/on-archivy/the-hubris-of-neutrality-in-archives-8df6b523fe9f.

14. Sharon P. Larade and Johanne M. Pelletier, "Mediating in a Neutral Environment: Gender-Inclusive or Neutral Language in Archival Descriptions," *Archivaria* 35 (Spring 1993): 99–109, https://archivaria.ca/index.php/archivaria/article/view/11889/12842.

for killing us."[15] Erasing or distorting the histories of Black people from the archival record, whether through collecting practices or descriptive practices, reinforces the dehumanization that leads to widespread anti-Black violence such as police killings, mass incarceration, and gentrification—each of which, in turn, have been the subject of analysis of their effects on Black people and the preservation of their histories.[16]

Emily Drabinski, while writing from a librarian's perspective, identifies an issue closely related to archival practice. She notes the problematic nature of hierarchical classification, stating that hierarchies privilege a single aspect of a subject, while making that privilege appear logical and neutral.[17] The same critique applies to archival description, as it is very intentionally hierarchical in nature, privileging the exposure of creators and collectors—those at the top of the hierarchical provenancial heap—over creators and subjects who fall for various reasons further down on the hierarchy. This is directly related to a core principle of archival work, that of provenance, described in the SAA Glossary as "a fundamental principle of archives, referring to the individual, family, or organization that created or received the items in a collection. The principle of provenance or the *respect des fonds* dictates that records of different

15. Bergis Jules, "Confronting Our Failure of Care Around the Legacies of Marginalized People in the Archives," *On Archivy*, November 11, 2016, https://medium.com/on-archivy/confronting-our-failure-of-care-around-the-legacies-of-marginalized-people-in-the-archives-dc4180397280.

16. Walidah Imarisha, "Keynote Address," Liberated Archive Forum, Society of American Archivists Annual Meeting, Portland, OR, August 22, 2017, http://www.walidah.com/blog/2017/8/22/transcript-of-walidahs-liberated-archives-keynote; Teressa Raiford, "#ArchivesforBlackLives: Archivists Respond to Black Lives Matter" panel, Liberated Archive Forum, Society of American Archivists Annual Meeting, Portland, OR, August 22, 2017; Society of American Archivists, "Issue Brief: Police Mobile Camera Footage as a Public Record, November 2017, https://www2.archivists.org/statements/issue-brief-police-mobile-camera-footage-as-a-public-record; Jarrett Drake and Stacie Williams, "Power to the People: Documenting Police Violence in Cleveland," *Journal of Critical Library and Information Studies* 1, no. 2 (2017): 1-27; Jarrett M. Drake, "Insurgent Citizens: The Manufacture of Police Records in Post-Katrina New Orleans and Its Implications for Human Rights," *Archival Science* 14, no. 3-4 (October 2014): 365-380.

17. Emily Drabinski, "Teaching the Radical Catalog," in *Radical Cataloging: Essays at the Front*, ed. K. R. Roberto (Jefferson, N.C.: McFarland, April 2008), 198–205, http://www.emilydrabinski.com/wp-content/uploads/2012/06/drabinski_radcat.pdf.

origins (provenance) be kept separate to preserve their context."[18] The provenance and context of records supplies much of their meaning, however, the concept of records-source-as-creator—who gets to be a collection creator/collector/main entry—determines whose names are deemed most important. Jarrett M. Drake questions the principle of provenance as a relic of colonialism and as a principle, asserting that the "patriarchal origins of provenance" embed themselves inevitably in archival description through the emphasis on the collection creator. Because of the legacy of colonialism inherent in the issues of who is able to generate, control, and transfer archival collections to archival repositories, the creators are more likely to be "wealthy, white, cisgendered and heterosexual men." The resulting provenance-based description serves "to valorize and venerate white western masculinity."[19]

The archives community is beginning to think beyond the traditional concept of provenance. The International Council on Archives' new Records in Contexts Conceptual Model (RiC-CM), may eventually prove useful in bridging the divide between traditional provenance-based methods of understanding context and new, more expansive ideas. RiC-CM is designed to take advantage of the semantic web and allow archivists to move from multilevel to multidimensional description. The model notes "While almost all archivists accept the theoretical validity of Provenance, many have become increasingly self-conscious and self-critical about the role that archivists and the application of archival principles play in what is remembered and how it is remembered."[20] RiC-CM provides a way to honor both the traditional application of provenance, while also using new communication technologies to accommodate new understandings

---

18. "Provenance," SAA Glossary, https://www2.archivists.org/glossary/terms/p/provenance.

19. Jarrett M. Drake, "RadTech Meets RadArch: Towards a New Principle for Archives and Archival Description," *On Archivy*, April 6, 2016, https://medium.com/on-archivy/radtech-meets-radarch-towards-a-new-principle-for-archives-and-archival-description-568f133e4325#.6w1a50egi.

20. International Council on Archives, *Records in Contexts*, September 2016, p. 6.

of archival context that represent the many contexts in which records are created and exist.

Little has been written about names in archival description, and even less on name authorities and archives. *Describing Archives: A Content Standard* (DACS), the primary descriptive standard used by archivists in the United States, contains a section on archival authority records. Here the importance of names to archival description is clearly stated: "The structure and content of archival materials cannot be completely understood without some knowledge of the context in which they were created." Without knowing who created or otherwise contributed to a collection of archival materials, the records lose meaning.[21]

Additionally, a simple authorized form of name is not sufficient for archival description. DACS requires not only a name, but biographical or historical information to provide context to the persons, individuals, or families themselves. DACS also emphasizes the usefulness of authority records systems as co-equal with collection descriptions. The standard notes that the model provided by the International Council on Archives' General International Standard for Archival Description (ISAD(G)) is the creation of standardized authority records maintained separately and embedded within archival description, rather than simply incorporating names as text strings into description. DACS declares that elements common to bibliographic authority records and archival authority records include a standardized access point, related or variant names, and information about the establishment and maintenance of the record. But DACS states that archival authority records must also include additional context and relationship information. Of course, with the implementation of RDA for the LCNAF and the increasing inclusion of name authorities from archival materials within the LCNAF, archival and bibliographic authorities are perhaps not so far apart.

One specific area of naming in archival description that has received attention is the issue of documenting names of enslaved people. In 1972,

---

21. *Describing Archives: A Content Standard* (DACS), 2nd ed. (Chicago: Society of American Archivists, 2013), 87.

Carole Merritt interrogated the damaging idea that "the Black past is unknowable." In her discussion of researching the history of enslaved people, she describes the types of records—census records, property and estate records, tax and court records—through which the lives of enslaved persons can be studied. She notes the issue of surnames of enslaved people, in that they often changed over time, and frequently (although not always) were the name of a current or former slave owner.[22] David E. Paterson proposes a system to include slaves' names in finding aids in the format: "[slaveholder last name, slaveholder first name] slave's first name/last name", i.e. "[Walter, Allen M.] Ginny Stamper," regardless of whether the enslaved person used the slaveholder's name in life. An exception would be allowed for "well known" slaves whose full names are well-documented.[23] This proposed solution dramatically and unfortunately reflects the tension between the archivist's desire to provide access to under-documented people within historical records with the violence of inflicting the white slaveholder's identity onto an enslaved person. It is this type of "solution" the authors of this chapter wish to avoid, instead seeking respectful and non-racist alternatives.

Archives for Black Lives in Philadelphia (A4BLiP)

Archives for Black Lives in Philadelphia (A4BLiP) was organized in August 2016. The group drew inspiration from the social justice work of many individuals in the field, including but not limited to Michelle Caswell, Stacie Williams, Bergis Jules, April Hathcock, Mario Ramirez, Samantha Winn, and Eira Tansey, but the main call to action came from Jarrett Drake's talk at the June 2016 ALA Annual Conference. He called on archivists to confront their own complicity in upholding structural inequalities and to build trust with communities being documented based

---

22. Carole Merritt, "Slave Family Records: An Abundance of Material," *Georgia Archive* 6, no. 1 (Spring 1978): 16–21, https://digitalcommons.kennesaw.edu/georgia_archive/vol6/iss1/12.

23. David E. Paterson, "A Perspective on Indexing Slaves' Names," *American Archivist* 64 (Spring/Summer 2001): 132–142, doi: 10.17723/aarc.64.1.th18g8t6282h4283.

on principles of allyship.[24] A4BLiP's name was derived from one of the hashtags Drake had created earlier in the year, #ArchivesForBlackLives.

More than a dozen archivists attended the initial A4BLiP meeting. As of February 2018, there are fifty-five members. Members are primarily white women, which reflects the demographics of the archival profession, as well as A4BLiP's belief that white archivists should actively do the work to create a more inclusive profession. Most members are employed at academic institutions rather than smaller cultural institutions or community archives.[25] The group began work by collaboratively creating a draft of an official position statement, via editing and comments within a Google Doc and feedback provided via email.

On January 9, 2017, the finalized statement was released on GitHub.[26] A4BLiP contacted formal and informal archivist groups to announce this initial document. The Concerned Archivists Alliance promoted the statement via social media, and in May, A4BLiP presented to Philadelphia Area Consortium of Special Collections Libraries (PACSCL). A4BLiP requested that one local Philadelphia area organization, the Delaware Valley Archivists Group (DVAG), formally endorse the statement, but they declined to do so. They did link to the statement from their website, with a preface explaining, "A4BLiP is not affiliated with DVAG, although we do encourage our members to read their statement and consider the issues it raises." Later, both DVAG and PACSCL agreed to fund refreshments for A4BLiP processing events. Although the overall reaction to the statement and to A4BLiP in general was positive, some

---

24. Jarrett M. Drake, "Expanding #ArchivesForBlackLives to Traditional Archival Repositories," *On Archivy*, June 27, 2016, https://medium.com/on-archivy/expanding-archivesforblacklives-to-traditional-archival-repositories-b88641e2daf6.

25. Rather than being a structured professional organization, A4BLiP is intentionally a loose affiliation of individuals who do most of their work remotely. Depending on inclination and availability, an archivist's involvement at any given time may wax or wane. The group's email list serves as a way to discuss issues of interest, including the race for Philadelphia District Attorney; conference and interest group announcements; discussions and formal talks about police body cameras, algorithm bias, and predictive policing; and a member's announcement of her addition of the "Black lives matter movement" heading to the Subject Authority Cooperative Program (SACO).

26. Rappel110 A4BLiP repository, GitHub, https://github.com/rappel110/A4BLiP.

archivists were unsympathetic, disparaging the group's aims or objecting to archivists involving themselves in politics as archivists. An early draft of the statement allowed for anonymous commenting, and reactions included rejection of white archivists' role in enforcing white supremacy (and negative comments on the use of the term "white supremacy" in general), expressions of negativity toward the Black Lives Matter movement, and concern that the statement weakened archivists' role as "objective" actors on archival collections.

A session about A4BLiP was part of the programming for the Liberated Archives Forum at the July 2017 Society of American Archivists conference in Portland. The "#ArchivesForBlackLives: Archivists Respond to Black Lives Matter" session provided an opportunity to discuss not just the statement but also the process by which it was created. In keeping with the theme of the Forum, Terry Baxter facilitated the pairing of three A4BLiP archivists with a community member: Teressa Raiford, a prominent voice for #BlackLivesMatter and founder of Don't Shoot Portland, who spoke after the A4BLiP co-presenters. Later in the day, she delivered a powerful closing statement on the importance of community memory, access, and control of archives.[27]

In August 2017, A4BLiP began discussing future goals. A poll of members indicated interest in two projects: partnering with community archives and conducting racism audits in repository catalogs and finding aids. A4BLiP created two working groups to focus on these areas. The community archives group's first project involved material collected by Rasheeda Phillips, an attorney, activist, and co-founder of the multidisciplinary Black Quantum Futurism Collective. Her collected material includes records of the Brewerytown Sharswood Community Civic Association (BSCCA), a one-month Community Futures Lab residency, and a zine library.[28] Phillips planned to donate the material to

27. An audio recording of the presentation, closing remarks, and the majority of conference sessions are available from SAA. https://www.pathlms.com/saa/events/941.

28. "Community Futurisms: Time & Memory in North Philly—Community Futures Lab," *Black Quantum Futurism* (website), https://www.blackquantumfuturism.com/community-futurisms.

the BSCCA in the hopes that it would serve as the kernel for an accessible community archives. In mid-December, four A4BLiP members visited the home of Rasheedah Phillips to survey the collection. They established that the collection could be collectively processed in a short amount of time. A "Processing Flash Mob" was scheduled for March 31, 2018, at the William Way LGBT Community Center, where volunteers began processing and the creation of a finding aid. In the fall of 2017, the racism audit group began work, which is described further below.

Names, Name Authorities, and Names of Black People in Archival Description

Working with names is a challenging aspect of archival description. The sheer number of names appearing in any given collection means that not every name can be included in higher-level description such as a biographical note, nor can they be made more prominent as a controlled access heading. Even knowing the names of those documented in archival collections is frequently difficult, as name forms are often partial, or undifferentiated, or must be transcribed as written. In addition to the practical difficulties of identifying names in archival collections, name authority work is hampered by a number of factors: the history of privileging published authors and subjects in name authority systems such as the LCNAF; barriers to archivists contributing to those systems; and issues of who is and who is not considered "important" to name within collection description, a factor often influenced by the archival principle of provenance.

The absence from name authority systems of the names of Black people represented in archival collections is a barrier to important research about the historical lives of Black people.[29] More diverse and

---

29. For one example, see April Armstrong's blog post on Princeton University's African American alumni in the 19th century. April C. Armstrong, "What Archival Silence Conceals—and Reveals. Recovering Princeton University's 19th-Century African American Graduate Alumni," *Mudd Manuscript Library Blog,* February 7, 2018, https://blogs.princeton.edu/mudd/2018/02/what-archival-silence-conceals-and-reveals-recovering-princeton-universitys-19th-century-african-american-graduate-alumni.

appropriate subject headings will do much to increase research access to a more accurate historical narrative, but individually naming people of color is also necessary to provide adequate access to records of marginalized communities. Those who are individually named are deemed important, and those whose names are established and controlled in authority systems such as SNAC[30] and the LCNAF are exponentially more visible and more easily researched than those who are not. Particularly in a discovery environment transitioning toward linked data, where an established name heading will connect to resources, entities, and relationships, those established headings vastly amplify the voices and stories of those whose names have been selected for inclusion. The lack of representation of Black people in name description and name authority systems skews the historical record toward white culture and people, effectively creating false silences. This silence and the privileging of certain names over others serves to reinforce the ongoing cultural erasure of Black lives, which in turn, as Bergis Jules states, enables the ongoing dehumanization of and violence against Black people.[31]

Armstrong explores how archives and archival description hid the existence of African American graduate students at Princeton during the late 19th and early 20th centuries. She describes how, even though these students were listed in some University publications as well as the Board of Trustees minutes, they were difficult to find. Navigating the University's records required laborious searches of outside sources which frequently did not mention individuals' names. Thus, while many of these men are not completely lost to time, the archival record and the way it is described means that recovering their histories is difficult and requires extensive research.

30. The archival community has begun to explore the creation of name authority records via the Encoded Archival Context-Corporate bodies, Persons, and Families (EAC-CPF) standard and the Social Networks and Archival Contexts (SNAC) project. EAC-CPF is an international standard for encoding information about the creators of records. The SNAC project is a joint effort by the United States National Archives and Records Administration, the University of Virginia, and the California Digital Library to develop a cooperative program for maintaining information about the people, organizations, and families documented by records. Similar to the Library of Congress's NACO program, it is designed as a cooperative cataloging program that archivists at various institutions can contribute to after receiving training. Once records are added to the SNAC web portal, collections related to the individual, family, or organization are connected through the EAC-CPF records on the site.

31. Bergis Jules, "Confronting Our Failure of Care Around the Legacies of Marginalized People in the Archives."

As described in the literature review above, librarians and archivists have been grappling with the issues of whiteness and neutrality (or lack thereof) in the profession. Whiteness—the socially constructed normalization and privileging of white culture—not only permeates all efforts to catalog and describe archival and library materials, but by its nature makes biases in that description difficult to see. The invisible imposition of whiteness on our work represents all identities not described above as "other," setting them apart and, frequently, rendering them invisible. Archivists have long claimed the ability to be neutral, as a means to objectively provide access to collections without influencing them or skewing their interpretation. However, the very foundations of libraries and archives are based on a society steeped in whiteness, as are the librarians and archivists employed within. While much of the examination of whiteness and the biases in library and archives work within the professional literature has focused on collecting biases, classification, and subject analysis, there is room to examine specifically the role of name description and name authorities within archival work. Names are important. Those who are named are empowered, and those who remain nameless are at best marginalized, and at worst erased. The exclusion of people's names from descriptions of historical records is not merely a barrier to scholarly research. Rather, it is both a symptom and cause of the violence of whiteness in our society.

There are several issues at work within archival description and name authority work that serve to privilege the naming of the white creators, collectors, and subjects over the naming of Black people represented in archival collections. One is the privileging of published authors and subjects of published works in the LCNAF. The history of who is published—as author or as subject—is, unsurprisingly, largely white and male. The historical emphasis on published works and their associated names privileges the types of people who have tended to publish works or have works published about them—white, male, wealthy and/ or educated. People less likely to appear in published works, even if they frequently appear in unpublished primary source materials such as archival collections, are less likely to be included in the LCNAF. While many people of color and members of other marginalized groups often appear as creators or subjects within archival collections, the unpublished nature of those materials means that their names have not been as readily contributed to the NAF. This is beginning to change as the NAF broadens its range of included names; however, as Moulaison's study demonstrates, the focus still remains white and male.[32]

Archival collections provide a diverse pool of names for inclusion in the LCNAF. In fact, Moulaison notes that most current authority records contributed by NACO-trained librarians are created during the process of original cataloging, that is, cataloging of materials not already cataloged by another institution: "the materials they are cataloging are unique, otherwise there would be cataloging copy available."[33] For many libraries, the bulk of this material is likely to be special collection materials, including archival collections. However, few archivists are trained to contribute records to the NAF, and the differences between cataloging and archival processing—not to mention the many and increasing demands for archivists to do more with less—raises barriers for archivists who may wish to do so. Many archivists have little to no training in MARC or RDA, making the participation in NACO training a daunting proposition. Coordinating with NACO-trained cataloging staff to contribute names from archival collections can be one solution; however, this assumes a certain level of institutional staffing and willingness among staff to undertake this work, and most likely an academic setting.

The efforts of archivists to implement archives-centric name authority systems face similar problems. The initial contributors to the SNAC portal as well as the initial member institutions are mostly large research universities, national archives, and well-resourced museums and research institutes in Europe and North America.[34] With the exception of Howard

32. Moulaison, "Authors and Authorities in Post-RDA Library Systems."

33. Moulaison, "Authors and Authorities in Post-RDA Library Systems," 4.

34. "Data Contributors," Social Networks and Archival Context website, http://snaccooperative.org/static/about/datacontrib.html; "2015-2017 Member Institutions," *Social Networks and Archival Context* (website), http://snaccooperative.org/static/about/members_cooperative.html.

University, all of the initial contributors are institutions likely to center whiteness and white people in their collecting and description. Another way in which newer projects such as SNAC carry forward the biases within the structure of our profession is in the use of LC subject headings—as established above, often problematic—in many SNAC records, such as those that refer to Indigenous people in North America as Indians. This practice serves only to reinforce the racism and colonialism of name authorities. Additionally, the time, training, and staffing levels needed to contribute to SNAC make it difficult for smaller repositories with fewer staff and less funding to be active contributors. This can exclude community archives or smaller repositories which specifically collect records of marginalized groups, just as surely as it creates a focus on name authorities only for published authors and subjects. At this point in the development of the project, it's unclear whether SNAC's approach to cooperative archival name authorities will address the problems with racism in archival naming practices.

As mentioned in the literature review, archival practice itself creates barriers to increasing representation of people of color, particularly though the principle and practice of provenance. In archival work, the context of records is as important as the informational content of the records. Through maintaining provenance, archivists hope to allow the original context of records to be understood by patrons, which is crucial in archival research. For example, information about enslaved persons is often found in plantation records, but those records are described with a focus on the slaveholder, who was the creator. While this provides important context for understanding the records and information that appears within them, the archival emphasis on context can also obscure and erase the human beings described as subjects in those records. The narrative of the slaveholder is preserved by archival description, but the lived experience of the enslaved person may be hidden or erased.[35]

---

35. Of course, provenance is not always straightforward. Records may have changed hands multiple times prior to arriving at an archival repository. Records may have been lost, or intentionally disposed of. Former owners may not have thought certain documents to be worth preserving--particularly those documenting marginalized people. In

The practical application of provenance in archival work results in an emphasis on the name of the originating source in both the collection title and as author/main entry. (One moderate exception to this is a group of records by one individual collected by another, which results in both names in the title: the Arthur Langley Searles Collection of H. P. Lovecraft Research Files, for example). It is important, however, to think about who has traditionally been empowered to collect archival materials, or create them, as well as whose materials have been collected. Just as published authors and those who have works published about them have traditionally been white and male, so too has it traditionally been white men whose papers have been collected, who have been at the head of organizations whose records have been preserved, and who have had the means and the sense of self-importance to create records of their activities in the first place.

The hierarchical nature of archival description places the name of the records originator or collector at the top of the descriptive pyramid, with all other names falling in layers underneath, with those who are least well-represented by the records in a collection at the bottom. Since the records are ideally maintained as the originator/creator left them, it is that person's or organization's biases and preferences that determine who has been documented and in what order. Description can do much to lift up the names of those who may not have originally been deemed important; however, this requires archivists to think closely about which names those might be, and how best to provide name access to those who according to traditional archival description would not have warranted naming.

A4BLiP Racism Audit Project

The racism audit group drew together members of A4BLiP interested in exploring racism against Black people inherent in archival description

---

these ways, provenance can sometimes be less illuminating that archivists might wish, while at the same time continuing to erase the history of marginalized people.

and the ways in which white archivists could develop anti-racist, inclusive description practices. The group began meeting regularly in the fall of 2017 via conference calls.

The group first created a bibliography of approximately eighty-two potentially relevant journal articles, blog posts, conference presentations, webinars, and bibliographies. They then focused on dividing up the resources to determine whether each resource was relevant, and, if it was, to create a brief abstract. This resulted in twelve resources being declared irrelevant or only somewhat relevant, leaving the group with seventy resources to draw on in developing best practices.

The initial bibliography was quite broad, addressing more than just description-related concerns. While many of the resources focused on name authorities, subject classification, and the process of archival description, others addressed the role of whiteness, white supremacy, and structural inequality in shaping the archival profession, as well as gender and sexuality issues. These wide-ranging readings helped provide a broad context for the work. By contextualizing the project in this way, the group is able to show how the work on anti-racist descriptive practices informs the project of creating a more ethical, inclusive, and anti-oppressive approach to archival description as a whole.

After completing the review of resources, the larger group divided into two smaller groups to work on best practices. One group focused on concerns related to archival theory about description, such as organizing collections by provenance. The other group focused on creating a recommended practices document for anti-racist archival description, addressing the specific language applied to Black people in finding aids, subject headings traditionally used to describe Black people and communities, and the use of name authorities as applied to Black people. While this document encompasses subject classification, language use, voice and style, titles, and collaboration with Black communities, several points focus specifically on names, including the following recommendations:

- Consider the extent to which describing a person by name is an act of affirming humanity.

- At the same time, when describing living creators or subjects, consider that description has the potential to put people from groups already subject to inordinate amounts of surveillance at greater risk.

- Revisit legacy description to provide better name access for Black people where possible, including names of subjects as well as creators of records.

- Acknowledge the limits of provenance-based description, and describe the subjects of collections documenting oppressed or marginalized peoples at least to the extent that you describe the creators or collectors of those collections.

- Recognize that the naming of enslaved persons within archival description has traditionally been ignored in favor of the naming of slave owners. If, for example, you have item-level description for a deed of purchase for an enslaved person and the seller and purchaser's names are included, include the name of the person being sold. Humanize these documents from all sides—not just from the side of the creator.

- Use terminology that Black people use to describe themselves, while recognizing that the Black community is not a monolith, and different people will have different and sometimes conflicting preferences.

- If you ask people from marginalized communities to help with description, be respectful of their time/labor and provide compensation. Do your homework first, and do not ask others to provide information you can easily find yourself. Pay them for their work.

- Stop writing flowery, valorizing biographical notes for predominantly white male collection creators. Remove and refrain from including evaluative terms like "preeminent," "renowned," or "genius" that serve to praise collection creators. Ask yourself: Does including this piece of information help users better understand the records? Evaluate existing biographical notes for aggrandizing language and remove it.

While A4BLiP's racism audit project is focused specifically on archives, many of the best practices could apply in other settings. Libraries and museums could benefit from some of the more general suggestions, such as considering referring to a person by name as affirming of his/her humanity and respecting the time and efforts of marginalized communities. Some of the more specific suggestions regarding how biographical notes are constructed may also prove helpful in other settings with modification to meet the needs of other types of organizations.

Once the racism audit group has finalized its recommendations for anti-racist archival description, the group plans to circulate the best practices to Black communities and Black archivists for feedback. Our goal with this practice is to ensure that any best practices we circulate to the wider community will truly advance the goal of anti-racist archival description, rather than reinforce the structural power of white archivists to determine standards for what anti-racist archival description should look like. We recognize that as white archivists, we have a responsibility to do this work, but also to avoid imposing our view of what qualifies as anti-racist description of affected communities without dialogue and collaboration. Additionally, A4BLiP is also planning to raise funds to compensate reviewers for their work, in compliance with the best practices. The group is currently discussing not only how we will raise the funds, but also how we will structure compensation and provide transparency about what we pay for and how much we pay for that work.

Conclusion

While name authorities, name access, and archival description have too often ignored and erased Black people from the archival record, the problem is not irreparable. The work of scholars and practitioners over the past two decades has helped illuminate the scope and contours of the problem. Naming practices and name authority work in archival description have traditionally been employed in an oppressive fashion that centers white people and their history; however, more recent work has begun to show how archival professionals can begin to overcome this tradition. These strategies include remediation of racist legacy description and proactively working to make new description inclusive and anti-racist; cooperative description; and a rethinking and critical analysis of the concept of the influence of provenance on descriptive practices. Most importantly, perhaps, archivists should develop an empathetic approach to description that considers the harms inflicted on Black people in our use of naming practices. We should strive for a future in which the concerns, identities, and cultures of all communities are represented in our application of name authorities and name access with the same attention, respect, and care historically reserved for white people.

Acknowledgements

The authors would like to acknowledge the readers of draft versions of this chapter, who generously volunteered their time and provided insightful and essential feedback and criticisms: Anastasia Chiu, Jarrett M. Drake, Fobazi M. Ettarh, Violet B. Fox, Margery Sly, Ruth Kitchin Tillman, and others who chose not to be named—as is their right.

Bibliography

A*CENSUS, Society of American Archivists, 2005. https://www2.archivists.org/initiatives/acensus-archival-census-education-needs-survey-in-the-united-states.

Adler, Melissa. "Case for Taxonomic Reparations." *Knowledge Organization* 43, no. 8 (2016): 630–40.

Adler, Melissa. "Classification Along the Color Line: Excavating Racism in the Stacks." *Journal of Critical Library and Information Studies* 1, no. 1 (2017): 1–32. doi: 10.24242/jclis.v1i1.17.

ALCTS Metadata Interest Group. "Diverse and Inclusive Metadata: Developing Cultural Competencies in Descriptive Practices." Presentation at the American Library Association Annual Conference, Orlando, Florida, June 2016.

Armstrong, April C. "What Archival Silence Conceals—and Reveals: Recovering Princeton University's 19th-Century African American Graduate Alumni." *Mudd Manuscript Library Blog*, February 7, 2018. https://blogs.princeton.edu/mudd/2018/02/what-archival-silence-conceals-and-reveals-recovering-princeton-universitys-19th-century-african-american-graduate-alumni.

Arroyo-Ramírez, Elvia. "Invisible Defaults and Perceived Limitations: Processing the Juan Gelman Files." *On Archivy*. October 30, 2016. https://medium.com/on-archivy/invisible-defaults-and-perceived-limitations-processing-the-juan-gelman-files-4187fdd36759.

Berman, Sanford. *Prejudices and Antipathies: A Tract on the LC Subject Heads Concerning People*. Metuchen, N.J.: Scarecrow Press, 1971.

Berry, Dorothy. "Lost in Aggregation: Towards Inclusive Metadata and Descriptive Practices in Digital Collections." Working session at DPLA Fest, Chicago, Ill., April 21, 2017.

Bourg, Chris. "Debating y/our humanity, or Are Libraries Neutral?" *Feral Librarian* (blog). February 11, 2018. https://chrisbourg.wordpress.com/2018/02/11/debating-y-our-humanity-or-are-libraries-neutral/.

Caswell, Michelle. "Teaching to Dismantle White Supremacy in Archives." *Library Quarterly* 87, no. 3 (July 2017): 222-35. doi: 10.1086/692299.

"Community Futurisms: Time & Memory in North Philly—Community Futures Lab." Black Quantum Futurism website. https://www.blackquantumfuturism.com/community-futurisms.

de jesus, nina. "Locating the Library in Institutional Oppression." *In the Library with the Lead Pipe*. September, 2014. http://www.inthelibrary-withthe- leadpipe.org/2014/locating-the-library-in-institutional-oppression/.

"Decolonizing Descriptions: Finding, Naming and Changing the Relationship between Indigenous People, Libraries and Archives." OCLC webinar. November 6, 2017. https://www.youtube.com/watch?v=w4HGdWx2WY8.

Drabinski, Emily. "Teaching the Radical Catalog." In *Radical Cataloging: Essays at the Front*, edited by K. R. Roberto, 198–205. Jefferson, N.C.: McFarland, April 2008. http://www.emilydrabinski.com/wp-content/uploads/2012/06/drabinski_radcat.pdf.

Drake, Jarrett M. "Expanding #ArchivesForBlackLives to Traditional Archival Repositories." *On Archivy*. June 27, 2016. https://medium.com/on-archivy/expanding-archivesforblacklives-to-traditional-archival-repositories-b88641e2daf6.

Drake, Jarrett M., "Insurgent Citizens: The Manufacture of Police Records in Post-Katrina New Orleans and Its Implications for Human Rights," *Archival Science* 14:3-4 (October 2014): 365-380.

Drake, Jarrett M. "RadTech Meets RadArch: Towards a New Principle for Archives and Archival Description." *On Archivy*. April 6, 2016. https://medium.com/on-archivy/radtech-meets-radarch-towards-a-new-principle-for-archives-and-archival-description-568f133e4325#.6w1a50egi.

Drake, Jarrett M. and Stacie Williams, "Power to the People: Documenting Police Violence in Cleveland," *Journal of Critical Library and Information Studies*, 1:2 (2017): 1-27.

Duarte, Marisa Elena, and Miranda Belarde-Lewis. "Imagining: Creating Spaces for Indigenous Ontologies." *Cataloging and Classification Quarterly* 53, no. 5-6 (2015): 677–702. doi:10.1080/01639374.2015.1018396.

Dunbar, Anthony W. "Introducing Critical Race Theory to Archival Discourse: Getting the Conversation Started." *Archival Science* 6, no. 1 (March 2006): 109–129.

EAC-CPF website. http://eac.staatsbibliothek-berlin.de/.

Frank Exner, Little Bear. "North American Indian Personal Names in National Bibliographies." In *Radical Cataloging: Essays at the Front*, edited by K. R. Roberto, 150-164. Jefferson, N.C.: McFarland, 2008.

Farnel, Sharon, Sheila Laroque, Ian Bigelow, Denise Koufogiannakis, Anne Carr-Wiggin, Debbie Feisst, and Kayla Lar-Son. "Decolonizing Description: Changing Metadata in Response to the Truth and

Reconciliation Commission." Presentation at Netspeed Library Technologies Conference, Edmonton, Alberta, Canada, October 3, 2017. doi: 10.7939/R3MS3KF68.

Farnel, Sharon, Sheila Laroque, Ian Bigelow, Denise Koufogiannakis, Anne Carr-Wiggin, Debbie Feisst, and Kayla Lar-Son. "Unsettling Our Practices: Decolonizing Description at the University of Alberta Libraries." Poster at Diversity by Design Symposium in Toronto, Ontario, Canada, September 14, 2017. doi: 10.7939/R3794175M.

Hathcock, April. "White Librarianship in Blackface: Diversity Initiatives in LIS." *In the Library with the Lead Pipe*. October 2015. http://www.inthelibrarywiththeleadpipe.org/2015/lis-diversity.

Hogan, Kristen. "'Breaking Secrets' in the Catalog: Proposing the Black Queer Studies Collection at the University of Texas at Austin." *Progressive Librarian* 34 (Fall 2010): 50–57. http://www.progressivelibrariansguild.org/PL/PL34_35.pdf

Iacovino, Livia. "Rethinking Archival, Ethical and Legal Frameworks for Records of Indigenous Australian Communities: A Participant Relationship Model of Rights and Responsibilities." *Archival Science* 10, no. 4 (December 2010): 353–372. doi: 10.1007/s10502-010-9120-3.

Imarisha, Walidah, "Keynote Address," Liberated Archive Forum, Society of American Archivists Annual Meeting, Portland, OR, August 22, 2017, http://www.walidah.com/blog/2017/8/22/transcript-of-walidahs-liberated-archives-keynote.

International Council on Archives. *Records in Contexts*. September 2016.

Jules, Bergis. "Confronting Our Failure of Care Around the Legacies of Marginalized People in the Archives." *On Archivy*. November 11, 2016. https://medium.com/on-archivy/confronting-our-failure-of-care-around-the-legacies-of-marginalized-people-in-the-archives-dc4180397280.

Larade, Sharon P. and Johanne M. Pelletier. "Mediating in a Neutral Environment: Gender-Inclusive or Neutral Language in Archival Descriptions." *Archivaria* 35 (Spring 1993): 99–109. https://archivaria.ca/index.php/archivaria/article/view/11889/12842.

Littletree, Sandra and Cheryl A. Metoyer. "Knowledge Organization from an Indigenous Perspective: The Mashantucket Pequot Thesaurus of American Indian Terminology Project." *Cataloging and Classification Quarterly* 53 (2015): 640–57.

Loewenthal, Anna B. "Comparing Representations of Race in Finding Aids Over Time." Master's thesis, University of North Carolina at Chapel Hill, 2015.

Long, Kara, Santi Thompson, Sarah Potvin, and Monica Rivero. "The "Wicked Problem" of Neutral Description: Toward a Documentation Approach to Metadata Standards." *Cataloging & Classification Quarterly* 55, no. 3 (2017): 107–128. doi: 10.1080/01639374.2016.1278419.

Matienzo, Mx A. "To Hell with Good Intentions: Linked Data, Community and the Power to Name." Mark A. Matienzo (website). February 11, 2016. http://matienzo.org/2016/to-hell-with-good-intentions/.

Merritt, Carole. "Slave Family Records: An Abundance of Material." *Georgia Archive* 6, no. 1 (Spring 1978): 16–21. https://digitalcommons.kennesaw.edu/georgia_archive/vol6/iss1/12.

Moulaison, Heather Lea. "Authors and Authorities in Post-RDA Library Systems: A Case Study." Paper presented at IFLA WLIC 2014, Lyon, France, August 16–22, 2014. http://codabox.org/147/2/086-moulaison-en.pdf.

Newman, Jon. "Revisiting Archive Collections: Developing Models for Participatory Cataloguing." *Journal of the Society of Archivists* 33, no. 1 (2012): 57–73.

Noble, Safiya Umoja. "Google Search: Hyper-visibility as a Means of Rendering Black Women and Girls Invisible." *InVisible Culture* 19 (2013). http://ivc.lib.rochester.edu/google-search-hyper-visibility-as-a-means-of-rendering-black-women-and-girls-invisible/.

O'Hagan Hardy, Molly. "The Practice of Everyday Cataloging: 'Blacks as authors' and the Early American Bibliographic Record." *Past is Present* (American Antiquarian Society blog). June 29, 2017. http://pastispresent.org/2017/good-sources/the-practice-of-everyday-cataloging-black-bibliography-and-the-early-american-bibliographic-record/.

Olson, Hope A. "The Power to Name: Representation in Library Catalogs." *Signs* 26, no. 3 (Spring 2001): 639–68.

Pagowsky, Nicole and Niamh Wallace. "Black Lives Matter! Shedding Library Neutrality Rhetoric for Social Justice." *College & Research Libraries News* 76, no. 4 (2015): 196–214. http://crln.acrl.org/index.php/crlnews/article/view/9293/10373

"Part II: Archival Authority Records." *Describing Archives: A Content Standard* (DACS), Second Edition. Chicago: Society of American Archivists, 2013.

Paterson, David E. "A Perspective on Indexing Slaves' Names." *The American Archivist* 64 (Spring/Summer 2001): 132–42. doi: 10.17723/aarc.64.1.th18g8t6282h4283.

Raiford, Teressa, "#ArchivesforBlackLives: Archivists Respond to Black Lives Matter" panel, Liberated Archive Forum, Society of American Archivists Annual Meeting, Portland, OR, August 22, 2017.

Ramirez, Mario H. "Being Assumed Not to Be: A Critique of Whiteness as an Archival Imperative." *American Archivist* 78, no. 2 (Fall/Winter 2015): 339–56. doi: 10.17723/0360-9081.78.2.339.

Rappel110 A4BLiP repository, GitHub, https://github.com/rappel110/A4BLiP.

Rawson, K. J. "Accessing Transgender // Desiring Queer(er?) Archival Logics." *Archivaria* 68 (Fall 2009): 123–40. https://archivaria.ca/index.php/archivaria/article/view/13234/14552.

Roberto, K. R. "Inflexible Bodies: Metadata for Transgender Identities." *Journal of Information Ethics* 20, no. 2 (2011): 56–64.

Sahadath, Catelynne. "Classifying the Margins: Using Alternative Classification Schemes to Empower Diverse and Marginalized Users." *Feliciter* 59, no. 3 (2013): 15-17.

Social Networks and Archival Context website. http://snaccooperative.org/.

Society of American Archivists, "Issue Brief: Police Mobile Camera Footage as a Public Record, November 2017, https://www2.archivists.org/statements/issue-brief-police-mobile-camera-footage-as-a-public-record.

Society of American Archivists, "Provenance," SAA Glossary, https://www2.archivists.org/glossary/terms/p/provenance.

Swanson, Raegan. "Adapting the Brian Deer Classification System for Aan-ischaaukamikw Cree Cultural Institute." *Cataloging & Classification Quarterly* 53, no. 5–6: Indigenous Knowledge Organization (2015): 568-79. doi: 10.1080/01639374.2015.1009669.

Wade, Carrie. "Whiteness and the Myth of Neutrality." *Library Barbarian* (blog). February 13, 2018.

Warren, Kellee E. "We Need These Bodies, But Not their Knowledge: Black Women in the Archival Science Professions and Their Connection to the Archives of Enslaved Black Women in the French Antilles." *Library Trends* 64, no. 4 (2016): 776–94. doi: 10.1353/lib.2016.0012.

Winn, Sam. "The Hubris of Neutrality in Archives." *On Archivy.* April 24, 2017. https://medium.com/on-archivy/the-hubris-of-neutrality-in-archives-8df6b523fe9f.

Chapter 16

AUTHORITY WORK AS OUTREACH

Tina Gross and Violet B. Fox

Introduction

Unlike any other resource, the National Authority File (NAF) is the result of decades of research conducted by librarians from the Library of Congress and those participating in the NACO (Name Authority Cooperative) program. The exacting standards in place for creating and editing name authority records have ensured that the quality of the data in the NAF is consistently high, especially when compared to the varying quality of bibliographic data in OCLC's WorldCat.

However, librarians have not necessarily been interested in collaborating with those outside the library world. In the process of creating personal name authority records, NACO participants usually do not attempt to contact people for whom authorized names are being established, even when the person is known to be alive and contact information is readily available. NACO training does not include much information about contacting creators; the training material available at https://www.loc.gov/catworkshop/courses/naco-RDA/index.html (as of May 2018) does not mention it. Emailing creators is framed as a last resort, to be done only when additional information (such as year of birth or middle initial) is needed to differentiate that person from others with the same name.

This chapter argues in favor of reframing authority work as a collaboration not just between librarians, but between librarians and the subjects of authority work. By reframing our work in this way, we shift our role from agents following opaque rules and gathering information on other people to partners mutually working towards accurate information.

Contacting Creators in the Later Years of AACR2

Before the adoption of RDA, when catalogers participating in NACO contacted a creator whose name they were establishing, it was usually because there was a conflict to break. If the creator's name was the same as that of one or more people already in the authority file, and no information to add to the heading was present in the resource being cataloged or readily available on the web, the cataloger would typically attempt to contact the creator to ask for such information.

Another common dilemma that would prompt a cataloger to contact a creator was when they could not determine whether the creator of the work in hand was the same or different from a previously established personal name in the authority file. As one of this chapter's authors once wrote to such a creator:

> In addition to "Cell tower deaths" and "An optimist in Haiti" (which are yours, yes?), the following works are attributed (I believe incorrectly) to the same Travis Fox: A 2007 golf instruction video titled "How to beat the bogey man," and a 2005 book on hypnosis titled "You want me to look where?" Those are not you, correct? They don't seem to fit in with your other work, but hey, you never know (in doing similar queries, I have sometimes been surprised to have the person confirm that they actually were indeed one and the same.)[1]

The need to contact creators occasionally to ask for conflict-breaking information was mentioned in NACO training, but how to go about doing it was not usually covered. Many catalogers felt the need for

---

1. Tina Gross, e-mail message to Travis Fox, July 26, 2012.

training and guidance, such as in Ohio's NACO funnel, where "catalogers mentioned the need for help with researching and contacting authors. This was eventually covered informally with their reviewer. Building that into the training would have saved time, and empowered them to take action quickly."[2]

Catalogers who contacted creators on a frequent basis often developed scripts or templates to use, which gave a basic explanation of library authority control practices as background to the request for information. These templates typically endeavored both to establish the legitimacy of the request (that it was a genuine request coming from a real library, not some kind of phishing attempt) and to introduce the creator to the basics of name disambiguation. They have been a topic on cataloging listservs on several occasions, with catalogers discussing ways of getting creators to respond and sharing their templates.[3] Examples are included in **Appendix I** at the end of this chapter.

In the authors' experience of contacting creators via email, the majority responded promptly with the requested information, often expressing gratitude to the library for adding their work to its collection or for making the effort to verify their name. Sometimes catalogers would receive an unusually enthusiastic or helpful response. For example, one of this chapter's authors emailed the producer of a film about Ghanaian dance to ask about contacting the featured dancer/choreographer to confirm the preferred form of his name. The producer responded by phone almost immediately to provide a short lesson on honorifics used in Ghana.

Occasionally, catalogers received responses that doubted the need for authority control with questions along the lines of "Wouldn't someone looking for me easily be able to distinguish me from the imposters?"

---

2. Melanie McGurr, Catherine Mason, and Michael Monaco, "Public and Academic Library Cataloging Collaboration in Ohio's NACO Funnel Project," *Cataloging & Classification Quarterly* 51, no. 1-3 (2013): 76.

3. AUTOCAT list, "Name inquiries that work!" Listserv thread beginning February 27, 2008, https://listserv.syr.edu/scripts/wa.exe?A2=AUTOCAT;b5cdafae.080 2D and PCCList, "Writing to authors to disambiguate their names," Listserv thread beginning June 11, 2013.

Unfortunately, errors that can result from the absence of systematic disambiguation are not difficult to demonstrate. The following email to a creator outlines one example of a tangle of conflicting metadata found on commonly visited reference sites:

> There's a lot more confusion in cases like this than you'd think. For example, Wikipedia has a page on American Primitive... You're listed as the producer, and your name is hyperlinked, but if someone clicks on your name, they're taken to the page for the Australian painter of the same name. In the IMDB, the record for you indicates that you were a writer for SNL… I couldn't be sure if that was true or not - it didn't really seem to fit with the rest of your body of work, and it seemed a possibility that you were being confused with the other James Egan who's an SNL writer (but he spells his name Eagan).[4]

It takes time and effort to identify disambiguation problems, but in most cases using such issues to make the case for authority control would not require much additional time, because the cataloger would have already discovered those problems when researching the name and attempting to complete the name authority record.

Under AACR2, it was possible to include a creator's contact information, work history, gender, birthdate, or other personal information in a personal name authority record. However, it could only be recorded in free text form in a note (not encoded in dedicated fields), and was not a common practice.

The Move to RDA

Changes to personal name authority work that came with the transition from AACR2 to RDA can be put in two broad categories. First, RDA rules provide for many additional methods of disambiguating a personal name, making it much easier to break a conflict with information provided within a resource being cataloged. Second, personal name authority records in RDA can contain significantly more biographical

---

4. Tina Gross, e-mail message to James Egan, March 12, 2008.

information about creators. Because of the expanded role for author-ity records put forward by IFLA with the adoption of the Functional Requirements for Authority Data (FRAD), "the original scope of a name authority record was broadened from simply that of a carrier of an authorized heading or access point to a description of an entity with the development of an expanded list of attributes that can be included in name authority records."[5]

Additional methods of disambiguation available in RDA have reduced the need to contact creators for information. AACR2 rule 22.19 and the associated Library of Congress Rule Interpretation did allow a per-sonal name to be qualified with a "descriptive phrase" that could be an occupation/profession in order to break a conflict, but only as a last resort to avoid creating an undifferentiated record. In RDA, adding the occupation or period of activity to an authorized access point to differentiate otherwise identical names is a routine practice. It is almost always possible to identify a piece of information to use as a qualifier, so catalogers rarely need to contact creators to ask for information to disambiguate their names.

While the increased flexibility in disambiguation under RDA has meant that catalogers don't need to contact creators as often as before, the proliferation of attributes that RDA calls for recording in personal name authority records raises issues that should compel catalogers to contact creators more frequently. These attributes include associated place (place of birth, country associated with the person), address, field of activity, affiliation (workplaces and organizations), gender, and language.

The practice of attempting to determine and record a creator's gender has drawn a great deal of concern and criticism. Catalogers attempt-ing to do so run the risk of misidentifying a person's gender based on false assumptions, or of outing a person as transgender without their knowledge or consent, thus actively causing harm.

---

5. Kelly J. Thompson, "More Than a Name: A Content Analysis of Name Authority Records for Authors Who Self-Identify as Trans," *Library Resources & Technical Services* 60, no. 3 (2016): 140, doi: 10.5860/lrts.60n3.

In 2014, Billey, Drabinski, and Roberto explained how the RDA rule on recording gender and its interpretation by LC codified a mistaken idea of gender as a binary in which all people experience gender as straight-forward and fixed (or changing only in linear fashion).[6] Interestingly, their argument includes an account of cataloging a work and creating a personal name authority record in the presence of its creator, and how that interaction impacted the record.

> But when we reached MARC tag 375, the field for the RDA element for gender, the author was confused about why that information mattered. This author did not feel comfortable disclosing and codifying gender in the authority record… Interestingly, this author was a cisgender woman with a name that our culture commonly reads as female; "cisgender" is a term used to refer to non-transgender people who identify with the gender that they were assigned at birth. Most catalogers would simply transcribe the gender as female from a glance at the title page, the author's biographical information, or physical appearance. But the author explained that gender was simply not an important aspect of the work in question, or the body of work the author intended to produce. Indeed, the author expressed hope that one day gender would no longer be a social marker. It made no sense that the Library of Congress (LC) would be interested in the author's gender; why would LC care about that! Once the cataloger explained that 375 was an optional field, we decided together to omit that information.[7]

This is a good illustration of how a cataloger cannot successfully anticipate or deduce a creator's views about what information about them should be shared. When consulted, a creator might express strong preferences that would otherwise remain unknown.

Gender stands out as the most-discussed potentially harmful attribute that can be included in RDA personal name authority records without the person's consent, but things such as name variations, date of birth, work affiliation, and address could be information that a person might not want to disclose or have permanently recorded as data that is publicly

---

6. Amber Billey, Emily Drabinski, and K. R. Roberto, "What's Gender Got to Do with It? A Critique of RDA Rule 9.7," *Cataloging & Classification Quarterly* 52, no. 4 (2014): 412-421, doi: 10.1080/01639374.2014.882465

7. Ibid., 413.

accessible online. The fact that personal name authority records can now take on the character of a miniature biography or CV is an indication that the person who is the subject of such a record should, whenever possible, be made aware of its contents and have input in what is included.

Authority Work as Outreach

Catalogers and metadata librarians are often "behind the scenes" workers; they may or may not have occasion to interact with library users, and users are often not aware of their efforts. Authority work presents a unique opportunity for catalogers to engage in user outreach and to demonstrate the value of the library's work in a tangible way. Just one email to a creator can establish that libraries see their work as important and relevant, and highlight the fact that librarians are working to represent information about them accurately and facilitate access to their work.

Although creators might not be familiar with terminology like authority control or disambiguation, they care about getting credit for the work that they've created. It is easy enough to explain the value of authority work using examples of bad metadata, such as that often found for less prominent authors on Amazon.com. Creators are interested in people being able to easily find their work, and the value that authority control provides can be viewed as just as worthwhile to creators as, for example, the promotion of popular books by public services librarians.

To assist librarians contributing to the NAF in reaching out to creators, the Program for Cooperative Cataloging (PCC) could create a landing page which provides information about the goals of authority work and examples of how the information collected by librarians would be used in disambiguating identities. The page could contain frequently asked questions about who uses the data collected and why certain data is more useful than others.

A landing page hosted at loc.gov would provide authority; after all, we often ask for personal information (such as birthdates and fuller forms of names). The fear of identity theft may be one reason why creators do not respond to librarians' requests for information. Being able to provide a link to a website which explains why librarians are looking for specific information may help convince creators to share their information. Of course, this landing page should fully explain that the information given will be made public and used in tandem with other linked data databases. Only when equipped with this information will creators be able to give fully informed consent when providing their personal data. In addition, a landing page could provide more detail on the purpose of a library authority record than can be explained in a short message; that is, a NAR does not necessarily document everything someone has ever created, but shows the range in topics that a person has produced within, as well as collocating differing forms of names for the same person.

When an institution has a collection development focus on materials in particular foreign languages or from particular locations, it may or may not be able prioritize employing catalogers with corresponding advanced language skills. It is not uncommon for catalogers to possess "bibliographic knowledge" of several languages, which allows them to catalog resources in those languages but to not be sufficiently fluent to feel comfortable contacting creators about their name authority records. This situation can cause a discrepancy between intended institutional priorities and the reality of readily making materials available to users. While this is a larger issue than the creation of name authority records, having help in the form of a landing page explaining concepts in multiple languages would help catalogers at many levels of expertise.

Even more important than explaining why librarians are collecting personal information, it is crucial for LC and PCC to provide a way for people to correct the information found on an authority record. Currently, there is no easy way for creators to know who is collecting information about them or how they might go about removing or correcting information. Upon finding erroneous information about themselves in a library catalog, they may try to contact their local library, which may or may not have the staff resources to address their concerns or to truly understand where the information in their catalog is coming from. An easily found form could help creators feel they have recourse when the information that libraries have about them is incorrect.

As a proliferation of data is linked among various sources, inaccurate data is nearly impossible to corral and correct once it has been distributed online or published. Contacting creators when initially creating an authority record is the most effective way to ensure that the information about them is accurate and consists of data which they feel is appropriate to share with the world. The purpose of this outreach work would not be simply to collect additional information to break conflicts but to ask the creator to confirm that the information they want to be present is available and that no information they want removed is kept. Information included or excluded according to creator's wishes should be noted in the NAR, and the provenance of data vetted by the creator themselves should be made explicit.

Catalogers or administrators may balk at the extra time and effort involved in emailing most or all the creators they establish authority records for. However, equipped with appropriate email templates and an explanatory landing page, there would be little need for back-and-forth emails. Catalogers could create spreadsheets where they keep track of who they have emailed and create records either when they hear back from a creator or after a certain amount of time has passed. There would be no need to keep a physical item from moving forward in processing during the wait; cataloging could be completed and the relevant information collected on the same form or as a pending draft in the bibliographic utility's save file. In the case that the workload of creating authority records is larger than a librarian would want to contact authors for, librarians can prioritize the work according to their institution's needs; for example, prioritizing contacting local creators or those creating work within the institution's collection specializations. Other priorities for creating authority records might include members of marginalized populations, such as people whose gender does not fit within a traditional gender binary, as the potential for harm in authority work may be higher than with cisgender people.

We suggest that contacting creators should be a recommended best practice, not necessarily a task required for every resource cataloged. Cataloging departments and librarians should develop policies based on their own resources and institutional priorities.

Related Efforts and Developments

In a recent survey, 66% of catalogers indicated that they use social media (such as LinkedIn, Facebook, Twitter or Instagram) to find information when creating authority records.[8] Viewing a creator's social media output is obviously not the same as contacting them directly, but the fact that catalogers are making it a regular practice to perform research for authority work on social media sites designed to enable users to connect with each other is significant. It suggests that the means to contact creators is frequently identified, even if it is not used to do so.

As discussed elsewhere in this volume, the Legislative Library of the Legislative Assembly of Nunavut and the National Library of Israel have developed approaches to authority work that involve contacting creators as a routine practice. The NLI provides forms for catalogers to send to creators to fill out, and then invites them to review the finished authority record in the OPAC or discovery layer. Creators who come into contact with the library for any reason are routinely asked "to review their authority record and contact us with corrections and more information."[9]

The OAQ (Online Author Questionnaire), developed by Harvard University Library, "is a library-hosted web application that automates publishers' processes for gathering author data and allows them to share a subset of that data with libraries to support the timely creation of

---

8. Ilda Cardenas, "Catalogers Cyberstalking Authors: Relationship Between Cataloging and Social Media," paper presented at ALCTS CaMMS Cataloging Norms Interest Group program at the American Library Association Midwinter meeting, Denver, CO, February 10, 2018.

9. Ahava Cohen, e-mail message to Violet Fox and Tina Gross, June 21, 2018.

discovery metadata."[10] Publishers receive support to use a customizable interface that facilitates asking authors to provide biographical and career information by filling out a web-based questionnaire. In turn, the library receives the data provided on the questionnaire as structured output to automatically create personal name authority records for those authors.

Efforts such as those put forward by the Nunavut Legislative Library, the NLI, and Harvard University Library are exemplary in making it simple for creators and publishers to contribute information which makes identification easier. Further study may be warranted to discover whether creators adequately understand how the data they provide is used by libraries.

Shifting Assumptions

When cataloging traditionally published books, librarians assume that the form of name on the title page is the author's preferred form. With non-book formats, decisions have been made about where to source the NACO-preferred form of name, but those decisions are somewhat arbitrary, and do not necessarily reflect an author's preference. As libraries move to collecting (and cataloging) less traditional materials, librarians often no longer have a title page or a clear preferred source of information about the work they are cataloging. When contact information is available, creators should be contacted to ensure their preferred form of name is established correctly.

While the move to linked data will place less emphasis on the label of the entity represented by an authority record, the issue of determining the human-readable form of name will not disappear. The shift will make name changes easier to deal with, as the URI will remain unchanging while the label can change as frequently as is required or requested. A desired future for authority control might look like an ORCID identity,

10. Online Author Questionnaire, accessed June 22, 2018, http://library.harvard.edu/oaq#.

where creators can claim their record and make edits to the publicly accessible label.

Regardless of how the technology involved handles the data of personal name records, with very few exceptions, the person who is being described should be viewed as the ultimate arbiter of any decisions to be made regarding the information collected about them. But in order to empower creators, we must first give them information about what data is collected about them. Contacting creators at the point of name authority record creation is the most effective way to ensure that authority work is truly a collaborative partnership.

Bibliography

Billey, Amber, Emily Drabinski, and K. R. Roberto. "What's Gender Got to Do with It? A Critique of RDA Rule 9.7." Cataloging & Classification Quarterly 52, no. 4 (2014): 412-421. doi: 10.1080/01639374.2014.882465.

Cardenas, Ilda. "Catalogers Cyberstalking Authors: Relationship Between Cataloging and Social Media." Paper presented at ALCTS CaMMS Cataloging Norms Interest Group program at the American Library Association Midwinter meeting, Denver, CO, February 10, 2018.

Harvard Library. "Online Author Questionnaire." http://library.harvard.edu/oaq#.

McGurr, Melanie, Catherine Mason, and Michael Monaco. "Public and Academic Library Cataloging Collaboration in Ohio's NACO Funnel Project." *Cataloging & Classification Quarterly* 51, no. 1-3 (2013): 72-81.

Thompson, Kelly J. "More Than a Name: A Content Analysis of Name Authority Records for Authors Who Self-Identify as Trans." *Library Resources & Technical Services* 60, no. 3 (2016): 140-155. doi: 10.5860/lrts.60n3.

Appendix I
Templates for Requesting Information from Creators

Template 1:

I am a cataloger at [Institution name], and I am cataloging [resource title]. Because there are multiple other people with the name [creator's name] in the Library of Congress name authority file, I need additional information to distinguish you. Will you let me know the year of your birth and/or your middle name?

This information will be used to contribute to the international authority record for your name and will help ensure that you get proper credit for the works you've contributed to.

Template 2:

Subject line: question about [title of work by creator]

My name is [XX], and I am the [position title] at [institution]. I am currently adding "[title]" to our library's collection and I'm writing to ask if it's possible to get a bit of information from you.

One of the things libraries do to make library catalogs more reliable and accurate is to create a unique "name heading" or access point for each author or creator, so that searchers can find all of their work without mistakenly retrieving things by other people with the same name. (The function is somewhat similar to "disambiguation" in Wikipedia, or the roman numerals used after names in the Internet Movie Database when there are multiple people with the same name, if you're familiar with either of those.)

I need additional information to establish such a unique heading for you. There are already several other people named [XX] in WorldCat, the global catalog of library collections where the record will be, and so in order to distinguish you from all of the others, I need to add an additional piece of information to the heading.

The most common and simple way to do this is to add your year of birth, but a middle name or middle initial can also be used. If you would be willing to provide this information, it would be very helpful.

Chapter 17

CREATING MULTILINGUAL AND MULTISCRIPT NAME
AUTHORITY RECORDS: A CASE STUDY IN MEETING THE
NEEDS OF INUIT LANGUAGE SPEAKERS IN NUNAVUT

Carol Rigby and Riel Gallant

Abstract

This case study examines the decision made by the Legislative Library of the Legislative Assembly of Nunavut to commit to a fully multilingual and multiscript library catalogue in order to meet the needs of its user community, the majority of whom are Inuit, and its legislated mandate to provide service in all of Nunavut's official languages: Inuktut (Inuit language), English, and French. This has resulted in the adoption of a multilingual and multiscript cross-referenced model of authority control, which represents Inuit people and organizations in their own language and scripts. Although this model may not be congruent with larger and more commonly shared authority systems, it does adhere to MARC coding standards and applies principles outlined in the IFLA *Statement of International Cataloguing Principles*. Challenges in using this approach include determining definitive versions of names, dealing with dialectal translation and historical transliteration variants, and sharing authority data with other systems that might have overriding unilingual authority control.

This study will consider some of the historical barriers to representing Inuit names in Inuit language, particularly those expressed in syllabics; the need for consultation with individuals and organizations to determine the best choices among many variant options; the need to track these variations for maximum accessibility to catalogue content; the need to continually advocate for cataloguing standards in both description and metadata coding that will support the creation of these cross-referenced records; the effort, expense, and specialized training required to create a unique authority database; and considerations going forward in sharing these authority records with other Nunavut libraries and with libraries outside of Nunavut and Inuit Nunangat.

It is hoped that this examination will demonstrate the Nunavut Legislative Library's commitment to ethical name authority practice in respecting the need for Indigenous peoples to be able to access materials in their own languages, through a catalogue that accurately represents both those languages and any script in which they may be expressed. It is also hoped that this practice will expand access to materials in various forms of Inuit language so that Inuit researchers will become more engaged and find the library catalogue to be a useful tool rather than yet another barrier. The Nunavut Legislative Library's practices have been adopted by other Nunavut libraries that share similar values. Perhaps one day these authority record standards will find more widespread acceptance.

Introduction

This case study examines the decision made by the Legislative Library of the Legislative Assembly of Nunavut to commit to a fully multilingual and multiscript library catalogue in order to meet the needs of its user community, which is chiefly Inuit, and its legislated mandate to provide service in all of Nunavut's official languages: Inuktut (Inuit language), English, and French. This has resulted in the adoption of a multilingual and multiscript cross-referenced model of authority control, which represents Inuit people and organizations in their own language and scripts.[1] It is hoped that by describing the social and jurisdictional context for and the development of these decisions, as well as some of the practical approaches used and the challenges faced in implementing these policies, other library systems may likewise consider approaches that allow entities to describe themselves more accurately in their own terms.

The Nunavut Context

Canada's youngest territory, Nunavut, is a rare political entity: a jurisdiction that is a public government but controlled by a population that is overwhelmingly of Indigenous descent, that is, Inuit. It was established in 1999 in fulfilment of conditions outlined in the settlement of the Nunavut land claim[2] between the Canadian government and the Tungavik Federation of Nunavut.[3] Consequently, efforts have been made to respect and encourage Inuit language and culture in the daily life of this territory through a number of mechanisms: the unique design of its public institutions such as the consensus-based Legislative Assembly; the operations of its civil service in the Government of Nunavut,

---

1. "Inuktut" is the term currently being used in Nunavut government and Inuit language circles to encompass all variants and dialects of Inuit language used in Nunavut. These include several dialects of Eastern Arctic Inuktitut, which can be represented either in syllabic script or roman orthography, and Inuinnaqtun, which uses roman orthography. See, for example, the proceedings of the Inuugatta Language Conference, held in Iqaluit in 2015. *Inuugatta: summary of presentations and recommendations* (Iqaluit, Nunavut: Government of Nunavut, 2015), http://assembly.nu.ca/library/ GNedocs/2015/001887-e.pdf.

2. Canada, *Agreement Between the Inuit of the Nunavut Settlement Area and Her Majesty in Right of Canada* (Ottawa: Indian and Northern Affairs Canada and Tungavik Federation of Nunavut, 1993).

3. *Nunavut Act.* S.C. 1993, c.28; *Nunavut Land Claims Agreement Act.* S.C. 1993, c.29. The *Nunavut Act* and the *Nunavut Land Claims Agreement Act* were both given royal assent in June, 1993, fulfilling the terms of the Nunavut Land Claim Agreement between the Government of Canada and the Tungavik Federation of Nunavut. The *Nunavut Land Claims Agreement Act* establishes the legal basis of the agreement; the *Nunavut Act* establishes the political entity of Nunavut in accordance with the terms of the agreement.

incorporating *Inuit qaujimajatuqangit* (traditional Inuit knowledge); the involvement of special "Institutions of Public Government" created under the Nunavut Agreement to support Inuit management of land and wildlife; and legislation developed in Nunavut to support, enhance, and preserve Inuit culture.[4]

In practical terms, however, it is much more difficult to implement these laudable goals and, for instance, make Inuktut a true working language in Nunavut, a goal targeted for the year 2020 by the Government of Nunavut (GN) in its initial Bathurst Mandate and recently reaffirmed by the current government.[5] Government systems and educational standards inherited from the previous Northwest Territories government operated primarily in English. The Canadian government, which still maintains a significant level of financial control over programs and services in the territory, operates in English and French. Despite the fact that the most recent census data from Statistics Canada indicates that a majority of *Nunavummiut* (residents of Nunavut) claims Inuit language as its mother tongue,[6] and that use of Inuktut is mandated by law,[7] many systems and services are still not available in Inuit language. In the national and international context, Inuit from Nunavut and other circumpolar jurisdictions are still expected to be able to operate within

---

4. For explanations of some of these developments, see, for example, Graham White, *Responsible Government in Nunavut: The "Consensus government" System* (2003), http://assembly.nu.ca/library/Edocs/2003/001487-e.pdf; Government of Nunavut, *Incorporating Inuit Societal Values* (2013) http://assembly.nu.ca/library/GNedocs/2013/001181-e.pdf; *Inuit Language Protection Act, S.NU 2008, c.17 (Nunavut)*

5. Nunavut, *Pinasuaqtavut : that which we've set out to do : our hopes and plans for Nunavut* = ᐱᓇᓱᐊᖅᑕᕗᑦ : ᓯᓂᑉᕆᔪᕐᓯᖃᒃ ᐊᒡᒪᑦ ᐸᖃᐅᖕᖅᑦ ᓄᓇᖃᒃ = *Pinasuaqtavut : voilà ce que nous cherchons à accomplir : nos espoirs et nos plans pour le Nunavut* = *Pinahuaqtavut : imaa titirarhimajuq : ihumagijavut upalungaijautillu Nunavunmi* (Iqaluit, Nunavut: Government of Nunavut, 1999); Nunavut, *Turaaqtavut* = ᑐᕋᖅᑕᕗᑦ (Iqaluit, Nunavut: Government of Nunavut, 2018)

6. According to the 2016 Census, 22,600 of Nunavut's population of 35,944, or 63%, claim Inuit language as a mother tongue and around 50% speak Inuit language as the first language at home. Statistics Canada. "Nunavut [Territory] and Canada [Country] (table). Census Profile," *2016 Census.* (Ottawa: Statistics Canada, 2017). http://www12.statcan.gc.ca/census-recensement/2016/dp-pd/prof/index.cfm?Lang=E.

7. *Official Languages Act*, S.Nu. 2008, c.10 (Nunavut); *Inuit Language Protection Act.*

the linguistic expectations of the societies surrounding them. As a result, the majority of Inuit are bilingual or multilingual, which helps those of us who do not possess fluency in Inuktut to work on providing respectful and helpful services in this family of languages. It does mean, however, that to provide barrier-free access to the information contained in library catalogues, and to have these catalogues genuinely represent Inuktut materials and their creators, a real effort must be made to have these catalogues be as multilingual and flexible as the people who use them. It is beyond the scope of this paper to consider all the various social, cultural, and linguistic factors that make it so difficult for Inuit to be able to use their own language in today's world of interconnected information systems.[8] However, certain very practical aspects can be examined in the library context for their impact on how library systems can, and should, handle service for their Inuit language users.

Authority control is a central practice to library catalogue management, collocating various possible references to a person or organization under one form for ease of reference and to ensure all works by one entity can be found together. In a world of linked data and shared cataloguing, centralizing this control and sharing authority records avoids a proliferation of variants. Unfortunately, the largely monolingual and Anglo-centric nature of most of today's largest authority control systems does not always adequately address the needs of users in systems where multiple languages, especially Indigenous languages, may be in use.

A major hurdle to including Indigenous language in shared library catalogues was overcome in 2000 with the inclusion of Unified Canadian Aboriginal Syllabics (UCAS) in Unicode 3.0.[9] Until that time, all cataloguing of Inuit language materials was predicated on the need to transliterate Inuktitut materials produced in syllabics into roman orthography for inclusion in automated catalogues. Authorities for the names of

---

8. See, for example, the extensive analysis of linguistic choices made by Nunavut Inuit in Louis-Jacques Dorais, *Inuit Discourse and Identity After the Advent of Nunavut* (Québec City: Université Laval, 2006).

9. Unicode, Inc., *The Unicode Standard 10.0 : Unified Canadian Aboriginal Syllabics Range 1400-167F*. (S. l.: Unicode, Inc., 2017), https://unicode.org/charts/PDF/U1400.pdf.

Inuit persons and organizations were consequently established either in an anglicized or a romanized version, which might or might not equate to how that person or organization self-represented. Another step forward was taken with the adoption in 2002 by the MARC21 community of a proposal put forward by the Canadian Committee on MARC (CCM) to accommodate records encoded using UCAS in records using Unicode.[10] Once commercial vendors began to incorporate Unicode-compatible software into their integrated library systems (ILSs), it became possible for those providing services to Inuktitut syllabics users to consider how to possibly integrate access through this language and script into their catalogues.

The Nunavut Legislative Library has always been at the forefront of attempts to expand library service in Inuktut. Founded in 1998, a year in advance of the first Sitting of the Legislative Assembly of Nunavut, the library's mandate included providing services to the incoming Members of the Legislative Assembly in their own language.[11] It took several years and considerable effort to procure a true-MARC ILS that would also accommodate Unicode text.[12] Initially, however, no library staff had sufficient knowledge or training to create records in Inuktut, particularly syllabic Inuktitut. Library staff were chiefly engaged in copy cataloguing, and therefore used national library records, with their associated authority records, that had a policy of transliterating syllabics for Inuktitut materials.

However, by 2005, in cooperation with other Nunavut library systems, several of the technical difficulties had been satisfactorily resolved, such as how to type in syllabics in the new system and how to ensure syllabics would display properly on online public access catalogue (OPAC)

10. Canadian Committee on MARC, *Proposal No. 2002-11: Repertoire Expansion in the Universal Character Set for Canadian Aboriginal Syllabics* (2002), https://www.loc.gov/marc/marbi/2002/2002-11.html. The proposal was approved July 11, 2002.

11. Yvonne Earle, "Ikajarutit: Delivering Legislative Library Services in Aboriginal Languages (Nunavut, Canada)," (presentation to the 2008 IFLA World Congress, Québec City, 2008), https://archive.ifla.org/IV/ifla74/papers/103-Earle-en.pdf.

12. Ibid., 3-4.

screens. It came down, at that point, to the libraries' willingness to push for Inuktitut cataloguing policy and staff willingness to learn and experiment with syllabic input.[13]

Establishing Name Authority Policies

The Nunavut Legislative Library took the lead in developing policies for creating multilingual and multiscript catalogue records encompassing all of Nunavut's official languages and scripts.[14] These policies were then adopted, with some institution-specific modifications, by the other major library systems in Nunavut, and have been described in other publications.[15] At the heart of all of the policy decisions taken, however, were certain objectives of IFLA's *Statement of International Cataloguing Principles*,[16] published in 2009 but in the process of being drafted at that time. These objectives reinforced the choice to make the catalogue serve primarily the needs of its users, rather than those of its cataloguers. Among those informing choices with regard to the establishment of name authority records were:

- Objective 1: Convenience of the user of the catalogue: "Decisions to be made for bibliographic description and controlled forms of access should be made with the user in mind."

- Objective 3: Representation: "Descriptions and names should be based on the way an entity describes itself."

---

13. Carol Rigby and Rae-Lynne Patterson, "A Catalogue in a Multilingual, Multiscript Environment: the Experience of Nunavut's Library Partnership," *Reaching Out: Innovations in Canadian Libraries*, Yvon-André Lacroix, ed. (Montréal: Les Presses de l'Université Laval, 2008), 46.

14. Legislative Library of Nunavut, "Cataloguing: Multilingual Records," *Cataloguing Policy and Procedures Manual* (Iqaluit, Nunavut: Legislative Library of Nunavut, 2009).

15. Carol Rigby, "Nunavut Libraries Online Establish Inuit Language Bibliographic Cataloging Standards: Promoting Indigenous Language Using a Commercial ILS," in "Indigenous Knowledge Organization," special issue, *Cataloging & Classification Quarterly* 53, no. 5-6 (2015): 615-639, doi 10.1080/01639374.2015.1008165

16. IFLA Cataloguing Section and IFLA Meeting of Experts on an International Cataloguing Code, *Statement of international cataloguing principles*, IFLA Series on Bibliographic Control, vol. 37 (Munich: K. G. Saur, 2009).

- Objective 4: Accuracy: "An entity should be faithfully portrayed."
- Objective 8: Standardization: "Bibliographic description and controlled access points should be provided in as standard a way as possible."[17]

The desire, therefore, was to create principles for authority records that would respect, insofar as possible, the governing library cataloguing standards of the day (at the time, AACR2, and now RDA descriptive cataloguing rules; MARC coding for bibliographic and authority records; etc.), while improving accessibility for Inuktut users. At first, concern was focused on accommodating materials and their authors in syllabic script, but the principles developed to answer these needs came to be applied to Inuktut in Roman orthography as well as other languages. These developments also went hand in hand with a general de-Anglicization of international cataloguing rules, with the eventual introduction of RDA as the descriptive standard, and the development over the last decade of a somewhat less Anglo-centric online environment, better able to handle multiple languages and non-roman scripts.[18]

Since the multilingual cataloguing policy was established, the Legislative Library has created thousands of local authority records under the following principles:

- In keeping with IFLA objective #1, the convenience of the user, all language expressions of a particular entity in Nunavut's official languages are considered of equal value. This decision was modeled on Library and Archives Canada's cross-referenced English/French authority files for subjects (LC/CSH/RVM)

---

17. Ibid., 1.

18. It should be noted, however, that English is still dominant on the Internet, which is why users of other languages must make special efforts to enhance and preserve their accessibility; see, for example, a recent article in *The Guardian* describing the challenges of keeping Icelandic alive, as "Iceland's mother tongue and cultural identity is drowning in an online ocean of English": Jon Henley, "Icelandic language battles threat of 'digital extinction'", *The Guardian*, international ed., February 26, 2018 https://www.theguardian.com/world/2018/feb/26/icelandic-language-battles-threat-of-digital-extinction

CREATING MULTILINGUAL AND MULTISCRIPT NAME AUTHORITY RECORDS:
A CASE STUDY IN MEETING THE NEEDS OF INUIT LANGUAGE
SPEAKERS IN NUNAVUT

359

and for names, especially official bilingual names of government departments.[19] Wherever possible, name authority files include references to the same entity in other languages and scripts as required. This respects the needs of a user searching in a particular language to find the entity in that language, and cross-references help those who do not use that language to find the appropriate form.

- In keeping with IFLA objectives #3 (self-description) and #4 (accuracy), the language and script used in cataloguing represent the item in hand in its totality of languages and scripts (i.e., true multilingualism). An item in Inuktitut syllabics is catalogued in Inuktitut syllabics, with any name authorities also in that script. An item containing more than one language would include a name authority in each language expression.

- With respect to objective #8, standardization, normal coding practices for authority records are observed. The chief difference from records derived from centralized sources such as OCLC is that there is not one "preferred" form of a name, but rather other language expressions are treated as "see also" rather than "see" references. This principle also recognizes the fact that many *Nunavummiut* do in fact use more than one language in their lives and work.

Also with respect to objective #8, authorities established by other agencies are used where appropriate, e.g. for English-language authors in commercial publication, but overridden by local need, usage, and knowledge if necessary. In the case of Inuit or Nunavut government entities, Nunavut usage and information derived from local knowledge or personal contact overrides any authority established by a body outside of Nunavut such as LAC or OCLC.

---

19. Library and Archives Canada, "Bilingual Cataloguing Policy," (2015), http://www.bac-lac.gc.ca/eng/services/cataloguing-metadata/Pages/bilingual-cataloguing-policy.aspx.

Historic and Ongoing Challenges in Establishing Inuktut Name Authorities

With these policy principles established, there are still numerous challenges in establishing "authoritative" forms of Inuit names.

A primary initial challenge was the long-standing history of transliterating Inuktitut names expressed in syllabics by national libraries such as Library of Congress (LC) and Library and Archives Canada (LAC). In fact, the transliteration standards established by LC in 2000 are still those currently in use for all cataloguing of Inuktitut syllabic materials received by LAC.[20] Because a name authority was not established in its original syllabic form, the name authority could be in a transliterated or an anglicized form. Anyone searching for the name in syllabics would be unsuccessful, and would have to know either how to transliterate the name according to the chosen standard, or the entity's preferred anglicized form of name.

As well, the currently accepted syllabic transliteration standard used in Nunavut, the Inuit Cultural Institute (ICI) standard roman orthography, was only adopted in 1976,[21] and many Inuit names appeared in print documents using different standards. Many Inuit would, as well, establish anglicized forms of their names for themselves for documentary or legal purposes, which would not necessarily correspond with an exact transliteration of their name in syllabics. This has led over the years to a multiplicity of forms of name for some people and institutions. In addition, for items translated into Inuktitut by authors with non-Inuktut names, these names would have to be transliterated into syllabics for the publication. Given the differences in available phonemes (e.g., there

---

20. Standards, Intellectual Management Office, Library and Archives Canada, *Inventory of Romanization Tools* (Ottawa: Library and Archives Canada, 2006), 5.

21. Kenn Harper, "Inuit Writing Systems in Nunavut: Issues and Challenges," *Building Capacity in Arctic Societies: Dynamics and Shifting Perspectives: Proceedings of the Second IPSSAS Seminar, Iqaluit, Nunavut, 2003*, François Trudel, ed. (Québec: Université Laval, 2005), 94.

is no "b" sound in Inuktut), a name transliterated into syllabics from, say, English, then back again for a catalogue entry, might end up some way from the original author's name. For example, the English name Rigby can be transliterated as ᕆᒡᐱ (Rigpi), ᕆᒡᕕ (Rigvi), ᕆᒃᐱ (Rikpi), or ᕇᒃᐱ (Riikpi), all of which have been found on Inuktitut publications for the same author.

For personal names, therefore, establishing name authorities for people publishing in Inuktut (and this does include non-Inuit) means dealing with variants both to and from Inuktitut syllabics, choosing appropriate sources of information, determining what is most "official," and consulting with individuals where necessary and possible with regard to personal use and preference. After some years of working with cross-referenced authority files, the Legislative Library is now drafting policy that provides specific guidance in these matters. The following sources have been identified as the preferred sources for authorized names for individuals, in order of authority.

- Personal communication from the individual or the individual's family, preferably in writing (letter, e-mail). This would also include any signature by that individual on correspondence, whether received directly or determined from a scanned document containing a signature (e.g. in correspondence tabled in the Legislature).
- For Members of the Legislative Assembly, the form of the Member's name used in the Hansard (the official transcript of proceedings). For other persons, the form of name appearing on legal or official documents (e.g. birth certificates, awards, licenses).
- For commercially published non-Inuit authors, the form of name established in their own language by national cataloguing authorities (e.g. Library and Archives Canada, Library of Congress, British Library).
- For other individuals, the name as represented in published works or documents. When there is a conflict between published versions of a name, some effort must be exercised to determine if one version of a name is used more frequently than others. This

is usually what gives rise to the need for personal communication as noted above.

- Where two forms of a name appear to be used with equal frequency or authority, and a preference cannot be established by personal contact, *both are treated as valid forms* and linked with cross-references (emphasis added).[22]

Generally, although personal communication is considered the most authoritative source for the forms of names, it is not always necessary to make personal contact if the forms that appear in print are consistent. It is when conflicting forms are found on published materials that the process of determining the most authoritative form becomes more complex. If it appears personal communication is required, e-mail or written correspondence is usually preferred over telephone conversations, in order to ensure the proper orthographic form is reproduced. One contact would in most cases be sufficient to deal with all variants, as most authors publishing in more than one language have their preferences in multiple orthographies already established. Authors of French and English materials use roman orthography, as do those who express their names in Inuinnaqtun and if asked, usually have a preference for the expression of their names in syllabics. Inuktitut speakers whose names are primarily expressed in syllabics usually indicate whether they have a preference for an "English" name, an Inuktitut expression strictly transliterated into roman from the syllabics table, or both.

Frequently, more than one potential source of information must be consulted to cover all of the different expressions of an individual's name. For example, a well-respected Inuit elder from Pond Inlet has been involved in a number of publications documenting Inuit traditional knowledge. Some have been published in Inuktitut syllabics, some in English. The Inuktitut spelling of her name is consistent in syllabics: ᐊᓕᓴᐱ ᐆᑑᒃ. This has appeared variously in English translation or in transliteration as Elisapie Ootova, Ilisapi Ootoova, Elisapee Ootoowak,

---

22. Nunavut Legislative Libraries, "Name Authorities (Draft)," *Cataloguing Policy and Procedures Manual* (Iqaluit, Nunavut: Legislative Library of Nunavut, 2018), 1-2.

and Elisapee Ootoova. The Legislative Library was, fortunately, able to contact a member of her family, who consulted with her. The form of name settled on for the "authorized" English/roman orthography entry was Elisapie Ootova: the form of her name that appears on her passport and on the citation of her Order of Canada.[23] All of the other variations have been added to the authority record for the "English" version of her name as "see" (MARC tag 400) references, to direct a roman orthography searcher to the preferred form of her name. The reverse would hold true in the case of an English name variously transliterated into syllabics: a preferred syllabic transliteration is chosen, and then all of the variant syllabic versions are traced as "see" references in the Inuktitut name authority file. In this way the variety of forms that appear on sources, and thus might be searched for, can be easily accessed, but the author's preference is also being respected.

An important point is to acknowledge that names may change and evolve over time, and that a person could be equally well known by possible variants on a name. One Inuit educator is well-known by his "English" name, David Serkoak, but has published works with his name in syllabics, ᑕᐃᕕᑎ ᓯᖁ, and in transliterated roman orthography, Taiviti Siqua. Likewise the famous Inuit artist who designed the Nunavut flag, ᐋᓄᓗ ᖃᐱᒃ, in the 1980s and '90s used the anglicized form of Andrew Karpik, but since 2000 has gone by Andrew Qappik; the transliterated form of his name using the current standard would be Aanulu Qaapik. In such cases, authority records need to acknowledge the equivalence of these forms, as they represent variant anglicized forms of his Inuit identity.

A little more problematic can be instances where persons might have been identified under a bureaucratic structure that did not necessarily equate to their self-identification. Traditionally, Inuit did not have surnames, and Inuit naming practices differed significantly from English ones, including a lack of gender bias.[24] As a measure of identification,

23. Philippa Ootoowak, personal communication by e-mail, April 21, 2006.

24. A. Barry Roberts, *Eskimo Identification and Disc Numbers: A Brief History* (Ottawa: Department of Indian and Northern Affairs, 1975), 2.

the federal government in the 1940s introduced a system of attaching "E-numbers" (i.e. Eskimo) to individual Inuit as they moved into settlements, issuing identification disks with the numbers on them like dog tags.[25] Eventually, in 1970, the government launched "Operation Surname" to identify family groupings and create surnames for all Inuit in conformity with practice elsewhere in Canada for official documents.[26] Some people of the transitional generations maintained their single-name identities, but most Inuit currently go by personal and family names. Authority records may need to track some of these variations. An interesting case in point was raised by a missing persons inquiry launched by the Nunavut government in 2007 for a person officially known as Qangualuk Uissatiaq.[27] He was commonly known simply as Qangualuk; other references in official documentation referred to him as Kangooalook No. 5449 (his E-number, attached to an older transliteration standard) and Kangualuk. The Legislative Library's name authority record for his name includes all of these variants as "see" references so the various versions of his identity can be traced.

Organizational or corporate name authorities, especially for Nunavut government departments and agencies, share similar challenges: determining the choice of "official" source, dealing with dialectal variants in the translation of names and determining how to trace or cross-reference them, and dealing with the ongoing evolution and reorganization of departments and agencies. The Legislative Library's preferred naming sources for corporate identities are as follows:

  1. For Nunavut government bodies, the form of name used in any wordmarks or visual identity programs. If the government

---

25. Ibid.

26. Michelle Filice, "Project Surname," *Historica Canada* (2015), http://www.thecanadianencyclopedia.ca/en/article/project-surname/. Abe Okpik, a prominent Inuk who was instrumental in carrying out the project, describes it in his biography: Abraham Okpik, *We Call it Survival: The Life Story of Abraham Okpik* (Iqaluit, Nunavut: Nunavut Arctic College, 2005).

27. Nunavut, "Draft Terms of Reference: Public Inquiry into the Qangualuk disappearance" (Iqaluit, Nunavut: Government of Nunavut, 2007), Tabled Document 57-2(4).

issues a list of official names for departments and corporations, this list takes priority.

2. When Nunavut and other government departments are reorganized, the name of the preceding department is cross-referenced to the name of the succeeding department or departments. If possible an explanatory note is included in the record. Government announcements or press releases are considered the authoritative source for this information.

3. Legislative Assembly standing and special committee names are established from the committees' terms of reference. If these are not available, the form of committee name used in the Hansard is preferred. The Assembly website is a supplementary source of information for names not translated in the Hansard or other official Assembly communications, particularly for Inuinnaqtun expressions.

4. For other corporate bodies, the form of name used in any corporate logo or wordmark is preferred. An organization's website is the next preferred option, followed by the name as found in publications. Again, if an organization's name changes over time or is re-translated in a new logo, both versions of the name are considered equally valid and are cross-referenced.[28]

The evolution of government departments and agencies is a particularly challenging aspect of maintaining cross-referenced, multilingual authority files. Not only does one need to track possible preceding and succeeding forms of a name, but also any dialectal variants that may crop up. This happens frequently with reports from government departments that have been translated into Inuktut, and the translator has not been given or chosen to use the "standard" department name but translated the name according to personal understanding. The authority record for the former Nunavut Department of Health and Social Services in Inuinnaqtun, officially identified as "Nunavut. Munarhiliqiyikkut Inuuhiriknikmullu," contains seven Inuinnaqtun

---

28. Legislative Library, "Name Authorities (Draft)" 2.

variant translations of the name that have appeared on various documents, traced in MARC 410 fields for "see" references, as shown in **Figure 1**.

110 1 $a Nunavut. $b Munarhiliqiyikkut Inuuhiriknirmullu.

410 1 $a Nunavut. $b Anniaktuliginikut Havakviat.

410 1 $a Nunavut. $b Aaniaqtuligiyit Inuligiyitlu Kivgaqtit.

410 1 $a Nunavut. $b Okoa Kavamat Mokhikakvilikiot Olasilikiot.

410 1 $a Nunavut. $b Munaqhiliqitikkut Inuuhiliqiyitkullu

410 1 $a Nunavut. $b Munagiyit Aniaktailigiyit ovalo Inuligiyit.

410 1 $a Nunavut. $b Aaniaqtailinikkut Inuuhilirinikkut Pilirivvik

410 1 $a Nunavut. $b Munaqhiliqiyitkut Inuuhiqattialiriyiit.

510 1 $a Nunavut. $b Department of Health and Social Services.

510 1 $a Nunavut. $b Ministère de la Santé et des Services sociaux.

510 1 $a ᓄᓇᕗᑦ. $b ᐋᓐᓂᐊᖅᑖᖃᕐᓂᒃᑐᑦᑎᑕᐅᖅᓯᒪᔪᒃ ᐃᓄᑦᑎᑕᐅᑦᑎᒥᒍᑦ.

510 1 $a Nunavut. $b Munarhiliqiyikkut.

510 1 $a Nunavut. $b Inulirijikkut.

680   $a Department divided in April 2013. Reorganized into the Department of Health and the Department of Family Services, which also includes Income Support, moved from the Department of Education

Figure 1: Inuinnaqtun Authority Record for Nunavut Department of Health and Social Services. Nunavut Legislative Library Catalogue, Last Amended October 15, 2013

Tracing a department or agency's evolution also has to be done equally for all language expressions. To avoid over-encumbering every authority record, the Library has adopted the following principle for the cross-references:

For preceding and succeeding forms of names for corporate bodies, the preceding or succeeding forms will be traced *for the language of the record* (emphasis added). Other language expressions of the name will be traced, but not other language expressions of preceding or succeeding bodies. Those will be traced in their respective applicable authority files. Thus the record for the Workers' Compensation Board of the Northwest Territories and Nunavut will reference both the preceding Workers' Compensation Board of the Northwest Territories and the succeeding Workers' Safety and Compensation Commission of the Northwest Territories and Nunavut, but only the Inuktitut and Inuinnaqtun equivalents of its own name. Those other language authorities will trace the preceding and succeeding names in their own languages.[29]

The example cited above is illustrated in **Figure 2**.

110 2 $a Workers' Compensation Board of the Northwest Territories and Nunavut.

410 1 $a Nunavut. $b Workers' Compensation Board.

410 1 $a Northwest Territories. $b Workers' Compensation Board.

510 2 $a ᐃᖃᓗᐃᖅᑖᕝᑎᒃ ᐊᑉᑎᐅᖅᑐᒃᕕᓗᑎᕆᓐᖏᒃᖃ ᑲᑎᒪᔩᖅᑎᒃ ᓄᓇᑦᑎᐊᕐᒥ ᓄᓇᕘᒥᓗ.

510 2 $a Commission des accidents du travail des Territoires du Nord-Ouest et du Nunavut.

510 2 $a Havaktinut Havalimaiqata Nalliqtaqvik Ukiuktaqtuni Nunavunmilu.

510 2$a Workers' Safety and Compensation Commission of the Northwest Territories and Nunavut.

510 2 $a Workers' Compensation Board of the Northwest Territories.

680 $a Name changed from Workers' Compensation Board to Workers' Safety and Compensation Commission with the coming into force of the Workers' Compensation Act, April 1, 2008.

Figure 2. English Authority Record for WCBNTN. Nunavut Legislative Library Catalogue, Last Amended November 10, 2009

This authority record has three parallel records for this particular agency in French, Inuinnaqtun and Inuktitut syllabics. The equivalent in Inuktitut is illustrated in **Figure 3**.

---

29. Ibid., 3.

110 2 $a ᐃᖃᓇᐃᓯᖅᑎᑦ ᓇᓪᓕᐅᒃᑯᒪᓕᕆᔩᒃᑯᑦ ᑲᑎᒪᔨᖏᑦ ᓄᓇᑦᑎᐊᕐᒥ ᓄᓇᕗᒥᒍ.

410 2 $a ᓄᓇᕗᒻᒥᑦ ᓄᓇᑦᑎᐊᕐᒧᓪᒍ ᐃᖅᑲᓇᐃᔭᖅᑏᑦ ᓇᓪᓕᐅᒃᑯᒫᖅᑕᐅᓯᒪᓂᖏᓐᓄᑦ ᑲᑎᒪᔩᑦ.

410 2 $a ᐃᖃᓇᐃᓯᖅᑎᑦ ᓇᓪᓕᐅᒃᑯᒫᓕᕆᔩᖏᑕ ᑲᑎᒪᔩᖏᑦ ᓄᓇᑦᓯᐊᕐᒧᑦ ᐊᒻᒪ ᓄᓇᕗᒧᑦ

410 2 $a ᐃᖃᓇᐃᓯᕐᑏᑦ ᓇᓪᓕᐅᑯᒫᓕᕆᔩᖏᑦᑕ ᑲᑎᒪᔩᖏᑦ ᓄᓇᑦᓯᐊᕐᒧᑦ ᐊᒻᒪ ᓄᓇᕗᒧᑦ

510 2 $a Workers' Compensation Board of the Northwest Territories and Nunavut.

510 2 $a Commission des accidents du travail des Territoires du Nord-Ouest et du Nunavut.

510 2 $a Havaktinut Havalimaiqata Nalliqtaqvik Ukiuktaqtuni Nunavunmilu.

510 2 $a ᐃᖃᓇᐃᓯᖅᑎᑦᓄᑦ ᐊᑦᑕᓇᖅᑐᓂᒃ ᐊᒻᒪ ᓇᓪᓕᐅᒃᑯᒫᓂᒃ ᖃᐅᔨᓴᖅᑎᑦ ᓄᓇᑦᑎᐊᕐᒥ ᓄᓇᕗᒥᒍ.

680 $a Name changed from Workers' Compensation Board to Workers' Safety and Compensation Commission with the coming into force of the Workers' Compensation Act, April 1, 2008

Figure 3: Parallel Inuktitut Record for WCBNTN. Nunavut Legislative Library Catalogue, Last Amended October 14, 2010

The Inuktitut records lists the English, French and Inuinnaqtun equivalents of the name, and the name of the succeeding agency in Inuktitut, as "see also" references (i.e. other valid headings). It also includes three variant Inuktitut translations as "see" references, for versions of the name that have appeared on documents but would not be considered official.

Clearly, the creation of these parallel and ever-evolving records, both for persons and corporate entities, involves significant commitment of time and resources on the part of the cataloguing agency. As the Legislative Library is often the first to receive and catalogue many Nunavut government documents, and has in its mandate the documentation of Nunavut's legislative history, it has the budget and institutional will to devote to this work. It also requires the cataloguers to have sufficient training to be able to create these records, and an interest in and connection to the community whose works are being catalogued.

Working with a relatively small population (35,944, as of the 2016 Census),[30] Nunavut's cataloguers are frequently in a position to be acquainted with members of the publishing community and to be well aware of changes in government departments or Inuit organizations. This is a personal connection frequently lacking in larger consortial cataloguing systems, and a luxury not always afforded to those creating original records in the context of bigger societies. The result is a personalized set of data that is helpful to the local population, but difficult to share with other institutions and consortia. Even within Nunavut, there is no current centralized cataloguing authority, so although similar approaches are applied by various Nunavut library systems, the authority records they arrive at may differ.

Future Challenges

The Nunavut Legislative Library continues to lead the way in advocating for Indigenous language cataloguing practices in Canada, but at the same time faces its own set of challenges. The energy and cost of maintaining a unique authority dataset remains high, while the pool of Inuit language cataloguers is low. As the founding developers of our multilingual cataloguing policies move towards retirement, much work needs to be done in terms of succession planning and the recruitment and training of the next wave of multilingual cataloguers.

The cost is high because libraries must dedicate a significant portion of staff working hours towards building and maintaining a multilingual authority dataset. Whereas library staff working in a unilingual or even an English/French environment can easily obtain copy cataloguing for most of their records, cataloguers in a multilingual environment must create their own records. Over the past ten years, monthly cataloguing statistics have indicated that approximately 85-90% of the cataloguing done at the Legislative Library involves the creation of original records. Unless more libraries begin cataloguing in Indigenous languages, libraries like the Nunavut Legislative Library will need to continue to spend

---

30. Statistics Canada, "Nunavut Census Profile."

a considerable amount of time and resources on creating their own records with a relatively small budget. The lack of cataloguers capable of cataloguing in Inuktut makes it even more challenging for the Nunavut Legislative Library. Though fluency is not required to catalogue in Inuktut, a certain degree of comprehension is needed, as well as familiarity with syllabic script for Inuktitut. Furthermore, these records are rooted in local history and culture, making it difficult for a cataloguer outside this sphere to have the knowledge base required to create such records.

In order to alleviate some of the stress put on these libraries, more effort is needed to encourage those with fluency or proficiency in Inuktut to choose a career in libraries, especially in cataloguing, in the hopes of developing another cohort of multilingual cataloguers. Training is a particular challenge in all of Canada's northern territories, as there are as yet no universities established and no library programs at the community college level. The only options for those in Nunavut wanting library training are to leave the territory for a college diploma or university degree, to engage in distance education, or to do training on the job. All three methods have been and are being used for current staff cataloguing at the Legislative Library, but it takes particular interest and dedication on the part of library staff to pursue these forms of education while developing careers. In addition, special training is required in order to apply locally developed standards, requiring additional commitment on the part of both those teaching and those learning, and from institutional management to support these ongoing costs.

The leaders in the multilingual cataloguing field must also continue to look for avenues to share knowledge and data with others in the cataloguing world. Some libraries may want to adopt multilingual cataloguing practices but are using systems with overriding authority control systems—this is an area where librarians working with a multilingual ILS can help.

LAC's recent decision to move to an OCLC-based national union catalogue could present yet another barrier in bringing libraries with multilingual authority datasets into their collective. Past practice for LAC, in Canada's national officially bilingual context, was to cross-reference English and French name and subject heading authorities. In particular, the names of government departments and agencies, being deemed to be legally equivalent and equally official, were always cross-referenced from English to French versions and vice versa, the principle adopted by the Nunavut Legislative Library for its multilingual authority practice. However, with the launch of Voilà, the new OCLC-managed national union catalogue for Canada, LAC has indicated that it has joined the Name Authority Cooperative Program (NACO), hosted by the Library of Congress, for English name authorities: "NACO libraries create standardized English-language forms of creator names to be used in the bibliographic records of all participating libraries. For English-language authority records, NACO will replace Canadiana Authorities."[31] However, the situation is less clear for French-language authorities:

> While many organizations around the world maintain French-language authority files, there is currently no international shared French-language authority program comparable to what is available in English through NACO. For this reason, LAC will continue to maintain its separate French-language name authority file. Once these authority records now maintained in AMICUS are migrated to OCLC, LAC will use OCLC's system for creating and updating French name authorities. LAC French-language authority data will continue to be freely accessible at viaf.org.[32]

It is not at all clear whether the French versions of names will be maintained as cross-references in the NACO English authorities, nor the English in the French ones, without a centralized Canadiana authorities file for reference. Nor is it clear how the political/legal side of name equivalence, especially for government entities, is going to be

---

31. Library and Archives Canada, "Will LAC continue to maintain Canadiana Authorities in English and in French?", *Questions and answers for Canadian libraries in light of LAC's contract with OCLC* (2018), http://www.bac-lac.gc.ca/eng/services/national-union-catalogue/Pages/questions-answers-contract-oclc.aspx

32. Ibid.

handled. This could have a significant impact going forward on how, and even whether, the Nunavut Legislative Library can share its Inuktut name authorities, and how it would manage English or French name authorities where local practice would differ from other institutions in providing cross-references. International cooperation and consistency in headings is a desirable good, but the Nunavut Legislative Library is probably not the only library or jurisdiction that might have local needs that are not met by authority files developed in another country or locality, and officially so established just because the other jurisdiction set them up sooner. While LAC has stated that they are still in the process of working out these issues, the Nunavut Legislative Library will continue to voice its concerns in the hopes that multilingual cataloguing needs are considered at the national and international level.

We must eventually determine whether or not an organization like OCLC is willing to accommodate this model and recognize our records as being equally authoritative, and if not, what other systems would be willing to accept the cross-referenced multilingual model. We must also explore the potential of participating in the emerging linked data environment to see if there is a way to incorporate our multilingual Inuit language authority datasets.

As ILSs become more sophisticated and user-friendly, there are opportunities to expand the effectiveness of multilingual authority datasets such as the one at the Nunavut Legislative Assembly. Unicode compliance is now a fairly standard feature in most new systems, making it possible to import and exchange data that might contain scripts such as Canadian Aboriginal Syllabics. More difficult is encouraging ILS developers to think in the context of multilingual catalogue users. Where more than one language option exists in a system, it is often assumed that users will want to switch from one language to another (for example, from English to French) and access the catalogue in the "other" language. Although having a preferred language interface is certainly helpful for the user, it is often the case that users want to be able to access materials in multiple languages, and to see references between them. Certainly in Nunavut it is the case that a government department might have issued a document in one language and not another; so, for example, a French-language speaker wanting to access a document issued only in Inuktitut and English will need to be able to determine the appropriate department name in one of those other languages in order to access the material. Someone conducting an authority search in one language does need to be able to see if other documents in other languages from the same entity are available.

If the ILS developer clearly understands this concept, browse searching for cross-referenced authorities is a fairly simple matter, as has been the case for the system originally adopted by the Nunavut Legislative Library. But as systems age and libraries migrate to other platforms, it becomes clear that this kind of multilingual searching is not understood or assumed by other ILSs. As the Legislative Library has discovered in a recent migration exercise, discussion of the management of authority files then becomes a key component in the assessment of data migration and in the design of public OPACs to make this carefully developed information available in practical terms to the general public.

In order for Inuit language authority control to continue to be sustainable, librarians must also find ways to better publicize catalogue content so that it becomes a more widely used tool for Inuktut-speaking researchers and library users. Many users are not aware, for example, that the Legislative Library's catalogue can actually be searched in syllabics. Likewise, the OPAC for the catalogue is available in English and French interfaces, but work needs to be done for full translation of the searching interface into Inuktut.

Conclusion

Clearly, maintaining multilingual and multiscript authority files of this complexity requires significant commitment on the part of the cataloguing agency. Effort is required to research and track variations, to make contact with persons or entities when possible, and to ensure that records remain up-to-date. Simple copy cataloguing from central-ized agencies will not meet the needs of Inuit language users of the catalogue, so cataloguing staff must have specialized training in the creation of original authority records and the ability to input text in different scripts. Library organizations must be committed to bearing the expense, whether in staff time or contract work, to create and main-tain these files. There must also be genuine commitment to supporting minority languages such as Inuktut, and to encouraging those for whom these languages are their mother tongue to take up work in this field.

Whether these choices are regarded as ethical or simply pragmatic in Nunavut's unique linguistic environment, they can serve as a possible model for others serving Indigenous or minority language populations. The chief question is whether they can be integrated into wider data linking networks and that still has to be determined.

Bibliography

Canada. *Agreement Between the Inuit of the Nunavut Settlement Area and Her Maj-esty in Right of Canada.* Ottawa: Indian and Northern Affairs Canada and Tungavik Federation of Nunavut, 1993.

Canadian Committee on MARC. *Proposal No. 2002-11: Repertoire Expansion in the Universal Character Set for Canadian Aboriginal Syllabics.* 2002. https://www.loc.gov/marc/marbi/2002/2002-11.html.

Dorais, Louis-Jacques. *Inuit Discourse and Identity After the Advent of Nunavut.* Québec City: Université Laval, 2006.

Earle, Yvonne. "Ikajarutit: Delivering Legislative Library Services in Aborigi-nal Languages (Nunavut, Canada)." Presentation to the 2008 IFLA World Congress, Québec City, 2008. https://archive.ifla.org/IV/ifla74/papers/103-Earle-en.pdf.

Filice, Michelle. "Project Surname." *Historica Canada.* 2015. http://www.thecanadianencyclopedia.ca/en/article/project-surname/.

Harper, Kenn. "Inuit Writing Systems in Nunavut: Issues and Challenges."
*Building Capacity in Arctic Societies: Dynamics and Shifting Perspectives:
Proceedings of the Second IPSSAS Seminar, Iqaluit, Nunavut, 2003,*
François Trudel, ed. Québec City: Université Laval, 2005: 91-100.
http://ipssas.ku.dk/publications/publindex2003/08_Harper.pdf

Henley, Jon. "Icelandic Language Battles Threat of 'Digital Extinction'." *The
Guardian,* international edition. February 26, 2018. https://www.
theguardian.com/world/2018/feb/26/icelandic-language-batt-
les-threat-of-digital-extinction.

IFLA Cataloguing Section and IFLA Meeting of Experts on an International Cataloguing Code. *Statement of international cataloguing principles.*
IFLA Series on Bibliographic Control, vol. 37. Munich: K. G. Saur,
2009.

Inuugatta: summary of presentations and recommendations. Iqaluit, Nunavut:
Government of Nunavut, 2015. http://assembly.nu.ca/library/
GNedocs/2015/001887-e.pdf.

Inuit Language Protection Act, S.NU *2008,* c.17 (Nunavut)

Library and Archives Canada. "Bilingual Cataloguing Policy." 2015. http://
www.bac-lac.gc.ca/eng/services/cataloguing-metadata/Pages/
bilingual-cataloguing-policy.aspx.

Library and Archives Canada. "Will LAC continue to maintain Canadiana
Authorities in English and in French?" *Questions and answers for
Canadian libraries in light of LAC's contract with OCLC.* 2018. http://
www.bac-lac.gc.ca/eng/services/national-union-catalogue/Pages/
questions-answers-contract-oclc.aspx, accessed April 3, 2018.

Library and Archives Canada, Standards, Intellectual Management Office. *Inventory of Romanization Tools.* Ottawa: Library and Archives Canada,
2006.

Nunavut. "Draft Terms of Reference: Public Inquiry into the Qangualuk
disappearance." Iqaluit, Nunavut: Government of Nunavut, 2007.
Tabled Document 57-2(4).

Nunavut. *Incorporating Inuit Societal Values.* 2013 http://assembly.nu.ca/library/GNedocs/2013/001181-e.pdf

Nunavut. *Pinasuaqtavut : that which we've set out to do : our hopes and plans for Nunavut* = ᐱᓇᓱᐊᖅᑕᕗᑦ : ᓂᑎᐅᕐᒥᒥᖕᔭᒃ ᐊᒻᒪᓗ ᐸᕐᓇᐅᑎᒃ ᓄᓇᕗᒃ = *Pinasuaqtavut : voilà ce que nous cherchons à accomplir : nos espoirs et nos plans pour le Nunavut* = *Pinahuaqtavut : imaa titirarhimajuq : ihumagijavut upalungaijautillu Nunavunmi.* Iqaluit, Nunavut: Government of Nunavut, 1999.

Nunavut. *Turaaqtavut* = ᑐᕌᖅᑕᕗᑦ. Iqaluit, Nunavut: Government of Nunavut, 2018.

Nunavut Legislative Library. "Cataloguing: Multilingual Records." *Cataloguing Policy and Procedures Manual.* Iqaluit, Nunavut: Legislative Library of Nunavut, 2009.

Nunavut Legislative Library. "Name Authorities (Draft)." *Cataloguing Policy and Procedures Manual.* Iqaluit, Nunavut: Legislative Library of Nunavut, 2018.

Nunavut Act. S.C. 1993, c.28 (Can.).

Nunavut Land Claims Agreement Act. S.C. 1993, c.29 (Can.).

Official Languages Act, S.Nu. 2008, c.10 (Nunavut).

Okpik, Abraham. *We Call it Survival: The Life Story of Abraham Okpik.* Iqaluit, Nunavut: Nunavut Arctic College, 2005.

Rigby, Carol. "Nunavut Libraries Online Establish Inuit Language Bibliographic Cataloging Standards: Promoting Indigenous Language Using a Commercial ILS," in "Indigenous Knowledge Organization," special issue. *Cataloguing & Classification Quarterly* 53, no. 5-6 (2015): 615-639. DOI 10.1080/01639374.2015.1008165

Rigby, Carol and Rae-Lynne Patterson. "A Catalogue in a Multilingual, Multiscript Environment: the Experience of Nunavut's Library Partnership." *Reaching Out: Innovations in Canadian Libraries*, Yvon-André Lacroix, ed. Montréal: Les Presses de l'Université Laval, 2008.

Roberts, A. Barry. *Eskimo Identification and Disc Numbers: A Brief History.* Ottawa: Department of Indian and Northern Affairs, 1975.

Statistics Canada. "Nunavut [Territory] and Canada [Country] (table). Census Profile," *2016 Census.* Ottawa: Statistics Canada, 2017. http://www12.statcan.gc.ca/census-recensement/2016/dp-pd/prof/index.cfm?Lang=E.

Unicode, Inc. *The Unicode Standard 10.0: Unified Canadian Aboriginal Syllabics Range 1400-167F.* S. l.: Unicode, Inc., 2017. https://unicode.org/charts/PDF/U1400.pdf.

White, Graham. *Responsible Government in Nunavut: The "Consensus Government" System.* 2003. http://assembly.nu.ca/library/Edocs/2003/001487-e.pdf.

Chapter 18

ETHICAL QUESTIONS IN NAME AUTHORITY CONTROL:
AN INDIGENOUS GLOBAL PERSPECTIVE OF POLICY, PRO-
CEDURES AND BEST PRACTICE

Naomi R. Caldwell

Language communicates one's identity, culture, value system, and perspective. Colonial language that is used to describe indigenous, aboriginal,
and First Nations people and cultures demoralizes, dominates, and is
created to justify abuses such as mass genocide and illegal land seizure.
Subtle practices of using language created to dominate are frequently
found in name authority files that describe indigenous peoples, cultures,
and homelands. This chapter calls attention to the indigenous worldview
of name authority history, political issues, policies, and best practices in
four countries: the United States, Canada, New Zealand, and Australia.

These countries each have a history of colonialism and share remarkable similarities in their treatment of indigenous peoples. A familiar
practice among these countries during colonial times was to disregard
indigenous perspectives languages and use language to dominate, assimi-
late, and devalue indigenous people. In postcolonial times, indigenous
peoples have worked with native speakers, cultural gatekeepers, elders,
educators, library and information professionals, and educators to create
protocols. The process of engaging indigenous people in the conversation to describe them is available in several policies. Digital authority
files are available to ethically describe indigenous topics. A practical
framework for ethical practices based on indigenous values and respect

and the decolonizing of name authority files is possible. Practical tips to foster effective advocacy and build coalitions with cultural gatekeepers for ethical name authority are also presented.

This chapter is designed to inform the reader about issues related to a global perception of indigenous name authority policy, procedures, and best practices. Careful attention is given to consulting documents that are vetted by indigenous peoples, native speakers and cultural gate-keepers, and librarians and educators.

The author became aware of the indigenous perspective on research, resources, and name authority issues and how these things are affected by colonial doctrines of domination at the First International Indigenous Librarians' Forum held at Waipapa Marae, University of Auckland, New Zealand.[1] There she was introduced to other indigenous librarians, archivists, library workers, cultural gatekeepers, and elders with similar personal and professional goals. We all gathered together to help each other and our people, and to contribute to our profession.

The author, a doctoral student at that time, was thankful to meet Dr. Linda Tuhiwai Smith (Maori) and learn about her classic textbook *Decolonizing Methodologies: Research and Indigenous People.*[2] Dr. Smith's presentation, subsequent Q&A session, and conversations with others brought to forefront of the author's mind the similarities in postcolonial existence experienced by indigenous elders, librarians, library workers, educators, scholars, and students worldwide. Forum participants gathered by invitation were indigenous.

We all sensed the honor granted us and the hospitable atmosphere provided by our Maori host. The serious work before us was woven together with lighthearted humor by our Maori facilitator who articulated our agreed-upon cultural protocols. We openly discussed our local and collective information issues in a safe environment and that gave voice

---

1. Robert Sullivan, ed., 2001, *International Indigenous Librarians' Forum, University of Auckland, 1999*, Wellington: Te Rōpū Whakahau.

2. Linda Tuhiwai Smith, *Decolonizing Methodologies: Research and Indigenous People* (London: Zed Books, 1999).

to many challenges that face individuals and communities who seek information by and about indigenous issues and topics.

Representatives of the Maori (Aotearoa New Zealand our host), Aboriginals (Australia), Sami (Sweden), First Nations (Canada), Aboriginal (Canada), and American Indian (United States) told stories about invasion, theft of homelands, genocide, war, domination, assimilation, and residential school trauma. To lighten the sobering truth of our shared histories, our Maori host told traditional stories in songs and dance between each session. One theme that resonated throughout the forum regardless of the session was the systematic effect of language used to dominate, subjugate, and justify colonialism. This chapter will provide a brief background on colonial language used to describe indigenous topics, and couple that historical perspective of language use with a second theme that resonated throughout the forum.

Forum participants agreed to begin with the global indigenous view of creation, which is the interdependence of all things animate, inanimate, tangible, and intangible. We acknowledged our responsibility to widen our circle of information advocates by sharing our point of view about what type of language we use to tell our story, history, and cultural information.

The advocacy theme is an important concern for all librarians and information specialists. Our professional training and experiences enabled us to be prepared to engage in conversations about building coalitions within our indigenous communities, as well as enlarging our circle to welcome others. Our professional code of ethics advocates for equal and ethical access to resources and information.[3] Attendees of the forum agreed that ethical use of information should require professionals who describe resources about indigenous topics to be knowledgeable of the cultural perspectives and demonstrate ethical use by consulting members of the community to ensure respectful use of language to provide access to resources.

---

3. American Library Association, "Professional Ethics," *American Library Association*, May 19, 2017, http://www.ala.org/tools/ethics.

We proceeded with several discussions about who "tells our story" and how these stories are perceived by those outside of our cultures. Most agreed that how information about indigenous people were historically described used colonial language that was disparaging, stereotypical, and inaccurate. The language used to describe cultural information is critical to ethical access and use of information about indigenous peoples. More about this will be shared in the section on best practices.

The first step for information professionals is the development of collaborative professional development opportunities to introduce and recognize that indigenous cultural perspectives and ways of being are valid. Globally, this recognition of indigenous cultural perspectives is not automatic. *The United Nations Declaration on the Rights of Indigenous Peoples* declares and "affirms that indigenous peoples are equal to all other peoples and recognize the right of all people to be different, to consider themselves different, and to be respected."[4] However, the countries discussed in this chapter delayed their official support of this declaration. Australia and New Zealand signed in 2009 and the United States and Canada in 2010.[5]

The International Federation of Library Associations and Institutions (IFLA) acknowledged the need to recognize indigenous perspectives in 2008 with the formation of IFLA Past President Alex Byrne's Presidential Task Force on Indigenous Matters.[6] A decade later, the IFLA Indigenous Matters Section was established. Fortunately, individual countries discussed in this chapter engaged indigenous communities in discussion about their information and service needs at a much earlier date.

---

4. United Nations, *United Nations Declaration of the Rights of Indigenous Peoples*, March 2008, http://www.un.org/esa/socdev/unpfii/documents/DRIPS_en.pdf.

5. K. M. Harrison, "Peace Instead of Policy: Indigenous and Autonomous Utopias," in *Policy for Peace: Language Education Unlimited*, ed. F. Tochon and K. Harrison (Blue Mounds, WI: Deep Education Press, 2016), 293.

6. *IFLA Indigenous Matters Section*, 2017, https://www.ifla.org/ES/about-indigenous-matters, 1.

New Zealand (Aotearoa) has the best record and documentation for the description of its indigenous people. It is important to share a bit of their collective history and library community advocacy. Aotearoa is a relatively young international nation that was established with the signing of the Treaty of Waitangi in 1841 by a representative of Queen Victoria and 500 Maori Chiefs. The Treaty is still honored. It provided the legal and moral basis for passage of the Maori Language Act in 1987 that established English and Maori as the national languages of the country.[7]

The Library Information Association of New Zealand (LIANA), which was founded in 1910, first established a Maori Library Services Committee in 1962. Ten years later in 1972, it endorsed Maori Language Day, followed by Maori Language Week in 1978.[8]

One of LIANZA's premier accomplishments is a collaborative project with Te Ropu Whakahu and Te Puna Matauranga O Aotearoa National Library of New Zealand.[9] This project demonstrates indigenous name authority with *Te Ara Tika (Guiding Voices)*, an online database of nationally recognized Maori subject headings.[10]

For those who collect, manage, and help to facilitate access to information, cultural perspective biases often go undetected by the uninitiated. Authentic respect for cultural differences occurs when one begins the process of acknowledging that personal biases exist. And yet one is always able to effect change for the good of the whole through successful efforts that will be discussed later in this chapter. But first let us examine the issue of language that has been used to describe differences and why.

It is relatively easy to acknowledge that differences among human beings exist. As children, we learn quickly how to discern visual differences among our peers. Some children have brown eyes; others have

7. New Zealand Ministry for Culture and Heritage, "History of the Māori Language," *Te Wiki o Te Reo Māori - Māori Language Week*, last modified October 10, 2017, https://nzhistory.govt.nz/culture/maori-language-week/history-of-the-maori-language.

8. *LIANZA History*, 2014, https://lianza.org.nz/node/59.

9. Te Ropu Whakahau, "Te Ropu Whakahau," https://lianza.org.nz/our-work/partnerships/te-rōpū-whakahau.

10. *LIANZA History*, 2014.

blue or green. Some have light-colored hair and others have dark-colored hair. Some have neon hair color. Some have straight hair. Some have curly. Some have short hair. And so on. Children also learn to discern different speech patterns and different ways of responding to sound and actions. They naturally look to the authority figures in their lives and communities for guidance on how to make assumptions and choices based on these differences.

Our first experiences with authority figures are with our parents or caregivers, family, extended family, and community members. As we mature, familial authority is expanded and transferred to those who continue teach us how to perceive the world. These "teachers" are educators, spiritual and religious leaders, coaches, peers, and print and digital media. All of these "tutors" communicate to us using sound, touch, movement, images, and language. We quickly learn to respond "good or bad" to the most prevalent messages. The sum of the communication we receive from these sources equates to our personal "Wikipedia" of semantics and language. Librarians, archivists, and information specialists understand that while Wikipedia may be a starting point, there is more to the story.

The language we use enables us to make sense of ourselves, and others. Nieto suggests that language is the foundation for all social interaction, and in turn, it is a symbol of national unity and a transmitter of cultural ideas and mores. He argues that the meaning of language is a continuous process that evolves by negotiation and is subject to being redefined according to cultural perception.[11]

Historical evidence of the use of language to dominate groups of people is widespread. Let us consider the first published grammar of the Castilian language by Antonio de Nebrija in 1492. Nebrija wrote that language had the ability to establish a powerful kingdom and helped to foster a sense of national unity. History recounts that Nebrija's thoughts

---

11. David Gonzalez Nieto, "The Emperor's New Words: Language and Colonization," *Human Architecture: Journal of the Sociology of Self-Knowledge*, 2007, https://scholarworks.umb.edu/humanarchitecture/vol5/iss3/21/.

about language were used by Spain to establish the use of Spanish among indigenous peoples—if they were to be perceived as "civilized."

Librarians are familiar with the story of Noah Webster, an American educator, lexicographer, and Yale University graduate. He is credited with the ambitious publication of the first American English language dictionary in 1828. Webster's goal was to unite the people of the United States by creating a dictionary for the country that reflected the terms used in America. Webster's political point of view supported a strong national government and American nationalism. Webster incorporated many words unique to this country, such as "raccoon" and "canoe." He used lists of words from the *King James Bible*. It is interesting to note how four "indigenous" topics are defined.

CANOE, noun
1. A boat used by rude nations, formed of the body or trunk of a tree, excavated, by   cutting or burning, into a suitable shape. Similar boats are now used by civilized men, for fishing and other purposes. It is impelled by a paddle, instead of an oar.
2. A boat made of bark or skins, used by savages.

MO'HOCK, noun, the appellation given to certain ruffians who infested the streets of London; so called from the nation of Indians of that name in America.

THANKSGIV'ING, participle present tense, Rendering thanks for good received.

THANKSGIV'ING, noun, the act of rendering thanks or expressing gratitude for favors or mercies.
A public celebration of divine goodness; also, a day set apart for religious services, specially to acknowledge the goodness of God, either in any remarkable deliverance from calamities or danger, or in the ordinary dispensation of his bounties. The practice of appointing an annual *thanksgiving* originated in New England.[12]

---

12. The practice of Thanksgiving first introduced to the Pilgrims in 1621 by Wampanoag Chief Massasoit and his people. The Wampanoag celebrated "thanksgiving" times to mark various crops during the year. See Gale Courey Toesning, "What Really Happened at the First Thanksgiving? The Wampanoag Side of the Tale the First Thanksgiving was a fact finding party," *Indian*

SAV'AGE, adjective [Latin silva, a wood, or silvicola, an inhabitant of a wood, or silvaticus.]
1. Pertaining to the forest; wild; remote from human residence and improvements; uncultivated; as a *savage* wilderness.
Cornels and *savage* berries of the wood.
2. Wild; untamed; as *savage* beasts of prey.
3. Uncivilized; untaught; unpolished; rude; as *savage* life; *savage* manners. What nation since the commencement of the christian era, ever rose from *savage* to civilized without Christianity?
4. Cruel; barbarous; fierce; ferocious; inhuman; brutal; as a *savage* spirit.

SAV'AGE, noun
1. A human being in his native state of rudeness; one who is untaught, uncivilized or without cultivation of mind or manners. The savages of America, when uncorrupted by the vices of civilized men, are remarkable for their hospitality to strangers, and for their truth, fidelity and gratitude to their friends, but implacably cruel and revengeful towards their enemies. From this last trait of the *savage* character, the word came to signify." [13]

The language Webster used and promoted to define indigenous peoples of America is evidenced by the definition of the word "savage" in his dictionary. It is a stereotypical definition that acknowledges the "hospitality...truth, fidelity, and gratitude" of indigenous, but places emphasis on their so-called "cruel and revengeful" ways with enemies.[14] One can see that from Webster's perspective a person was considered uncivilized if he or she were not "Christian." Webster cannot take sole responsibility for the term "savage." This term was used by the many colonists who relocated from their homelands to other lands they wished to settle. It was a term used to justify illegal land seizure and genocide. All of the countries considered for this chapter used similar disparaging connotations to initially describe their indigenous people and topics.

Country Today, Nov. 23, 2017, https://indiancountrymedianetwork.com/history/events/what-really-happened-at-the-first-thanksgiving-the-wampanoag-side-of-the-tale/.

13. Noah Webster, 2018, "American Dictionary of the English Language," *Webster's Dictionary 1828 - Online Edition,* http://webstersdictionary1828.com.

14. Ibid.

"Savage" is a term that was acceptable and used in newspapers, textbooks, nonfiction, fiction, children's books, radio, television, and movies. As a result, its popular use influenced the mindset of those who created library cataloging schemes. Needless to say, indigenous people were not consulted on how to properly define, reference, or cite them.

A dramatic shift in regard to how indigenous peoples were categorized worldwide began in the 1960s. This shift in the use of language was a result of civil unrest and civil rights protests among ethnic peoples and women, including those who voiced the inequities in terms of respect and fair treatment. The protests that extended into the 1970s and 1980s called for a more inclusive and respectful portrayal of ethnic groups. Members of traditional library and information science associations recognized that the shift in mainstream societal attitudes and the activism on the part of indigenous peoples meant they needed to address information services and resources for indigenous people. A natural response to this change in the provision of services and resources was the issue of name authority files. Modern use of words like "savage" have become unacceptable worldwide, due in part to ethnic library association members, and progressive and activist librarians like Sanford "Sandy" Berman in the United States.

Sandy Berman was Head Cataloger, Technical Services Division Principal Librarian, who worked over several decades to help change subject headings for indigenous and other peoples. He worked closely with members of the American Indian Library Association to develop lists of appropriate subject headings to reference Indigenous topics and subjects.[15] He met with some success, though it has been a slow process. The American Indian Library Association members continue with the work of informing on indigenous name authority files and cataloging.

The major concern that is voiced by critics of Library of Congress Subject Headings (LCSH) and authority files is the outdated and inappropriate use of terminology. Libraries need to localize terminology

---

15. Sanford Berman, "When the Subject is Indians," *American Indian Libraries Newsletter* 18, no. 2 (Winter 1995), http://www.nativeculturelinks.com/ailanewsW95_LCindians.html.

based on the need of each library community.[16] Many are of the opinion that LCSH serves as a tool for imposing a United States worldview in a neocolonial way, since many countries use either LCSH or a translation of LCSH to describe the materials in their collections.

The Library of Congress (LC) has established a project called the Name Authority Cooperative Program (NACO). This program is an attempt to invite institutional participants to contribute new name authority records and that may facilitate changes to the existing authority records. The process is described on the LC webpage.[17] It details project funnels (groups of libraries or catalogers) that may join together to contribute to the development of name authority file records. There are many funnels that have been formed. At the time of this writing, none represents the indigenous peoples of North America. However, the Latin American and Indigenous Peoples of the Americas SACO Funnel has reached out to the members of the American Indian Library Association to join.

Canadian efforts with regard to the establishment of Aboriginal and First Nation authority records have advanced beyond the efforts of those in the United States. A study conducted by Deborah Lee, Indigenous Studies Portal Librarian, Murray Library, University of Saskatchewan, surveyed indigenous leaders at five indigenous-focused conferences about LC subject headings and the idea of creating an alternative method of organizing materials.[18] The respondents agreed that changes are needed and suggested that a system less linear and non-hierarchical would be useful to express indigenous knowledge systems.

Canada has completed work to recognize the use of Aboriginal names to preserve and strengthen languages and cultures. The former practice

---

16. Deborah Lee, "Indigenous Knowledge Organization: A Study of Concepts, Terminology, Structure and (Mostly) Indigenous Voices." *Canadian Journal of Library Information Practice and Research* 6, no.1 (2011), doi:10.21083/partnership.v6i1.1427: 3, 6, 27.

17. Library of Congress, "Library of Congress NACO Program of Program for Cooperative Cataloging," https://www.loc.gov/aba/pcc/naco/parameters.html.

18. Deborah Lee, "Indigenous Knowledge Organization," 3, 6, 27.

of renaming places by colonizers demonstrated a lack of understanding of the close cultural ties that indigenous peoples have to the land. Among indigenous people, their relationship with the land is a vital part of their cosmology and their relationship with creation. The Geographical Names Board of Canada (GNBC) consulted with members of Aboriginal communities, cultural associations, and heritage groups to collect names and meanings. Together they established a practice of seeking the advice of Aboriginal experts to develop policies and procedures, and to date hundreds of indigenous place names have become official. In some cases, one place might have three names.[19]

Aboriginal and First Nations librarians acknowledge the Library and Archives of Canada (LAC)[20] review of Canadian Subject Headings (CSH). However, the LAC discovered after the fact that there is no consensus on better terminology. They recommend changing headings on an individual, case-by-case basis.

Australia has made greater strides in terms of how Aboriginal and Torres Strait Islander peoples are described than in how the people are treated in mainstream society. The publication of *The Aboriginal and Torres Strait Islander Thesaurus (ATSIT)*[21] by Heather Moorcroft and Alana Garwood discussed the unacceptable mainstream classification system. Past practice described Aboriginals and cataloged them as "savages" or "primitive," and in contrast referred to and cataloged Western industrials as "advanced" and "complex."[22] The work done by Moorcroft and Garwood promoted awareness of how to describe Aboriginal ways of being and how to dispel fear caused by stereotypical descriptions.

19. Geographical Names Board of Canada, 2016, "Indigenous Naming Activities in Canada," 23 June 2017, https://unstats.un.org/unsd/geoinfo/UNGEGN/docs/29th-gegn-docs/WP/WP70_16_Indigenous%20Naming%20Activities%20in%20Canada.pdf.

20. Deborah Lee, "Indigenous Knowledge Organization," 8.

21. Heather Moorcroft, Alana Garwood and National Library of Australia, *Aboriginal and Torres Strait Islander Thesaurus* (Canberra: National Library of Australia, 1997).

22. Martin Nakata, Alex Byrne, Vicky Nakata, and Gabrielle Gardiner, "Libraries Indigenous Australians and a Developing Protocol Strategy for the Library Information Sector," *Australian Academic & Research Libraries* 36 no. 2 (June 2005): 185-199.

The Australian Institute of Aboriginal and Torres Strait Island Studies (AIATSIS) has devoted the last half century to advocating for a better understanding of indigenous peoples and cultures by collecting material, organizing it, and preserving a "national" collection. AIATSIS has guidelines about research, cultural protocols, and developing an understanding of indigenous knowledge systems. They have done much to dispel the traditional "scientific method" of collecting and naming indigenous cultural materials.[23] AIATSIS is well known for its Pathways thesauri online project and its steady use of technology to provide access.

One of the most remarkable projects is the development of a framework that combines indigenous knowledge systems and linked data. This new framework acknowledges indigenous knowledge systems and provides for greater access and culturally appropriate use of materials in the GLAM (galleries, libraries, archives, and museums) sector. This project is exciting news because the technology has developed to facilitate understanding the complexities of linked data for use by a myriad of potential users. It uses tBibframe[24] which allows users to annotate data by tagging and adding their own content. AIATSIS guidelines help to inform this process. This project allows for a more culturally holistic and authentic approach to descriptive categories and is a more organic method for doing so.

New Zealand, among all the nations discussed in this paper, has the most honorable and consistent record of acknowledgment, engagement, and description the Maori people and their culture. The Maori Language Act of 1987 established Maori, along with English, as one of

---

23. Jodie Dowd and Jenny Wood, "Indigenous Knowledge Systems and Linked Data." *ALIA Online Conference, February 14, 2017*, https://informationonline17.alia.org.au/content/indigenous-knowledge-systems-and-linked-data-0.

24. Ibid., 7. Bibframe (Bibliographic Framework Initiative) was developed to replace MARC. Bibframe uses linked data principals and provides a new way to present records and allows for a variety of formats such as video, digital pictures and documents to be linked and viewed via the internet. The user has the ability to click on certain words in the Bibframe and link to other sources of information that are referenced in on a computer or table screen. These references can be clicked on and expanded for additional relevant.

the country's official languages.[25] Public schools began to offer Maori language immersion classes. The National Library of New Zealand established a permanent Maori language expert to help describe and translate terms. As a result, there is an ongoing Maori Subject heading website.

Each of the countries studied for this brief survey of indigenous name authority issues and developments have produced information about the process. This information also includes nuggets of tried and successful advice that can inform the process of building advocacy groups to further improve indigenous name authority policies and procedures. Below is a short list to get started and engaged.[26]

- Seek ongoing consultation with local authorized indigenous representatives and gatekeepers.
- Develop collections in myriad formats about indigenous cultures that reflect all key perspectives on issues.
- Gain information about the kinds of indigenous materials that might be culturally sensitive from an Indigenous perspective.
- Work with community representatives to consider cataloging terminology.
- Invite recognized community leaders to provide continuing professional development about indigenous topics for staff.
- Inquire about indigenous formal research policies and procedures.
- Develop institution and community-based agreements of cooperation.
- Arrange for reciprocal visits to build strong long-term relationships.
- When in doubt ask questions.
- Still not sure? Ask again.
- Join Indigenous Library Associations and visit their webpages.

Authentic respect for cultures occurs when one dispels deep-set personal biases. Often one is unaware of her or his internal biases

---

25. New Zealand Ministry for Culture and Heritage, "History of the Māori Language.»

26. First Archivists Circle, 2007, "Protocols for Native American Archival Materials," 19-20, http://www2.nau.edu/libnap-p/protocols.html.

until one becomes aware of subtle and not-so-subtle distinctions in the language they use to describe themselves and others. The good news is that if one can dispel the initial intimidation and learn about and understand one's own culture and use of language, one can also learn about another culture and their use of language. As librarians and information professionals, we are well prepared to learn, effect change, and enjoy the process.

Bibliography

American Library Association. "Professional Ethics." *American Library Association*. May 19, 2017. http://www.ala.org/tools/ethics.

Berman, Sanford. "When the Subject is Indians." *American Indian Libraries Newsletter* 18, no. 2 (Winter 1995). http://www.nativeculturelinks. com/ailanewsW95_LCindians.html.

Dankowski, Terra. "Removing Barriers to Indigenous Knowledge." *American Libraries*. August 18, 2016. https://americanlibrariesmagazine.org/ blogs/the-scoop/removing-barriers-to-indigenous-knowledge/.

Dowd, Jodie and Jenny Wood. "Indigenous Knowledge Systems and Linked Data." ALIA Online Conference. February 14, 2017. https:// informationonline17.alia.org.au/content/indigenous-knowledge-systems-and-linked-data-0.

Echavarria, T. and A. B. Wertheimer. "Surveying the Role of Ethnic-American Library Associations." *Library Trends* 46 no. 2, (1997): 373-392. http://hdl.handle.net/2142/8160.

First Archivists Circle. "Protocol for Native American Archival Materials." 2007. Protocols for April 9. http://www2.nau.edu/libnap-p/protocols.html.

Geographical Names Board of Canada. "Indigenous Naming Activities in Canada. 2016." April 29. https://unstats.un.org/unsd/geoinfo/ UNGEGN/docs/29th-gegn-docs/WP/WP70_16_Indigenous%20 Naming%20Activities%20in%20Canada.pdf.

Harrison, K. M. "Peace Instead of Policy: Indigenous and Automous
    Utopias." In *Policy for Peace: Language Education Unlimited*, edited by
    F. Tochon and K. Harrison, 283-306. Blue Mounds, WI: Deep
    Education Press, 2016.

IFLA Indigenous Matters Section. 2017. https://www.ifla.org/ES/about-
    indigenous-matters.

Lee, Deborah. "Indigenous Knowledge Organization: A Study of Concepts,
    Terminology, Structure and (Mostly) Indigenous Voices." Partner-
    ship: *Canadian Journal of Library Information Practice and Research* 6, no.
    1 (2011). 2011. doi: 10.21083/partnership.v6i1.1402.

LIANZA History. 2014. https://lianza.org.nz/node/59.

Library of Congress. "Library of Congress NACO Program of Program
    for Cooperative Cataloging." https://www.loc.gov/aba/pcc/naco/
    parameters.html.

Library of Congress Program for Cooperative Cataloging. https://www.loc.
    gov/aba/pcc/naco/funnels.html..

Moorcroft, Heather, Alana Garwood and National Library of Australia.
    Aboriginal and Torres Strait Islander Thesaurus. Canberra: National
    Library of Australia, 1997.

Nakata, Martin, Alex Byrne, Vicky Nakata, and Gabrielle Gardiner. "Librar-
    ies Indigenous Australians and a Developing Protocol Strategy
    for the Library Infomation Sector." *Australian Academic & Research
    Libraries* 36 no. 2 (June 2005): 185-199.

Nieto, David Gonzalez. "The Emperor's New Words: Language and Colo-
    nization." *Human Architecture: Journal of the Sociology of Self-Knowledge.*
    2007. https://scholarworks.umb.edu/humanarchitecture/vol5/
    iss3/21/.

Smith, Linda Tuiwai. *Decolonizing Methodologies: Research and Indigenous Peoples*.
    London: Zed Books, 1999.

Sullivan, Robert. *International Indigenous Librarians' Forum, University of Auck-
    land, 1999*. Wellington: Te Rōpū Whakahau.

Te Ropu Whakahau. "Te Ropu Whakahau." https://lianza.org.nz/our-work/partnerships/te-rōpū-whakahau.

New Zealand Ministry for Culture and Heritage. "History of the Māori Language." *Te Wiki o Te Reo Māori - Māori Language Week*. Last modified October 10, 2017. https://nzhistory.govt.nz/culture/maori-language-week/history-of-the-maori-language.

Tirado, Michelle. "News from Indian Country." The Wampanoag Side of the First Thanksgiving Story from the Native perspective: The True Story of Thanksgiving. November 23, 2011. https://indiancountrymedianetwork.com/news/the-wampanoag-side-of-the-first-thanksgiving-story/.

Toesning, Gale Courey. "What Really Happened at the First Thanksgiving? The Wampanoag Side of the Tale: The First Thanksgiving was a Fact Finding Party." *Indian Country Today*. November 23, 2017. https://indiancountrymedianetwork.com/history/events/what-really-happened-at-the-first-thanksgiving-the-wampanoag-side-of-the-tale/.

United Nations. *United Nations Declaration of the Rights of Indigenous Peoples*. March 2008. http://www.un.org/esa/socdev/unpfii/documents/DRIPS_en.pdf.

Webster, Noah. 2018. "Webster's Dictionary 1828 - Online Edition." *American Dictionary of the English Language*. http://webstersdictionary1828.com.

About the Contributors

Kalani Adolpho received their MLIS from the University of Wisconsin, Milwaukee in May 2017 and is currently in their second year of a three-year Diversity Resident Librarian position at the University of Wisconsin at Madison. They spent their first year at College Library (UW's undergraduate library), and will be spending their second and third years processing archival collections and cataloging for the University Archives and Special Collections departments. Their research interests include decolonizing cataloging and classification (and everything else), the history of books and printing (especially in Hawai'i), race/gender/sexuality in LIS, and social justice.

Fatemeh Ahmadinasab has a PhD in linguistics. She is currently a faculty member in the Department of English Language and Literature, Shahid Chamran University of Ahvaz, Iran. She is interested in linguistic issues in information management and translation studies.

Alexis A. Antracoli is Assistant University Archivist for Technical Services at the Seeley G. Mudd Manuscript Library, a part of the Princeton University Library. She also teaches in the archival studies graduate program at the Rutgers University School of Communication and Information.

Sholeh Arastoopoor is currently a faculty member in the Department of Information Science and Knowledge Studies at the Ferdowsi University of Mashhad. She has also worked for over six years as a researcher in Regional Information Center for Science and Technology.

Naomi R. Caldwell, PhD, MSLS, is an Associate Professor and coordinator of the Library Education Media Online Program, College of Education, Alabama State University. She is past president of the American Indian Library Association and an active member of the American Library Association.

Ahava Cohen is the Head of Hebrew Cataloguing at the National Library of Israel and a member of the Israel National Cataloguing Committee. She also serves as Executive Secretary of the European RDA Interest Group (EURIG) and as the backup European representative to the RDA Steering Committee. Ahava is a doctoral candidate in Bar Ilan University's iSchool, writing her dissertation on the implementation of RDA in Israel.

Katherine M. Crowe has been the University of Denver (DU) Curator of Special Collections and Archives since 2012, and prior to that, supervised metadata and physical processing for the DU Libraries. Her research focuses on critical information literacy and pedagogy, creating inclusive, diverse, and equitable collections, and community-driven archives.

Erin Elzi is the Design & Discovery Librarian at the University of Denver (DU), where she works to make the discovery layer, the library, and the world in general a better place for everyone. Prior to this role, she spent a number of years working in cataloging, and teaches Metadata Architectures in the DU LIS program.

Violet B. Fox is a cataloging and metadata expert who received her MLIS in 2013 from the University of Washington iSchool. Her research interests and publications center on the ethics of controlled vocabularies and best practices in library cataloging and classification.

Riel Gallant is the Legislative Librarian for the Legislative Assembly of Nunavut. He is originally from Wellington, Prince Edward Island and obtained his Master of Library and Information Studies at Dalhousie University.

Tina Gross is the Catalog Librarian at St. Cloud State University. She received her MLIS from the University of Pittsburgh in 1998, and is currently working on an MFA in creative writing at Minnesota State University, Mankato. She co-authored the 2005 study "What Have We Got to Lose? The Effect of Controlled Vocabulary on Keyword Searching Results" with Arlene G. Taylor and a follow-up study in 2015 with Taylor and Daniel N. Joudrey. She recently served as chair of the CaMMS Subject Analysis Committee Working Group on the LCSH "Illegal aliens."

Heather K. Hughes is currently the Middle East Studies Librarian at the University of California, Santa Barbara. She holds an MA in Middle Eastern Studies from the University of Washington and an MSIS from the University of Texas. She has lived and worked in Turkey.

Michelle M. Kazmer is a Professor in the School of Information at Florida State University. Her research focuses on distributed knowledge, and she maintains a research agenda bringing information science theoretical perspectives to the works of Agatha Christie. She teaches in the areas of information organization, information policy, information literacy, and qualitative research methods. Her PhD is from the School of Information Sciences at the University of Illinois at Urbana-Champaign, her MLS is from the University of Pittsburgh, and her BS in mechanical engineering is from Columbia University. She has worked as a rare book cataloger, as an academic engineering/digital librarian, and as a technical information specialist for an automotive manufacturer.

Jennifer M. Martin is the Cataloging and Metadata Services Librarian at Salisbury University, where she catalogs everything from rare books to scholarly works to hot-off-the-press popular fiction.

Anchalee (Joy) Panigabutra-Roberts is Associate Professor and Head of Cataloging and Metadata Services at the University of Tennessee Libraries in Knoxville, Tennessee since November 2016. She is also the coordinator for the Tennessee Name Authority Cooperative Funnel since June 2017. Her work experience has been in cataloging and metadata in academic libraries including positions as Head of Cataloging and Metadata at the American University in Cairo Libraries, New Cairo, Egypt (2013-2016); Cataloging and Metadata and Multicultural Services Librarian and a faculty affiliate with Women's and Gender Studies Program at University of Nebraska-Lincoln (2007-2013); Catalog Librarian at St. Cloud State University in Minnesota (October 2005-July 2007); and assistant professor in the Master Programme in Library Science at University of Western Ontario in London, Ontario, Canada (2002-2005). She has also worked as a Thai-language specialist at Olin Library, Cornell University and at Memorial Library, University of Wisconsin-Madison. She received her MLIS from the University of Wisconsin-Madison, her BA in English (Literature) from St. Olaf College, Northfield, Minnesota and her BA in English (Linguistics) from Chiangmai University, Chiangmai, Thailand. She has published journal articles on research resources on human trafficking in the United States and book chapters on diversity issues in librarianship. Her current research interest is on researcher identifier systems.

Hale Polebaum-Freeman graduated from UCLA's Graduate School of Education & Information Studies with their MLIS in 2017. They recently began their adventures in librarianship by moving their young family 2864.7 miles to the Berkshires, where they work as Reference and First Year Outreach Librarian at Williams College.

Katy Rawdon is the Coordinator of Technical Services for the Special Collections Research Center, Temple University Libraries. She received her BA from Smith College and her MLS from Simmons College, and has worked previously at the Barnes Foundation, the Philadelphia Museum of Art, the American College of Physicians, and the Beinecke Library at Yale University. She is active in the Society of American Archivists and the Mid-Atlantic Regional Archives Conference, and is a member of the Rare Books and Manuscripts Section of ACRL.

Carol Rigby is an independent cataloguer specializing in the creation of multilingual and multiscript original bibliographic and authority records, with a focus on Inuit language, including Inuktitut syllabics. She has more than two decades' experience in working in school, public, and special libraries in Canada's Eastern Arctic, both in front-line public service and in technical services, and since 2004 has been providing cataloguing services on contract to such clients as the Nunavut Legislative Library, the Pond Inlet Library and Archives Society, and Nunavut Public Library Services. She is a member of the Nunavut Library Association, the Canadian Technical Services Network, and the Cataloguing and Metadata Committee of the Canadian Federation of Library Associations, and an advisory member on the Canadian Committee on Metadata Exchange, working with the national library community in Canada on developing cataloguing standards for Inuit language and advocating for the right of indigenous languages to be presented on their own terms in library catalogues.

Jane Sandberg is the Electronic Resources Library at Linn-Benton Community College, where she does system administration, software development, and cataloging.

Naomi Shiraishi is the Japanese Cataloging Librarian for the C.V. Starr East Asian Library at the University of California, Berkeley. She received her MLS and PhD (philosophy) from the University of Wisconsin-Madison.

Kelly Swickard has been in academic libraries for ten years as a cataloging/metadata librarian. She previously worked as an archivist at the Georgia O'Keeffe Museum Research Center, and learned valuable lessons about artists' privacy even if they are many years deceased. She holds graduate degrees in archaeology and art history. She enjoys working with student artists and absorbing their enthusiasm for zines as well as their excitement in having their zines in the library collection.

Ruth Kitchin Tillman currently works as the Cataloging Systems and Linked Data Strategist at the Penn State Libraries, where she also acts as product owner for discovery work. She has previously held metadata and digital collections positions, managing metadata for institutional repository and cultural heritage materials. Her research interests include labor in GLAM, ethical questions within librarianship (particularly cataloging and system design), and the praxis of lowering barriers to technical library work. She'd like to make it easier for people to do technical work, to engage with them in the ethical conversations which arise, and for all of us be compensated and treated well for it and all forms of labor.

Travis L. Wagner is currently a doctoral student in the University of South Carolina's School of Library and Information Sciences. Travis also received a Graduate Certificate in Women's and Gender Studies from USC's Department of Women's and Gender Studies, where they continue to serve as a lecturer. Travis also spends time working closely with multiple community archives within Columbia, SC helping organizations to create cost-effective strategies for the digital preservation of archival content.

Thomas A. Whittaker is the Head of Media Cataloging at Indiana University, Bloomington. He has held previous appointments as the Metadata Librarian and Audiovisual Cataloger at the University of Maryland, College Park, where he also received his MLS in 2007. His professional interests include library authority control and identity management, cataloging education, and descriptive metadata of film and video.

INDEX

CPSIA information can be obtained
at www.ICGtesting.com
Printed in the USA
BVHW040918120621
609180BV00007B/830